Livable Cities From a Global Perspective

Livable Cities From a Global Perspective offers case studies from around the world on how cities approach livability. They address the fundamental question, what is considered "livable?" The journey each city has taken or is currently taking is unique and context specific. There is no thing as a one-size-fits-all approach to livability. Some cities have had a long history of developing livability policies and programs that focus on equity, economic, and environmental concerns, while other cities are relatively new to the game. In some areas government has taken the lead, while in other areas grassroots activism has been the impetus for livability policies and programs. The challenge facing our cities is not simply developing a livability program. We must continually monitor and readjust policies and program to meet the livability needs of all people.

The case studies investigate livability issues in such cities as Austin, Texas; Helsinki, Finland; London, United Kingdom; Warsaw, Poland; Tehran, Iran; Salt Lake City, United States; Rio de Janeiro, Brazil; Sydney, Australia; and Cape Town, South Africa. The chapters are organized into such themes as livability in capital city regions, livability and growth and development, livability and equity concerns, livability and metrics, and creating livability. Each chapter provides unique insights into how a specific area has responded to calls for livable cities. In doing so, the book adds to the existing literature in the field of livable cities and provides policy makers and other organizations with information and alternative strategies that have been developed and implemented in an effort to become a livable city.

Roger W. Caves is Professor Emeritus of City Planning, School of Public Affairs, San Diego State University. He is the author of *Land Use Planning: The Ballot Box Revolution* (1992), editor of *Exploring Urban America: An Introductory Reader* (1995), co-author of *Planning in the USA: Policies, Issues, and Processes* (2003, 2008, and 2014), editor of *Encyclopedia of the City* (2005) and co-editor of *Community Livability: Issues and Approaches to Sustaining the Well-Being of People and Communities* (2012) with Fritz Wagner. His research areas include urban planning, direct democracy, smart cities, housing and information technology, and community development.

Fritz Wagner is Research Professor Emeritus in the Department of Urban Design and Planning at the University of Washington (Seattle). He directs the Northwest Center for Livable Communities and teaches part time. Before joining the University of Washington, he was at the University of New Orleans for 26 years, where he founded the College of Urban and Public Affairs and served as its Dean.

Livable Cities From a Global Perspective

Edited by
Roger W. Caves and Fritz Wagner

NEW YORK AND LONDON

First published 2018
by Routledge
711 Third Avenue, New York, NY 10017

and by Routledge
2 Park Square, Milton Park, Abingdon, Oxon, OX14 4RN

Routledge is an imprint of the Taylor & Francis Group, an informa business

© 2018 Taylor & Francis

The right of Roger W. Caves and Fritz Wagner to be identified as the authors of the editorial material, and of the authors for their individual chapters, has been asserted in accordance with sections 77 and 78 of the Copyright, Designs and Patents Act 1988.

All rights reserved. No part of this book may be reprinted or reproduced or utilised in any form or by any electronic, mechanical, or other means, now known or hereafter invented, including photocopying and recording, or in any information storage or retrieval system, without permission in writing from the publishers.

Trademark notice: Product or corporate names may be trademarks or registered trademarks, and are used only for identification and explanation without intent to infringe.

Library of Congress Cataloging-in-Publication Data
Names: Caves, Roger W., editor. | Wagner, Fritz W., editor.
Title: Livable cities from a global perspective / [edited by] Roger W. Caves and Fritz Wagner.
Description: New York, NY : Routledge, 2018.
Identifiers: LCCN 2017059190 | ISBN 9781138696747 (hardback) | ISBN 9781138696754 (pbk.)
Subjects: LCSH: Urbanization—Social aspects. | City planning—Social aspects. | Community development. | Urban policy.
Classification: LCC HT361 .L789 2018 | DDC 307.76—dc23
LC record available at https://lccn.loc.gov/2017059190

ISBN: 978-1-138-69674-7 (hbk)
ISBN: 978-1-138-69675-4 (pbk)
ISBN: 978-1-315-52341-5 (ebk)

Typeset in Sabon
by Apex CoVantage, LLC

To my late brother, Ronald L. Caves
You are missed

and

To Ryan F. Wagner, son, and
Melanie K. Wagner, daughter

Contents

List of Figures ix
List of Tables xi
Notes on Contributors xii
Acknowledgments xvii
Preface xviii

1 **Livable Cities: From Concept to Global Experience** 1
   HILDA BLANCO

PART I
Livability in Capital City Regions 15

2 **Livability in New Urban Helsinki** 17
   TUOMAS ILMAVIRTA

3 **Livable Cities: UK and London** 30
   JUDITH RYSER

4 **Place-Making and Livability in Ottawa and the National Capital Region** 45
   ANGELA FRANOVIC AND CAROLINE ANDREW

PART II
Livability and Growth and Development 59

5 **Struggling Toward Livability in Austin, Texas** 61
   ELIZABETH J. MUELLER

6 **Livable or Lovable? Framing the Revitalization Projects in Warsaw, Poland** 79
   ANNA DOMARADZKA

7 **Pune Metropolis: Unlivable Cities Within a Livable Metropolis** 93
   CHRISTOPHER BENNINGER

PART III
Livability and Equity Concerns — 109

8 Livable Sydney: Livable for Whom? — 111
ROBERTA RYAN AND YVETTE SELIM

9 Making Tokyo Livable for a Super-Aging Society — 127
HIDEKI KOIZUMI

10 Livability for Whom? Vancouver's Conundrum — 138
PENNY GURSTEIN

PART IV
Livability and Metrics — 149

11 A Global Perspective on Building a Livable City: Singapore's Framework — 151
TENG CHYE KHOO AND HWEE JANE CHONG

12 Livability in Salt Lake City — 166
HOLLY LOPEZ AND RALPH BECKER

13 Livability and Access to Urban Goods in Melbourne — 176
HEATHER MACDONALD

PART V
Creating Livability — 189

14 The Search for Livability in Third World Segregated Cities: The Entrepreneurial City and the Possibilities of Overcoming Historical Inequalities in Rio de Janeiro — 191
LUCIA CAPANEMA-ALVARES AND JORGE LUIZ BARBOSA

15 Livable Cities: The Case of Cape Town, South Africa — 208
DAVID DEWAR

16 Livability and the Challenge of Planning in Tehran — 224
ALI MODARRES

Final Remarks — 237
Additional Information on Livability for Cities Covered in the Book — 239
Index — 241

Figures

2.1	The Center of Kalasatama Will Consist of Eight High-Rise Buildings and a Large Shopping Center—A Visible Exception in an Otherwise Low Silhouette of Helsinki	25
3.1	Location of UK Livable Cities (according to quoted indices)	36
4.1	National Capital Region of Canada (NCR)	46
4.2	Hendrick Farm Prior to Development (left)—Hendrick Farm Development Plans Created by DPZ (right)	54
5.1	Austin HOLC Map	65
5.2	City of Austin Watershed Regulation Areas	66
7.1	Map of Pune Metropolitan Region	94
7.2	Balewadi High Street	95
7.3	Consumption Distribution by Multipliers of Subsistency	96
7.4	Shaniwar Wada Citadel	98
7.5	Slum on Parvati Hill, Pune	101
8.1	Income Levels in Sydney	116
8.2	Housing Tenure in Sydney	118
8.3	Relationship Between Different Forms of Spatial Disadvantage	120
9.1	Changes of the Number of Households in Tokyo Metropolitan Area 2000–2005 and 2005–2010	132
9.2	Distribution of Vacant Lots and Houses in Sennari-danchi, Sakura City, Chiba Prefecture	133
10.1	View of Development in North and South False Creek From South Side	143
11.1	The CLC Liveability Matrix	151
11.2	The Singapore Liveability Framework	152
11.3	Under the ABC Waters Programme, the Kallang River at Bishan-Ang Mo Kio Park Was Transformed From a Concrete Canal to a Naturalistic River for the Community to Enjoy	155
11.4	Implicit Principles of Integrated Master Planning and Development	156
11.5	Implicit Principles of Dynamic Urban Governance	159
11.6	Today, Chek Jawa Is a Popular Spot for Nature Lovers to Gather and Observe Wildlife	161
11.7	View of the Guggenheim Museum, an Icon of Bilbao's Transformation Into an International Cultural Center, From the Iberdrola Tower, the Tallest Building in Bilbao	162
12.1	9-Line Community Garden: Salt Lake Partnered With Wasatch Community Gardens to Provide Gardening Opportunities on City-Owned Lands	171

13.1	Index of Relative Socio-Economic Advantage and Disadvantage	179
14.1	Summary of Desirable Livability Aspects According to Authors and Institutions Under the Three Sustainability Dimensions	194
14.2	First World Style Refurbishment in Rio's Port Area	198
14.3	Cultural Manifestations in Rio Favelas	201
16.1	Nighttime at a Park at Chitgar Lake, Western Tehran	225

Tables

1.1	Top Ten Livable Cities by Major Global Rating Systems	6
2.1	Frame for the Production of Urban Livability in Helsinki	20
3.1	Comparative Table of Selected City Livability Indices of Rank Order: UK	33
3.2	Comparative Livability Index: London Rank Order in Global Indices	37
7.1	Percentage of Income Expended on Basic Needs	100
8.1	Top Ten Ranking Cities From Selected Livability Indices and Surveys	114
8.2	What Matters to People in NSW in Relation to Transport	117
8.3	Comparison of the Housing Tenure in Sydney in 1991 and 2011	117
9.1	Population Change in Tokyo Metropolitan Area	128
10.1	Median Household Incomes and Average Home Prices in Greater Vancouver	139
13.1	Components of the Economist Intelligence Unit City Ranking	180

Notes on Contributors

Caroline Andrew is the director of the Centre on Governance at the University of Ottawa. Her research interests focus on partnerships between equity-seeking community groups and municipal governments to create and develop programs around the better integration of immigrants, enhancement of women's rights, and elimination of violence against women. She is a member of the Order of Canada.

Jorge Luiz Barbosa holds a degree in Geography from the Federal University of Rio de Janeiro (1980), a master's degree in Geography from the Federal University of Rio de Janeiro (1990), a PhD in Geography from the University of São Paulo (2002), and a postdoctoral degree in Human Geography from the University of Barcelona–Spain (2010). He is currently an associate professor at the Graduate Program in Geography at the Fluminense Federal University. He is the director of the Favelas Observatory in Rio de Janeiro and works with Urban Geography, particularly with landscape, politics, and culture matters.

Ralph Becker is a 43-year resident of Salt Lake City, where he served two terms as mayor (2008–2015). He also served in the Utah State Legislature as a member of the House of Representatives for 11 years (1996–2007). For most of that tenure, he was in legislative leadership positions, including five years as House Minority Leader. In 2015, he served as President of the National League of Cities. In his political career, he focused attention on serving the public interest through solution-orienting, inclusive governance practices. He became known for his work improving conditions for the LGBT community around discrimination; sustainability practices and protection of lands and resource; and changes to improve equity in education, access to the outdoors, and community development. In 2017, he held a Leadership in Government Fellowship with the Open Society Foundation. He was an adjunct professor in the University of Utah College of Architecture and Planning, teaching classes each semester in Environmental Planning and Law, Public Involvement and Governance, Public Lands Planning and Management, and related courses and lectures. He holds an undergraduate degree from the University of Pennsylvania, and from the University of Utah, he holds a JD and a MS in planning.

Christopher Benninger was born in the United States, studying urban planning at MIT and architecture at the University of Florida and at Harvard, where he later taught. He has lived in India since 1971, when he founded the Faculty of Planning at CEPT University, where he is a board member. In 1976, he founded the Centre for Development Studies and Activities with Aneeta Gokhale, focusing on watershed management, decentralized, and microlevel planning in rural and urban areas. His planning work covers cities in Sri Lanka, India, and Bhutan, where he prepared the capital city plan of Thimphu and designed the Supreme Court of Bhutan. He is a Statutory Member of the Andhra

Pradesh Capital Region Development Authority. His book, *Letters to a Young Architect*, appeared on the Top Ten Best Selling Non-fiction Books of India. Rizzoli in Manhattan, with SKIRA in Milan, recently published his book *Christopher Benninger: Architecture for Modern India*.

Hilda Blanco holds master's and PhD degrees in City and Regional Planning from the University of California, Berkeley. She held tenured appointments at Hunter College Department of Urban Affairs (1988–1996) and the University of Washington (1996–2009), where she chaired the Department of Urban Design and Planning (2000–2007) and is currently an Emeritus Professor. From 2010 to 2016, she was a research professor and Interim Director of the Center for Sustainable Cities at the University of Southern California, and is currently the Project Director of the Center for Sustainable Cities. Her research areas include sustainable and livable cities, urban growth management, cities and climate change, water policy, and renewable energy policy. She is the North American editor of the *Journal of Environmental Planning and Management* and member of the editorial boards of *Progress in Planning* and the *Journal of Emergency Management*.

Lucia Capanema-Alvares holds a degree in Architecture and Urban Planning from the Federal University of Minas Gerais (1988), a master's degree in City and Regional Planning from Memphis State University (1992), a PhD in Regional Planning from the University of Illinois at Urbana-Champaign (1999), and a postdoctoral degree in Urban and Regional Planning at the Institute for Urban and Regional Planning and Research, IPPUR-UFRJ (2011). She is currently an associate professor at the Graduate Program in Architecture and Urban Planning of the Fluminense Federal University, working with community planning, urban revitalization, social movements and urban conflicts, integrated sustainability, landscape, and tourism planning.

Roger W. Caves is Professor Emeritus of City Planning, School of Public Affairs, San Diego State University. He received his PhD in Urban Affairs and Public Policy from the University of Delaware in 1982. He is the author of *Land Use Planning: The Ballot Box Revolution* (1992), editor of *Exploring Urban America: An Introductory Reader* (1995), co-author of *Planning in the USA: Policies, Issues, and Processes* (2003, 2008, and 2014), editor of *Encyclopedia of the City* (2005) and co-editor of *Community Livability: Issues and Approaches to Sustaining the Well-Being of People and Communities* (2012). His research areas include urban planning, direct democracy, smart cities, housing and information technology, and community development.

Hwee Jane Chong is a manager at the Centre for Liveable Cities, where she focuses on knowledge management, research administration, and publication projects spanning various urban domains. She graduated with First Class Honours in English Language from the National University of Singapore.

David Dewar is Emeritus Professor and Senior Research Scholar in the School of Architecture, Planning and Geomatics at the University of Cape Town. He is author or co-author of nine books (with three others forthcoming) and over 250 monographs and articles on issues relating to urban and regional planning. He consults widely in these fields in South, Southern, and Eastern Africa and has received numerous national and international awards for his academic and professional work.

Anna Domaradzka is a sociologist, an assistant professor and Associate Director for Research at Robert Zajonc Institute for Social Studies, University of Warsaw. Between 2011 and 2012, she was a Senior Fulbright Researcher at the Institute for Social Research at University of Michigan, in 2016–2017 invited as a visiting Scholar to San Diego State

University (US) and INCAE Business School (Costa Rica). Her main research interests concern the issues of civil society organizations, social movements, and local activism in urban context. She specializes in intersectional and international comparative research in the areas of gender sociology and urban studies and works in several international projects concerning urban development, civil society, and welfare state issues. At the moment, her main research focus is on participatory planning processes, neighborhood associations, "right to the city" movement, and social entrepreneurship in comparative perspective. Since 2015, she has been involved in the creation of the Warsaw Development Strategy 2030 as an expert on social issues.

Angela Franovic is a PhD student at the University of Ottawa (Political Studies). In her role as researcher at the Centre on Governance, Angela examines the relationship between public transportation and the notion of social equity and accessibility as important organizational goals as well as livability and urban planning in the National Capital Region.

Penny Gurstein is Professor and Director of the School of Community and Regional Planning and the Centre for Human Settlements at the University of British Columbia. Her research focus is on housing access and affordability.

Tuomas Ilmavirta is a university teacher of land-use planning at Aalto University. His research interests lie in urban branding, discursive production of urban space, and emerging urban planning methods.

Teng Chye Khoo is currently the Executive Director of the Centre for Liveable Cities, Ministry of National Development (MND), Singapore. He was formerly the Chief Executive of PUB, Singapore's National Water Agency (2003 to 2011), President and Chief Executive Officer of Mapletree Investments and Managing Director (Special Projects) of Temasek Holdings (2002 to 2003), Chief Executive Officer/Group President of PSA Corporation (1996 to 2002) and Chief Executive Officer/Chief Planner at the Urban Redevelopment Authority, URA (1992 to 1996). He is an adjunct professor at the School of Civil and Environmental Engineering (CEE), NTU, and at the Lee Kuan Yew School of Public Policy, NUS. He is Senior Fellow of the URA Academy and Chairman of Urban Land Institute (ULI), Singapore. He graduated with First Class Honours in Civil Engineering from Monash University, Australia. A President-cum-Colombo Plan Scholar, he also holds a Master of Science in Construction Engineering and a Master of Business Administration from the National University of Singapore.

Hideki Koizumi is a professor at the University of Tokyo's community development laboratory. He is extracting the methodology of urban planning and community development while working on the practice of urban planning in many areas of Japan and Asia. He also contributes to the reform of the urban planning system, such as involving the Ministry of Land, Infrastructure and Transport of the Japanese government in establishing a proposal system for urban planning.

Holly Lopez is a PhD candidate in the Metropolitan Planning, Policy and Design program at the University of Utah, where she is researching the connection between urban density and water consumption. She earned a Master of Public Policy with an emphasis in environmental and water policy and a Bachelor of Psychology from the University of Utah. She worked as the Project and Policy Manager for the Salt Lake City Mayor's Office under the Becker administration, where she has worked on projects such as the North Temple Viaduct and TIGER Streetcar Funding requests and currently works for the Park City Public Utilities Department as an executive assistant and Water & Energy Conservation project manager.

Heather MacDonald is Head of the School of Built Environment in the Faculty of Design Architecture and Building at the University of Technology Sydney. She received her PhD in Urban Planning at Rutgers, the State University of New Jersey (US). Her research has focused on affordable housing finance, spatial analysis, and estimating the economic and social impacts of public investments. She has published two books on GIS and urban planning (*Unlocking the Census With GIS*, 2005, and *Urban Policy and the Census*, 2011) and numerous articles in top-ranked academic journals. Since moving to Sydney in 2008, she has been Chief Investigator on two Australian Research Council Discovery grants. Her recent research has investigated the planning reform process in NSW, the impacts of rail investments on housing prices, the impacts of planning regulation on housing prices, and ethnic discrimination in the Sydney rental market.

Ali Modarres is Director of Urban Studies at University of Washington Tacoma. From 1999 to 2017, he served as Editor-in-Chief of *Cities: The International Journal of Urban Policy and Planning*. He earned his PhD in Geography from the University of Arizona and holds master's and bachelor's degrees in Landscape Architecture from the same institution. He has published in the areas of social geography, immigration, urban development, planning, and policy. Some of his recent publications appear in *Current Opinion in Environmental Sustainability*, *Current Research on Cities*, *Journal of Transport Geography*, and *International Journal of Urban and Regional Research*. He is a member of the advisory board for a book series on Demography and Political and Social Change in the MENA region (Middle East and North Africa). He also serves on the editorial boards of the *Journal of Urban Affairs*, *Cities*, and *Sociologica Urbana e Rurale* (Italy). He has focused a significant portion of his public scholarship on economic development through an equity lens that includes global labor migration and subject formation within larger political and economic discourses.

Elizabeth J. Mueller is Associate Professor of Community and Regional Planning and Social Work at the University of Texas at Austin and Graduate Adviser in the Community and Regional Planning Program. Before coming to University of Texas, she was an assistant professor of Urban Policy at New School University in New York City. Her current work focuses on the development of strategies for preventing displacement of low-income renters due to transit-oriented planning. Other recent projects include case studies on conflicts between planning goals and preservation of low-income communities, a comparative assessment of city housing needs and programs in Texas, a review of evidence for the connection between stable, affordable housing and education and health outcomes, and an assessment of how state and local governments target housing funds they control. Her academic work has appeared in the *Journal of the American Planning Association*, *Journal of Planning Literature*, *Journal of Planning Education and Research*, *Housing Policy Debate*, *Community Development*, *Economic Development Quarterly*, *Policy Studies Journal*, and *The Journal of Ethnic and Migration Studies*. Her article "Sustainability and Vulnerability: Integrating Equity Into Plans for Central City Redevelopment" (*Journal of Urbanism*, fall 2011, with co-author Sarah Dooling) won the 2012 University Cooperative Society Research Excellence Award.

Roberta Ryan is Director of the Institute for Public Policy and Governance and the Centre for Local Government at the University of Technology Sydney. She is a leading social research and policy, program evaluation and stakeholder engagement practitioner and researcher with over 30 years' experience. She is widely recognized for her work in developing new approaches to government policy research and practice in the areas of land use and infrastructure planning, housing, human services, environment and sustainability, arts and culture, and community and stakeholder engagement. She has published extensively and is the Regional Vice-President (Australasia), IASIA International Association of Schools and Institutes of Administration.

Judith Ryser is qualified as an architect and urbanist, with an MSc in Social Sciences. She is dedicating her cosmopolitan professional life to the built environment, its sustainability, and its contribution to the knowledge society. Her research activities in Paris (French Ministry of Works/Arnaud Consultancy), Berlin (Candilis, Josic, Woods), Stockholm (KKonsult/SCBR), Geneva (United Nations), Brussels (EU), Madrid (Fundacion Metropoli), and London (UCL/AA/LSBU) in public sector posts, private practice, and at universities focused on cities and development strategies. Based in London, she carries out research and consultancies, advises international agencies, is teaching and guest lecturing, engages with community groups, writes articles, and edits publications at home and abroad. She is a member of the International Advisory Council of the Fundacion Metropoli, Madrid, engaging in their projects and writing and editing books for them. Past vice-president and life member of ISOCARP (International Society of City and Regional Planners), she carried out many executive functions and was the general rapporteur for the 50th anniversary congress in 2015 and editor of the *International Manual of Planning Practice* and author of *ISOCARP: 50 Years of Knowledge Creation and Sharing*. She is a member of the Urban Design Group and its editorial board and a member of The Chartered Institute of Journalists.

Yvette Selim is a lecturer and senior research associate at the Institute for Public Policy and Governance at the University of Technology Sydney. She has an academic background in law, conflict resolution, bioethics, and medical science. Her research interests include transitional justice, peacebuilding, development, and human rights. Her forthcoming book with Routledge is entitled *Transitional Justice in Nepal: Interests, Victims and Agency*. In addition to her extensive research in Nepal, she has conducted research on a range of issues including social planning, monitoring and evaluation, local government, indigenous governance, and community engagement. Yvette was also a Visiting Fellow at the University of Oxford and the Australian National University.

Fritz Wagner is Research Professor Emeritus in the Department of Urban Design and Planning at the University of Washington (Seattle). He directs the Northwest Center for Livable Communities and teaches part time. Before joining the University of Washington, he was at the University of New Orleans for 26 years, where he founded the College of Urban and Public Affairs and served as its Dean.

Acknowledgments

The origin of this book came from the many discussions we and others have had regarding the multidimensional topic of livability. It is our hope that the material contained in this book leads to more discussions on this important topic throughout the globe. It is a topic that must be interdisciplinary in nature. Discussions must be collaborative in nature and not be the purview of one individual group. Benefits should be directed to everyone and not to one specific group. This is a lesson echoed throughout this book. We would like to thank the authors of the various chapters; Kunal Rakshit, Research Associate, India House, Pune, India for his technical assistance with the figures in the book; Robert Whelan for his guidance on organization; and the many individuals who we encountered over the years who strive to make cities more livable today and tomorrow.

Roger W. Caves and Fritz Wagner

Preface

The term "livable city" has become a commonly used term throughout the globe. It can be found in articles, reports, and books. We hear the term in public meetings, on the radio, on television shows, and especially see it discussed on the Internet. All levels of governments, the private sector, and nonprofit sector have addressed the term in one way or another. It is everywhere. However, for as widespread as its use is, we have many definitions for what actually constitutes a "livable city". We use it interchangeably with such other terms as a sustainable city, smart city, eco-city, resilient city, intelligent city, or green city. Common attributes of each term include the need for walkability, the need for a variety of housing types, mixed land uses, preservation of open space, opportunities for civic engagement, job opportunities for all, respecting community character and local heritage, quality educational facilities, low crime rates, balanced transportation options, and so forth. These are all quality of life attributes that cities desire.

The term "livable" means different things to different people. Cambridge Systematics define livability in the following manner:

> Livability is most often used to describe the diverse aspects of society, surroundings, and shared experiences that shape a community. Livability is focused on the human experience of place, and is specific to the place and time in question. It includes an interrelated set of economic, spatial, and social components that together are challenging to understand and measure in the defined world of planning and development. As such, it is best defined by the state, region, association, or community in question, and is best measured at a geographic scale where definitional consensus about livability can be found.[1]

Another organization, Partners for Livable Communities, believes "Livability is the sum of the factors that add up to a community's quality of life—including the built and natural environments, economic prosperity, social stability and equity, educational opportunity, and cultural, entertainment and recreation possibilities."[2]

However we define "livable," we will continue to witness debating the attributes that constitute a "livable city". Areas want information. They want to know how areas go about achieving the goal of livability. They want to know the efforts that other areas have tried. Have these areas been successful? How long have they been successful? Is everyone able to enjoy the livable city or just certain groups? What are the obstacles areas face in their quests for achieving livability? These and other questions are addressed in the chapters contained in this book.

There is no one-size-fits-all approach to becoming a livable city. Cities are unique. Many cities have been proactive is becoming a livable city. Others has procrastinated so long hoping that things get better without any true guidance. These are areas without direction. Areas need effective leadership if they are to become livable in the eyes of its citizens.

With the world becoming increasingly urbanized, this book aims to address how residents and areas around the world have responded to calls for developing livable cities. The book offers case studies on a broad selection of cities and examines how these cities are attempting to achieve the goal of becoming a livable city. It draws on the interdisciplinary expertise of both academics and practitioners from areas around the globe. Chapters examine the following questions:

- How is "livable" defined?
- Is there an official policy trying to reach it?
- How did the area get to be livable?
- What tools/techniques were used to achieve livability?
- Are there any metrics for determining livability?
- Is the area livable for everyone or certain groups?
- How do we keep a city livable?

The book commences with a strong introduction into the various dimension of livability. It discusses the concept of livability, a discussion of movements related to livable cities, a review of various ranking systems of livability and concludes with a discussion on how it relates to sustainability and to resilience.

The remainder of the book is divided into five parts, with each part containing case studies of three cities from around the globe. Part I examines the idea of how livability is viewed in three different capital city regions. Part II discusses three areas dealing with livability and growth and development issues. Part III investigates how three areas are confronting issues associated with livability and equity concerns. Part IV focuses on how three areas are dealing with livability and metrics. Part V discusses how three areas are actually creating livability. The book concludes with final remarks on livable cities from a global perspective and a list of websites for readers to get more information on livability for the cities covered in this book.

Notes

1. Porter, C. (2010). *Ask the experts: Planning for sustainable and livable communities*. Medford, MA: Cambridge Systematics. Retrieved August 15, 2017, from www.camsys.com/insights/ask-experts%E2%80%93planning-sustainable-and-livable-communities
2. Partners for Livable Communities. (n.d.) *What is livability?* Washington, DC: Partners for Livable Communities. Retrieved August 15, 2017, from http://livable.org/about-us/what-is-livability

1 Livable Cities
From Concept to Global Experience
Hilda Blanco

Introduction

The professions involved in urban planning and development, management, and the provision of urban services have long concerned themselves with what makes for a good city from their specific standpoints. Is a city safe? Does its built environment reflect a rich history? Is it economically vibrant, providing employment opportunities for its residents? Does it house its population adequately? Are there great economic inequalities in its population? Does it have adequate parks, medical care, roads, transit, and so forth? Because cities have become the dominant human habitat, and according to the United Nations' latest population projections, by 2050, 66% of the world's population will live in urban areas (UNDESA, 2014), cities and their qualities have transcended professional domains and have become the subject of public attention. Popular global indexes focus on the quality of cities. A city's livability, its sustainability, its resilience are concerns that transcend specific professional interests and engage larger publics. These concepts are multidimensional and intersecting. The essays in this volume provide profiles of cities around the world through the lens of livability. They make clear the multidimensional aspects of the concept of livable cities as well as its limitations. In particular, many of the essays raise the issues of whether livable cities are sustainable cities and whether livable cities are just cities.

This introduction will first discuss the concept of livable cities, as it became popular in the 1980s and 1990s in the urban planning and design professions and related movements, including the new urbanism, smart growth, healthy cities, biophilic cities, and resilient cities movements. It will then review major ranking systems and reflect on their relation to the livable communities/cities movement in urban development. The final section will discuss the relation of the concept of livable cities to sustainability and to resilience, addressing issues of future generations, human rights, ecological sustainability, and resilience to disasters.

Emergence of the Concept of Livable Communities/Cities

A livable place is a place suitable for human living, worth living in, according to dictionary definitions. As such, a livable city or community is commonly recognized as a place with qualities that are suitable or good for human life. Although urban livability concerns such as overcrowding, the quality of housing, air quality, green spaces, safe and adequate supplies of water, and sanitation are issues that have been at the core of urban planning, public health, and other urban professions that emerged in the early 20th century, the concern with community or urban livability is more recent (Whelan, 2012). In the US, the quality of places has been an object of study since the 1980s. In the same decade, a major rating of urban places, Rand McNally's *Places Rated Almanac* (Boyer & Savageau, 1981) began to be published. In the 1970s and 1980s, a growing interest in what makes for livable communities and cities led to the development of a new field in psychology, environment-behavior studies, pioneered by Kevin Lynch's *The Image of the City* (1960, which emphasized the quality of places and the effect of places and their quality on people's behavior.[1] Appleyard's *Livable Streets* (1981) focused on the characteristics of streets and how their quality affects the quality of neighborhood life, a continuing major focus of livable cities' efforts. Partners for Livable Places (now Partners for Livable Communities) organized as a national nonprofit in the US in 1977 to foster livability in the built environment. In 1981, Pressman edited a volume, *International Experiences in Creating Livable Cities*, a collection of essays focused on the experiences with policies to improve the livability of cities around the world, primarily in Europe and Canada, but also including lessons from Australia, Brazil, South Africa, and Japan. Many of the essays were focused not only on cities' efforts to tame motor vehicles and to improve pedestrian safety, but also on urban regeneration and planning, although the topics varied among countries. For example, the concern with livable cities or communities was evident and a focus of political agendas in the Netherlands since the 1960s, with a specific emphasis on a need to improve citizen participation in livability policy (Kaal, 2011). International conferences for urban design and planning professionals with the explicit focus on making cities livable began to be held in 1986 (International Making Cities Livable, 2017).

Lynch's Theory of Good City Form

Kevin Lynch's *A Theory of Good City Form* (1984) identified several dimensions of urban form that are important to the concept of livable cities. Lynch's dimension of *vitality* is particularly relevant. By vitality, Lynch meant the extent to which a city or places in a city support "the vital functions, the biological requirements and capabilities of human beings". Lynch identifies three aspects to vitality: sustenance, safety, and consonance. Sustenance refers to the ability of a city to provide an adequate supply of food, energy, water, and air and proper disposal of waste, all the physical and natural goods that humans need to survive in an urban place. Safety, according to Lynch, refers to the absence or control of hazards, poisons, disease in a settlement. Consonance refers to the match of a settlement form with the biological structure of humans, for example, whether a settlement can maintain the internal temperature of people or provide optimum sensory input. Thus, Lynch's dimension of vitality is very close to what the ordinary meaning of a livable place is in terms of enabling human life. Other dimensions of place in Lynch's theory are often incorporated in concepts of livable communities: *access* and *fit*. By access, Lynch meant the degree to which people have access to public places, to other people, places of employment, schools, information sources, and so forth. This dimension concerns the range and quality of things or people or activities to which people desire access. In a more abstract way, Lynch was referring to the means of transportation and communication that provide us access to all types of economic and social goods. By fit, Lynch referred to the degree of match between the place and the customary behavior of people in a place. For example, how well does the suburban home fit an elderly resident, or how well does a narrow sidewalk fit the needs for daily walking of residents? Lynch's normative theory of urban form identified major dimensions of how urban form can sustain basic human needs. His theory was a normative one, describing multidimensional values, which he did not operationalize. To apply these criteria, a designer or an evaluator would need to interpret the dimensions in measurable ways.

The New Urbanism and Smart Growth Movements

The livable cities movement has been strongly identified with the new urbanism movement and the smart growth movement in the US (Godschalk, 2004). The early focus of New Urbanism, an urban design movement that emerged in the US in the mid-1980s, was mainly on reforming suburban development into more compact and livable places. It sought to replace suburban subdivisions with more traditional town plans incorporating interconnected street grids, better defined lot/block and block/street patterns, and higher densities than existing suburbs (Duany & Plater-Zyberk, 2006). Moving beyond suburban development, the emphasis of the new urbanism movement has been on the quality of urban places and the public experiences and behavior that well-designed places can facilitate. It has also emphasized diversity of housing types to promote affordable housing options and more inclusive urban places. Peter Calthorpe, an urban designer who brought a strong environmental ethos to the new urbanism movement (van Der Ryn & Calthorpe, 1986), initiated the concept of transit-oriented development in the late 1980s and early 1990s (Calthorpe, 1993; Carlton, 2007). This concept, geared to reduce automobility, enhance mobility, and develop more compact development, has been incorporated into the new urbanism agenda.

In the 1990s, reacting to lack of progress in containing sprawl, the smart growth movement, a movement in urban planning that evolved from the earlier urban growth management movement (DeGrove & Miness, 1992) advocated several similar measures as the new urbanism: limiting expansion of new development through urban growth boundaries or utility districts, increasing residential densities in existing and new growth areas, promoting more mixed-use and pedestrian amenities to minimize car use, emphasizing public transit to reduce the use of private vehicles, and revitalizing older existing neighborhoods. (American Planning Association, 1998; Burchell et al., 2000; Downs, 2001). The association of new urbanism and smart growth with livable places and communities in the US was made explicit through the Ahwanee Principles[2] (Calthorpe et al., 1991) advocated by major new urbanists and smart growth advocates, including Calthorpe and Duany and Plater-Zyberk in 1991.

The Healthy Cities Movement

In the late 1970s, the World Health Organization's (WHO) concept of health began to shift from absence of disease to well-being, and its goals began to go beyond medical intervention to include disease prevention and health promotion (World Health Organization, 2005). The notion that people's health in cities is as much dependent on their social and physical environment as on their access to medicine began to emerge in the 1980s, with the support of WHO. A growing movement among public health professionals began to coalesce around the healthy cities concept, which is defined as a process rather than a particular health status, and by a commitment to improve social and physical conditions to support the quality of life of residents (Duhl & Sanchez, 1999). Regional associations of Healthy Cities and Healthy Communities under WHO number hundreds, if not thousands, of members. In Europe alone, 90 cities in 31 countries belong to the regional association, and 28 countries have national networks involving 1,400 towns and cities (Hancock, 2014). The physical aspects of the Healthy Cities agenda overlap significantly with the livable communities' agenda, with a greater emphasis on promoting active living, that is, opportunities for walking and biking. In the US, the active living agenda, prompted by the increasing incidence of obesity, has brought together urban design and public health academics to conduct joint research on the urban form aspects of the agenda (Moudon,

2005; Berke et al., 2007; Frank et al., 2007; Giles-Corti et al., 2016; Goenka & Andersen, 2016). But the Healthy Cities program also highlights, especially in the context of low-income countries, the importance of environmental infrastructure for health, such as water, sanitation, and waste disposal.

Biophilic Cities

The more recent movement promoting *biophilic* cities also gains its support from environment-behavior studies focused on the effect of exposure to nature on psychological and physical health (Velarde et al., 2007; Mitchell & Popham, 2008; Bowler et al., 2010) and the argument of E. O. Wilson that humans have a natural inclination to affiliate with nature (Wilson, 1984). Biophilic cities' agendas focus on providing close and ongoing contacts with nature and facilitating "an awareness and caring for this nature" (Beatley & Newman, 2013, 3329; see also Beatley, 2011; Downton et al., 2016). The focus is on ensuring greenery and green elements in cities, natural daylight, proximity to parks and green space, as well as in promoting pro-nature behavior and attitudes.

Resilient Cities

The early focus of the *resilient* cities movement was on preparing for and reducing the impacts of natural hazards on communities (Mileti, 1999; Godschalk, 2003), with an emphasis on vulnerability assessments of communities, preparation for hazards, and reduction of existing vulnerabilities. In the 2000s, the resilient cities literature began to incorporate resilience to terrorism (Godschalk, 2003). Today, the resilient cities literature focuses on both preparations for natural hazards, terrorism, and climate change impacts (Desouza & Flannery, 2013; Jabareen, 2013; Stumpp, 2013; Wamsler et al., 2013; Johnson & Blackburn, 2014) and since the early 2010s, is being increasingly used almost interchangeably with sustainability (Stumpp, 2013). The resilient cities movement has been promoted by the United Nations International Strategy for Disaster Reduction (UNISDR) which began a Making Cities Resilient Campaign in 2010. Since then, over 2,600 local governments in 98 countries have signed up (UNISDR, 2017). Also important is the related Hyogo Framework of Action, which fosters disaster risk reduction by providing tools, technical assistance, and training for local governments (Johnson & Blackburn, 2014). The concept of resilience in the natural hazards literature emphasized the importance of a community's organizational capacity to respond to disasters, as well as a focus on vulnerable populations, because natural disasters typically have greater impacts on vulnerable populations. As a result, resilient city agendas pay attention to both organizational capacity to respond to disasters and the importance of strategies to prepare for and reduce the impact of disasters on vulnerable populations.

Rating Systems for Livable Cities

While the urban professions have been focused on documenting conditions in cities and developing theories and policies to improve their livability, the rating or ranking of cities along livability dimensions is being popularized through several well-known global ranking systems, including the Economist Global Liveability Index (EIU, 2016), the Mercer Quality of Living Index (Mercer, 2017a), the Monocle Quality of Life Survey (Monocle, 2016), and the PricewaterhouseCoopers (PwC) Quality of Living Indicators in their Cities of Opportunity Ranking (PwC, 2016). Rating systems can be based on available data or surveys of population.[3] The most popular ranking systems use data readily available for a range of cities.

Quality of Life Surveys in EU Cities

The European Commission has been conducting quality of life surveys of population in European capitals and other cities every 3 years since 2004. The most recent one for which results are available was conducted in 2015. It surveyed more than 40,000 people in 79 cities and four city regions (European Union, 2016), with 500 people surveyed in each city. The surveys probe people's satisfaction with living in their city, including questions on satisfaction with the infrastructure and facilities of the city, employment opportunities, housing situation, presence and integration of foreigners, safety and trust, city administrative services, their satisfaction with the natural environment, including air quality, noise level, cleanliness, green spaces, and fight about climate change, as well as people's personal satisfaction with their personal situation. The survey ends by asking respondents for the three most important issues facing their city. In all, except six cities, 80% of people surveyed expressed overall satisfaction to living in their city (European Union, 2016, 12). But an important finding in the 2015 survey was that in more than one half of the cities surveyed, especially in capital cities, the majority of respondents disagreed that it was easy to find good housing at a reasonable price. The three most important issues facing their cities, respondents noted, were health services, unemployment, and education and training (Ibid., 17).[4]

Popular Global City Rating Systems

The most popular global rating systems, based on available data, vary in their focus, range, and methods used. For example, the PwC Quality of Living indicators are included under categories of Transportation/Infrastructure, Health, Safety and Security, Sustainability and the Natural Environment, and Demographics and Livability, whereas the EIU Global Livability Index includes categories of Stability, Healthcare, Culture and Environment, Education, and Infrastructure.

The rating systems vary in the range of cities surveyed: whereas the PwC rating system rates only 30 cities, which it selects as cities of opportunity, the EIU includes 140 cities, and Mercer includes 450 cities. The major objective of Mercer's Quality of Living Index is to aid corporations in providing compensation for relocated international workers beyond cost of living increases. The EIU Global Livability Index has a similar orientation and uses some of the data in Mercer's index. PwC Index is more policy oriented, aiming to understand policies and approaches that work best for economies and people in an urbanizing world. Table 1.1 includes the most recent ratings for the top ten cities. Notice that in both EIU and Mercer, only European, Australian, and Canadian cities achieve rankings in the top ten. This may be, to a large extent, explained by the underlying purpose of Mercer's rankings—to provide additional compensation for expatriate workers. Workers relocated to top-ranked cities should not expect extra hardship compensation. The Monocle ranking is more of an editorial decision and varies the indicators that it uses to rank cities. It takes into account public transport networks and the cost of monthly transit cards, international connections, general safety, quality of urbanism, and architecture. Recently, Monocle's survey has been focused on nightlife and other urban amenities particularly attractive to tourists, for example, the time restaurants and clubs close, the number of independent bookshops (Monocle, 2017).

6   Hilda Blanco

Table 1.1 Top Ten Livable Cities by Major Global Rating Systems

EIU Global Livability Index (30 indicators in five categories) (2016)	Mercer Quality of Living Index (39 indicators in ten categories) (2017)	PwC Quality of Living[5] in their Cities of Opportunity (22 indicators in four categories) (2016)	Monocle Quality of Life Survey (11 indicators) (2016)
1. Melbourne	1. Vienna	1. Stockholm	1. Tokyo
2. Vienna	2. Zurich	2. Toronto	2. Berlin
3. Vancouver	3. Auckland	3. Berlin	3. Vienna
4. Toronto	4. Munich	4. Paris	4. Copenhagen
5. Calgary	5. Vancouver	5. Sydney	5. Munich
6. Adelaide	6. Dusseldorf	6. San Francisco	6. Melbourne
7. Perth	7. Frankfurt	7. Amsterdam	7. Fukuoka
8. Auckland	8. Geneva	8. London	8. Sydney
9. Helsinki	9. Copenhagen	9. New York	9. Kyoto
10. Hamburg	10. Sydney	10. Singapore	10. Stockholm

Sources: EIU (2016); Mercer (2017a); PwC Quality of Living (2016); Monocle (2016)

In PwC's Quality of Living rating, half the cities in the top ten are European and two US cities are included, as well as one Asian city. Monocle's Quality of Life Survey, a more eclectic rating system, includes three Asian cities, five European cities, and two Australian cities in their top ten.

Focusing on the more policy-oriented PwC, note that the actual ranking in their overall ranking for Cities of Opportunity is rather different from the ranking for their Quality of Life issues, which is only one of four categories used in their overall Cities of Opportunity ranking, as PwC defines them. In their overall ranking, geared to economic opportunity, London, Singapore, Toronto, Paris, Amsterdam, New York, Stockholm, San Francisco, Hong Kong, and Sydney are the top ten cities in order. Stockholm, seventh in PwC's overall ranking, is rated as their top city for quality of living, whereas London, PwC's top city of opportunity, is rated eighth for its quality of living. Also, note that the cost of living, which Mercer tracks through a different cost of living rating system, is not explicitly included in several of these livable cities rating systems. In Mercer's 2017 cost of living ranking, Luanda, Angola, was ranked the city with the highest cost of living, followed by Hong Kong, Tokyo, Zurich, and Singapore (Mercer, 2017b).

The availability of affordable housing, which should be an important variable in livable cities rating systems, does not seem to be an influential indicator in these major ranking systems. Evidence for this is available from the latest European Union quality of life surveys described earlier. In Paris, Munich, Geneva, Stockholm, and Zurich, top-ranked cities for their livability in major rating systems, over 90% of respondents to the question "Is it easy to find good housing at a reasonable price in their city?" answered that they strongly disagreed. And over 80% of respondents strongly disagreed in Hamburg, Helsinki, Amsterdam, Copenhagen, Berlin, Oslo, and London, other top-ranked cities in these rating systems (EU, 2016, 72–73). Even in Vienna, which has a strong social housing policy, 75% of those surveyed disagreed (40%) or strongly disagreed (35%) with the statement (Ibid., 73). These findings provide good evidence that the major global rating systems are not rating cities from the standpoint of their residents but from the standpoint of visitors or affluent populations.

In addition, Conger's (2015) recent article points out the many problems with quality of life, livable cities ranking systems, including (a) boundary issues, namely, which are the boundaries of the city being measured, that is, municipal, metropolitan, mega-city region; (b) changing metrics, that is, all the popular ranking systems change their methods and include different indicators; (c) methodological biases, for example, both EIU and Mercer are focused on the values of "traveling corporate executives, academics and researchers targeted by such surveys" (Kotkin, 2009), and clearly there are biases for German- and English-speaking cities in the EUI and Mercer rankings, and to a lesser extent in PwC's ranking system.

Livability, Sustainability, Resilience: Standpoints, Horizons, Linkages

Livability and sustainability are closely interrelated concepts, as indicated earlier, for example, PwC's rating system uses a subcategory of Sustainability and the Environment to define its Quality of Living Rating system. How are the concepts related? How do they differ? How does the concept of livability relate to sustainability? Do we need to choose between them?

The Expanding Notion of Sustainable Cities

There are two canonical definitions of sustainability: the Brundtland Commission's and balancing "the three E's". The 1987 UN Commission on Environment and Development report (or the Brundtland Commission) identified sustainable development as development "that meets the needs of the present generation without compromising the ability of future generations to meet their own needs"(United Nations General Assembly, 1987). Sustainable development is even more widely defined as balancing the three E's of environment, economy, and equity (Daly & Cobb, 1989; Campbell, 1996; Godschalk, 2004). Sustainability, however defined, is a nebulous concept. The Brundtland Commission report was followed up by the UN Conference on Environment and Development held in Rio de Janeiro in 1992 (widely known as the Earth Summit), where Agenda 21 was developed. Part of this agenda identified a local scale for sustainable development, known as Local Agenda 21. ICLEI-Local Governments for Sustainability, an NGO founded in 1990, began to provide technical assistance to local governments around the world to develop Agenda 21 plans (Tang et al., 2010). Today, over 1,500 local governments around the world belong to ICLEI. This international NGO has been instrumental in assisting local governments to develop sustainability plans and programs, and its analytic tools and software have expanded since their original focus on Agenda 21 sustainability plans. In 2017, the organization's overarching goal is still the creation of sustainable cities, which they define as:

> an environmentally, socially, and economically healthy and resilient habitat for existing populations, without compromising the ability of future generations to experience the same. They aim for sustainability in a comprehensive and inclusive manner. They integrate policies across sectors to connect their ecological and social goals with their economic potential, rather than addressing challenges through fragmented approaches that meet one goal at the expense of others
>
> (ICLEI, 2017).

However, to respond to the related agendas of livability, resilience, climate change mitigation and adaptation, healthy cities, and biophilic cities, ICLEI has expanded their technical services to their local government members beyond their overarching agenda into nine related local agendas: Low-carbon City; Resource-efficient and Productive City (Eco-Cities); Resilient City; BiodiverCity; Smart City; Eco-Mobile City (Sustainable Urban Mobility); Happy, Healthy and Inclusive Communities; Sustainable Local Economy and Procurement; and Sustainable City-Region Cooperation (ICLEI, 2017). This expansion in the scope of technical assistance that ICLEI provides to local governments illustrates vividly the evolving nature of the concept of sustainable cities, and its overlaps with livable cities agendas and biophilic and resilient cities agendas. Note, however, that this broad set of agendas does not explicitly include a Livable City agenda. How, then, are the concepts of sustainability and livability related?

Contrasting Spatial and Temporal Standpoints

The livability standpoint is a human standpoint: how does a place, a city, support human life in its many dimensions? The sustainability standpoint is broader, it includes not only the human standpoint, but also other species' standpoints, as well as ecosystems, both regional and planetary, such as the atmosphere and oceans. The temporal aspect of sustainability is also broader, spanning generations, if not hundreds of years, whereas the concept of livability does not incorporate such a long-term horizon (Gough, 2015). When we discuss livable cities, we are taking a contemporary standpoint, we are posing the issue of the livability of a city from our standpoint now, and from our needs as humans in an urban context. When we discuss sustainable cities, we cannot help but frame this question from some future horizon, and from a larger ecological standpoint that necessarily extends beyond any city or mega-city context. But the concepts are related. As humans, with increasingly longer life spans, we need to question how sustainable is a city's livability, and how livable are a city's sustainability measures.

Differences and Overlaps

How do the agendas of sustainable cities and livable cities differ and overlap? What aspects are shared, which are neglected? The sustainable city agenda includes a strong emphasis on reducing greenhouse gas (GHG) emissions, urban expansion (to reduce loss of forested and agricultural lands, biodiversity, water resources), energy use, extraction of materials, and the use of raw materials used in production and in production processes. It advocates recycling, reuse, and more circular economies. In this agenda, there are important overlaps with a livable cities agenda. In particular, the reduction of vehicle kilometers traveled (VKT), which is strongly correlated with automobile dependency (a major source of GHG emissions in high- and middle-income countries), through better transit and other forms of mobility, land use mix and higher densities, is a major goal of new urbanist and smart growth agendas (Ewing & Cervero, 2010). The reduction in VKT is also important for a livable cities agenda, with its promise of reducing regional air pollution.

On the other hand, the concept of sustainability incorporates a social dimension, the recognition that the sustainability of a way of life includes not only ecological and economic aspects, but also social aspects. In particular, the three E's definition of sustainability emphasizes the importance of social equity to sustainability. To what extent are social goods or environmental harms equitably distributed within a population? Major livable cities rankings, and even policies, do not directly incorporate a social equity dimension, although both smart growth and new urbanism, planning and design movements that have been at the core of livable communities agendas, incorporate concerns with housing affordability, mobility, and access to jobs. Another neglected aspect of the major livable cities ranking systems is local participation in planning and budget allocation processes (Blanco, 2012).

Sustainability and Resilience

Sustainability and resilience are also related, and to some extent because of the broadness of the concept of sustainability and the recent focus on the need for cities to begin to plan for climate change impacts, the concept of resilient cities has been gaining ground. There are reasons for this. A resilient agenda is more contained, focused on natural hazards and potential climate impacts. The core of the concept relies on a well-defined analytic methodology, namely, vulnerability assessment. It is less problematic, for example, in contrast to a sustainability agenda; it does not question the existing economy and insist on its overhaul. A resilience agenda is also human focused and need not incorporate a strong ecosystem and biodiversity agenda. Its time horizon is not as distant as that of urban sustainability, but rather extends the present outlook of urban livability to the foreseeable future.

Livable Cities and Human Rights

The evaluative lens of livable cities/communities is fundamentally connected to human rights, especially Article 25 in the UN's Universal Declaration of Human Rights (1948), the right to an adequate standard of living, adequate for the health and well-being of persons and their families, including food, clothing, housing and medical care, and necessary social services. Article 7 is also relevant articulating the right to equality of treatment and nondiscrimination. In 2015, the UN adopted a set of sustainability goals to end poverty, protect the planet, and ensure prosperity for all as part of a new sustainable development agenda. Goal 11 of this agenda calls for making "cities inclusive, safe, resilient and sustainable". In 2016, the Habitat III Conference held in Quito developed a new urban development agenda, which includes targets for basic services for all citizens, including access to housing, safe drinking water and sanitation, and other basic goods and services. In particular, the new urban development agenda is centered on housing and the role of urban planning. The position paper on the new agenda calls for urban planning to use "housing as the integrating, central element of urban planning". It points out that "place matters and that urban areas will not be inclusive without providing access to housing, services and livelihood for all", emphasizing location and transportation. It calls for urban planning and legislation "to maximize affordable housing and spatial inclusion". It argues that "sustainable housing is a litmus test of sustainable cities" programs, and that "urban planning and programs should be geared towards the progressive realization of adequate housing for all". It concludes with a call for "a continuous, participatory, and inclusive urban planning process as a starting point for integrating housing into urban growth and development strategies" (UN Habitat, 2015, 16–17).

The United Nations new urban development agenda has been prompted by the rapid growth of urban development in the Global South and concern for informal settlements, but its objectives, grounded on basic human rights, are also important for many cities in high-income countries as well, as the concerns with housing affordability from the EU Quality of Living survey of major European cities make clear (United Nations, 2017).

Concluding Remarks

Livability concerns deepen and humanize sustainability issues in many ways. Urban livability is focused on basic goods and services and experiences essential for human life: opportunities for work; availability of housing, its quality and affordability; food access, quality and affordability; clean air, clean water and sanitation services; transport access and mobility; availability and affordability of energy for lighting, refrigeration, cooking, and so forth; health services; educational services; public safety services; safety from natural hazards. Urban livability is enhanced by strong connections to nature, through parks, vistas, street trees, proximity to natural areas; by sociability or a strong sense of public life—a sense of belonging to and participation in a community which is facilitated by public places, such as streets, parks, plazas, which are accessible to all, and where all are welcome; by urban solidarity, through neighborhoods that are integrated in terms of economic and racial/ethnic class and by local governments with strong participatory practices in urban planning, local government policies, and budgeting processes.

We have discussed the similarities and differences among the concepts of sustainable cities, livable cities and other recent movements in urban development. We should also note that some of the dimensions of livability may work against one another. Cities may concentrate capital or economic activities to such an extent that housing becomes unaffordable to large segments of their populations. Or clean air, a basic requirement for human life and health, could be, and is often, compromised by industrial development and/or widespread automobility in many urban areas.

Cities differ in the way that they respond to these livability concerns or conflicts. The essays in this volume, rich in detail, present profiles of cities as they address and try to resolve livability challenges in an era where the global environmental challenge of climate change and its anticipated regional impacts loom large on the horizon. As the dominant human habitat, the livability of cities is inextricably intertwined with the sustainability of the planet. Global sustainability challenges will be fundamentally addressed in the 21st century in cities, through the restructuring and reforming of city functions, which will be, to a large extent, planned and implemented by city residents. Improving the livability of people in cities under any circumstances is a noble task; in the 21st century, it will be essential, because we will be relying on the population of cities to initiate and test radical changes to our economies and our ways of life.

Notes

1. The research journal *Environment and Behavior* was launched in 1969.
2. The principles include mixed use, walking distance among uses, transit accessibility, diversity of housing types to ensure affordability, range of jobs to ensure employment for a diverse community; a central area combining commercial, civic, cultural, and recreational use; ample open space; public places, a well-defined edge; well-designed streets, pedestrian and bike paths; parks or greenbelts; conservation of resources and minimizing of waste; efficient use of water; street and building orientation to contribute to energy efficiency of buildings, and so forth. The principles were developed for the Local Government Commission, a California nonprofit providing leadership services and networking to local leaders and communities.
3. See Okulicz-Kozaryn (2013) for a comparison of results between Mercer's Quality of Living Index and the European Commission's periodic survey of residents' satisfaction with the quality of life in European cities.
4. The city of Vienna has been conducting its own quality of life surveys periodically since 1995. The latest was conducted in 2013: 140 questions with 8,000 respondents (Vienna, 2017).
5. Quality of Living is one of four categories in PwC's Cities of Opportunity ranking system. The ranking of Quality of Living for PwC survey was calculated by the author from the data provided in PwC's report on *Cities of Opportunity 7* in their Quality of Living indicators.

References

American Planning Association (APA). (1998). *The principles of smart development*. PAS Report 479. Chicago, IL, USA: Author.
Appleyard, D., Gerson, M. S., & Lintell, M. (1981). *Livable streets*. Berkeley: University of California Press.

Beatley, T. (2011). *Biophilic cities: Integrating nature into urban design and planning.* Island Press. Retrieved from https://books.google.com/books?hl=en&lr=&id=H9Y4z68WSgUC&oi=fnd&pg=PR5&dq=biophilic+cities&ots=ZkIm5CURwc&sig=97zHFSbLUn_Le0FbngyiIP-vt_A

Beatley, T., & Newman, P. (2013). Biophilic cities are sustainable, resilient cities. *Sustainability, 5*(8), 3328–3345.

Berke, E. M., Koepsell, T. D., & Moudon, A. V. (2007). Association of the built environment with physical activity and obesity in older persons. *American Journal of Public Health, 97*(3), 486–492.

Blanco, H. (2012). Public participation in neighborhood planning, a neglected aspect of community livability: The case of Seattle. In F. Wagner, & R. Caves (Eds.), *Community livability: Issues and approaches to sustaining the well-being of people and communities.* New York: Routledge.

Bowler, D. E., Buyung-Ali, L. M., Knight, T. M., & Pullin, A. S. (2010). A systematic review of evidence for the added benefits to health of exposure to natural environments. *BMC Public Health, 10*(1), 456.

Boyer, R., & Savageau, D. (1981). *Places rated almanac.* Chicago: Rand McNally.

Burchell, R., Listokin, D., & Galley, C. C. (2000). Smart growth: Less than a ghost of urban policy past, less than a bold new horizon. *Housing Policy Debate, 44*, 821–879.

Calthorpe, P. (1993). *The next American metropolis.* Princeton, NJ: Princeton Architectural Press.

Calthorpe, P., Corbett, M., Duany, A., Moule, E., Plater-Zyberk, E., & Polyzoides, S. (1991). *Ahwahnee principles for resource-efficient communities.* Retrieved from www.lgc.org/ahwahnee/principles.html

Campbell, S. (1996). Green cities, growing cities, just cities? Urban planning and the contradictions of sustainable development. *Journal of the American Planning Association, 62*, 296–312.

Carlton, I. (2007). Histories of transit-oriented development: Perspectives on the development of the TOD concept. *IURD Working Paper 2009–02.* Institute of Urban and Regional Development, UC Berkeley. Retrieved from http://escholarship.org/uc/item/7wm9t8r6

Conger, B. (2015). *On livability, liveability and the limited utility of quality-of-life rankings.* Retrieved from https://papers.ssrn.com/sol3/papers.cfm?abstract_id=2614678

Daly, H. E., & Cobb, J. B. (1989). *For the common good: Redirecting the economy toward community, the environment, and a sustainable future.* Boston, MA: Beacon Press.

DeGrove, J., & Miness, D. (1992). *The new frontier for land policy: Planning and growth management in the states.* Cambridge: Lincoln Institute of Land Policy.

Desouza, K. C., & Flanery, T. H. (2013, December). Designing, planning, and managing resilient cities: A conceptual framework. *Cities, 35*, 89–99. doi:10.1016/j.cities.2013.06.003

Downs, A. (2001). What does "Smart Growth" really mean? *Planning, 67*, 20–25.

Downton, P., Jones, D., & Zeunert, J. (2016). Biophilia in urban design: Patterns and principles for smart Australian cities. *IUDC 2016: Smart Cities for 21st Century Australia: Proceedings of the 9th International Urban Design Conference 2016,* 168–182. Association for Sustainability in Business, Canberra, ACT.

Duany, A., & Plater-Zyberk, E. (2006). *Towns and town-making principles.* New York: Rizzoli.

Duhl, L. J., & Sanchez, A. K. (1999). *Healthy cities and the city planning process.* WHO Report EUR/ICP/CHDV 03 04 03. Copenhagen, DK: WHO.

Economist Intelligence Unit. (2016). *A summary of the livability ranking and overview.* August 2016. Retrieved from www.eiu.com/public/topical_report.aspx?campaignid=liveability2016

European Union. (2016). *Quality of life in European cities: Flash eurobarometer 419.* European Commission, Directorate for Regional and Urban Policy. Retrieved from http://ec.europa.eu/regional_policy/sources/docgener/studies/pdf/urban/survey2015_en.pdf

Ewing, R., & Cervero, R. (2010). Travel and the built environment: A meta-analysis. *Journal of the American Planning Association, 76*(3), 265–294.

Frank, L. D., Saelens, B. E., Powell, K. E., et al. (2007). Stepping towards causation: Do built environments or neighborhood and travel preferences explain physical activity, driving, and obesity? *Social Science and Medicine, 65*(9), 1898–1914.

Giles-Corti, B., Vernez-Moudon, A., Reis, R., Turrell, G., Dannenberg, A. L., Badland, H., Foster, S., et al. (2016). City planning and population health: A global challenge. *The Lancet, 388*(10062), 2912–2924.

Godschalk, D. R. (2003). Urban Hazard mitigation: Creating resilient cities. *Natural Hazards Review*, *4*(3), 136–143. doi:10.1061/(ASCE)1527-6988(2003)4:3(136)

Godschalk, D. R. (2004). Land use planning challenges. *Journal of the American Planning Association*, *70*(1), 5–13.

Goenka, S., & Andersen, L. B. (2016). Urban design and transport to promote healthy lives. *The Lancet*, *388*(10062), 2851–2853.

Gough, M. Z. (2015). Reconciling livability and sustainability: Conceptual and practical implications for planning. *Journal of Planning Education and Research*, *35*(2), 145–160.

Hancock, T. (2014). The little idea that could: A global perspective on healthy cities and communities. *National Civic Review*, *103*(3), 29–33.

ICLEI-Local Governments for Sustainability. (2017). *ICLEI's ten urban agendas*. Retrieved from www.iclei.org/agendas.html

International Making Cities Livable. (2017). *History*. Retrieved from www.livablecities.org/conferences/history

Jabareen, Y. (2013). Planning the resilient city: Concepts and strategies for coping with climate change and environmental risk. *Cities*, *31*, 220–229.

Johnson, C., & Blackburn, S. (2014). Advocacy for urban resilience: UNISDR's making cities resilient campaign. *Environment and Urbanization*, *26*(1), 29–52.

Kaal, H. (2011). A conceptual history of livability: Dutch scientists, politicians, policy makers and citizens and the quest for a livable city. *City*, *15*(5), 532–547.

Kotkin, J. (2009, August 10). Why the "livable cities" rankings' are wrong. *Forbes*. Retrieved from www.forbes.com/2009/08/10/cities-livable-elite-economist-monocle-rankings-opinions-columnists-joel-kotkin.html

Lynch, K. (1960). *The image of the city* (Vol. 11). Cambridge, MA: MIT Press.

Lynch, K. (1984). *Good city form*. Cambridge, MA: MIT Press.

Mercer. (2017a). *Quality of living: City rankings*. Retrieved from https://mobilityexchange.mercer.com/quality-of-living-rankings

Mercer. (2017b). Cost of living. *Newsroom*. Mercer's annual *Cost of Living Survey* finds African, Asian, and European cities dominate the list of most expensive locations for working abroad. Retrieved from www.mercer.com/newsroom/cost-of-living-2017.html

Mileti, D. (1999). *Disasters by design: A reassessment of natural hazards in the United States*. Washington, DC: Joseph Henry Press.

Mitchell, R., & Popham, F. (2008). Effect of exposure to natural environment on health inequalities: An observational population study. *The Lancet*, *372*(9650), 1655–1660.

Monocle. (2016, July–August). Top 25 livable cities. *Global*, *10*(95), 42–65. Retrieved from https://monocle.com/magazine/issues/95/top-25-liveable-cities/

Monocle. (2017, July–August). Where to live well? *Global*, *11*(105), 46–69. Retrieved from https://monocle.com/magazine/issues/105/where-to-live-well/

Moudon, A. V. (2005). Active living research and the urban design, planning and transportation disciplines. *American Journal of Preventive Medicine*, *28*(2), 214–215.

Okulicz-Kozaryn, A. (2013). City life: Rankings (livability) versus perceptions (satisfaction). *Social Indicators Research*, *110*(2), 433–451.

Pressman, N. E. P. (1981). *International experiences in creating livable cities*. Waterloo, Ontario: University of Waterloo.

PwC. (2016). *Cities of opportunity 7*. PwC. Retrieved from www.pwc.com/cities

Stumpp, E.-M. (2013, June). New in town? On resilience and "resilient cities". *Cities*, *32*, 164–166. doi: 10.1016/j.cities.2013.01.003

Tang, Z., Brody, S. D., Quinn, C., Chang, L., & Wei, T. (2010). Moving from agenda to action: Evaluating local climate change action plans. *Journal of Environmental Planning and Management*, *53*(1), 41–62.

U.N. Habitat. (2015). *Housing at the centre of the new urban agenda*. Nairobi: U.N. Habitat. Retrieved from https://unhabitat.org/housing-at-the-centre-of-the-new-urban-agenda/

UNISDR & Gencer, E. (2017). *Local government powers for disaster risk reduction: A study on local-level authority and capacity for resilience - UNISDR*. Retrieved from www.unisdr.org/we/inform/publications/54156

United Nations. (1948). *Universal declaration of human rights*. Retrieved from www.un.org/en/universal-declaration-human-rights/

United Nations. (2017). Sustainable development goals. *17 Goals to Transform our World*. Retrieved from www.un.org/sustainabledevelopment/sustainable-development-goals/

United Nations Department of Economic and Social Affairs. (2014). *2014 revision of the world urbanization prospects*. New York: United Nations Department of Economic and Social Affairs, Population Division. Retrieved from http://2014-revision-world-urbanization-prospects.html

United Nations General Assembly. (1987). *Resolution adopted by the General Assembly*. 42/1987. Report of the World Commission on Environment and Development (UNWCED). A/RES/42/1987. Retrieved from www.un-documents.net/a42r187.htm

Van der Ryn, S., & Calthorpe, P. (1986). *Sustainable communities: A new design synthesis for cities, suburbs and towns*. San Francisco: Sierra Club.

Velarde, M. D., Fry, G., & Tveit, M. (2007). Health effects of viewing landscapes: Landscape types in environmental psychology. *Urban Forestry & Urban Greening*, 6(4), 199–212.

Vienna. (2017). *New survey on quality of life in Vienna*. Retrieved from www.wien.gv.at/english/politics-administration/survey-quality-of-life.html

Wamsler, C., Brink, E., & Rivera, C. (2013). Planning for climate change in urban areas: From theory to practice. *Journal of Cleaner Production*, 50(1), 68–81.

Whelan, R. K. (2012). Introduction to community livability. In F. Wagner & R. Caves (Eds.), *Community livability: Issues and approaches to sustaining the well-being of people and communities* (pp. 1–6). Abingdon, UK: Routledge.

Wilson, E. O. (1984). *Biophilia*. Cambridge, MA: Harvard University Press.

World Health Organization. (2005). *Statement of mayors and political leaders of the WHO healthy cities network and the European national cities network on "designing healthier and safer cities: The challenge"*. Bursa, Turkey: WHO. Retrieved from www.euro.who.int/__data/assets/pdf_file/0020/101477/bursa_statement_E.pdf

Part I
Livability in Capital City Regions

Introduction

Capital cities play key roles in the development our urban areas. They are seats of government. They are centers of economy. They influence the growth of surrounding areas. In other words, they attract people and all of the positive and negative attributes associated with more people and growth.

Part I examines how three capital city regions have responded to the livability. Chapter 2 investigates the actions and reactions to Helsinki, Finland's actions toward livability. With a reputation of being a livable city in various rankings, Helsinki has to determine if it is meeting the needs of changing demographics. Recognizing Helsinki and its surrounding region attracts most of the country's in-migration, the pressures on the city and region are immense. It must make sure that livability policies and actions must be properly developed and implemented. However, as we all know, what is written down often gets lost in translation. Nevertheless, Helsinki continues to seek out proper means of maintaining and enhancing livability for everyone.

Chapter 3 examines livability in London, England, and its surrounding region. London recognizes livability is affected by a multitude of factors. Over time, the city has recognized livability is an important part of planning. Because many local actions transcend local boundaries, the city realizes the issue of livability cannot be separated or discussed in isolation from other important topics such as education, quality of life, income equality, and so forth. The key question in such a large area remains—livability for whom? There currently exists an imbalance between groups. This imbalance offers many challenges to local government's actions to improve the residents' quality of life.

Chapter 4 explores how the Ottawa, Canada, region has responded to and is responding to the myriad of issues surrounding livability. Ottawa recognizes government is a factor in what it does. Different decision-making structures in the region certainly complicates matters, making interaction between the various structures critically important. In-migration to the area from other parts of Canada and from other countries has also offered challenges. This change has pushed growth out of the urban core. Ultimately, the wise use of various policy tools is of paramount importance. It is important to devise multiple programs that meet the needs of the various populations and to listen to all sectors of the population in developing the programs.

Part I

Livability in Capital
City Regions

2 Livability in New Urban Helsinki

Tuomas Ilmavirta

Helsinki has a reputation of being a livable city. It ranks relatively high, for instance, in The Economist's and Monocle's livability and quality of life indices (The Economist, 2016; Monocle, 2011). Traditionally, the Nordic welfare state has provided good healthcare and proper social services for everyone, Finland is a country of one of the lowest income inequality in the world, and basic living standards in Finland have already been relatively high for decades (OECD, 2016a, 2016b). Helsinki has plenty of green space, and the crime rates are low. In recent years, Helsinki has also become an increasingly lively city with plenty of world-class events and cultural services. This all contributes to success in livability rankings.

Finland has urbanized exceptionally late; the first wave of urbanization took place in the latter part of the 19th century. As late as in 1850, only 5% of the Finnish population lived in cities. Industrialization started to urbanize the country, but Finland remained a predominantly agricultural society until the 20th century. The second wave of urbanization took place only after the Second World War: the 1960s was a time of rapid urbanization, and by the 1970s, more than half of the Finnish population lived in the cities. As a consequence, a lot of the residential areas in Helsinki follow the planning and housing principles of the modernist era. In these modernistic satellite suburbs, it was considered Finnish novelty to add more nature to the mix by building close to nature and leaving a lot of untouched nature around the buildings. These residential areas have sometimes been called *Forest suburbs*—a Finnish interpretation of the international modernistic suburban housing estates (Sundman, 1991). Through the decades, planning ideologies in Helsinki evolved following international trends. But due to the late urbanization of Finland, a lot of Helsinki's housing stock has been built around and after the 1960s. These suburbs provided decent housing for the workers of moderately growing city with—presumably—rather homogenous housing needs, but the society and ways of residing have changed, and critics argue that the way Helsinki has been built in the modernistic era, but also in the recent decades, doesn't meet the needs of contemporary, diversifying society: changing demographics and differentiating urban cultures with varied lifestyle preferences (e.g., Andersson et al., 2017; Vaattovaara & Kortteinen, 2003). However, in the 21st century, there has been a clear change in the more "urbanistic" direction in Helsinki's planning policies. According to the recent national survey (Strandell, 2017), Finns' residential aspirations have also urbanized—more and more people prefer to live near services in an urban environment.

This chapter discusses the livability of Helsinki by analyzing the strategic visioning, planning, and building of "the new urban Helsinki". How is livability brought up and framed in visions and planning documents, and how does it fold in public debate and eventually in the built environment? How is urban livability produced "discursively"? The topic will be studied in light of recent planning discourse in Helsinki. Development of the Fish Harbour area, Kalasatama, an ongoing site of urban regeneration, will be used as a case to illustrate the planning and development policies. The primary sources consist of planning documents and, most importantly, a new master plan of Helsinki 2050 stratified in 2016 (City of Helsinki, 2013) and the vision for the development of Helsinki (City of Helsinki, 2009), as well as other texts produced on urban development—such as marketing material of apartments in Kalasatama, and so forth, and public discussion on urban development and planning.

Politics of Livability

Lowe et al. define livable places as "safe, attractive, socially cohesive and inclusive, and environmentally sustainable; with affordable and diverse housing linked to employment, education, public open space, local shops, health and community services, and leisure and cultural opportunities; via convenient public transport, walking and cycling infrastructure" (Lowe et al., 2013, 11; see also Schmidt-Thomé, 2015, 30). The Washington-based organization Partners for Livable Communities (2017) uses the following definition: "Livability is the sum of the factors that add up to a community's quality of life—including the built and natural environments, economic prosperity, social stability and equity, educational opportunity, and cultural, entertainment and recreation possibilities." These are typical, almost all-encompassing, definitions of livability. The problem with them is that they touch on so many aspects of human life and social interaction, that one is tempted to ask what is left outside. Another aspect is that along with increasing ethnic, cultural, and religious diversity in our societies and, on the other hand, due to rapidly emerging technologies and environmental constraints, it is extremely challenging to create a generally applicable definition of livability, however all-inclusive it would be (Ruth & Franklin, 2014, 22). Definitions vary and are context specific by nature. This has led to attempts to frame the concept into a more manageable form. One way to have a more concrete grip on livability has been to make it quantifiable. Livability indices and rankings attempt to frame these multifaceted phenomena, operationalize them and make them comparable in terms of public discussion. While index-thinking seems to be necessary for governing and measuring urban environments (e.g., Kuoppa, 2016), quality of life and livability indices condense numerous aspects of human interaction and built environments into one number, and the concept inevitably loses its nuances. Rankings create comparisons and competition, and indices have become useful tools to market and brand cities. Post-industrial cities have been drawn into a global competition for skilled workers, tourists, and direct foreign investments, which in part create demand for such rankings. Livability becomes a measure not only for quality of life, but also of the market value of cities, and thus, a political tool.

This development emphasizes the symbolic values of livability and other qualitative elements of urban life. Urbanity, livability, and walkability become factors in the discussion on economic development and competition. From the city's perspective, planning and building a livable city not only is a service for its citizens, but also contains a promise of economic prosperity. The discussion on creative cities has been vivid in the past decade. A well-known argument by Richard Florida (2002) is that most skilled workers tend to move to the most desirable living environments, and jobs will follow. For a city, the primary promise of livability does not seem to be the quality of life for its existing citizens, but the promise it entails of a more prosperous future. This logic is also evident in Helsinki, and Helsinki's new master plan sets its goals accordingly:

"The urban living environment creates opportunities while also providing stimuli with indisputable value to the appeal and thus the competitiveness of the city" (City of Helsinki, 2013, 16).

From this perspective, the concept of livability can be seen as a political tool. By the same token, Shaun Teo divides the concept of livability into two realms: "state's appropriation of livability as a political tool, and residents' understandings of livability as a unique and embodied experience" (Teo, 2014, 917). Harm Kaal argues that a discussion on livability often reflects the interests of elites, who pursue an agenda of urban growth and represent upper- and middle-class interests (Kaal, 2011, 534–535). For Kaal, livability is a discursive frame that contributes to legitimizing political agenda and policy initiatives (McCann, 2004, 1913 cited in Kaal, 2011, 534–535). One of the problems in representing livability as a unanimous goal for urban development is that it overshadows the contested nature of urban development. Different resident groups and stakeholders have differing needs and preferences, which cannot be covered under one conceptual umbrella. Whose livability is favored, or what are the spatial preferences of development? (see Godschalk, 2004 on conflicts of livability and development). Within critical urban studies, this notion is linked with a broader discussion on a "just city" or a "right to the city" that criticizes neoliberal urban planning and development policies that have been claimed to support gentrification, spatial segregation, and privatization of public space, rather than equity and socially just urbanism (see, e.g., Brenner et al., 2009; Mitchell, 2003; Smith, 1996). Even though this debate has been marginal in Finland, there are studies on the effects of neoliberal policies on Finnish planning and city development (e.g., Mäntysalo et al., 2015, for an international take, see, e.g., Sager, 2011).

Some of the changes that have been recognized are the rise of so-called soft urban planning instruments and non-statutory planning methods. These include urban visions and strategies initiated and prepared by, for instance, ad hoc think tanks, living labs, and networks of public and private actors (Mäntysalo et al., 2015). One of the key characteristics of these instruments is their "informality"; they do not operate within statutory planning's frame either in terms of documentation or the process, but nevertheless, they still strongly contribute to the planning and urban development. Visioning and strategic planning take place in new ways and in new coalitions, bypassing statutory planning. This development has been considered problematic from various viewpoints, perhaps most importantly in regards to its legitimacy (Mäntysalo et al., 2015, 350).

Visioning and strategic planning, with their alternative visualization methods, emphasize the development where urban change is increasingly driven by imagery and symbolic factors. Symbolic capital—the image of the city and its neighborhoods—has become an essential element in developing cities within the public sector as well. Urban developers and planners aim at not only changing the built environment, but also affecting the image of the city and the symbolic values tied to it. This affects the social structure of the city, and thus, livability, too. It implies the uses and users the city or a neighborhood is planned and meant for. Brands and concepts such as livability don't aim at providing an objective representation of reality, but instead shaping it, and they are becoming increasingly important in creating the built environment (see also Kaal, 2011, 535). Also, narratives and storytelling have become central in creating the overall socio-spatial feel of neighborhoods (see Throgmorton, 2003; and on narratives in planning, see Ameel, 2015). In Helsinki, the strategic plan "Development Perspective" was created to help guide the future planning of the city. It is a development document produced by the city planning office, and its aim is to be a vision for the future Helsinki. However, the document has no official legislative power, but its purpose is to steer statutory planning (City of Helsinki, 2009), and it also widens the scope of urban planning. The strategic plan is a good example of a planning instrument that attempts to affect the identity, symbolic perception and even the social space of the city directly. The plan states, "In Helsinki, there is a new kind of awareness that represents the improvement of the social space as spatial planning target. For the development of the cityscape, ten general identities have been profiled on the Housing map" (City of Helsinki, 2009, 23).

Helsinki's strategic urban planning aims at affecting the social space of neighborhoods and creating identities for them. This is a very straightforward take on utilizing symbolic values in urban development. As Sharon Zukin sums up:

> Building a city depends on how people combine the traditional economic factors of land, labor and capital. But it also depends on how they manipulate symbolic languages of exclusion and entitlement. The look and feel of cities reflect decisions about what—and who—should be visible and what should not, on concepts of order and disorder, and on uses of aesthetic power.
>
> (Zukin, 1995, 7)

Frame for Analysis

On the basis of the theoretical review, it seems meaningful to study urban development from the perspective of the discursive production of space. For the analysis of Helsinki's livability in planning, I will introduce a theoretical frame, where "production of urban livability" is divided into three categories or realms: "soft city", "institutional city", and "soft planning". The soft city represents civic society: urban civic activism, grassroots initiatives, social interaction in urban environment and bottom-up urban dynamics in general (on everyday urbanism, see also Kelbaugh, 2007). The institutional city includes statutory planning with legally binding planning instruments—most notably, detailed planning and master planning instruments as well as construction permits. It also contains the construction process conducted within planning permits often in partnership with public and private parties. This category forms the "hard institutional and economical frames" for creating urban environment.

Between these two categories, there is a fuzzier realm, which can be labeled as "soft planning". It partly overlaps the previous two categories and also mediates between them. Emerging planning instruments such as visions and "informal" strategic urban planning as well as marketing efforts by construction companies—the symbolic, visual and discursive production of urban livability done by both the public sector and the private sector either in partnership or based on statutory plans can be included into this category. I will argue that soft planning instruments utilize the symbolic value and imagery created by the "soft city", but the content doesn't seem to translate into detailed planning and built environment (see Table 2.1).

Table 2.1 Frame for the Production of Urban Livability in Helsinki

Soft City	Soft Planning	Institutional City
Life worlds and cultures of city, bottom-up approach, new urban movements, everyday life, urban civic activism	Discursive production of space, strategic plans, visions, brands, narratives in planning, marketing	Statutory plans, implementation of visions, construction permits, construction/ realization of plans

Source: Tuomas Ilmavirta

Planning and Livability in Helsinki

In the recent years, globalization along with the structural changes—economic as well as sociological ones—have significantly accelerated migration to the biggest cities in Finland. At the same time, there has been a change in planning ideology in the bigger towns. Helsinki, most notably, has taken a turn for a more "urban" direction in its planning. The new master plan, called the "Urban plan" of Helsinki, states:

> The Helsinki of 2050 is a boldly urban metropolis pulsating with life. Urban Helsinki means: more street-level shops in blocks of flats, bicycle lanes, the clatter of trams, coffee at the market place, international flavour, urban productivity, beach saunas, district events and pedestrian streets.
>
> (City of Helsinki, 2013, 13)

Following global mega trends, urbanity has also become more popular and desirable in Helsinki (Strandell, 2017). More and more families are moving back to the center (e.g., Lilius, 2015), and the need to mitigate climate change has affected housing and transportation policies and also supported the popularity of increased density in recent urban planning solutions.

Helsinki is the undisputed center of Finnish economy, and the Helsinki region attracts most of the in-migration; therefore, there is an increased need for new apartments and urban areas in Helsinki. The city of Helsinki's housing policies has traditionally stressed equity and the importance of social housing with mixing all income levels within all new residential areas, producing socio-spatially relatively equal urban structure. Recently, however, some scholars have recognized a shift in policies from solving "the housing question" to catering to more diverse and differentiated housing needs (e.g., Ilmonen, 2016, 35–38). However, in terms of neighborhood diversity, Helsinki is still a rather homogenous city (e.g., Andersson et al., 2017). It has been considered a rare exception in Europe in retaining a relatively equal spatial structure, but some studies (Bernelius & Vaattovaara, 2016; Vaattovaara & Kortteinen, 2003) have found signs of increasing social polarization, and gentrification of some urban inner-city neighborhoods, such as Punavuori and Kallio, has been a recurring topic of popular discussion.

Recent migration pressure on Helsinki has caused housing prices to increase. This has been especially evident in more central locations, and housing markets in Finland have been polarized between bigger cities and smaller towns, but also within cities (OSF, 2017). Affordability of housing has suffered severely, and Helsinki's urbanization has been described as "uncontrollable" (Talouselämä, 2017). During the past ten years, prices of apartments in the center of Helsinki have increased by twice as much as those in outer suburbs (OSF, 2017). Even though the increase in prices has still been somewhat modest compared with some of Helsinki's European counterparts, this development has raised concerns over livability. A recent study found that less than 20% of inhabitants agree that it is easy to find good housing at a reasonable price in Helsinki. This, nevertheless, goes for many other European capitals as well (Eurostat, 2016).

New (or More) Urbanity for Helsinki

Public discussion on urban development and livability has been very active recently, and the debate has seen some new active participants. Finnish politics have typically been consensus oriented, and the same can be said about the discussion on urban development. However, culture is changing, and, for example, social media has opened up new channels to voice concerns over urban planning and development issues. The Facebook group *Lisää kaupunkia Helsinkiin* [LKH; more urbanity for Helsinki] has been one of the factors that has significantly contributed to semi-public discussion on urbanism and livability. The group is normative by nature: it demands denser urban development, and it is also politically active. The core group of the discussion channel creates alternative plans for topical planning cases and tries to affect media coverage on urban matters as well as aim to achieve official positions in Helsinki's municipal politics. Their main aim is to "build more city/urbanity in Helsinki" (LKH, 2017).

Furthermore, other urban civic activist groups are affecting urban development. Loosely organized and place- or situation-based citizen groups have been vocal in commenting on as well as contributing to urban development, for example, by organizing bottom-up urban events such as Restaurant Day, Recycling Day, and block parties. This has been a rather visible shift in Finnish urban civic activism and participation culture. Urban grassroots movements have started to raise urban issues to the planning agenda, but also—through direct action—have changed the way Finnish urban livability and urbanism are understood (see also Hernberg, 2012b). In many inner-city neighborhoods as well as numerous suburbs, citizen-driven events are now a part of the sense of neighborhood. Urban movements and activist groups make claims on space and shape the ways urban livability is perceived, lived, and talked about. As Pasi Mäenpää and Maija Faehnle conclude:

> [the rise of civic activism] leads to changes in civil society and thereby also changes in cities and how they are planned and developed. . . . The question is not of participating in decision making in society, but of acting directly to improve the urban environment, its spaces, its service and cultural offering and its operationality.
> (Mäenpää & Faehnle, 2017, 69)

Change in Planning Policies—Urbanism to the Fore

As opposed to sub-urban or "forest urban" (Sundman, 1991) planning of the modernistic era, there has been a clear turn toward a more urban approach in Helsinki's planning as well. This has been visible both in strategic visioning and land-use planning. Following the argumentation of the Facebook group by the same name, the recently stratified master plan titled "Urban plan" states that "Urban Helsinki means more city in the city" (City of Helsinki, 2013, 13). Also, in transportation planning, there has been a shift in policies toward a smaller scale: walking and cycling have been prioritized in the planning guidelines. A main newspaper in Helsinki titled its article on the new planning policies "A coup in the car-oriented city—In the future, Helsinki will be planned for walking and cycling" (HS, 2016). Also, the new master plan has a very urban take on transportation: "In the centres, the pedestriin is king" (City of Helsinki, 2013, 13). The plan has an evident focus on urban livability:

> First and foremost, Helsinki is a city with a human scale. Urban spaces will be designed on terms that suit pedestrians, not vehicular traffic. In the future, fun cities that are pleasant to live in, where everyday life runs smoothly, and where the range of opportunities is ever-expanding will be the successful ones.
> (City of Helsinki, 2013, 5)

The Plan takes a strong stance on livability, but also—in line with the discussion on creative cities—links it with economic competition: according to the Plan, a smooth, every day, fun city and "ever-expanding" range of opportunities is the recipe for success.

Case Kalasatama—Symbolic Values of Urban Livability

Fish Harbour, Kalasatama, is one of the main regeneration areas in Helsinki. It is located north-east of Helsinki's city center, adjacent to eastern downtown. The land was freed up for development when Helsinki built a new cargo terminal further east. The location of Kalasatama is excellent, and it is one of the prime examples of planning and developing a new urban Helsinki—rarely can a city develop such a large area so close to the city center. The plan is to continue the downtown-like urban structure of Helsinki by building a new mixed-use area for 25 000 inhabitants and 10 000 jobs (Uutta Helsinkiä, 2017).

Helsinki's strategic plan lays out the housing identity for the area:

> Metropolis symbolism will be used in the development of the area. The identity consists of industrial and labour history and the positive image factors of the neighbouring area of Kallio, which are, for example, urban life, tolerance and urbanity. The area will be marketed as an area of cultural heritage in which families, single persons, students, professionals and foreigners live.
>
> (City of Helsinki, 2009, 28)

It is an explicit goal of the plan to utilize the positive image factors of the neighboring area of Kallio, which is known for its urban civic activism and robust urbanism. Applying the categorization presented before, here "soft planning" utilizes the symbolic value created by a "soft city" in development of the Kalasatama. Public planning in cooperation with private developers is producing symbols of livability and urbanity in order to affect the social space as well as the real estate value of the forthcoming urban neighborhood (see also Ameel, 2016, 225).

Interestingly, private developers but also the City of Helsinki utilize urban livability and urbanism in creating symbolic value for Kalasatama area —the reference point is general and rather vague and, thus, can be interpreted in a variety of ways. Condominium flats in Kalasatama are being marketed with the theme of "getting more out of everyday". There is also a story of the history of Kalasatama harbor on the website of the development project, painting a rather romantic picture of seafarers operating in the area in the past: "Already a hundred years ago people dreamt of skyscrapers in Helsinki. This dream is becoming a reality in the new residential area of Kalasatama" (Redi, 2015). Kalasatama condominium towers are marketed to be livable in a new way:

> For urbanites, REDI [name of the centre] means a whole new way to live. . . . REDI means an adventure to the future, where seafarer's quest for freedom combines with the city-dweller's dream of a better life. . . . Here everyday life takes on a whole new course.
>
> (Redi, 2015)

On the marketing website of one of the condominiums, there is an article about a bicyclist who visits a café in Kalasatama (Redi, 2017b). The text paints an attractive picture of a picturesque and robust café, operating in a former industrial site. The article is a marketing text for the apartments in Redi towers, advertising the "urban everyday" of Kalasatama for the future homebuyers; however, the café itself is not part of the future plans of Kalasatama, and it will have to close down or find new premises once development takes place (Ihana kahvila, 2017). Here, again, the "soft city" is appropriated for marketing purposes.

Sharon Zukin writes,

> A city is original if it can create the experience of origins. This is done by preserving historic buildings and districts, encouraging the development of small-scale boutiques and cafés, and branding neighborhoods in terms of distinctive cultural identities. . . . Whether it's real or not, then, authenticity becomes a tool of power.
>
> (Zukin, 2010, 3–4)

Branding of the condominiums stresses the historical connection to the areas past as well as authenticity, be it a reference to a unique history of the area or an example of a vernacular culture having taken place in the area (see Hernberg, 2012a on the urban activism in Kalasatama).

The symbolic value linked to the notions of urbanity and livability is used to increase the economic value of urban development. For example, the café in question in and of itself has only instrumental value, its purpose is to represent urbanism, it is an amenity of livable urban environment for the construction company. In a way, this follows the logic of gentrification: the ones who create the symbolic value that contributes to the urban development are eventually out-priced once the development takes place. Or, at least, they are not considered significant enough to be included in the future neighborhood.

Sharon Zukin writes about the TV series *The Sopranos*: "Two of these Italian-American gangsters are standing in a café that looks like Starbucks and one of them says to another, 'You know, we Italians invented espresso but now everyone else is profiting from it'" (2017, 9). Zukin notes that often, products become detached from the original ethnic and cultural context and become commodities for someone else's benefit. The very same idea can be linked with the urban branding of Kalasatama. The logic here is that by branding, one aims at attaching values to an urban development site that otherwise wouldn't exist—a lot of this imagery is symbolic value created by urban activism, popular culture, or just everyday urban social interaction.

In Kalasatama's Redi, these are rather vague notions of urbanity and livability, but they are also references to other regeneration areas. On the Redi website, there is an article that illustrates the future development of Kalasatama, following "the footsteps of the world's trendiest dockland areas" (Redi, 2017a). One of these is the Meatpacking district, that is, the site writes, "currently one of New York's trendiest corners, and a prime tourist location" (Redi, 2017a). Finns are said to have weak "urban self-esteem" because of the late urbanization and young urban culture of the country, and therefore, they are said to undermine Finnish urbanity. This may be one explanation for the need to look at other cities for reference. However, in this case, the Meatpacking district may have been chosen as a reference point because of the symbolic values it represents in terms of lifestyle and urban aesthetics. Unlike in the Meatpacking district, in Kalasatma, there are hardly any reused or preserved buildings. For example, the REDI center, with its shopping mall and adjacent residential towers, is built from scratch. Such branding seems to be an attempt to attach values of urban history, lifestyle and livability to a newly built construction project—and to also present a case of how symbolic values can increase real estate value as well as frame the intended social atmosphere of the future Kalasatama.

Redi Centre—Discrepancy Between Plans and Realization

The center of Kalasatama will consist of eight towers built around a metro station. Six towers will be dedicated to residence, one tower will be a hotel, and the last one will be an office tower. In addition, there will be a shopping center (see Figure 2.1). Although

Figure 2.1 The Center of Kalasatama Will Consist of Eight High-Rise Buildings and a Large Shopping Center—A Visible Exception in an Otherwise Low Silhouette of Helsinki
Source: Helin & Co Architects/Voima Graphics

traditionally, smaller scale shopping and storefront businesses are seen to contribute to urban life and are considered more "urban" than shopping malls, the Redi shopping mall is advertised as "the most urban shopping centre in Helsinki" (Redi, 2017c).

For the master plan of Kalasatama area (City of Helsinki, 2008), an evaluation was made on the impacts of the Kalasatama plan. The aim of the master plan, as well as the strategic plan (City of Helsinki, 2009), is to create a lively urban neighborhood that is "seamlessly connected to downtown", and the plan states that the overall feel of the neighborhood should be "extremely urban"—including small-scale storefront shopping, diverse housing options and a downtown feel (City of Helsinki, 2008, 24). In the plan, the city planning office evaluates that the maximum amount of commercial space in Kalasatama by the year 2030 should be 20 000–25 000 square meters, half of which, at maximum, could be built in a single large retail unit or a shopping mall. Anything more, according to the city planning office, would threaten the economic viability of the street-level shops in the area, and hence, jeopardize the fundamental aim of the plan (City of Helsinki, 2008, 37–38).

In the detailed plan (City of Helsinki, 2011) stratified three years after the master plan, the volumes have, nevertheless, changed dramatically. The number of towers at the center has increased from four to eight, and the height of the towers has risen drastically. The shopping mall space that is allowed to be built in Kalasatama has multiplied to 60 350 square meters. This is more than two and half times the maximum overall commercial space in the neighborhood and approximately five times the shopping mall space that was allowed in the master plan. This is heavily in conflict with the planning offices' evaluation on the maximum commercial space and its effects on the goals of the plans for the area: having more street-level shops, street life, and a downtown feel (City of Helsinki, 2009, 2013). Different levels of planning are in stark contrast.

In addition, in the detailed plan and impact assessment documents thereof, there is not a word on the effects of the increased shopping mall floor space on urban space of Kalasatama or the economic viability of the stores in neighboring districts. Instead, the impact assessment concentrates on various detailed issues on, for instance, how the wind situation changes due to the building of the towers, the visual impact of the towers, and so forth. In one of the city's most important regeneration project for decades, Helsinki is allowing a huge shopping mall to be built against its own planning policies and evaluations. The development of Kalasatama seems to be detached from the values the planning aims to achieve. The aims of the strategic and master plans are either overridden or heavily reinterpreted in detailed planning. There is a clear contradiction in the discursive and symbolic production of urban space between the actual urban environments that are being built based on the plans.

Similar conflicts and discrepancies have been noted elsewhere, too. Lieven Ameel has studied the rhetoric and "storytelling" of the planning process in Kalasatama. He, too, notes the emphasis on creating urbanity and an urban environment in the planning documents, but argues that the projected built environment, on the basis of the analysis of the plans, reminds one more of a suburban area, than a city center (Ameel, 2016; Image, 2016). Also, Lapintie (2014) has noted a related phenomenon in Helsinki's planning, when studying immigration and multiculturality in planning. On a general level of planning, there are goals to integrate and address immigration and multiculturalism in future urban developments; however, the more detailed level of planning is at hand, the less there are mentions of and policies for these resident groups, and the realization of recent urban areas in Helsinki has neglected the housing needs and preferences of ethnic enclaves (Lapintie, 2014). There have also been doubts about how apartment towers of Kalasatama would contribute to the planning goals of the area: livability, vivid street life, and diverse housing provision (Hasu & Staffans, 2014).

Based on Kalasatama, urban livability is a clear planning goal on a strategic and general level of planning, but it gets lost in translation in detailed planning and the construction phase. In Kalasatama, it seems that livability and urbanism as concepts are being used to legitimize plans and projects whose realization doesn't necessarily correspond with the content and aims of the plans. There seems to be a mismatch between the intentions and realization in planning urban livability. At the same time, symbolic values around notions of livability and urbanism, presumably, increase the economic value of the projects. Interestingly, in Helsinki, both private developers and public planning officials utilize urban branding, and it is also conducted in public-private partnerships. Soft planning instruments are mediating between "soft city" and statutory planning and aiming to affect the symbolic image of the city. Soft planning and development instruments utilize the imagery brought up and created by the civic society, but the values behind the brand don't translate into the built environment—they seem to remain on the upper level of vision and plans. By appropriating cultural and symbolic value created by the "soft city", soft planning instruments on one hand, are legitimizing plans and regeneration projects, and on the other hand, are producing urban environment discursively.

Conclusions

Symbolic values have gained importance in urban planning. In Helsinki, urban livability has been one of the key elements of the planning debate in the recent year, and both planners and urban developers have acknowledged the economic significance of urban livability as well as that of symbolic values created by bottom-up urbanism groups. As a concept, a livable city entails various human-centered aspects of the urban environment and everyday life. It aims at understanding attributes of a balanced and desirable life in an urban environment. However, in the context of symbolic values and competition for residents and investments, livability also becomes a political and economic development instrument. Soft meanings and symbolic values are being utilized for marketing, but the content of the built environment does not seem to reflect the planning discourse. Planning and marketing are utilizing the symbolic values revolving around urban livability, but in the process, detach them from their cultural meanings and functions. From this point of view, livability can be seen as a style, rather than contents deriving from residents' life worlds.

One of the challenges with branding-oriented production of urban livability is that it aims at appropriating certain elements of urban life, for example, the grassroots-driven urban action, for commercial use. Although it creates a symbolic representation of an urban neighborhood, it also implies the preferred social setting of urban livability. By the same token, such urban development for economic competition between cities may undermine many of the values related to livability: equity, diversity, affordability, public space, suburban living, and so forth. Discrepancy between aims of the plans and realization of the projects does not support the human-centered and place-specific local identity. As Sharon Zukin (2017) notes, urban environment becomes commodified and detached from the values it is branded with.

Following the categorization of Teo (2014), it seems to be meaningful to divide livability to the conceptual livability of global competition and the livability emerging from residents' everyday life worlds. In the latter sense, Helsinki is very livable in many ways: safe, green, and a relatively just city with good public services. However, based on Kalasatama, the recent planning of Helsinki seems to emphasize the livability of a symbolic level and global competition and undermine that of the residents' experience and existing urban cultures. The Finnish tradition of a welfare state has provided an excellent basis for diversifying and developing the urban livability in Helsinki. The city is changing quickly. With new urban areas being built and new far-reaching planning decisions being made, the key question for Helsinki is how the city can continue to become a livable city for all of its current and future residents: creative professionals and wealthy urbanites as well as immigrants, children, senior citizens, and blue-collar workers. One is tempted to think that the key for Helsinki's success—also in the global competition—could lie in embracing the locally specific, unique qualities in a diverse and inclusive way.

References

Ameel, L. (2015). Narrating Helsinki's Kalasatama: Narrative plotting, genre and metaphor in planning new urban morphologies. In G. Strappa, A. R. D. Amato, & A. Camporeale (Eds.), *City as organism: New visions for urban life: 22nd ISUF International Conference*, 22–26 September 2015, Rome Italy.

Ameel, L. (2016). Emplotting urban regeneration: Narrative strategies in the Case of Kalasatama, Helsinki. In J. Rajaniemi (Ed.), *Re-city: Future city—combining disciplines* (DATUTOP, Vol. 34). Tampere: Tampere University of Technology, School of Architecture.

Andersson, R., Brattbakk, I., & Vaattovaara, M. (2017). Natives' opinions on ethnic residential segregation and neighbourhood diversity. *Helsinki, Oslo and Stockholm, Housing Studies*, 32(4), 491–516. doi: 10.1080/02673037.2016.1219332

Bernelius, V., & Vaattovaara, M. (2016). Choice and segregation in the "most egalitarian" schools: Cumulative decline in urban schools and neighbourhoods of Helsinki, Finland. *Urban Studies*, 53(15), 3155–3171.

Brenner, N., Marcuse, P., & Mayer, M. (2009). Cities for people, not for profit. *City*, 13(2), 176–184.

City of Helsinki. (2008). Sörnäistenrannan ja Hermanninrannan osayleiskaava Osayleiskaavan selostus. *Helsingin kaupunkisuunnitteluviraston julkaisuja*, 11.

City of Helsinki. (2009). *City of Helsinki strategic plan: Development perspective*. Helsinki City Planning Department publications 2009:8. Retrieved from www.hel.fi/hel2/ksv/julkaisut/julk_2009-8.pdf

City of Helsinki. (2011). Kalasatman keskus 10. kaupunginosa, Sörnäinen. Osa korttelia 571, korttelit 10593 ja 10595–10598. *Asemakaavan uutoksen nro 12070 selostus. Helsingin kaupunkisuunnitteluvirasto, asemakaavaosasto, 12070.*

City of Helsinki. (2013). Helsinki city plan: Urban plan—the new Helsinki city plan. *Reports by the Helsinki City Planning Department General Planning Unit, 23.* Retrieved from www.hel.fi/hel2/ksv/julkaisut/yos_2013-23_en.pdf

The Economist. (2016). The world's most liveable cities. Retrieved June 2017, from www.economist.com/blogs/graphicdetail/2016/08/daily-chart-14

Eurostat. (2016). *Urban Europe: Statistics on cities, towns and suburbs.* Luxembourg: Publications Office of the European Union, 2016. Retrieved from http://ec.europa.eu/eurostat/statistics-explained/index.php/Urban_Europe_-_statistics_on_cities,_towns_and_suburbs

Florida, R. (2002). *The rise of the creative class.* New York: Basic Books.

Godschalk, D. R. (2004). Land use planning challenges: Coping with conflicts in visions of sustainable development and livable communities. *Journal of the American Planning Association, 70*(1), 5–13. doi: 10.1080/01944360408976334

Hasu, E., & Staffans, A. (2014). Korkean rakentamisen pilvilinnat (High rising dreams). *Article in the Finnish Journal of Urban Studies (Yhdyskuntasuunnittelu), 52*(4).

Hernberg, H. (2012a). Kalasatama temporary. In H. Hernberg (Ed.), *Helsinki beyond dreams* (pp. 90–101). Helsinki: Urban Dream Management.

Hernberg, H. (Ed.). (2012b). *Helsinki beyond dreams.* Helsinki: Urban Dream Management.

HS. (2016). Vallankaappaus autokaupungissa – Helsinkiä suunnitellaan nyt kävelyn ja pyöräilyn ehdoilla. *Helsingin Sanomat.* Retrieved from www.hs.fi/kaupunki/art-2000002881668.html

Ihana kahvila. (2017). *www-site of the café Ihana kahvila.* Retrieved June 2017, from http://ihanakahvila.fi

Ilmonen, M. (2016). Diversity of residential experiences: On housing preferences and residential choices. In *Ways of residing in transformation: Interdisciplinary perspectives.* London & New York: Routledge.

Image. (2016). Kalasatama on urbaani Prisma, sanoo tutkija. *An Article in Image Magazine.* Retrieved June 2017, from www.image.fi/image-lehti/kalasatama-on-urbaani-prisma-sanoo-tutkija

Kaal, H. (2011). A conceptual history of livability. *City, 15*(5), 532–547. doi: 10.1080/13604813.2011.595094

Kelbaugh, D. (2007). Toward an integrated paradigm: Further thoughts on the three urbanisms. *Places, 19*(2). Retrieved from http://escholarship.org/uc/item/25d4w94z

Kuoppa, J. (2016). *Kävelyn lupaukset kaupungissa. Kolme tapausta kävelijöiden arjesta ja kokemuksista sekä kaupunkisuunnittelusta.* Tampere: Acta Universitatis Tamperensis 2147.

Lapintie, K. (2014). Miksi monikulttuurisuus ei mahdu suunnittelijan suuhun—eikä päähän? *Yhdyskuntasuunnittelu, 52,* 3. Retrieved from www.yss.fi/journal/miksi-monikulttuurisuus-ei-mahdu-suunnittelijan-suuhun-eika-paahan/

Lilius, J. (2015). Is there room for families in the inner city? Life-stage blenders challenging planning. *Housing, Theory and Society, 29*(6), 843–861.

LKH. (2017). *Lisää kaupunkia Helsinkiin—Facebook Group.* Retrieved from www.facebook.com/groups/184085073617/

Lowe, M., Whitzman, C., Badland, H., Davern, M., Hes, D., Aye, L., Butterworth, I., & Giles-Corti, B. (2013). *Liveable, healthy, sustainable: What are the key indicators for Melbourne neighbourhoods?* Melbourne: Place, Health and Liveability Research Program, University of Melbourne.

Mäenpää, P., & Faehnle, M. (2017, January). Civic activism as a resource for cities. *Helsinki Quarterly.* Retrieved from www.kvartti.fi/en/articles/civic-activism-resource-cities

Mäntysalo, R., Jarenko, K., Nilsson, K. L., & Saglie, I.-L. (2015). Legitimacy of informal strategic urban planning: Observations from Finland, Sweden and Norway. *European Planning Studies, 23*(2), 349–366. doi: 10.1080/09654313.2013.861808

McCann, E. (2004). "Best places": Interurban competition, quality of life and popular media discourse. *Urban Studies, 41,* 1909–1929.

Mitchell, D. (2003). *The right to the city: Social justice and the fight for public space.* New York and London: The Guilford Press.

Monocle. (2011). *Most liveable city: Helsinki.* Retrieved June 2017, from https://monocle.com/film/affairs/most-liveable-city-helsinki/

OECD. (2016a). *OECD Income Distribution Database (IDD): Gini, poverty, income, methods and concepts.* Retrieved from www.oecd.org/social/income-distribution-database.htm

OECD. (2016b). *Income distribution and poverty.* Retrieved from https://stats.oecd.org/Index.aspx?DataSetCode=IDD

Official Statistics of Finland (OSF). (2017). *Real estate prices [e-publication].* ISSN=2342–8902. Helsinki: Statistics Finland [referred: 1.6.2017]. Retrieved from www.stat.fi/til/kihi/index_en.html

Partners for Livable Communities. (2017). *Website of the organization.* Retrieved June 2017, from http://livable.org/about-us/mission-a-history

Redi. (2015). *www-site of the Redi centre.* Retrieved from www.redi.fi

Redi. (2017a). *Redi.fi www-site of the Redi centre.* Retrieved from www.redi.fi/en/kalasatama-is-following-in-the-footsteps-of-the-worlds-trendiest-dockland-areas/

Redi. (2017b). *Redi.fi www-site of the Redi centre.* Retrieved from www.redi.fi/naista-evaista-syntyy-kesan-paras-pyorailypiknik-2/

Redi. (2017c). *Redi.fi www-site of the Redi centre.* Retrieved from www.redi.fi/en/shopping-centre/

Ruth, M., & Franklin, R. S. (2014). Livability for all? Conceptual limits and practical implications. *Applied Geography, 49*, 18–23. ISSN 0143–6228. http://dx.doi.org/10.1016/j.apgeog.2013.09.018

Sager, T. (2011, November). Neo-liberal urban planning policies: A literature survey 1990–2010. *Progress in Planning, 76*(4), 147–199.

Schmidt-Thomé, K. (2015). *Between fulfilment and vitiation – Discerning incapacitation in urban regeneration.* Aalto University publication series doctoral dissertations, 176/2015.

Smith, N. (1996). *The new urban frontier: Gentrification and the revanchist city.* New York: Routledge.

Strandell, A. (2017). Asukasbarometri 2016 – Kysely kaupunkimaisista asuinympäristöistä. *The Finnish Environment Institute Series 19/2017.* Helsinki: Finnish Environment Institute: Helsinki.

Sundman, M. (1991). Urban planning in Finland after 1850. In T. Hall (Ed.), *Planning and urban growth in the Nordic countries* (pp. 60–115). London: Spon.

Talouselämä. (2017). Suomi kaupungistuu Osmo Soininvaaran mielestä nyt hallitsettomasti. *Article on Newspaper Talouselämä.* Retrieved from www.talouselama.fi/uutiset/us-suomi-kaupungistuu-osmo-soininvaaran-mielesta-nyt-hallitsemattomasti-muuttopaine-helsinkiin-on-liian-suuri-6658281

Teo, S. (2014). Political tool or quality experience? Urban livability and the Singaporean state's global city aspirations. *Urban Geography, 35*(6), 916–937. doi: 10.1080/02723638.2014.924233

Throgmorton, J. (2003). Planning as persuasive storytelling in a global-scale web of relationships. *Planning Theory, 2*(2), 125–151.

Uutta Helsinkiä. (2017). *City of Helsinki website on regeneration projects.* Retrieved June 2017, from www.uuttahelsinkia.fi/fi/kalasatama

Vaattovaara, M., & Kortteinen, M. (2003). Beyond polarisation versus professionalisation? A case study of the development of the Helsinki region, Finland. *Urban Studies (Sage), 40*(11), 2127–2145.

Zukin, S. (1995). *Cultures of cities.* Oxford: Blackwell Publishing.

Zukin, S. (2010). *Naked city: The death and life of authentic urban places.* New York: Oxford University Press.

Zukin, S. (2017). *Conference presentation.* Retrieved June 1, 2017, from www.cpu.gov.hk/doc/en/events_conferences_seminars/e-zukin.rtf

3 Livable Cities
UK and London

Judith Ryser

What Is a Livable City?

The pendulum of cities from livability to non-livability has swung back and forth throughout urban history: three hundred years ago, London rose from the ashes of the Great Fire, and in the 20th century, it resurrected itself from the Second World War blitz. The livability of cities is affected by many factors, natural and man-made disasters (earthquakes, fires, floods, and epidemics as well as wars, nuclear accidents, pollution, and crime), as well as socioeconomic, environmental and psychological reasons. Livability is intrinsically linked to place and time, thus unique to each city and its inhabitants. This is how the livability of cities in the UK and in particular of London is considered here.

In the UK as regards design and planning, livability has been shaped by Ebenezer Howard's (1902) Garden City movement at the beginning of the 20th century in reaction to the ills of industrialisation, and in the interwar period by functional design advocated by the Congrès Internationaux d'Architecture Moderne (CIAM), which also influenced the New Towns created after the Second World War to decongest UK's large cities and especially London by creating livable self-contained cities beyond their green belts. More recent attempts at livable cities are compact cities with mixed uses.[1]

In the UK, seeking better livability of cities has been an integral part of urban planning, accompanied by 'creative destruction' (Schumpeter, 1942) as condition of such betterment. Livability is inherently culture-bound, which explains how the British dream of 'my home is my castle' has turned housing into commodity by means of government support to acquire homes with gardens in green settings, near facilities and public transport. Livability also applies to neighbourhoods, characterised by location, proximity to good schools, health services, transport, shops, leisure and other facilities, jobs, well-maintained collective open spaces, but also feeling safe due to low crime rates, which often translates into types of neighbours. Livability thus applies to both social and material values whereby objective as well as subjective individual and collective factors shape cities and are often drivers of gentrification.

Measuring Livability of Cities in the UK

Against the background of this wider context this chapter aims to identify current characteristics that typify the livability of cities in the UK and of London in particular. It has to be kept in mind that London, with its 8.8 million cosmopolitan inhabitants (GLA datastore 2016 estimate) and growing, and its 19.1 million foreign visitors per annum, is larger and more complex than many nation states (Prynn, 2016, ONS 2016 estimate). It operates in a global perspective and is not typical of most UK cities.

A wide range of institutions, such as Mori, Mercer, Monocle, Deloitte, PricewaterhouseCoopers, *The New York Times*, and the Economist Intelligence Unit, has quantified the livability of cities and rank ordered it globally as well as regionally according to criteria that reflect their objectives of promoting cities. At the global level, livability indices provide background information mainly targeted at the footloose elite whose mobility depends on the globalisation process. This metric is also widely used by London to highlight its attractiveness in the context of global competitiveness and for city branding. Other more specialised criteria have been devised and may also apply to UK cities. These mainly quantitative metrics have been selected to characterize the relative livability of London and UK cities, although qualitative aspects may well determine where people choose to live.

Livability indices have their critics. They claim that indices do not rank cities but issues, often related to specific purposes, such as benchmarking cities for the purpose to determine expat allowance packages, or for their connectedness which enables global headquarters to keep their outposts on call. Others consider the indices too narrow, favouring 'well manicured older European cities, and (white) new world metropolises'.[2] Others still see a bias towards cities that are least challenging for residents, excluding personal preferences in favour of standard criteria.[3] It may be judicious to conclude that livability is a very elusive concept and perhaps not the best measure to characterise the worth of cities or the desirability to live in them.

Livable Cities in the UK

The UK has a chequered history of livability. It was first in the world to industrialize with unprecedented impacts on the livability of cities as well as rural areas. Factories were polluting the air and water, work conditions were harsh and living conditions dire as depicted by the industrialist Engels in his writings about workers' housing.[4] When factories were located in cities in the north of England or in East London, livability was neither for the working class, nor for many women. Reacting to these unlivable conditions at the end of the 19th century, philanthropists developed alternative concepts of cities and created 'model dwelling companies' to build homes for workers, and some are still in operation today, such as The Peabody Trust. In response to insalubrity in Victorian cities, progressive housing and planning legislation aimed to improve the quality of life of workers already before the First World War. With one of the oldest housing stock in Europe, the UK retains a physical heritage of that period, although heavily transformed and often gentrified. Post-industrialism created new problems affecting the livability of cities, such as high unemployment among unskilled workers connected to poor education and health. Various regional policies to redress deficiency of urban livability were introduced, but the north-south divide persisted, together with the primacy of London.

Livability is a socioeconomic construct closely linked to other factors, such as income equality, education and quality of life. Livability is understood differently in the constituent nations of the UK. Scotland had sovereignty over its own housing while planning for a long time, whereas planning and housing powers have been devolved only recently to Northern Ireland, Wales and London to varying degrees reflecting different aspirations. It was more common, for example, to live in collective housing tenements in Scotland than in England, and this model was reproduced in the early compact new town of Cumbernauld outside Glasgow. In the south, low-density suburban sprawl was more widespread and, with continuous decentralisation, had leapfrogged out to market towns and villages while larger cities were losing population. The return to the city reversed this trend to some extent. Compact cities were offering more urban services, and stigma of urban living was waning. In the late 1980s, London had gained population for the first time since before the Second World War. Similar population losses and gains occurred in provincial UK cities. In recent years, in- and out-migration of cities have accelerated in both directions for a wide range of reasons, not least the end of jobs for life. The seminal assumption that mixed uses would improve livability for people by living near their workplace proved erroneous, as proximity to family, leisure activities, transport hubs and change of lifestyle had become equally important in people's pursuit of livability.

Some are seeking livability in the countryside to escape the urban rat race. Yearning for autarchy has old roots in the UK, promoted by social reformers like Robert Owen and experimented in New Lanark, but new material forms of self-containment have emerged. 'Transition Towns' express people's desire to adopt a more ecological way of life. Totnes in the West Country was the first to endorse the transition model, and Rob Hopkins, its initiator, created the Transition Network, which manifested itself even in London.[5] In 2007, the Labour government launched the 'eco-town initiative' aimed to assist 'eco-friendly living as well as high quality design and architecture'.[6] It is not clear, though, whether these self-declared social experiments amount to greater livability for its participants.

Conversely, others, often young people, are attracted to cities thanks to their better employment prospects and urban lifestyles. The Centre for Cities found that young people (20–29) congregate mostly in large city centres, but also in medium and small city centres, where they are on par with young professionals (30–44), although they are less prominent in London, which is shared by more people over 45.[7] Such population movements could be considered a valid indicator of livability. In the UK, movements between cities and hinterland have accelerated both ways, and this population dynamic has contributed to blur the urban-rural dichotomy.

Yet the UK system of cities persists, reflecting a very centralised country. It is characterised by massive concentration of population, urban functions, financial flows and wealth in the capital London (8.6 million population, GLA est.) and the metropolitan area around it, comprising a number of small- and medium-size cities including fast-growing academic Oxford and Cambridge, amounting to some 20 million people (out of a total UK population of estimated 65.6 million in 2016, ONS) and growing. Other metropolitan areas of over 1 million population have emerged around ten core cities (2011 data).[8] Urban concentration occurs in all four UK nations, and the defenders of economies of scale argue that metropolisation is facilitating better infrastructure and services and thereby increasing livability.

An inherent mismatch between urban change and urban boundaries hampered livability and led to a new definition of the city: 'primary urban areas'.[9] The Centre for Cities' perception of livability is essentially economic related to competitiveness, without taking into account internal differentiation of the cities' physical and social fabric. According to their research core cities, the drivers of the economy are most livable because they are able to attract a dynamic workforce.[10]

'Foresight', also focusing on the economy, found that smaller UK cities have performed more strongly over the past 30 years, a crucial trend for UK's long-term economic competitiveness, which they link intrinsically to well-being and livability.[11]

Yet other than economic criteria may continue to motivate people in the UK in their choice of places to live. The 'noble savage' imagery yearning for a countryside with urban comfort remains strong in the British psyche. These aspirations do not represent contemporary British society, though, and lead to conclude that livability remains firmly in the eyes of the beholders.

Measured Livability of UK Cities

Livability of UK cities was measured by academic research, commercial indices and sectorally (urban economy, development industry, travel, culture, social, spatial criteria, everyday life). One academic example is the livable cities project[12] led by four UK universities[13] that were exploring what makes a city livable, with implications for next generation infrastructure services.[14] Their underlying assumption was that design and engineering is able to improve livability of cities.

Four main UK indices are commercially generated by MoneySuperMarket, uSwitch, UK Money and OPP. *The Telegraph* produces also a series of livability indices based on subjective surveys, besides sectoral indices (see Table 3.1).

Table 3.1 Comparative Table of Selected City Livability Indices and Rank Orders: UK

UK					
indices authors	*type of index*	*author objective*	*target users*	*criteria*	*ranked cities*
'Happiest cities' rank order OPP with Deloitte (2016)	happiest cities index	city competitiveness attractiveness	UK city decision makers Investors	well-being quality of environment happiness	(Ten cities UK) survey sample 2 500 workers UK-wide) Norwich 1 Liverpool 2 Birmingham 3 Brighton 4 Plymouth 5 Sheffield 6 Nottingham 7 Manchester 8 Southampton 9 Bristol 10
MoneySuper Market MSM (2013)	most livable cities in Britain	city economic competitiveness	UK city decision makers, businesses, citizens	disposable income average salary, cost of living, house prices, rent levels, mortgage costs low unemployment life satisfaction	(Twelve cities UK) Bristol 1 Edinburgh 2 Cardiff 3 Liverpool 4 Leeds 5 Manchester 6 *London 7* Belfast 8 Glasgow 9 Birmingham 10 Sheffield 11 Bradford 12
uSwitch independent price comparison (2015)	Best Place to Live	Life ranking: best and worst area quality of life	Consumers	quality of life 26 factors in total: costs (house, rent, energy, food, insurances) equipment (schools, broadband, car registration), life related (mortality, life expectancy)	(138 UK NUTS3 regions) Edinburgh 1 Solihull 2 Hertfordshire 3 Northumberland 4 South Lanarkshire 5 Berkshire 6 Darlington 7 North Lanarkshire 8 York 9 (Outer London S 15, N&W 33, N&E 75, E 84)

(Continued)

Table 3.1 (Continued)

UK

indices authors	type of index	author objective	target users	criteria	ranked cities
UK Money (2015)	Best big city to like in UK	**quality of life** life satisfaction		high wages, affordable rents, low crime levels, low unemployment rate	(23 cities UK) Edinburgh 1 Belfast 2 Birmingham 3 Bradford 4 Bristol 5 Cardiff 6 Glasgow 7 Leeds 8 Liverpool 9 *London 10* Manchester 11 Sheffield 12
Creative Boom (UK sectoral) (2015)	culture creative industries	**innovative jobs**	job seekers in creative industries social entrepreneurs artists	creative knowledge industries arts media receptive diverse population heritage digital infrastructure retail variety waterfronts	Manchester 1, Liverpool 2 Bristol 3 Newcastle upon Tyne 4 Birmingham 5 Cardiff 6 Brighton 7 Dundee 8 Bournemouth 9 Nottingham 10
Telegraph (travel) (2016)	travel	**visit, play not stay**	holiday makers, visitors, culture, free time	historic heritage, cosmopolitan culture and people, new areas, food, music, festivals landscape, museums, market cafes, shopping waterfront themed walks	Edinburgh 1 *London 2* York 3 Bath 4 St Davids Wales 5 Cambridge 6 Wells 7 Durham 8 Chester 9 Oxford 10 Winchester 11 Lincoln 12 Chichester 13 Liverpool 14 Salisbury 15 Cardiff 16 Canterbury 17 Norwich 18 Truro 19 Newcastle 20

UK					
indices authors	type of index	author objective	target users	criteria	ranked cities
Travellers Point (UK sectoral) (2015?)	leisure, travel	**travel holiday making**	travellers, visitors, holiday makers	sports facilities, leisure places, nightclubs, bars, pubs, beaches, fresh food	Newquay 1 *London (but too expensive, dirty) 2* Brighton 3 Manchester 4 Liverpool 5 Newcastle 6 Birmingham 7 Sheffield 8 Oxford 9 Cambridge 10 Cardiff 11 Swansea 12 Edinburgh 13 Glasgow 14
Telegraph (UK subjective)	family friendly	**estate agents**	home seekers with families	good school access to nature kid=friendly amenities cycle paths low crime reasonable house prices slow living	(20 cities regions) Cheltenham 1 North Norfolk 2 Stamford Lincs 3 Great Missenden 4 Edinburgh 5 Tunbridge Wells 6 *[Outer London last and second last]*

Source: © Compiled by Judith Ryser 2016
Source: © Compiled by Judith Ryser, based on the comparative tables of city indices presented in this chapter

Figure 3.1 shows that these indices and rank orders do not produce a unified picture of the livability of UK cities that were found throughout the UK.

Interestingly, neither the capitals of the UK's four nations, nor cities in the more prosperous south, nor post-industrial cities are dominating the top places, although Manchester, a core city, appears in several indices. This wide variety may be explained by the fact that standpoints, criteria and sample sizes vary considerably between the selected indices, although they all contain economic indicators. The broad range of cities may reflect implicit individualistic preferences, which may be related to omitted criteria, such as being born in the city respondents consider most livable, having strong kinship ties with them, hosting their favorite football team or sports facilities to name but a few. Climate does not seem to weigh particularly, nor does city size.

36 *Judith Ryser*

UK
UK cities:
Livability indices

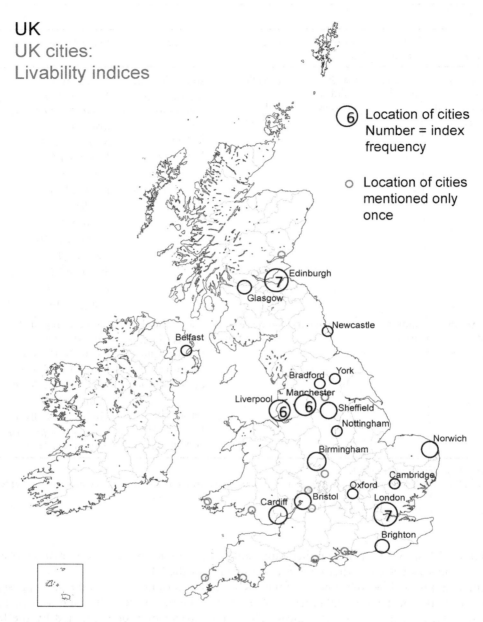

Figure 3.1 Location of UK Livable Cities (according to quoted indices)
Source: Judith Ryser

London's Livability

One thing is clear, London does not top city livability in any of the major UK indices and is often absent. Does this mean that London is not livable, or that it is livable for different types of people than those living in provincial British cities? Indeed, London appears in the top rank of international city livability indices, indicating that its quality of life criteria relates to the global world rather than the UK (see Table 3.2).

Table 3.2 Comparative Livability Index: London Rank Order in Global Indices

author of index	type of index	criteria	London's rank
MMF Mori Memorial Foundation	GPCI Global Power City Index (global competitiveness)	livability economy R&D cultural interaction accessibility environment	London 1 (40 world cities) 2015
Mori Institute for Urban Strategies	CPICI Global Power inner-city Index (urban functions)	Super-rich, footloose urbanites arts FDI industry	London 2 (ex equo) (35 world cities) 2015
Mori Memorial Foundation	GLCI Global Liveable Cities index (sustainability urban functions)	economy vibrancy security stability governance	London 22 (64 cities worldwide) 2015
Monocle Media	quality of life index (human individual aspects)	business context employment connectivity community affordability	London N/A (25 cities worldwide) 2016
Mercer HR & financial services	Most Attractive City (re: work and living)	work relations hygiene access to goods personal services	London 38 (230 cities worldwide) 2015–2016
PwC International accountants	Cities of opportunities	dynamic livable sectoral optima	London 1 (30 cities worldwide) 2014
EIU Economist Intelligence Unit	liveability index (global competitiveness)	quality of life stability healthcare education	London 22 (140 cities worldwide)

Source: © Compiled by Judith Ryser

Socially cosmopolitan with its 300 languages and 240 nationalities, London could be likened to a one-off microcosm garnering a vast array of urban spaces, each with its specific characteristics and aspects of livability, appealing to a broad range of people. Although the London myth of an amalgam of village life has little grounding, its fabric is nevertheless fragmented and segregated along income, ethnic, religious and class divides. This is reflected in the growing number of gated communities or selective free and faith schools. A number of factors accelerate segregation. Property speculation is annexing public land and rights of way.[15] It is also eradicating specialized communities.[16] The corporate sector is taking over public realm for private functions. Rapidly increasing population is exacerbating divisiveness, and generalised surveillance is infringing privacy.

In the light of all this, London's renewed growth cannot be attributed to a sudden increase in livability. It tends to be explained by the deregulation of the financial sector (the 'big bang' in 1986), which brought about liberalisation also of other markets, real estate in particular, and led to population influx from the European Union and the rest of the world in similar numbers. Far from improving London's livability, this growth increased income polarisation and put pressure on housing and urban services as well as affordable workplaces for SMEs and artists. Conversely, it helped higher education, culture and the hospitality sector to flourish. London has traditionally been an open city, but since the big bang, it became more livable mainly for the wealthy to the detriment of the resident population whose eroding living standards are being denounced by many pressure groups. The UK's decision to leave the European Union may compound effects on London.

Dealing With London's Livability Deficits

The key question is livability for whom? As indicated before, London is a very mixed society with a fast-growing population. Its 2015 resident population is estimated at 8.6 million and projected to reach 10 million by 2025. Add well over 17 million foreign tourists per annum, and the pressure on public services becomes self-evident. Internationally, more people move to London than move from London abroad. Conversely, UK-wide, more Londoners move out than people immigrate to London from other parts of the UK. 77% of London's population is British, 12% EU nationals, and 11% others. Among the 77% British nationals, 36.7% were foreign born in London, including 24.5% outside Europe according to the 2011 census.[17]

Browsing through a month's worth of the *Evening Standard*,[18] London's widely read free newspaper provides an admittedly anecdotal but revealing cross section of what are perceived as London's ills. Not surprisingly, London's economy ranks high and its future outside the European Union preoccupies the financial and corporate sectors. Sadiq Khan, the recently elected first Muslim London mayor, is pleading with the previous mayor, now government foreign secretary for the UK, to remain in the Single European Market. Similarly, he makes a case for London's need of highly skilled foreign workers who have always contributed to London's buoyancy. 'Brexit[19] must not stop London from laying the UK's golden eggs', argues Simon Jenkins (2016), but he and Iain Martin remain staunch believers in London's ability to weather any storm, as it did after the Great Fire in 1666, commemorated by burning a model of the medieval city in the Thames 300 years after the event (Kenyon, 2016) or, most recently, after the 2008 global financial crash.[20] Russell Lynch believes that the 'work-permit plan can only deal a body blow to the London economy',[21] whereas Anne McElvoy asks how London can continue to get the workforce it needs.[22] London's universities are also alarmed by Brexit,[23] and some are responding by becoming footloose and digital only.[24] Other obstacles to London's prosperity and thus its livability are of national making, such as the growth of precarious self-employment (Ashton, 2016). Conversely, property tycoons are doing well with temporary office lettings during periods of uncertainty.

At the London level, the extension of the Underground to night travel will help the leisure industry, and the London property industry seems to extend its activities beyond speculative housing and offices to provide room for theatres, rooftop playgrounds and space for start-ups (Tobin, 2016). However, all is not well in London's real estate sector on both ends of the spectrum. 'Foreign super-rich drive out old money'[25] and 'our communities are being driven out by foreign money'.[26] Fighting back is piecemeal and seldom wins. A pub has been priced out due to its own success, to be converted into luxury flats) like 497 others in London in 2015 alone.[27] Even when one development proposal is turned down, a new one is accepted that is not less out of scale or adverse to the local population.[28] Residents and small businesses, retailers and artists are all pushed further out, beyond London or into closure. The last working Art deco cinemas are going down the same route, and even a 100-year-old tree is not spared from commodity greed,[29] although a basement tax may slow down the underground extensions of large houses to accommodate 'must have' swimming pools, gyms, cinemas, wine cellars and panic rooms.[30] Any activities on public land, even football stadia,[31] are under pressure to sell off land to private developers, and a grammar school is being converted into a luxury Indian hotel on London's South Bank that has over 260 skyscrapers, with development permits in the pipeline.

Despite these frantic development activities, London's housing crisis does not show any sign of waning. Yet the illusionary remedy of building the problem out of the way persists. The now twice-weekly property pages of the *Evening Standard* do not lack vacancies, ranging from vertical villages to trendy suburb offers as well as to premises in not-yet-gentrified districts. Besides the advocates of building over the green belt, others want forced sales of all publicly owned land, regardless of what it is kept for.[32] The problem remains housing for ordinary Londoners. The London mayor wants to use public land for affordable housing that means only up to 20% below market value in the UK.[33] Provision of social housing provided by the public sector could contribute to a solution. House prices are rising relentlessly and make housing unaffordable to buy for Londoners below an annual income of £140,000, let alone on a median salary of £30,000, even to rent. Those among the 'generation rent' who can move out of London to buy a home are doing so, unless they can use the 'mum-and-dad bank'. The legacy of vanity projects like the 2012 Olympics can neither cover the long-standing housing deficit, nor redress the most urgent need of housing for the most deprived Londoners. One of the *Evening Standard* campaigns, 'The Estate We Are In', is an innovative example of how stigmatised social housing estates can be turned around and become livable for their inhabitants as well as their surrounding neighborhoods. The campaign started with the Angell Estate in south London and is being rolled out throughout London.[34]

London's infrastructure has been improved in parts. Public rail transport is being expanded (Crossrail 1 and 2), upgraded (Thameslink, the first rail track crossing London) and refurbished (stations are gaining retail but losing ticket offices). However, the inherited fragmentation of public transport prevents integrated commuter services. Many transport interventions are contested: a third runway for Heathrow airport located within London; the extension of City airport; the terminus of HS2 high speed rail connecting London with the north; the conversion of the private, ailing cable car into a drinking club[35] instead of integrating it into the public transport system; the removal of conductors of the new buses, curtailing easy access. Other infrastructures are wanting: the utilities from Victorian times, the sewers, gas, electricity and water networks are crumbling; the cycling network is only slowly extended throughout London; even the garden bridge, yet another vanity project, lacks funding. Meanwhile, developers are resorting to Business Improvement Districts (BIDs) to privatize public space,[36] while public budget pressures are forcing local authorities to sell their assets, which drives space-consuming, low value-added businesses out or into bankruptcy. Prevention of temporary uses are also thwarting creative social entrepreneurship.

Some well-intentioned interventions to improve the quality of life in London have unexpected side effects. For example, land prices get inflated around new Underground stations, relaxation of use classes are pushing out workplaces from the city centre and creating empty ghost quarters, and accelerated and simplified planning conditions are exacerbating social cleansing.

These shortcomings, together with social problems, most of all poverty and crime,[37] are inherent in large cities, together with rough sleepers, beggars and street gamblers. London is no exception.[38] Too much deprivation may lead to rebellion, which repression may not be able to appease. Tensions are also mounting between community groups as well as intolerance and frictions with the police or the local state. Yet not all is doom and gloom in London—quite the reverse. What makes London attractive is its rich, diverse cultural offer, public art, festivals, and nightlife as well as many fringe activities which, like the large number of tech start-ups, are contributing to the creativity and vibrancy of London and thereby to its livability.

Enhancement of London's Livability for All

First and foremost, there is a need to rebalance life chances among London inhabitants, to stop pushing the least affluent Londoners out of the city, and to provide better chances for all to have access to reasonably paid jobs, places to live, education for their children, services for the elderly and care for the disadvantaged. The institutional powers have yet to materialize though, together with political will to induce such profound changes. This remains difficult without devolution of powers to London and its mayor.

London is not without universal provisions, such as free museums, protection of heritage assets and many well-maintained green spaces. A host of cultural events are free and open to all, and freedom passes for public transport are improving mobility for pensioners. Although overstretched, the health service remains free at the point of need in the many excellent London teaching hospitals, and free state education for children still prevails. It is fair to mention the time and money private homeowners are putting into maintaining, improving and expanding their homes, including in conservation areas that contribute to London's heritage and attractiveness. Similarly, Londoners cultivate their gardens and contribute to London's ecology and biodiversity. Grassroots movements have started to grow food in unused public spaces and keep bees on roofs. A host of charities takes care of Londoners in need, and the privately owned *Evening Standard* runs various campaigns for deprived Londoners, the most recent against London's massive food waste and how to get it to the hungry.

How much planning can contribute to improve London's livability imbalance remains to be seen, considering that the central government is retaining many development powers despite the mayor of London lobbying for more devolution. Shared planning powers between the London mayor and the 33 London Boroughs complicate London-wide planning strategies, and in particular, efforts to redress inequalities London-wide. However, the London Legacy Development Corporation (LLDC), which is directly controlled by the London mayor and has planning powers over the whole Olympic site and its surroundings, seems to have done little to rebalance Londoners' needs in that historically deprived area. Although the LLDC is maintaining and animating the park, land is sold to developers with few conditions, not even a timetable for housing development or a proscribed housing mix. The LLCD Local Plan 2015–2031 does not mention livability as such, except in terms of 'creating a sustainable place to live and work'. Nor is it particularly concerned about the displaced residents and businesses who had to give way to the Olympic park development. Their voices have been researched, but they still seem to struggle to retain and regain access to their London area.[39]

London planning has made various efforts to improve livability. It has created conditions to shift people from car use to public transport including at night, fostered more cycling by building designated cycle highways, and made walking safer by widening pavements and slowing motor traffic. However, car pollution remains unacceptably high on many London streets and airbound noise pollution from flight a path of planes and helicopters over the city is increasing and accident rates are not waning. Central government austerity policy continues to put pressure on cities, also on London, and Londoners ask why the London mayor is not more entrepreneurial in clawing back some income, or collecting a tourist tax like most world cities.

How to redress unequal livability among all Londoners remains a prime issue. 'Just Space' is one of many community-led networks that aim to counteract London's trend to polarisation. Assisted by 84 community and volunteer groups, it devised a 'Community Led London Plan'[40] with counterproposals to the London Plan. Its main demands for 'a more liveable London for all' are genuine public participation, an economically fair city, a just provision of housing with a much broader offer of tenures and more protected user rights, a reduction of the need for transport by creating lifetime suburbs and a better environment by turning London into a blue-green city. It points to specific areas where livability of London could be enhanced for all and even proposes new delivery mechanisms for its policies. The work of Just Space, aimed at influencing decision makers, is a good example of how to harness the rich knowledge base of Londoners who feel that they are not given an appropriate say on the future of London, compared with the development industry or the gentrifiers.

Other pressure groups are taking care of neglected public spaces and organize pop-up events. Social housing tenants are fighting for their 'right to the city' and demanding to form 'community land trusts'. Many nongovernmental organizations have contributed ideas to improve London's livability, each from their particular standpoints. CPRE has launched a campaign for a livable London.[41] Although focused on the countryside, CPRE advocates a green infrastructure for London as a contribution to the 'Total Economic Value'. It seeks people-centred solutions to meet London's housing needs and proposes to build partnerships for livable neighborhoods to enhance mutual learning. In 2015, the Greater London Authority Green Infrastructure Task Force recommended to enhance 'natural capital' in a green infrastructure for a Future London. A green grid may also assist the capital's growth in East London.

Many voices point to the deficiencies of London's livability, which needs improving if London is to remain on top of global city ranking and reach a better position on UK livability indices. London claims with some justification that it is the economic engine of the UK as a whole, but innovators and creators may choose less stressful and expensive places for their experimentation that may prove harmful for London's future.

Conclusion

A 'livable city' may provide a material framework but does neither necessarily makes the city livable, nor guarantees quality of life for all. Livability of cities in the UK is influenced by their neoliberal context and how it has come under pressure, especially since the 2008 financial crisis. The presence of 'Occupy' in London's heart of capitalism in 2011 'to fight for a new political and economic system that puts people, democracy and the environment before profit'[42] was one manifestation of discontent. Among other attempts to imagine a system which would favor more just, livable cities for all are Paul Mason's post-capitalism (2016). The Just City alternative for London planning is another.

Like elsewhere, the livability of UK cities varies across geographic levels and with people's expectations. The city rank indices used to characterise livability of UK cities and London reflect such variances, notwithstanding their own limitations. They favour economic indicators, especially at the global level, and may not capture implicit individual and cultural preferences at city level, and they may rank issues rather than cities. By their sheer existence, they may influence livability policies of cities. Despite these reservations, the indices applied to UK cities show that neither climate nor city size or location seem to matter much.

Thus, livability may conceivably depend more on what people living in cities are making of their own lives and immediate environments. They have very uneven and often limited means to achieve this. Yet signs of greater solidarity seem to appear and willingness of people in UK cities to engage more in co-determination, even co-production of their cities,

Notes

1. Taken on board by OECD. (2012). *OECD, compact city policies: A comparative assessment*. OECD Green Growth Studies Series. Retrieved September 14, 2016, from www.oecd.org/greengrowth/greening-cities-regions/compact-city.htm
2. Kotkin, J. (2009, August 11). Why the livable city rankings are wrong. *Forbes*. Retrieved from www.forbes.com/2009/08/10/cities-livable-elite-economist-monocle-rankings-opinions-columnists-joel-kotkin.html#9f47cd218130
3. Conger, B. *Critique of Liveable Rank Ordering (by EIU)*. SPP research paper no. 7-4, 04/06/15, SSEN social science research network, Calgary, Canada: University of Calgary, School of Public Policy.
4. Engels, F. *The Housing Question, 1872, Volksstaat* (various numbers). Reprinted by Progress Publishers Moscow in 1970, prepared for the internet 1997 by David J Romagnolo.
5. See Transition Town Network. Retrieved from https://transitionnetwork.org, no author.
6. www.ecobicester.org.uk/cms/node/37#.V9-3zYX5rTw. This website lists all of the transition initiatives in London. However, this programme has disappeared without trace, except for a single small town, Bicester, pursuing eco-objectives without explicit inclusion of livability.
7. Thomas, E. Serwicka, I., & Swinney, P. *Urban Demographics: Why People Live Where They Do, November 2015*. (Centre for Cities, resident population of 59 cities within England and Wales).
8. https://en.wikipedia.org/wiki/List_of_metropolitan_areas_in_the_United_KingdomThe second city, Birmingham, a polycentric post-industrial metropolis with a 2.4 million population (2011) encompasses Wolverhampton, Coventry, Nuneaton and several other medium-size, formerly industrial cities. The third city, Manchester, with a 1.9 million population extends to Manchester metropolitan area, with a 2.8 million population. The Leeds-Bradford metropolitan area encompasses a 2.3 million population. Liverpool, with 0.79 million population, is forming a metropolitan area of 2.2 million population (2011 est.), with Birkenhead and other smaller cities. Glasgow, with a 1.2 million population, forms part of a metropolitan area of 1.8 million population. Newcastle, with 0.83 million population, is part of Tyneside metropolitan area of 1.6 million population. They are followed by Sheffield, South Hampshire, Nottingham Derby, Cardiff Newport, Edinburgh, Bristol metropolitan areas, all with over 1 million population, and Belfast metropolitan area with just under a million population.
9. Centre for Cities, City definition, PAUs, primary urban areas. Retrieved September 15, 2016, from www.centreforcities.org/puas/
10. Ibid.
11. Future of Cities: Foresight for Cities, Government Office for Science, Foresight, 2016. https://www.gov.uk/government/uploads/system/uploads/attachment_data/file/516443/gs-16-5-future-cities-foresight-for-cities.pdf
12. Retrieved September 16, 2016, from http://liveablecities.org.uk/content/liveable-cities-project
13. The University of Birmingham, Lancaster University, University College London and University of Southampton supported by the Engineering and Physical Research Council (EPSRC) were developing a city analysis methodology (CAM). Retrieved November 12, 2016, from http://liveablecities.org.uk/challenges/city-analysis-methodology. CAM aims to design and engineer UK cities "taking cognisance of one planet living, one world resources and individual and societal well-being."
14. They also examined whether sustainability measures may constrain urban design creativity. Joanne M. Leach et al. (2015). Do sustainability measures constrain urban design creativity? *Urban Design and Planning*. Retrieved from www.icevirtuallibrary.com/doi/full/10.1680/udap.13.00034
15. Vasgar, J. (2012). *Public spaces in Britain's cities fall into private hands*. Retrieved from www.theguardian.com/uk/2012/jun/11/granary-square-privately-owned-public-space
16. The latest is the jewellers in Hatton Garden.
17. All this may change with 'Brexit', UK's decision to leave the European Union, by popular referendum, in June 2016.
18. All the examples quoted have figured in the *Evening Standard* during end of August and end of September 2016, www.standard.co.uk/.
19. British exit from the European Union.

20. Martin, I. (2016, September 14). The Big Bang and a crash didn't stop the City reinventing itself. *Evening Standard*.
21. Lynch, R. (2016, September 15). Work-permit plan can only deal blow to the London economy. *Evening Standard*.
22. McElvoy, A. (2016, September 7). What should we do to get the workforce we need in London? *Evening Standard*.
23. Bentham, M. (2016, September 15). *Evening Standard*, warnings by UCL Provost Prof Michael Arthur.
24. New Model in Technology and Engineering, Hereford, university without lectures at £12,000 annual fee for students worldwide conceived by Peter Goodhew and Kel Fidler.
25. Prynn, J. (2016, 31 August) "Super-rich foreigners forcing the old money elite out of London's prime post codes." Evening Standard https://www.standard.co.uk/news/london/superrich-foreigners-forcing-the-old-money-elite-from-Londons-prime-postcodes-a3332961.html
26. Peter York, *Evening Standard*, September 1, 2016, about massive regeneration of Battersea power station and surroundings, Nick Curtis on the West London the redevelopment of the BBC TV center, *Evening Standard*, August 26, 2016, or 'MiniManhattan, on City Island opposite Canary Wharf, London's second financial center in East London which may be joined by the English National Ballet school and the London film school.'
27. McCoy, F. (2016, August 25). *Evening Standard*. How rent hikes called last orders for the Truscott Arms. *Evening Standard*. Retrieved from https://www.standard.co.uk/go/london/restaurants/the-truscott-arms-a3329156.html
28. For example, 'The Poll' London's tallest 72 story proposal has been replaced by a 'groundscraper of 18 floors occupying 38,000 sq.ft. office space, both designed by Renzo Piano of 'the Shard' fame, London's currently tallest skyscraper.
29. *Evening Standard*, residents fight to save 100-year-old horse chestnut from basement dig, September 8, 2016.
30. *Evening Standard*, Westminster City Council is proposing this very contested measure, September 2, 2016.
31. For example, Millbank football stadium in East London, a very popular Working-class venue; Prynn, J., & Bloomfield, R. (2016, September 30). London 'green belt grab' could lead to loss of football pitch where Sir Trevor Brooking honed his skills. *Evening Standard*. Retrieved from https://www.standard.co.uk/news/london-green-belt-grab-could-lead-to-loss-of-football-pitch-where-sir-trevor-brooking-honed-skills-a3357966.html
32. For example, Daniel Bentley, *Evening Standard*, September 2016.
33. Khan orders TfL to sell unused land for housing, *Evening Standard*, August 23, 2016 https://www.standard.co.uk/news/mayor/sadiq-khan-orders-tfl-to-sell-unused-land-for-housing-a3327236.html. In addition, the Office for National Statistics has published a study on 'affordable housing' which relates house prices to income and market values of housing – 'Housing summary measures analysis 2015.' This study brings together a range of data sources on housing to present 16 housing summary measures that provide a broad overview of the availability and affordability of privately owned and social housing for local authorities in England and Wales. See also: BBC, Reality check, what is affordable housing? November 23, 2016 (no author cited). https://www.ons.gov.uk/peoplepopulationandcommunity/housing/articles/housingsummarymeasuresanalysis/2015#house-prices

    See also: Shelter NGO, What is affordable housing, August 10, 2015. Blog.shelter.org.uk/2015/08. See also: The London Plan, Policy 3.10 Definition of affordable housing. https://www.london.gov.uk/what-we-do/planning/london-plan/current-london-plan/london-plan-chapter-3/policy-310-definition.
34. Lebedev, E. (2015, October 5). The Estate We're in: A Lifeline for Angell Town. *Evening Standard*. Retrieved from https://www.standard.co.uk/news/london/the-estate-were-in-a-lifetime-for-angell-town-a3082961.html
35. *Evening Standard*, cable car should be cheap transport not a nightclub, August 31, 2016.
36. See Vasagar, J. (2012). *Public spaces in Britain's cities fall into private hands*. Retrieved from www.theguardian.com/uk/2012/jun/11/granary-square-privately-owned-public-space; Private-owned public space (csv). *Table providing information of spaces mainly in London but also elsewhere in the UK*. Retrieved from https://fusiontables.google.com/DataSource?docid=1lrNKscwda7NNc9rrq_Si9dhBqZAbv1Cv2Bx-o7s#rows:id=1
37. Knife stabbings, pickpockets in public places, muggings, theft, domestic violence, drug overdosing, gang warfare, even honor and race hate killings.
38. Even a 100-year-old Londoner was assaulted brutally in broad daylight.

39. See: Watt, P. (2016). A nomadic war machine in the metropolis, en/countering London's 21st century housing crisis with Focus E15. *City, 20*(2), 297–320, Routledge; Watt, P. (2016). It's not for us, regeneration, the 2012 Olympics and the gentrification of East London. *City, 17*(1), 99–118, Routledge; Watt, P., & Minton, A. (2016). London's housing crisis and its activism. *City, 29*(2), 204–221, Routledge; Games Monitor was a website created to provide an outlet for those opposing the Olympic park construction, in particular local residents whose housing had been demolished, local businesses and construction workers who were blacklisted due to their protests. The articles are written by various authors, for example, Gary Cox. An introduction to the social impacts of the Olympics, 1996. http://gamesmonitor.org.uk/
40. Just Space. (2016). *Towards a community-led plan for London: Policy directions and proposals.* London: Just Space.
41. CPRE: Campaign to Protect Rural England, The Liveable City Project, Report London. (2014). Retrieved from www.cprelondon.org.uk/projects/item/2161-liveable-london-campaign
42. Occupy London. http://occupylondon.org.uk/about-2/; Jan Taylor, Occupy London was a degree in politics for the streets. *New Statesman*, October 11, 2016. https://webcache.googleusercontent.com/search?q=cache:P-DuvJHeXAJ
    https://www.newstatesman.com/politics/staggers/2016/10/occupy-london-was-degree-politics-streets+&cd=12&hl=en&ct=clnk&gl=uk&client=firefox-b

References

Ashton, J. (2016, September 16). Self-employed are on the rise but pay the price in work rights. *Evening Standard*. Retrieved from www.standard.co.uk/comment/comment/james-ashton-selfemployed-are-on-the-rise-but-pay-the-price-in-work-rights-a3345826.html

Conger, B. W. (2015). *On livability, liveability and the limited utility of quality-of-life rankings* (Vol. 7, Issue 4). Calgary: University of Calgary School of Public Policy.

Howard, E. (1902). *Garden cities of to-morrow* (2nd ed.). London: Swan Sonnenschein & Co. Retrieved from http://archive.org/details/gardencitiestomO0howagoog

Jenkins, S. (2016, September 6). Brexit must not stop London from laying the UK's golden eggs. *Evening Standard*. Retrieved from www.standard.co.uk/comment/comment/simon-jenkins-brexit-must-not-stop-london-from-laying-the-uk-s-golden-eggs-a3338096.html

Kenyon, N. (2016, August 30). The lessons of the Great Fire on how to recreate our capital. *Evening Standard*.

Mason, P. (2016). *Postcapitalism*. New York: Penguin.

ONS (Office of National Statistics). (2016). *Leisure and tourism, visit and visitors to the UK*. Retrieved from https://ons.gov.uk/peoplepopulationandcommunity/leisureandtourism

Prynn, J. (2016, May 18). Record year as 19 million tourists visit London. *Evening Standard*. Retrieved from www.standard.co.uk/news/london/record-year-as-19m-tourists-visit-london-a3542271.html

Schumpeter, J. S. (1942). *Capitalism, socialism and democracy*. New York: Harper and Brothers.

Tobin, L. (2016, September 5). Rooftop playgrounds and new theatres: how property developers are curating communities in London. *Evening Standard*. Retrieved from https://www.standard.co.uk/lifestyle/london-life/rooftop-playgrounds-and-new-theatres-how-property-developers-are-curating-communities-in-london-a3336696.html

4 Place-Making and Livability in Ottawa and the National Capital Region

Angela Franovic and Caroline Andrew

> All quotes and particular information regarding Hendrick Farm were received during an interview with Hendrick Farm and LandLab founder Sean McAdam.

Introduction to the National Capital Region and Governing Sub (Urban) Spaces

The objective of this chapter is to think about the concept of livability in urban spaces very different from those that existed even 20 years ago, given continued suburban and ex-urban development, along with what governments, community groups, and the private sector are currently doing in order to ensure livability. We have chosen to look at Canada's Capital, which requires a slightly more complicated definition than it might appear. In 1867, with the creation of Canada, the capital was to be the City of Ottawa, but over time, this seemed to be in contradiction with the increasing recognition given to the bilingual nature of Canada (more timidly with Prime Minister Lester "Mike" Pearson, who established a Royal Commission on Bilingualism and Biculturalism and adopted a distinctly Canadian flag and more robustly after the electoral victory of Pierre Elliott Trudeau in 1968).

In 1969, Prime Minister Trudeau received approval from the provinces to create the National Capital Region (NCR) (see Figure 4.1) including the City of Ottawa (located in the Province of Ontario), the City of Gatineau (located in the Province of Québec) and considerable rural and semi-rural territory in both provinces that better reflected bilingualism in Canada (for greater detail, see Andrew, in Nagel, 2013). The NCR separates the two provinces by the Ottawa River, but the lived reality is that the population of both sides of the provinces are constantly moving across the bridges at all times of the day; this is largely due to the heavy presence of the federal government within the NCR. A large number of Québec residents work in Ontario and the reverse is true for Ontario residents. Until the 1970s, the majority of federal government office buildings were in Ontario, but by the early 1980s, some 10,000 federal government workers were located in the different phases of Place du Portage, which is located across the river in Québec (Andrew et al., 1981).

As well as locating federal employment on the Québec side of the river, Trudeau wanted a symbolic balancing of the two sides of the Ottawa River and located two new museums—the first permanent home of the National Gallery on the Ontario side and, on the Québec side, the Museum of Civilisation (renamed the Museum of History) designed by Douglas Cardinal, an internationally recognized Aboriginal architect.

The second unique part of NCR's story concerns the municipal amalgamations, both on the Ontario side and on the Québec side. In 2001, the new City of Ottawa was created by

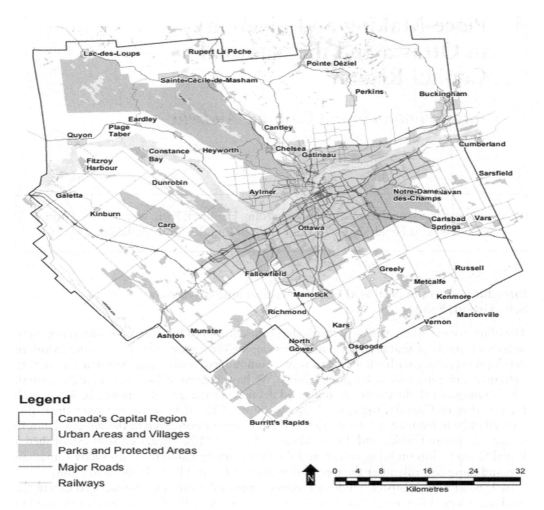

Figure 4.1 National Capital Region of Canada (NCR)
Source: City of Ottawa

putting together the former Regional Municipality of Ottawa-Carleton, the former cities of Ottawa, Nepean, Kanata, Gloucester, Vanier, and Cumberland, the former townships of West Carleton, Goulbourn, Rideau, and Osgoode, and the former village of Rockcliffe Park into the new City of Ottawa. Similarly, on the Québec side the amalgamation put together the former city of Gatineau, the cities of Aylmer and Hull, the town of Buckingham, and the township of Masson-Angers. These amalgamations have led to a limited number of municipal institutions, which certainly facilitates decision-making processes.

In what we are describing as Canada's Capital, there are currently three important decision-making structures, two municipal and one federal: the City of Gatineau, the City of Ottawa, and the National Capital Commission (NCC). The Mayors of Gatineau and Ottawa now sit on the Board of the National Capital Commission, currently as non-voting members but have been promised full membership once the current government is able to change NCC's legislation. Because there are countless and necessary interactions between the aforementioned groups, this chapter will focus on using the National Capital Region (NCR) as the territory of the Canadian Capital.

Having defined the region being discussed, we now need to explain how we are going to examine the governing of suburbia, place-making, and livability in the Canadian Capital. We are going to combine two frames or bodies of literature: the frame of governance and the frame of place-making, as these two complement each other. Governance essentially refers to the process, and place-making about content.

In terms of governance, for this chapter, we have been inspired by the work of the Global Suburbanisms Research project, led by Roger Keil through the City Institute at York University, and in particular the book edited by Pierre Hamel and Roger Keil *Suburban Governance: A Global View* (2015). They go on to propose a method of how to examine the governance of suburbia in practice. There is material to be examined: institutions, practices, discourses, ideologies, and representations that affect how different spaces and processes are produced, contested, and experienced. The solutions to these processes involve both democratic deliberation and social conflict. For the purpose of this chapter, we will focus specifically on the policies and mechanisms put in place to increase livability and place-making in the City of Ottawa but will use the City of Chelsea to exemplify how communities and developers also have a key role in introducing and maintaining notions of livability and place-making in the NCR.

The processes of governance and importance of place-making become increasingly important as two major demographic trends increase, both globally and specifically in the NCR; the aging of the population (on May 3, 2017, Statistics Canada released the 2016 Census, which indicated that 16.9% of Canadians were 65 and older as compared with 16.6% who were under 15, thus confirming this major population shift) and the growing ethno-cultural diversity of the population, who are increasingly pushed out of city centres (urban core). As our analysis is focused on improving the conditions of the most marginalized parts of the population, we focus on the impact governance of new urban spaces has on the elderly and the recent immigrant and refugee population. The increasingly widespread patterns of urbanization make public transit solutions impractical, if not impossible, and therefore increase the focus on the private car. But our two groups demographically challenged, the elderly and recent immigrants, are those penalized by the emphasis on the private car: the elderly becoming dependent on younger drivers and the recent immigrants penalized by the costs of the private car. Ensuring livability and place-making within the City of Ottawa would lessen the burden and need for a private car and would increase health, accessibility, and sustainability, yet efforts continue to be made much more for urban centres rather than suburban and rural areas.

The Concept of Place-Making and Livability

The idea of place-making and livability has gained intensity in response to what is understood as the problem of urban sprawl and has come primarily from the philosophy associated with new urbanism, which focuses on "people and functions in lively public spaces" and in doing so plans for "creating diversity, walkability, and sustainability" (Fishman, 2012, 65). The urban sprawl problem has been defined in a variety of ways including developing suburbs with unforeseen negative consequences (Dunham-Jones & Williamson, 2008; Martin, 2012) or planning that relies primarily on automobiles (Speck, 2013), and it often leads to the ad hoc development and creation of suburbs that is market-driven in nature and innately car-centric. Instead of urban sprawl, tenets of new urbanism, which include place-making and livability, go hand-in-hand with re-developing existing spaces in both a purposeful way, ensuring that suburban development can have an "urban" lifestyle (Dunham-Jones & Williamson, 2008), and a way that will give citizens an enjoyable place to live. When considering development, the social benefit of said development is at the forefront.

Many authors have noted that livability can have several definitions and meanings and there is not one single, accepted definition of the two terms (Palermo & Ponzini, 2015; Whelan, 2012), although they seem to share certain core principles including a focus on community, sustainability, walkability, and interconnectedness. Furthermore, Whelan explains that livability focuses on "economy, ecology, and equity" when considering the use of public space, transit, and building design (Whelan, 2012, 1). This new urbanist push came from the frustration associated with the quality of urban and suburban conditions and the lack of focus on communities and social interest, and it sought to make places better for its citizens (Healey, 2010; Carmona et al., 2003; Healey, 2010; Palermo & Ponzini 2015). Place-making and livability would ideally be able to create spaces where there would be housing, access to community services, sustainability, walkability throughout the neighborhood and/or region, and public transit and would focus on the need and benefit of the community. These two concepts do not forego the need for traditional standards in development, such as the need to evaluate water supply and climate/soil in the region; instead, it is a multifaceted approach that further includes the need to enhance our natural environments in both a sustainable and enjoyable way.

Livability and place-making can be seen as inextricably linked with Edward Soja's concept of "third space". According to Karen Wall, the third space "may be a literal physical space, a cognitive space of dialogue, or a combination" (Wall, 2016, 304). The first place is associated with one's home, the second place is work, and the third place is a neutral, social place where a community is built and conversation and belonging occurs (Dunham-Jones & Williamson, 2008; Oldenburg, 1999). Indeed, Palermo and Ponzini note that livability and sustainability are maintained through the transformation of public spaces, which allows for the interaction of multiple actors, and can generate common meaning and can ultimately impact public policy and social norms (Palermo & Ponzini, 2015). They further add that in order to have success in creating these spaces, the public space must ensure social cohesion and a common good that can enhance the quality of life and capabilities of those who use it, the public space would need to be developed in a way that ensures sustainability and equity, there would need to be a betterment of existing conditions, and there would need to be a distinct appreciation for ethical and social responsibilities (Palermo & Ponzini, 2015, 77). As a result, this movement theoretically incorporates the rights of citizens and their role in controlling urban space and the need for urban transformation and design to respond to the needs of its citizens. For example, this movement was implemented by the Penalosa brothers in Bogotá, Colombia, who rejected the modern urbanist designs of the 1960s, and realized that cities should maximize the utility and happiness for all of its citizens, to use their city in a way that is different from car use only, in order to increase not only the happiness but also the health of its citizens (Montgomery, 2013).

How do we go about making such significant changes? Ellen Dunham-Jones has advocated for re-inhabitation, retrofitting/re-developing, and re-greening of existing spaces. This would mean that cities would need to focus on converting existing developments that are either lacking or unsuccessful (Dunham-Jones uses the example of a dead mall that is transformed to a community centre), whereas other strategies could be to revive nature and parks. Others, such as Jeffrey Speck, focus on the need to ensure that a city is walkable. Speck, along with several other health advocates and studies, insists that the more walkable your city or neighbourhood is, the healthier the people will be (less time spent in a vehicle, or sitting at home, and increasing activity), and the more sustainable and environmentally friendly your region will be. Another key success to place-making and livability would be transit. Freeing up the road space is necessary in controlling urban sprawl and not going "beyond the border" in order to build parks, extra housing, and/or employment; would allow for more walkability; and would allow transit to become the primary service provider in getting people around when they aren't on foot. In North America, many programs have been implemented in order to increase some of the aforementioned ideas and have also been implemented to lessen the effects of urban sprawl (Martin, 2012; Speck, 2013). Vancouver, which has both topical and physical constraints on urban sprawl, have been leaders in urban planning when it comes to the creation of a livable region (Hutton, 2011). Vancouver's history of livability goes back to the 1970s, with their livable region program, and has since focused on issues of growth management, urban structure, preservation of parks and public spaces and, more recently, sustainability (Hutton, 2011).

Livability, Walkability, and Sustainability in Ottawa

Although the City of Ottawa has introduced the notion of walkability, livability, and sustainability, there are still very few policy tools that are being thoroughly used to ensure that future developments adhere to these aforementioned notions in a way that is unified and interrelated. With the city's move towards more urban intensification, it has become even more vital not only to correct issues surrounding urban sprawl in suburban and rural areas, but also to ensure that future projects are being conducted with a larger vision in mind instead of small corrections and projects, which is the city's current approach to enhancing livability, walkability, and sustainability.

Currently, the main policies put forward by the City of Ottawa that address the notion of urban planning, transit, livability, walkability, and sustainability are the Pedestrian Plan, the Ottawa Cycling Plan, the City's Transportation Master Plan, the Infrastructure Master Plan (which are under the Official Plan, the main policy framework in place that governs growth in the City of Ottawa) and the Complete Streets plan. The latest versions of the latter plans have not been updated since 2013, and renewals of policies like the master transportation plan are held up due to appeals made by developers. It is worth mentioning that the City has other programs that focus on safer roads, most of which are done in partnerships with the Ottawa Paramedic Service, Ottawa Police Service, and Pubic Health, but these programs are largely focused on safety issues and collisions rather than enhancing quality of life and enjoyment of public space. Although many strides have been made, it is important to note that there is often a divide between urban planning, transportation, and multimodal use of our roads and increasing place-making outside of the urban/downtown core of Ottawa, areas that are increasingly inhabited by vulnerable populations. The City of Ottawa noted in 2005 in their Official Plan that more and more individuals will be living past the Greenbelt area (suburban and rural areas past Ottawa's urban core), including vulnerable populations as well, and that there has to be proper planning that would include neighborhoods that have access to walking, transit, work, and recreation. However, citizens who live in these suburban areas continue to rely on their automobiles to get most of their errands done and to work, and walking is not as accessible as it should be.

Moreover, the policy tools in place are still in the stage of planning and goal setting and neither incorporate the role of private developers and their responsibility in enhancing livability and sustainability in Ottawa, nor see place-making and livability as a tool to increase equity and to enhance the quality of life for vulnerable populations. This goal becomes even more difficult when we take into consideration current budgetary caps on municipal funding put in place by city council.

The Transportation Master Plan, the Official Plan, and the Infrastructure Master Plan are the three main overarching plans that the City of Ottawa has created. According to the City of Ottawa, "the Official Plan and related Master Plans work together to direct how the city will grow, what infrastructure is needed to support that growth and how the City will pay for the infrastructure" (City of Ottawa, 2013e, 1). In order to accommodate the intensification and growth in Ottawa, along with its changing needs, the City introduced new policy proposals, which were based on public consultation, in their report entitled "Building a Liveable Ottawa 2031", where the focus was, in fact, on financial feasibility and affordability, removing the presence of cars, and the increasing need for an improved interconnected transit system. Although the report is trying to highlight the importance of walking, cycling, and public transit, and understanding that context matters, the Transportation Master Plan is still created without much conversation with the city's urban planners; the city continues to work in silos rather than increasing cooperation between departments.

Although, the report, like many others before it, features walkability, cycling, and transit the follow-up to this report is unclear. As a result, the main policies and reports in place continue to be the master plan that was initially approved, along with the pedestrian plan and cycling plan. This is not the only time the city has introduced the notion of livability and then lacked the proper development and clarity. After the report being published in 2013, there has been no more mention about next steps that are available publicly. Another promising venture that took into account the special context of the National Capital Region and livability was a plan entitled "Choosing Our Future". This report was funded by the City of Gatineau, the City of Ottawa, and the National Capital Commission. The particulars of the initial plan are not available; however, the follow-up to the initial research was created and entitled "Framing Our Future". This latter research focuses on building flexibility and adaptability in the region, building complete neighbourhoods, protecting green space, using a sustainability lens, supporting proper growth through zoning and design guidelines, and so on, but more importantly, it focused on cooperating with partners (City of Ottawa, City of Gatineau, and National Capital Commission), community groups, and other stakeholders (City of Ottawa, 2012).

This project was promising on several levels: not only did it represent the National Capital Region, but also it was a joint and concerted effort towards making livability in the city a priority, with concrete goals that range from environment to proper urban design models. This sort of cooperative planning is necessary, especially in Ottawa, as it aims to renew its public transit system through the implantation of a light rail system. Unfortunately, the initial plan, which was tabled in 2009, had only one real follow-up plan (the aforementioned "Framing Our Future") in 2012, and was then buried. The website for the venture no longer functions, and the initial research is unavailable. Finally, similarly to the other livability policy plans, there has been no mention of the plan or its priorities since 2012 that is accessible to the public. One can posit that the plan has been tabled temporarily. We do not know if this was due to a budgetary issue or whether the policies align with current political interests; the reasons for tabling the plan remain unknown. The NCC (National Capital Commission) has made efforts towards providing a framework for the NCR from 2017–2067; however, the only concrete plans and policies that remain in place for the City of Ottawa are the Pedestrian Plan and Cycling Plan, the Transportation Master Plan and Official Plan, and the Complete Streets plan.

Pedestrian Plan and Cycling Plan

The City of Ottawa's Pedestrian and Cycling Plans focus on "sustainable mobility" and "multi-modal synergies" by ensuring both safe cycling networks that are also connected to the City's transit system and a "walkable urban environment encourages social interaction and local economic vitality" (City of Ottawa, 2013a, 1, 2013c, B-2). The Ottawa Cycling

Plan has the goal of connecting bikes to the new LRT (light rail system) and existing transit way, allowing cyclists to leave their bikes at certain points and take public transit (this goal has not yet been achieved, because the LRT won't be completed until 2020), making sure that the City is doing its part in allowing cycling to be a yearlong option (i.e., ensuring proper snow removal and creating local cycling routes as well as routes throughout major employment hubs (City of Ottawa, 2013a). The benefits of implementing these action items are enhancing public health, environment and affordable modes of transportation and allowing people to interact with public spaces (City of Ottawa, 2013a), all subjects that coincide with the basic tenets of livability. There will need to be continued efforts in bringing proper infrastructure (ultimate network concept) to rural and suburban areas especially. Indeed, the City of Ottawa has shown that cycling is highest in the downtown core, inner urban areas (where there is mixed land use and where the environment was built with cyclist and pedestrians in mind as intensification increases) and lowest in the rural areas. This is most likely due to the lack of purposeful urban development, leaving many people with car-centric mobility.

According to the Pedestrian Plan, the City of Ottawa's focus on pedestrians and walkability came from the International Charter resulting from the Walk21 conference in 2014 (Walk21 is a group that focuses on promoting walking as a mode of transportation internationally); the principles were listed as inclusive mobility, creating spaces and places for people, creating networks, supporting land and spatial planning, increasing road safety, reducing crime, and creating a culture of walking (City of Ottawa, 2013c). The ultimate goal is to ensure that Ottawa becomes a fully walkable city in a way that is both friendly, safe, and functional. Like cycling, there are important benefits to being able to walk including limiting physical and mental health conditions and allowing for increased social interactions, as well as economic and environmental benefits. The City of Ottawa notes that

> the automobile, which has become a primary form of transportation in many communities, has had a profound influence on the built environment of North American cities and suburbs. This has contributed to decreases in physical activity levels . . . and that in Ottawa only 22% of youth meet recommended daily physical activity targets, and only 30% of adults average 10,000 steps or more per day, the target for health benefits based on best practice literature.
>
> (City of Ottawa, 2013c, 6)

It was further found that there has been a decrease in walking trips between 2005 and 2011, and that the majority of walking is typically short and occurs in the inner urban areas of Ottawa, whereas in all other sectors of the city the automobile was the main mode of transportation. The denser (commerce, housing, population) the area is in Ottawa, the more likely it is that the environment can be "walkable". Current changes to enhance walkability (i.e., increasing infrastructure that is both safe and useful) are fragmented and limited to certain areas and have only just begun and will go into the year 2031.

Complete Streets

Another project that was introduced to the City of Ottawa in 2015 was the idea of complete streets. According to the City of Ottawa,

> Complete Streets incorporate the physical elements that allow a street to offer safety, comfort and mobility for all users of the street regardless of their age, ability, or mode of transportation", and that complete streets are meant to "accommodate multiple

modes, incorporate context-sensitive design principles, and can be used as a way to improve neighborhoods and support liveability

(City of Ottawa, 2015, 1)

Complete streets is an idea that has been adopted in both the US and Canada but is not a Federal level initiative and has instead been adopted by cities such as Ottawa and Toronto. In order to do achieve a complete street, the City has introduced the complete streets implementation framework, which ensures that when building specific projects, they consider all modes of transportation (Ecology Ottawa, 2015). Ottawa has already completed audits on several neighbourhoods (all located in the inner urban core of Ottawa), and some streets have even undergone a "complete streets" retrofitting. Unfortunately, the reviews of these projects are mixed: some have said that there is more confusion on the roads, whereas others have noted the traffic congestion and difficulty driving on the new and narrower roads. Regardless of these criticisms, complete streets have slowed down traffic (in fact, part of their intended purpose), they do make extra space for other modes of transportation, and they start to think of the pedestrian and cyclist as equally important as the automobile driver. This policy places accessibility of various modes of transportation at the forefront. Unfortunately, most cases of complete streets in Ottawa are pilot projects in the urban core.

Community Advocacy in the City of Ottawa

Many of the plans to enhance mobility, walkability, sustainability, and livability have been pushed and advocated by several community partners including but not limited to the Council on Aging Ottawa (Age-Friendly Ottawa), City for All Women Initiative (CAWI; they pushed for a low-income transit plan that was finally accepted and is being implemented and also ensured that the Equity and Inclusions Lens was applied to public transit), Social Planning Council of Ottawa, Ottawa Neighbourhood Study (providing walking scores), Healthy Transportation Coalition (providing research and advocacy on issues of transportation), Federation of Citizens' Associations of Ottawa, and the Community Development Framework. The Council on Aging of Ottawa, along with community and neighbourhood groups, conducted walking audits to show the struggles seniors and other vulnerable populations face in areas inside and outside of the downtown core. According to their annual report, key findings were that infrastructure was lacking, crossing times were not long enough, prevention and education regarding increasing road safety was essential, access to public transit needs to be easily accessible, safety of walkways and neighbourhoods needs to be ensured, winter cleaning was sub-par and made many sidewalks inaccessible and so on. It was noted, though, that the largest problem is that very few projects ever come to fruition because the City's budget does not allow it, due to the mayor's promise to put a cap on property taxes in Ottawa; a contentious move that has led to a lack of funds for community funding and cuts to city staff. The overall findings of the report and at the annual meeting to review the report were that small changes are being made but that the City has a lot of work ahead in order to make seniors and other vulnerable populations feel like walking, sustainability, and livability is a yearlong option in Ottawa.

Similarly, our previous research showed that recent immigrants are scattered throughout the city and that immigrant women and elderly immigrant populations in particular are faced with challenges in enjoying and accessing public services due to the lack of proper suburban design and public transit infrastructure. Public transit in Ottawa is exceedingly based on dense areas and where government workers reside and work and overlooks at times the needs of individuals who rely on public transit the most. Organizations like CAWI have given a voice to these populations and have been successful in lobbying an increase in bus routes to suburban areas, as well as an implementation of a low-income bus pass. The importance of the role of organizations such as CAWI or Age-Friendly are undeniable, and without them the city would undoubtedly disregard those who are in less dense or which are outside of the downtown core. These groups ensure that development is not limited to the densification of the urban core and that services, accessibility, and livability of the city is not limited to the majority only.

Is Place-Making, Livability, and Sustainability Possible in the NCR? Case Study: Hendrick Farm Development

The City of Ottawa and the National Capital Region in general have remarkable parks and pockets of walkability, which are largely accessible throughout the urban core; but part of our interest was to see to what extent livability and sustainability was a primary concern and option to private developers outside of the urban core and whether it was even possible. Private development in the NCR has been booming (renewed IT interest), but as previously mentioned, there is little push to ensure that developments safeguard and encourage communities that provide a lifestyle that is enjoyable, sustainable, and healthy for its population. One new project, entitled Hendrick Farm, caught the eye of the authors, a community with the intention of preservation of nature and the goal of place-making and walkability.

Hendrick Farm is developed by LandLab and designed by DPZ (urban planners Duany Plater-Zyberk) and is located in Old Chelsea, Québec (a 10- to 15-minute drive from downtown Ottawa). It is arguably one of Canada's first adaptive developments. Chelsea, Québec, is officially a part of the National Capital Region and is North of Ottawa and Gatineau. Much of Chelsea is made up of the Gatineau Park and Hills (Federal Park that spans just over 360 km) and has the unique reality of doubling as both a suburb to Ottawa (even though it is not in the same province or city), and an urban centre of its own, albeit a small urban centre.

According to LandLab, Hendrick Farm is a "mixed-use agricultural, commercial, residential, and recreational development" that is designed on "the principle that a sustainable, living, breathing community must be composed of a mix of uses that places the needs of people and their environment ahead of an artificially defined set of zoned uses". The ultimate goal of Hendrick Farm is to have created a place where its population can work, play, and interact both socially and economically. Figure 4.2 shows the land prior to development, along with the organic farm that was, in fact, put in by LandLab and was not on the land when they first purchased it. The photo on the right shows the plans made by DPZ that includes a market, boutiques and cafes, parks, single homes, semi-detached homes, and apartments along with manicured trails. At the time of this publication, single homes have been constructed, semi-detached homes commenced construction, and the trails and organic farm were already completed and running.

The plans undoubtedly give rise to the concept of place-making, livability, and sustainability. Although we know that one of the main goals is to build homes and make a profit from a business perspective, as private developers, they have extended that goals into ensuring place-making, livability, and sustainability was a huge part, if not the driving factor, in the development process.

Although there was no legal obligation for the City of Chelsea or Hendrick Farm to consult the public prior to the development, Sean McAdam, lead developer, met with citizens 2 years prior to filing the development application with the municipality. These consultations were informal in nature, but all meetings with neighbours and other interested parties had the aim of understanding what those stakeholders wanted to see within their

Figure 4.2 Hendrick Farm Prior to Development (left)—Hendrick Farm Development Plans Created by DPZ (right)
Source: LandLab and Hendrick Farm

community and what was important to them. McAdam also hosted events when the plan was completed so that individuals could come and share their feedback; this consultation process all occurred prior to the developers officially filing their plans with the city. Each month the developers spoke at council meetings, as did other citizens that were both for and against the project, and both were active in voicing what the project should look like and how it should proceed. Although there was no official public consultation process, the municipality of Chelsea had previously completed a visioning exercise, where the Hendrick Farm development was mentioned and where public opinion on the development was shared. After the developers had filed their plans and were approved, each milestone of the project was shared online via a website so that individuals could follow the evolution of the development.

In addition to listening to the citizens of Chelsea and what they wanted, the developers believe that it was of the utmost importance to "listen to the land", meaning that when creating and planning a development they need to look at the history and intended purpose of that land. As a result, Sean McAdam, founder of LandLab, maintains that listening to the land leads to what he calls adaptive development. Adaptive development, according to him, would mean that each development is unique, as it would have to be designed in order to complement its existing community, its history, its geography, its people, and its land. Applying this thought process to Hendrick Farm, the developers discovered that this land, which is on the cusp of the Gatineau Park, was historically used for agricultural purposes and was rezoned several decades later for housing (700+ houses); housing was never achieved even if it was rezoned to be used as such and agricultural activities stopped decades before then. Hendrick Farm, as a result, became an ode to the two previous conceptualizations, a mix of residential and agricultural, and now commercial, models.

In order to ensure place-making, livability, and spaces that the community would socially benefit from, they not only created the organic farm (the focal point of the project), but they also ensured that over 50% of the land would be preserved. Furthermore, the way in which the homes were built, clusters and networks of sidewalks and green space, allows for more walkability. According to LandLab,

> Through road jogging, a built environment that is appealing and human scale, and distances that work within the idea of the "pedestrian shed" (a distance that can be covered in five minutes at a normal walking pace—typically shown on a plan as a circle with a quarter-mile radius), Hendrick Farm has been designed specifically with pedestrians in mind.
>
> (Interview with Sean McAdam)

Finally, the way in which homes are placed, with porches up front, garages and main roads behind the homes, and sidewalks and walkways either at the front or to the side of the home, puts social interaction at the forefront rather than vehicles. The form of the community is reminiscent of older villages where its community can work, play, and interact easily and rely on one another.

The project was not met with immediate enthusiasm, and the biggest challenges to ensuring that place-making, livability, and sustainability were maintained were, in fact, zoning and other government regulations. The contractors and developers were confronted with zoning that did not traditionally mix agricultural, commercial, and residential zoning. Traditionally, agriculture is far removed from residential zoning, presumably to protect agriculture and ensure its integrity. Similarly, LandLab noted that government regulation did restrict infrastructure engineering, road design, and building types in ways that take away from the social benefit lens. Unfortunately, governments (municipal and otherwise) have not yet realized the benefit in safeguarding for place-making and livability principles in private developments, and municipalities and specific private developments still very much work in silos, often forgetting the place that these types of communities have in the larger national capital region and the larger impact they can have.

Although the project is one to aspire to, it is not without its pitfalls and criticism. Although the houses do range from single homes, townhomes, and apartments (phase 3 of the development), they are predominantly targeted to a middle to high-income bracket and do not do much to attract more vulnerable populations. Arguably, this might be in part because governments do not do much to subsidize projects that encourage place-making and do even less to encourage projects similar to these for vulnerable populations that live in suburban areas. Conversely, the walkability and accessibility aspect allows for individuals with disabilities to more easily access the community and enjoy its parks, walkways, and market place.

Another discrepancy that might be resolved in the future is the lack of public transit in the Chelsea area. The reality is that a large part of the Gatineau and Chelsea population are employed in Ottawa and vice versa. Yet Ottawa has continued to do very little to ensure that public transit meets the needs of those living in suburban and rural areas surrounding the urban core. Chelsea, only a 10- to 15-minute drive to Ottawa, does not have a direct line to Ottawa, leaving much of its population to rely on using automobiles. Ottawa and the National Capital Region continue to expand their borders, yet they fail to increase the infrastructure necessary to ensure connectivity between communities that share employment and housing. Hendrick Farm is hoping that Ottawa/Gatineau will realize that not only does Chelsea bring in almost 3 million tourists that visit staples in Chelsea including Gatineau Park, the Nordik Spa, the golf club, Camp Fortune Ski Centre, and various restaurants, but also the Hendrick Farm too will house hundreds more residents and will have a multifaceted community that will contain a commercial stretch as well. They believe that it will become self-evident that the city of Ottawa and Gatineau will see the need in ensuring proper connectivity to the area. Although this fact might be true, historically OC Transpo (the main provider of public transportation in Ottawa) and STO (the main provider of public transportation in Gatineau) have been slow to realize and develop the important role public transit plays in ensuring a properly functioning national capital region that guarantees livability and connectivity between urban, suburban, and rural areas.

For all of its limitations, Hendrick Farm is an example that place-making is a possibility in urban and suburban development and that mixing traditionally separate zoning areas is not only possible but enhances the social benefit and enjoyment of a particular community. Future steps to ensure place-making and livability in the NCR would be the need for municipal and the federal government to realize its place in brokering and communicating amongst advocacy groups, communities, and urban developers. The municipal and federal governments have zoning and other governance tools that can enhance the social benefit of urban development and can ensure that developments are not only looking for profit but also listening to the needs of its community. We believe that this can truly be done only by listening to the voices of all sectors (government, civil society, and the private sector) and putting the social well-being of its citizens to the forefront.

References

Andrew C., Bordeleau, S., & Guimont, A. (1981). *L'Urbanisation: Une affaire*. Ottawa: Éditions de l'Université d'Ottawa.
Andrew, C. (2013). The Case of Ottawa. In K.-J. Nagel (Ed.)., *The problem of the capital city: New research on federal capitals and their territories* (pp. 83–103). Barcelona: Institut d'Estudis Autonomics.
Carmona, M., Heath, T., Oc, T., & Tiesdell, S. (2003). *Public spaces, urban spaces: The dimensions of urban design*. Oxford: Elsevier.
City of Ottawa. (2012). *Framing our future: A plan for sustainability & resilience in Canada's capital region*. Retrieved May 6, 2017, from http://ottawa.ca/calendar/ottawa/citycouncil/ec/2012/02-21/03-Document%203%20-%20CoF_Sust%20Plan_FINAL%5B1%5D.pdf
City of Ottawa. (2013a). *Ottawa cycling plan*. Retrieved May 6, 2017, from http://documents.ottawa.ca/sites/documents.ottawa.ca/files/documents/ocp2013_report_en.pdf
City of Ottawa. (2013b). *Master transportation plan*. Retrieved May 6, 2017, from http://documents.ottawa.ca/sites/documents.ottawa.ca/files/documents/tmp_en.pdf
City of Ottawa. (2013c). *Ottawa pedestrian plan*. Retrieved May 6, 2017, from http://documents.ottawa.ca/sites/documents.ottawa.ca/files/documents/opp_2013_en.pdf
City of Ottawa. (2013d). *Official plan*. Retrieved May 6, 2017, from http://ottawa.ca/en/city-hall/planning-and-development/official-plan-and-master-plans/official-plan
City of Ottawa. (2013e). *Building a liveable Ottawa 2031*. Retrieved May 6, 2017, from http://greenspace-alliance.ca/wp-content/uploads/2017/02/OP-2014-preliminary_proposals.pdf
City of Ottawa. (2015). *Complete streets in Ottawa*. Retrieved May 6, 2017, from https://documents.ottawa.ca/sites/documents.ottawa.ca/files/documents/complete_streets_en_0.pdf
Dunham-Jones, E., & Williamson, J. (2008). *Retrofitting suburbia: Urban design solutions for redesigning suburbs*. Hoboken, NJ: Wiley.
Ecology Ottawa. (2015). *A guide to the complete streets implementation framework for the city of Ottawa*. Retrieved May 6, 2017, from https://ecologyottawa.ca/2015/07/31/a-guide-to-the-complete-streets-implementation-framework-for-the-city-of-ottawa/
Fishman, R. (2012). New Urbanism. In B. Sanyal, L. J. Vale, & C. D. Rosan (Eds.), *Planning ideas that matter: Livability, territoriality, governance, and reflective practice*. Cambridge and London: MIT Press.

Hamel, P., & Keil, R. (2015). *Suburban governance: A global view*. Toronto: University of Toronto Press.

Healey, P. (2010). *Making better places: The planning project in the twenty-first century*. Houndmills, Basingstoke: Palgrave Macmillan.

Hutton, T. A. (2011, August). Thinking metropolis: From the "livable region" to the "sustainable metropolis" in Vancouver. *International Planning Studies*, 16(2), 237–255.

Janssen-Jansen, L. B., & Hutton, T. A. (2011, August). Rethinking the metropolis: Reconfiguring the governance structures of the twenty-first-century city-region. *International Planning Studies*, 16(3), 201–215.

Martin, J. A. (2012). Public policy promotion of livable cities. In B. Sanyal, L. J. Vale, & C. D. Rosan (Eds.), *Planning ideas that matter: Livability, territoriality, governance, and reflective practice*. Cambridge and London: MIT Press.

Montgomery, C. (2013). *Happy city*. New York: Farrar, Straus and Giroux.

Oldenburg, R. (1999). *The great good place: Cafes, coffee shops, bookstores, bars, hair salons, and other hangouts at the heart of a community*. New York: Marlowe & Company.

Palermo, P. C., & Ponzini, D. (2015). *Place-making and urban development: New challenges for contemporary planning and design*. London and New York: Routledge.

Speck, J. (2013). *Walkable city: How downtown can save America, one step at a time*. New York: North Point Press.

Wall, K. (2016). Gathering place: Urban indigeneity and the production of space in Edmonton, Canada. *Journal of Urban Cultural Studies*, 3(3), 301–325.

Whelan, R. K. (2012). Introduction to community living. In F. Wagner & R. Caves (Eds.), *Community livability: Issues and approaches to sustaining the well-being of people and communities*. London and New York: Routledge.

Part II
Livability and Growth and Development

Introduction

Growth and development issues offer challenging conditions to develop and maintain livability in our cities. This is the thrust of Part II. Chapter 5 examines how Austin, Texas, has struggled with this issue. With growth comes issues surrounding whether everyone will have opportunities. Will all people benefit from government actions? We know that property values increase with growth. Will this lead to displacement and gentrification? What are the consequences of redevelopment? As different groups emerge, a true city vision for livability is needed. Unfortunately, the presence of multiple groups adds complications to issues associated with livability. There needs to be discussions regarding the relationship between development and housing affordability. The vulnerability of neighborhoods must also be addressed in any discussion of revitalization.

Chapter 6 examines the issue of livability in Warsaw, Poland. Warsaw is the country's growth machine. Livability must be addressed, as the country's population shifts from rural to urban. Changes have occurred and with changes comes complaints. These complaints are the results of new demands from residents and grassroots activist groups. This chapter looks at how the city is coping with the problems associated with growth in its quest to be livable in the minds of its residents. It covers actions that need to be developed and implemented if it is to be a livable city.

Chapter 7 investigates livability in the Pune, India, metropolis. The Pune area is a magnet attracting people for jobs. As Pune has grown, satellite towns have surrounded it to handle the growth. Many low-income people have ventured to it for jobs. One important issue that must be understood about all areas is the area's history. History must be taken into consideration when considering and developing livability strategies. This is especially true with the presence of squatter settlements. Infrastructure projects are critical in such areas and need to be considered when examining policy and program options for livability.

5 Struggling Toward Livability in Austin, Texas

Elizabeth J. Mueller

Introduction

Civic boosters in Austin, Texas, routinely highlight the city's high ranking on many "best of" lists, culminating in its place atop *U.S. News and World Report*'s 2017 list of best places to live (U.S. News and World Report, 2017). Since 2011, the city has ranked high on 50 lists, which the city tracks under the headings of economy, environmental leadership, education, qualify of life and real estate (City of Austin, Texas, 2017). Most such lists emphasize job opportunities and lifestyles appealing to new, young migrants. At the same time, other recent rankings have highlighted the region's ongoing patterns of social separation and inequality: in 2015, Florida and Mellander ranked the region as first among large metro regions on its index of overall economic segregation (Florida & Mellander, 2015, p. 56) marking it "the place where wealthy, college-education professionals and less-educated, blue collar workers are least likely to share the same neighborhoods" among large US metropolitan areas (Badger, 2015). Another study placed the city ninth among large US cities in income segregation and found that the share of the population living in mixed-income neighborhoods had declined over time (Bischoff & Reardon, 2013). A 2011 Brookings study ranked the region high among large metros in its growth in suburban poverty (Kneebone & Berube, 2013).

The polarized nature of the city's rankings highlights the tensions between its rapid economic growth and the uneven landscape of opportunity and quality of life across groups and neighborhoods within the city:

> We celebrate what we're doing right to be ranked first, recognizing it also highlights the accompanying affordability, equity and mobility challenges that our city faces. . . . Inherent in that ranking is the strength to manage growth so we can preserve Austin's special spirit. —Austin Mayor Steve Adler
>
> (Theis, 2017, par. 7).

These tensions are evident in current struggles over plans and policies that will shape the growth of the city moving forward and will determine whether and how growth will reshape current patterns of exclusion and polarization. This chapter chronicles this period, focusing on key decisions and the positions taken by groups operating under varied assumptions about what constitutes a livable Austin. To frame this discussion, we begin with an overview of the different meanings of the term "livable" and how these shape agendas for action.

Conflicting Visions of Livability

Livability is inherently a socially constructed concept, rooted in the relationships between people and the environments that contribute to their well-being (Kaal, 2011; Pacione, 1990). For city residents, livability is intertwined with urban life and the factors that shape it. Early discussions of urbanism, focused on the rise of large cities in renaissance Europe and later during the industrial revolution, emphasized the new social relations associated with urban life and with the creation of an urban class and city culture (Mumford, 1937). Contemporary discussions focus either on advocating for the importance of particular factors to urban life or on the threats posed by new urban projects to current residents—especially for groups most vulnerable to harm. Based on these purposes, livability then becomes linked to particular projects or policy agendas.

Economic development and growth that dominate popular discussions of urban livability in US cities are presented as engines of creativity and innovation (Florida, 2005; Glaeser, 2011), harkening back to earlier portrayals of cities as places that liberated their residents from the constraints of rural social hierarchies and allowed some greater freedom to define their own social position (Kashef, 2016) and where civic culture both emerged from and reinforced urbanity (Mumford, 1937). US urban economic development agendas are set in the context of resource-poor city governments and depend heavily on the formation of governing regimes whose agendas are dominated by land development interests (Molotch, 1976; Stone, 1989). Critics have noted that unequal power in agenda setting works against integration of equity goals (Oden, 2016). Nowadays, such regimes commonly advocate for a platform characterized by "reduction of public subsidies and regulations, the aggressive promotion of real estate development . . . and the privatization of previously public services" (Hackworth, 2007, 16). Livable cities are thus characterized (and ranked) as places that offer a set of policies consistent with these goals, thought crucial for robust economic development (Fisher, 2013; Kaal, 2011).

At the same time, rising concern for the relationship between urban growth, environmental degradation and population health has fostered a movement for new forms of planning and settlement. Environmental livability agendas focus on maintaining the health of urban ecosystems and reducing the impact of urbanization on the natural environment (Kashef, 2016). The environmental, economic and health challenges associated with urban sprawl are well-documented (Burchell & Mukherji, 2003; Ewing et al., 2008; Ewing et al., 2003; Frumkin, 2002). Policy guides, development benchmarks and best practices recommended by professional planning organizations seek to foster sustainable development by promoting a greater mix of land uses and focusing density to support higher transit use and reduce vehicle miles traveled by residents (American Planning Association, 2000, 2002, 2008, 2012; ICMA and Smart Growth Network, 2002, 2003). Of course, mixed-use, transit-oriented development is not inconsistent with the development agendas described earlier: it enables higher returns for developers and greater property and sales tax revenue generation for cities. Tensions revolve around the consequences of redevelopment on a scale large enough to foster new, more sustainable patterns and around who will inhabit newly redeveloped central neighborhoods (Pollock et al., 2010).

In rapidly changing cities, the tensions between groups motivated by different livability agendas will be high. Local economic development agendas are often viewed as natural and thus inevitable (Hackworth, 2007; Marcuse & Kempen, 2008). Yet the rich contemporary case study literature on the differences in urban development across cities suggests that political struggles and resulting policies can shape development (Marcuse & Kempen, 2008). The environmental justice movement has pushed to broaden the conception of the environment in local discussions to include social justice dimensions (Agyeman et al., 2003;

Dobson, 1998; Pulido, 1996). Environmental justice activists have reframed quality of life goals in terms of their ability to ensure that all types of people have a decent quality of life (Gauna, 2008). Yet linking local (often neighborhood-based) concerns and struggles to city-level agenda setting and policies remains difficult—particularly for the historically marginalized groups and places that are most often the target of current redevelopment agendas.

Neighborhoods are often at the center of discussions of livability. Because they constitute the scale at which we organize the social landscape of cities, integrating race and class dimensions of political marginalization and vulnerability with redevelopment, they are often where reaction to new agendas is organized. Neighborhood-based struggles have spawned a growing movement toward neighborhood representation in city decision-making, including forms of self-governance. Threatened communities have called for a "right to the city" that allows them to have a say in its governance, that gives them meaningful and full urban citizenship (Harvey, 2003; Kaal, 2011). In many cities, demands for improved conditions or a seat at the local policy table have been translated into neighborhood level councils or participatory processes that are connected to city-level policy making (Fung, 2006; Thomson, 2001). Although presented as democratic and open to all, such processes place a premium on community self-organization (Chen et al., 2009; Fagotto & Fung, 2006; Molina Costa, 2015).

In this chapter, we use the case of Austin, Texas, to consider how efforts to foster new forms of urban living have been received by residents, the particular ways that conflict has emerged and the decisions that have resulted. We will discuss the struggle to define a local livability agenda in Austin and the key events and conflicts that have emerged as the city attempts to adopt policies ostensibly aimed at implementing a citywide vision. In particular, we will focus on the view of neighborhoods in this process, the way that threats to livability are framed and how they relate to the city's underlying landscape of inequity.

The Context for Livability in Austin

Austin has sustained a steady pace of growth for most of its history, growing from a modest-sized city of 250,000 in 1970 to one containing more than 920,000 by 2015—an increase of 268%. During the same period, the broader metropolitan area grew from 400,000 to over 2 million (Robinson, 2016). It has gone from a city whose workforce was dominated by moderate income state and university workers to a diversified, technology oriented, regional economy with greater extremes of wealth and poverty. Its low cost of living and large public university helped spawn a unique culture and music scene. By 2014, Austin had transformed from one of the most affordable small cities in the country, to the 11th largest city in the nation and the least affordable housing market in the state of Texas. The region was the fastest growing of the nation's largest metropolitan areas in 2011, with an annual growth rate of 3.9% (Mueller & Kaplan, 2014).

The region's rapid growth and shifting wage structure has been driven in part by the rise of new sectors in the regional economy and the reduced share of overall employment comprised by government workers. Between 1991 and 2011, the share of regional workforce employed by state and local government fell from 29% to 23%(Texas Workforce Commission, 2011). Although the rise of the technology sector has been heralded as an engine of regional growth and wealth, there has been a parallel rise in service jobs with low average wages. Of the ten largest occupational categories in the MSA, only three had annual incomes above $60,000 in 2015. The other seven occupations were service jobs with mean annual wages between $19,800 and $34,100 per year (Texas Workforce Commission, 2011).

Over the past 50 years, the city's environmental footprint has also grown. The city's urbanized area expanded from 86 square miles in 1970 to 524 square miles in 2015–five times its earlier size. Citywide, population density declined sharply between 1970 and 1990, while building back to nearly 1970 levels by 2015. As growth expands outward, the share of regional population captured by the city has declined, from 63% in 1970 to 46% in 2010 (Robinson, 2016). The amount of driving is also on the rise; whereas vehicle miles traveled per person declined at the state level, it rose in the Austin metro area from 2008 to 2014 (Community Advancement Network, 2016). One consequence was a rise in congestion—six city corridors made the list of 100 most congested corridors in the US (INRIX, 2015). Finally, in addition to threats to water quality, growth has put a strain on the region's water supply and also contributed to flooding in neighborhoods along the many creeks in the city (Wheater & Evans, 2009). In response, FEMA has updated maps of local flood plains, which now encompass many existing homes ("New FEMA Maps for Central Texas Expand Flood Plains," 2015). A major flood event on October 31, 2013, highlighted the growing vulnerability of low-lying neighborhoods to flooding. Flooding was most dramatic in the Onion Creek neighborhood, whose boundaries were based on 1970s-era FEMA maps. Environmental justice activists have charged that the city's approach to flood mitigation neglects the needs of neighborhoods in east Austin (Almanza et al., 2016).

Concerns regarding the impact that growth might have on existing neighborhoods have been a central theme in city plans and policy disputes over the past 40 years. In the 1970s, these concerns focused on preventing encroachment of denser development into traditional residential areas (City of Austin, Texas, 1979). Although such concerns continued, by the 1990s, attention was focused on shifting development from the west side of town to the east, ostensibly to protect the city's karst aquifer and the iconic Barton Springs pool (Swearingen, 2010; Tretter, 2016). By the turn of the century, attention was focused on rapidly rising property values and property taxes, particularly in central core neighborhoods where values were rising most dramatically in percentage terms (Robinson, 2017).

Rapid and sustained growth has been overlaid on a racial landscape that has been shaped by segregationist government policies and private real estate practices. Beginning with the early settlement of the city, a pattern was set through the use of restrictive property deed covenants that set allowed uses, development intensity and—in some cases—prohibited people of color from occupying properties.[1] The city's first comprehensive plan, adopted in 1928, codified these patterns by creating a "negro district" in central east Austin, which was the only area where separate-but-equal public services would be provided to African Americans (Koch & Fowler, 1928). In 1935, the federal Home Owners Loan Corporation, in consultation with the local real estate community, created a "residential security" map that graded particular areas of the city according to the risk they posed to lenders (see Figure 5.1). Such maps were based on criteria set during the Great Depression that favored new construction, single family homes and white communities (Massey & Denton, 1993; Rothstein, 2017). They reinforced the racial and economic patterns in place, coloring central east Austin red ("hazardous") and affluent west Austin and nearby undeveloped areas green ("desirable"). In the 1950s, the city further undermined the value of property in minority neighborhoods by overlaying industrial zoning on central east Austin. In the 1970s, urban renewal areas were designated in both downtown and central east areas, although not all were fully implemented due to resistance (Busch, 2011; Naishtat, 1972).

By the 1990s, attention had shifted to protection of the hilly west side over the aquifer from development, and city policy began to favor redevelopment of the low-density downtown, with support from environmentalists. The city's Smart Growth strategy created a new "desired development zone" in the center and east side of town and offered

Struggling Toward Livability in Austin, TX 65

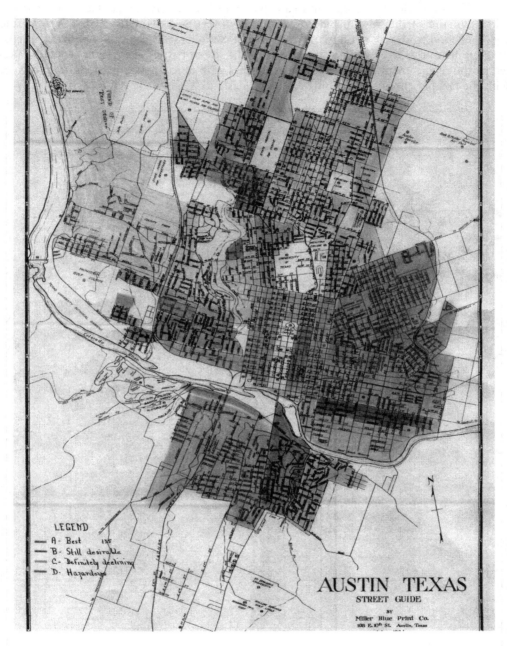

Figure 5.1 Austin HOLC Map
Source: National Archives and Records Administration (NARA) II RG 195, Entry 39. Folder "Austin, Texas," Box 153

various incentives for growth in these areas while constraining development in the west side "drinking water protection zone" (McCann, 2007; Tretter, 2016). A low-income Latino neighborhood on the southeast edge of downtown was the site of a protracted battle over rezoning as it was incorporated into the renewed downtown. The end result illustrates the worst fears of long-time residents: redevelopment produced new, high-end, high-rise condos and apartments and the conversion of the modest homes of former residents into

66 *Elizabeth J. Mueller*

bars and restaurants, both adjacent to a newly built Mexican American Cultural Center—a key demand of the now displaced community (Tretter & Mueller, 2018). The Latino neighborhood to the east of downtown, across the interstate, began to experience intense development pressure. By 2010, this area was the site of battles over rising property taxes fed by the replacement of existing, modest homes with upscale, custom homes out of sync with the neighborhood's scale and vernacular design.

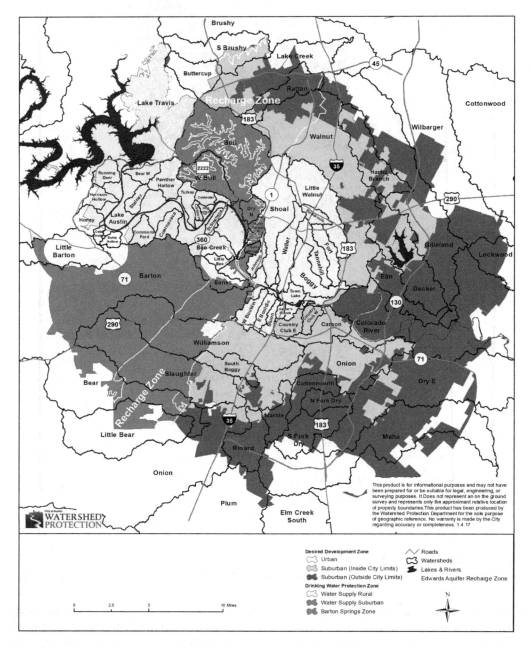

Figure 5.2 City of Austin Watershed Regulation Areas
Source: City of Austin

The city's previous attempts to shape city-scale growth patterns, through planning, have been largely ineffectual and have encompassed both regional, non-binding visioning processes and the creation of district or neighborhood scale plans. City-scale efforts have been particularly weak: the 1979 plan, *Austin Tomorrow*, was a vision plan with few details about implementation. Efforts in the 1980s to create a more robust plan foundered after a long public process and a change in the composition of the city council (Gregor, 2010). Restrictions on development over sensitive watersheds were adopted by citizen referendum in 1992, rather than through formal planning (but were later undercut by the state legislature) (Swearingen, 2010). By the 1990s, the city had shifted strategy away from the development of a citywide comprehensive plan. Instead, it focused on development of neighborhood plans, which were then appended to the 1979 plan. In addition, the city created other district scale plans for the central business district, for areas adjacent to stations on the city's one light rail line, along selected transit corridors and for areas opting into the use of new mixed-use zoning (called vertical mixed-use zones). At the same time, the city participated in a regional planning effort, Envision Central Texas, aimed at building consensus around a less sprawling regional growth pattern, amenable to regional transportation planning. The non-binding scenario selected has had little effect on government policy, the pattern of transportation investments governed by the Capital Area Metropolitan Planning Organization, or the dynamics of sprawling growth.

Over time, the limitations of planning in this way became apparent. An audit of the city's Long-Term Planning in 2006 found that "the city has not laid out a citywide vision for growth to effectively guide long range planning decisions" and that "the city of Austin pursues various planning efforts that form a patchwork of plans; however these plans are not formally integrated to achieve a unified vision" (City of Austin, 2006, 5). The report noted that neighborhood planning had come to dominate local planning efforts but that it was narrowly focused on land use. In describing the outdated nature of the 1979 plan, the report noted that "one of the stated characteristics to result from implementation of this plan is that most new residential construction would be low density single family units" (18–19). This goal was established when the city's population was approximately 349,000—roughly 38% of its current population (Robinson, 2016). In addition, the process of creating neighborhood plans proved to be time consuming and slow, with only 45% of the city's population living in areas with an adopted neighborhood plan by 2016, with few in lower income neighborhoods (City of Austin, 2016). In addition, such processes have also been criticized as unrepresentative of the residents of their planning areas and lacking transparency (City of Austin, 2016).

From this point onward, a series of initiatives and events have brought the tensions between different views of livability into high relief. The city's effort to develop a new comprehensive plan set off a sequence of related initiatives and conflicts that are far from resolved. The central theme running throughout these efforts is how growth will affect the existing city and who will bear the burden—or reap the benefits—of rapid change.

Defining the Livable City: *Imagine Austin*

By 2009, momentum was growing for the creation of a new comprehensive plan for the city. From the start, the process was contentious: membership on the citizens' advisory group was by appointment by city council members and county commissioners, who were allowed to veto a certain number of their colleagues' appointments. The plan advisory group developed the initial vision statement, with extensive community input, over a nine-month period:

> As it approaches its 200th anniversary, Austin is a beacon of sustainability, social equity and economic opportunity; where diversity and creativity are celebrated; where community needs and values are recognized; where leadership comes from its citizens and where the necessities of life are affordable and accessible to all.
>
> Austin's greatest asset is its people: passionate about our city, committed to its improvement, and determined to see this vision become a reality.
>
> (City of Austin, 2012, 74)

The plan then breaks this statement down into seven components including "Austin is Livable":

> One of Austin's foundations is its safe, well-maintained, stable, and attractive neighborhoods and places whose character and history are preserved. Economically mixed and diverse neighborhoods across all parts of the city have a range of affordable housing options. All residents have a variety of urban, suburban, and semi-rural lifestyle choices with access to quality schools, libraries, parks and recreation, health and human services, and other outstanding public facilities and services.
>
> (City of Austin, 2012, 76)

Within this brief livability statement lie the seeds of the battles that have been (and continue to be) fought out over the city's future. Creating economically mixed neighborhoods—including affordable housing—would require the inclusion of multifamily rental housing in areas currently zoned for and often deed-restricted to provide only low-density, single family housing. Providing residents a choice of neighborhood types, ranging for low to high density, implies that some areas will not include this housing mix (or not much of it). And providing equitable access to public services implies, perhaps at a more fundamental level, an undoing of the city's deeply embedded pattern of economic segregation.

Not surprisingly, the combatants in the battle over adoption of the plan focused on the issue of neighborhood change in central Austin. Central neighborhoods both east and west of the interstate (the city's historic dividing line) opposed adoption of the plan on the basis of fears of how it might encourage redevelopment or the addition of density to existing neighborhoods. For east Austin residents, this concern was voiced as yet another example of how east Austin was being taken advantage of, of "expelling the have nots so that the haves can redevelop the land" (Houston, 2012). Others objected to the public process, which they felt had marginalized current citizens at the expense of powerful interests, who believed that it was important to favor new residents as the "saviors of Austin" (Bartz, 2012). The vehicle for protecting neighborhoods was the neighborhood plan: a letter sent by the Austin Neighborhoods Council to the Planning Commission in opposition to adoption of the comprehensive plan called for the plan to be shelved until all areas of the city had such plans, which would then be the basis for the new comprehensive plan (Aleman, 2012). In contrast, although affordable housing advocates embraced the idea of using the plan to create "complete communities" throughout the city, they were less effective at building support for this message.

Imagine Austin was adopted by City Council unanimously on June 15, 2012. The final resolution included an amendment put forward by a council member with strong ties to neighborhood groups that made clear that it would not override existing neighborhood plans or prevent the development of future such plans "and not predetermine decisions made" in these plans. At the same time, the plan was amended to make clear that the growth concept map should indicate the areas that would protected from growth—namely, "environmentally sensitive areas . . ." and to protect the character of neighborhoods by directing growth to areas identified by small area plans." A statement was added to make clear that the growth concept map should be consistent with existing neighborhood plans (Morrison, 2012). Thus, adoption of the plan came with conditions that prevented changes to neighborhoods covered by such plans. This issue would be debated again as the city moved forward to revise its land development code to be consistent with the plan.

Challenging the Local Regime: Geographic Representation

As the comprehensive plan was moving toward adoption, an alliance was forming to push for a vote on a new form of city council representation. A new system was promoted as a way to increase the diversity of the council, improve voter turnout and increase the connection between council members and their constituents (Annette Strauss Institute for Civic Life, 2015). Discontent over the decisions of the current at-large city council brought together a coalition united by a view that the current at-large council structure represented central neighborhoods at the expense of other parts of town and interest groups. The coalition brought together minority neighborhoods, more suburban neighborhoods and the development community. Austinites for Geographic Representation gathered 33,000 signatures on a petition to put a measure on the ballot to have a nonpartisan commission draw ten districts. An alternative proposal to include two at-large seats on the council, and to allow the council itself to approve the district maps, was opposed by 10–1 proponents as patronizing and potentially corrupt because it implied that the at-large seats were for the "smart people, for the ones who really grasp the big issues . . ." and that control over the map would constitute a "gentlemen's agreement 2.0,[2] 2012 edition" (Garza, 2012). Both measures were placed on the ballot as separate propositions. The 10–1 measure passed by a higher margin and was adopted.

The new council elected in November of 2014 was more diverse on several dimensions: it included three Latinos, one African American, seven women—and three Republicans. The races themselves were qualitatively different. A total of 78 candidates competed for the ten seats, some in very crowded fields. Debates and forums allowed candidates to discuss district level concerns in greater depth.

The new council brought both a more locally grounded and comparative perspective to city issues. A study on the new council during their first year in office, based on interviews with community leaders, found concern about the socioeconomic, racial and political divides across and within districts, along with optimism that the new system could help better represent diverse viewpoints (Annette Strauss Institute for Civic Life, 2015). The business community, who had supported the 10–1 proposition, expressed some buyers' remorse, fearing that the change would "reverse the push to make Austin a 'world class' city" (Diaz, 2014). Advocates for low-income and minority constituencies felt their issues were better represented by the new council (Velasquez, 2016).

The city's declining affordability was a central theme in the council elections. The new council debated a proposal to grant tax relief to homeowners by creating an exemption for a percentage of assessed value of owner-occupied properties. The issue highlighted the power of homeowners both within neighborhoods and across the city. Despite several studies documenting the transfer of wealth away from users of various city services to owners of high value properties, council passed the first of what was described as several steps toward a 20% exemption—a promise in several council district campaigns (King, 2014; Tynan, 2015). The measure was adopted as part of the budget process. An attempt by a council member representing a poor, primarily renter district to reduce the exemption and redirect the equivalent of the foregone 1% exemption to tenant support programs was voted down (Casar, 2015). In short, despite representing a majority renter city, and increasing attention to renter issues, the new council still reflected the strong voice (and vote) of homeowners and their neighborhood associations.

Code Next: Facilitating, Blocking, or Changing Development?

The tensions between neighborhood plans and neighborhood representation and the future vision for the city were brought back into relief as the city moved forward on one of its priority programs under the new comprehensive plan—the rewrite of the land development code. This process was dubbed "Code Next". Once again, the tensions between the goals embodied in the "Austin is Livable" statement were apparent. Neighborhood associations, environmental organizations, professional groups representing development interests and urbanist organizations voiced their concerns, working through a variety of groups and coalitions. Neighborhood organizations were represented both by a citywide umbrella organization and by individual associations and coalitions whose concerns differed by area of the city. Environmental groups included citywide groups, groups focused on particular creeks, lakes or neighborhoods and environmental justice groups. Development groups included the real estate council, the board of realtors—but also, at times, nonprofit affordable housing developers. Urbanists included architects and planning professionals, millennials, bicycle and transit advocates and a nascent group of alternative neighborhood associations that included small-scale infill developers.

The purpose of the code rewrite was ostensibly twofold: first, to clarify the rules by integrating the layers of exceptions, unique overlays and neighborhood plan elements applying in different parts of town into a clear set of zoning codes, and second, to direct growth in a pattern consistent with the vision presented in *Imagine Austin*. In both cases, there was concern about the impact of the rewrite. Central city neighborhood groups were concerned that the new rules would not really embody all that was agreed to in the neighborhood plans; development groups and urbanists were worried that they *would* embody these constraints and thus that no meaningful change would occur. East Austin neighborhoods feared that even sticking with current zoning would result in their ongoing displacement and that any further change would only accelerate the dramatic pace of redevelopment in their communities, which were highly vulnerable as a result of a history of permissive zoning.

The tensions and strange bedfellows engaged in the Code Next process are best seen through the view taken of low-density, single family neighborhoods by various groups. A speaker at a community advisory group meeting charged current residents of low-density neighborhoods with enforcing segregation:

> We can't ignore the effects that our density limits have in central Austin. Density limits force people to purchase a certain amount of land to buy a home. These land purchase requirements are what have made us the most economically segregated city in the country. It's not something that just happened to us. Economists around the country are telling us that we did this. Single family neighborhood is a segregationist term. If you can afford a single family home in central Austin, congratulations. Buy it and invite me over sometime. But if I can only afford enough land for a townhouse, no law should prevent me from living anywhere in central Austin. If I can only afford to share land in an apartment no law should prevent me from living anywhere in central Austin. Pushing people away from our great parks, frequent transit and central

living with a short commute is wrong. The people who are asking to preserve single family neighborhoods are asking to preserve segregation because they like the way their neighborhoods look. And that's a request that we should reject. We can't just tweak our segregation laws. We can't adjust our segregation laws. We must repeal our segregation laws.

(Babalola, 2016)

Urbanist organizations began to focus on the need to open up older, low-density, single family neighborhoods to new development or redevelopment as a fair housing issue. A frequent speaker to the Code Next advisory group, representing a broad coalition of urbanist, environmental and development groups repeatedly made this point at monthly meetings:

Mixing housing options does not damage neighborhoods.... It's also what's basically fair. I don't know why any citizen in our town should be told that because you don't make enough money you don't have access to a certain neighborhood or a certain part of a neighborhood... The market's going to cause some of that unfairness, but for us to exacerbate that problem, that unfairness by actual government policy, I think is wrong.

(Harren, 2016a)

A representative of central east Austin, a long-time Latino community leader active in the Austin Neighborhoods Council responded, focusing on the ownership aspect of this housing rather than the form:

I heard that somebody was telling you guys that single family housing is racist. Is that true? Did somebody come and say that to you all? I'm here to tell you that single family housing is one of the main ways that people of color have been able to prosper in our country and in our city. Without homeownership there is no prosperity. Whoever is telling you this has some kind of secret agenda cause that absolutely is not true. This city has more renters than homeowners ... we need to have ownership of apartments, of homes so people can build equity.... Homeownership of single family housing is anything but racist ... when I was growing up, those who did not buy homes, their kids had less of a chance. Homeownership is where it's at. It's anything but racist.

(Llanes, 2016)

While the battle over the single family zoning raged, others attempted to return attention to the vision justifying change. The *Imagine Austin* plan called for the creation of "complete communities" throughout the city:

A complete community is a great place that meets your daily needs within a short trip of where you live or work. A community is "complete" when it provides access by foot, bike, transit or car to jobs, shopping, learning, open space, recreation, and other amenities and services. That means no matter what part of Austin you live in ... nearby amenities help you in the pursuit of your desired quality of life. Simultaneously, we want complete communities that preserve identity, culture, and sense of place.

(City of Austin, Texas, 2013)

At issue was whether it would be possible to create such communities without changing existing single family neighborhoods—particularly those that are uniformly low density. The battle here was between neighborhood advocates and urbanists of various stripes.

Neighborhood advocates feared that their neighborhood plans would not be respected, or that development on adjacent corridors would drive up their property taxes. They focused their demands on ensuring that plans would be respected and that any changes to rules regarding adjacent areas would not affect them. On the other side of the argument, urbanists claimed that it would not be possible to realize the goal of creating complete communities without changing neighborhoods. They argued that limiting redevelopment to the "centers and corridors" marked on the growth concept map was a misinterpretation of *Imagine Austin*:

> We ought to allow all price points in all neighborhoods and that proposal is completely supported by *Imagine Austin*. If you look at what the comp plan actually says . . . We are going to create and maintain affordability throughout the city. That's not one mention of centers and corridors in that program. Not one mention. You go to the first sentence of *Imagine Austin*: We are going to be a beacon of social equity. Then you go to page 107 where it talks specifically about what types of redevelopment will occur under the comp plan, outside of corridors and centers. What is that area? Our neighborhoods. It says that we will redevelop everything from single family housing up to large apartment projects, in areas outside of centers and corridors. Plus office, plus commercial, plus institutional needs. I don't know how clear we could be . . . Why should we segregate housing types? Particularly in our neighborhoods?
>
> (Harren, 2016b)

The mayor weighed into the fray when he delivered his State of the City address in January of 2017. He clearly sided with the view that new development should be directed away from existing neighborhoods. In what was described as the "Austin bargain" he stated that "we will protect our neighborhoods" while delivering the "increased housing supply we need to make it more affordable by building on corridors and not forcing density into the middle of [single family] neighborhoods" (King, 2017).

Existing low-income communities remained concerned about the vulnerability of their neighborhoods—not only to displacement through gentrification. Central east Austin has historically been the repository of many unwanted industrial uses that were not allowed in other residential neighborhoods. For example, the leader of a local environmental justice group pointed out that despite successful efforts to rezone industrial sites occupied by residential uses in central east Austin, many existing industrial sites had been allowed to keep their industrial zoning. She argued that industrial zoning for these grandfathered, often hazardous uses, in the middle of historically minority residential areas, should be revoked (Almanza, 2016).

The Strategic Housing Plan: More Housing vs. Fair Housing?

The push to adopt the city's first Housing Plan added intensity to the debate over the relationship between development and affordability. After discussing the need for a local housing plan for years, the city's Housing department initiated a public process for developing a plan in early 2016. As it moved forward, the discussion of affordability became conflated with the land development code discussion, and the emphasis shifted to the need for greater housing supply. The need for more supply was increasingly used as an argument for overriding any restrictions on infill development in central, residential neighborhoods. Urbanists continued to argue for loosening up zoning restrictions to serve both overall supply goals and to address fair housing issues.

Once again, the tensions focused in on central Austin. Affordable housing advocates argued for setting goals for production of housing affordable to low-income residents and also for access to high opportunity areas of the city, and to locations providing accessibility, via transit, to jobs and services. Urbanists often cited academic studies on the link between zoning and income or racial segregation (Lens & Monkkonen, 2016; Pendall, 2000). Less often noted was that these studies find the strongest effects in the most affluent jurisdictions or neighborhoods, where low-density zoning is most effectively employed as an exclusionary tactic. In Austin, the groups fighting over where infill should be allowed were generally focused on central neighborhoods that were among the most diverse in terms of housing type in the city. These areas were often incorrectly identified as sites of white flight, when most had been developed well before the city's school integration initiative of the 1970s. Instead, the wealthy west side enclaves that such research highlighted were largely untouched—and undiscussed—locally. In part, this was because such areas were largely understood to be closed to change due to restrictions attached to property deeds and thus beyond the purview of local zoning rules.

Neighborhood advocates opposed the housing plan as another tool for increasing pressure on central neighborhoods. They saw the supply arguments put forward by urbanists, linked to production of "missing middle" housing types, to be a sort of Trojan horse for pushing through the kind of changes to their neighborhoods they feared would be adopted in the new land development code.

Nonetheless, after much debate and a protracted process, the Strategic Housing Plan (renamed a Blueprint) was adopted and appended to the comprehensive plan. In essence, the Blueprint set goals for production of affordable housing, for integration of subsidized housing into all areas of the city and for preservation of existing housing vulnerable to loss in the centers and corridors identified in *Imagine Austin*. It left unresolved how such goals would be achieved. In particular, it left unclear how goals would be met for integrating housing affordable to extremely low-income households into low-density, suburban districts currently lacking rental housing. As a result, the council adopted a follow-up resolution called on staff to propose a strategy for implementation which included discussion of how they would be integrated into the neighborhood planning process. Thus the battle over such changes is still to come.

The issue of race and the historical context for these discussions was brought back into focus when the mayor established a task force on institutional racism in early 2017. Working intensely, the group produced a report by the end of March. The real estate and housing working group challenged the idea that segregation was simply an outcome of market processes, beyond the reach of policy:

> What accounts for the residential economic and racial segregation of Austin? Some argue that it is driven primarily by the housing market. As Austin becomes a destination city, those with means move here from other parts of the country at a rapid clip, thus raising housing prices and, subsequently, property taxes, especially in the more attractive areas of the urban core. In turn, longstanding residents, particularly those with modest means, can no longer afford to live in the heart of the city . . . The focus on market forces suggests that the racial segregation we are witnessing today is . . . beyond the purview of government remedies. But, this line of argument fails to account for the ways in which past government policies which were explicitly racially discriminatory—including laws, ordinances, and city planning—were directly responsible for segregation and gentrification driven displacements we witness today. City government has yet to take full responsibility, much less redress these past racial injustices. Our working group believes it should.
>
> (City of Austin, Mayor's Office, 2017, 18)

74 *Elizabeth J. Mueller*

Although the report included a long list of ideas for addressing institutional racism, there was a discouraging lack of consensus among task force members regarding appropriate solutions and no clear mandate for moving forward.

Conclusion

The debate over realizing the livability vision put forward in Austin's comprehensive plan and related policies reflects underlying disagreements about what it means to be a livable city. At its heart, these disputes center on whose views are considered most valid or important to the features of livability each group values. In Austin, these battles are between old and new residents, across lines of race and class, and housing tenure, and across age cohorts. These divisions prevent the articulation of a more inclusive, forward-looking livability agenda in the face of strong growth pressures and development interests.

The neighborhood has become the central site of conflict in Austin's battle over livability. Long-time homeowners in central neighborhoods focus on maintaining the character of their existing neighborhoods and resisting dramatic changes. Their concerns are embodied in the adopted neighborhood plans for many central neighborhoods and defending these plans has become the focus of these groups. For long-time minority residents, livability goes further to acknowledge the distinct vulnerability of their neighborhoods and the role of public actions in its creation. Long-time residents—whether white, African American or Latino—want acknowledgment of the history of their particular neighborhoods and of their past efforts to protect them. Historically segregated communities want additional protection to address their extreme vulnerability to change.

For more recent younger migrants to the city, and for renters with lower incomes, livability means having access to the city, including central neighborhoods. This takes several forms—finding a place to live and having access to jobs and services, but also having a voice in discussions of city goals. For these residents, the dominance of traditional neighborhood groups in city politics feels exclusionary. They have formed common cause with urbanists and urban developers to have a voice in city discussions. Their demands for access have been transformed into demands for more housing across all neighborhoods, regardless of historic context.

The concentrated focus on central residential neighborhoods in Austin is problematic for several reasons. First, it has districted attention from other areas of the city. For example, it has distracted attention from the truly exclusionary suburban neighborhoods, where low-density zoning and, in some cases, deed restrictions, have been most effective in limiting housing choices. And important environmental concerns—at both the city-regional scale, and for particular sites—have not gotten enough attention or have been framed primarily to serve neighborhood preservation goals. Second, it has supplanted a conversation about the public, civic realm that could be envisioned and created in the city. The focus on neighborhoods and on neighborhood scale organization leaves to the side discussion of other spaces and forms of representation that might help build a broader conversation about urban life and livability. In the context of ongoing growth pressures and dramatic redevelopment in the center of the city, this means that the physical spaces that might support this civic realm are likely being lost.

We began with a discussion of early aspirational visions of the power of urbanism. These visions of the city as a place where social interaction among people or groups unlike each other would produce new forms of life and new ideas hinged on the urban public realm. The battle in Austin is leaving to the side the questions that need to be answered in order to define a more aspirational vision and move toward it: what sites should be the focus of action aimed at fostering a livable city? What constitutes the civic realm in the livable city, and who has access to it?

Notes

1. Such racial restrictions were overturned by the Supreme Court in 1948.
2. The current at-large council, in order to comply with the voting rights act, operates under a "gentlemen's agreement" where one seat is understood to be the black seat, and thus should be a contest between black candidates, whereas another is the Hispanic seat.

References

Agyeman, J., Bullard, R., & Evans, B. (2003). *Just sustainabilities: Development in an unequal world*. Cambridge, MA: MIT Press.

Aleman, S., & ANC President. (2012, March 27). *Austin neighborhoods council letter to Austin's planning commission re imagine Austin*.

Almanza, S. (2016). *Citizen communication on industrial zoning*. Code Next Community advisory group meeting. Austin, TX.

Almanza, S., Granados, E., & Zeh, A. (2016). *Drainage fees, capital improvements and equity in the city of Austin*. Austin, TX: PODER.

American Planning Association. (2000). *Policy guide on planning for sustainability*. Adopted April 16, 2000. Retrieved from http://www.planning.org/policy/guides/adopted/sustainability.htm

American Planning Association. (2002). *Policy guide on smart growth*. Adopted April 15, 2002. Retrieved from http://www.planning.org/policy/guides/adopted/smartgrowth.htm

American Planning Association. (2008). *Policy guide on planning and climate change*. Adopted April 27, 2008. Retrieved from http://www.planning.org/policy/guides/pdf/climatechange.pdfAmerican Planning Association. (2012). *Policy guide on smart growth*. Retrieved from https://www.planning.org/policy/guides/pdf/smartgrowth.pdf

Annette Strauss Institute for Civic Life. (2015). *Civic engagement in Austin: Views on 10–1 geographic representation*. Austin, TX: University of Texas.

Babalola, N. (2016). Citizen communication at Code Next Community Advisory Group meeting. Austin, TX.

Badger, E. (2015, February 23). The wealthy are walling themselves off in cities increasingly segregated by class. *Washington Post*, Wonkblog. Retrieved from https://www.washingtonpost.com/news/wonk/wp/2105/02/23/the-wealthy-are-walling-themselves-off-in-cities-increasingly-segregated-by-class/?utm_term=.a39cfdba9efc

Bartz, J. (2012). *Public hearing on imagine Austin*. Austin City Hall.

Bischoff, K., & Reardon, S. F. (2013). Residential segregation by income, 1970–2009. In *The lost decade? Social change in the U.S. after 2000*. Retrieved from www.s4.brown.edu/us2010/Projects/Reports.htm

Burchell, R. W., & Mukherji, S. (2003). Conventional development versus managed growth: The costs of sprawl. *American Journal of Public Health*, 93(9), 1534–1540. https://doi.org/10.2105/AJPH.93.9.1534

Busch, A. (2011). *Entrepreneurial city: Race, the environment, and growth in Austin, Texas, 1945–2011*. Austin, TX: University of Texas.

Casar, G. (2015). *Discussion of tenant based rental assistance proposal by Council member Gregorio Casar*. Austin City Hall.

Chen, B., Cooper, T.L., & Sun, R. (2009). Spontaneous or constructed? Neighborhood governance reforms in Los Angeles and Shanghai. *Public Administration Review*, 69(1), 108–115.

City of Austin. (2012). *Imagine Austin comprehensive plan*. Austin, TX: City of Austin, adopted by city council.

City of Austin, Mayor's Office. (2017). *Mayor's taskforce on institutional racism: Final report*. Austin, TX: City of Austin.

City of Austin, Office of the City Auditor. (2006). *Long range planning*. Austin, TX: City of Austin.

City of Austin, Office of the City Auditor. (2016). *Audit of neighborhood planning*. Austin, TX: City of Austin.

City of Austin, Texas. (1979). *Austin tomorrow comprehensive plan*. Austin, TX: City of Austin, Department of Planning.

City of Austin, Texas. (2013, February 25). What is a complete community? *Imagine Austin* [Blog post]. Retrieved from http://www.austintexas.gov/blog/what-complete-community

City of Austin, Texas. (2017). *City stage: Local and national rankings*. Austin. Retrieved from www.austintexas.gov/department/local-and-national-rankings

Community Advancement Network. (2016). *CAN dashboard 2016: Key socioeconomic indicators for greater Austin and Travis County*. Austin, TX: Community Advancement Network.

Diaz, J. (2014, August 18). Could the hyper local focus of 10–1 reverse the push to make Austin a "world class" city? *KUT*. Retrieved from http://kut.org/post/could-hyperlocal-focus-10-1-reverse-push-make-austin-world-class-city

Dobson, A. (1998). *Justice and the environment: Conceptions of environmental sustainability and theories of distributive justice*. Oxford: Oxford University Press.

Ewing, R., Bartholomew, K., Winkelman, J., Walters, J., & Chen, D. (2008). *Growing cooler: The evidence on urban development and climate change*. Washington, DC: The Urban Land Institute.

Ewing, R., Schmid, T., Killingsworth, R., Zlot, A., & Raudenbush, S. (2003). Relationship between urban sprawl and physical activity, obesity and morbidity. *Journal of Health Promotion*, 18(1), 47–57.

Fagotto, E., & Fung, A. (2006). Empowered participation in urban governance: The Minneapolis Neighborhood Revitalization Program. *International Journal of Urban and Regional Research*, 30(3), 638–655.

Fisher, P. (2013). *Grading places: What do the business climate rankings really tell us?* (2nd ed.). Washington, DC: Good Jobs First.

Florida, R. (2005). *Cities and the creative class*. Abingdon, UK: Routledge.

Florida, R., & Mellander, C. (2015). *Segregated city: The geography of economic segregation in America's metros*. Retrieved from www.diva-portal.org/smash/record.jsf?pid=diva2:868382

Frumkin, H. (2002). Urban sprawl and public health. *Public Health Reports*, 117(3), 201.

Fung, A. (2006). *Empowered participation: Reinventing urban democracy*. Princeton, NJ: Princeton University Press.

Garza, D. (2012). *Statement at charter revision committee of committee member Delia Garza, § city of Austin charter revision committee*. Austin, TX.

Gauna, E. (2008). El dia de los muertos: The death and rebirth of the environmental movement. *Environmental Law*, 38(2), 457–472.

Glaeser, E. (2011). *Triumph of the city*. Oxford: Macmillan.

Gregor, K. (2010, February 5). Austin Comp Planning: A brief history. *Austin Chronicle*.

Hackworth, J. (2007). *The neoliberal city: Governance, ideology, and development in American urbanism*. Ithaca, NY: Cornell University Press.

Harren, F. (2016a). *Citizen communication on the need for housing diversity in neighborhoods*. Austin, TX.

Harren, F. (2016b). *Citizen communication the need to change neighborhoods to achieve Imagine Austin goals*. Austin, TX.

Harvey, D. (2003). The right to the city. *International Journal of Urban and Regional Research*, 27(4), 939–941.

Houston, O. (2012). *Public hearing on imagine Austin, § Austin city council meeting*. Austin, TX: Austin City Hall.

ICMA and Smart Growth Network. (2002). *Getting to smart growth: 100 principles for implementation*. Washington, DC: ICMA Press.

ICMA and Smart Growth Network. (2003). *Getting to smart growth II: 100 more policies for implementation*. Washington, DC: ICMA Press.

INRIX. (2015). *INRIX 2015 traffic scorecard*. Retrieved from http://inrix.com/scorecard/

Kaal, H. (2011). A conceptual history of livability: Dutch scientists, politicians, policy makers and citizens and the quest for a livability city. *City*, 15(5), 532–547.

Kashef, M. (2016). Urban livability across disciplinary and professional boundaries. *Frontiers of Architectural Research*, 5, 239–253.

King, M. (2014, November 21). Point Austin: Color me exempt, the homestead exemption money flows uphill. *Austin Chronicle*.

King, M. (2017, March 31). Point Austin: The Mayor's Tightrope: Tiptoeing our way toward a consensus on housing supply. *The Austin Chronicle*.

Kneebone, E., & Berube, A. (2013). *Confronting suburban poverty in America*. Washington, DC: Brookings Institution Press.

Koch and Fowler. (1928). *A city plan for Austin, Texas—1928*. Austin, TX: City of Austin.

Lens, M. C., & Monkkonen, P. (2016). Do strict land use regulations make metropolitan areas more segregated by income? *Journal of the American Planning Association*, 82(1), 6–21. https://doi.org/10.1080/01944363.2015.1111163

Llanes, D. (2016). *Citizen communication on single family homeownership*. Austin, TX.

Marcuse, P., & Kempen, R. van. (2008). Conclusion: A changed spatial order. In *Globalizing cities: A new spatial order?* (pp. 249–275). Blackwell Publishing Ltd. Retrieved from http://onlinelibrary.wiley.com/doi/10.1002/9780470712887.ch12/summary

Massey, D. S., & Denton, N. A. (1993). *American apartheid: Segregation and the making of the underclass*. Cambridge: Harvard University Press.

McCann, E. (2007). Inequality and politics in the creative city-region: Questions of livability and state strategy. *International Journal of Urban and Regional Research*, 31(1), 188–196.

Molina Costa, P. (2014). From plan to reality: Implementing a community vision in Jackson Square, Boston. *Planning Theory & Practice*, 15(3), 293–310.

Molotch, H. (1976). The city as a growth machine: Toward a political economy of place. *American Journal of Sociology*, 82(2), 309–332.

Morrison, L. (2012). *Statement of council member Morrison during city council vote on Imagine Austin*. Austin City Hall.

Mueller, E. J., & Kaplan, C. (2014). *Coming home: The benefits of housing choice for low-wage commuters in Austin, Texas*. (Sustainable Places Project). Austin, TX: Center for Sustainable Development, University of Texas.

Mumford, L. (1937). What is a city? *Architectural Record*, 92–96.

Naishtat, E. (1972). *The evolving concept of citizen participation: An historical study with a case analysis of urban renewal and the Blackshear Residents Organization*. Austin, TX: University of Texas Press.

New FEMA Maps for Central Texas Expand Flood Plains. (2015, August 24). *Insurance Journal*. Retrieved from www.insurancejournal.com/news/southcentral/2015/08/24/379433.htm

Oden, M. D. (2016). Equity: The awkward E in sustainable development. In S. A. Moore (Ed.), *Pragmatic sustainability: Dispositions for critical adaptation* (2nd ed., pp. 30–47). New York: Routledge.

Pacione, M. (1990). Urban livability: A review. *Urban Geography*, 11(1), 1–30.

Pendall, R. (2000). Local land use regulation and the chain of exclusion. *Journal of the American Planning Association*, 66(2), 125–142. https://doi.org/10.1080/01944360008976094

Pollock, S., Bluestone, B., & Billingham, C. (2010). *Maintaining diversity in America's transit-rich neighborhoods*. Boston, MA: Dukakis Center for Urban and Regional Policy, Northeastern University.

Pulido, L. (1996). *Environmentalism and economic justice: Two Chicano struggles in the Southwest*. Tucson, AZ: University of Arizona Press.

Robinson, R. (2016). *Austin area population histories and forecasts*. Austin, TX: City of Austin, Department of Planning. City Demographer.

Robinson, R. (2017). *Top ten demographic trends*. Austin, TX: City of Austin, Department of Planning. Retrieved from http://austintexas.gov/page/top-ten-demographic-trends-austin-texas

Rothstein, R. (2017). *The color of law: The forgotten history of how our government segregated America*. New York: Liveright Publishing Company.

Stone, C. (1989). *Regime politics: Governing Atlanta, 1946–1988*. Lawrence, KS: University of Kansas Press.

Swearingen, W. S. (2010). *Environmental city: People, place, politics, and the meaning of modern Austin*. Austin, TX: University of Texas Press.

Texas Workforce Commission. (2011). *Austin-round rock MSA wages*. Texas Workforce Commission, Labor Market & Career Information Department. Retrieved from www.tracer2.com/?PAGEID=67&SUBID=151

Theis, M. (2017, February 6). Austin is no. 1 on prestigious U.S. News "best places to live" ranking. *Austin Business Journal*. Retrieved June 9, 2017, from www.bizjournals.com/austin/news/2017/02/06/austin-is-no-1-on-prestigious-u-s-news-best-places.html

Thomson, K. (2001). *From neighborhood to nation: The democratic foundations of civil society*. Hanover, NH: University Press of New England.

Tretter, E. (2016). *Shadows of a Sunbelt city: The environment, racism, and the knowledge economy in Austin*. Atlanta: University of Georgia Press.

Tretter, E., & Mueller, E. J. (2018). Transforming Rainey Street: Decoupling equity from environment in Austin's Smart Growth Agenda. In K. Ward, A. E. G. Jonas, B. Miller, & D. Wilson (Eds.), *The Routledge handbook of spaces of urban politics*

Tynan, D. (2015, June 9). Election Austin: Notes/errors/corrections: Austin city council homestead exemption work session video. *Election Austin* [Blog post] Retrieved from http://electionaustin.com/homesteadexnotes/

U.S. News and World Report. (2017). *100 best places to live in the USA* (Rankings). Retrieved from http://realestate.usnews.com/places/texas/austin

Velasquez, J. (2016, October 26). Local organizations weigh in on how Austin's 10–1 council is faring 2 years in. *Community Impact Newspaper*.

Wheater, H., & Evans, E. (2009). Land use, water management and future flood risk. *Land Use Futures*, 26(Supplement 1), S251–S264. https://doi.org/10.1016/j.landusepol.2009.08.019

6 Livable or Lovable? Framing the Revitalization Projects in Warsaw, Poland

Anna Domaradzka

Introduction

This chapter aims at deconstructing the definition of livability, analyzing Polish national policy measures as well as assumptions and effects of urban revitalization projects conducted in Warsaw.[1] Although the goal of most of the revitalization projects to date was to raise the quality of public space, scale up the neighborhood or create places that would attract tourists and residents alike, seldom did this change bring the positive effect in terms of quality of life of residents or usability of the space itself. As a result, the subsequent phases of the revitalization projects are now planned with participation of residents and other local stakeholders, thus redefining the livability idea, so it would include different interests, feelings and needs of the city users. In this process, I argue the new ideas and ways of measuring the livability of the city are being defined and re-defined, influencing the city social policy as well as urban planning practices. On the other hand, we can argue that the process of defining the livability is driven by needs of specific social groups (mainly middle class and young professionals), therefore focusing more on aesthetics and scaling up of the neighborhood, than making it more democratic, accessible or inclusive for everyone. Those processes lead to gentrification of many areas of Warsaw, making them unlivable for less affluent residents.

On a more general level, using cases of Warsaw urban development programs as well as national government policies, we can describe the struggles in the field of polish urban policy, resolving between public (local and national administration), private (business) and civil society actors (urban movement grassroots initiatives). This struggle is strongly connected with the concept of community livability (Wagner & Caves, 2012) and plays out around different narratives and norms present in the strategic action field of Polish urban policy (Domaradzka & Wijkström, 2016).

The chapter will discuss the issue of livability from the perspective of quality of life studies, which define residents' well-being as the level of fulfillment of various basic and complex needs. Those are connected with all of the important spheres of life, such as health, education or work, but also with building meaningful relationships with others, and participation in social life. What makes fulfillment of those needs even more difficult is that they differ according to age, gender, stage of life and socioeconomic status. Thus, every city faces the challenge of serving the whole variety of needs and more often than not fails to deliver goods or services that some of the residents expect to receive. This, in turn, stimulates grassroots groups to either pressure the city government to introduce some improvement or to take matters into their own hands and create alternative sources of services or goods that the city doesn't supply (Domaradzka & Matysiak, 2015).

In recent years, this intensifying social activity, often called "the grassroots urban movements" (Jacobsson, 2015), became clearly visible in Polish cities. This indicates a shift in a way people perceive the urban environment and the rise of expectations for greater participation in local policies and planning. One of the main reasons for this change is the visible domination of money-driven (not people-driven) investments and the lack of clear vision for cities development in terms of urban design (Domaradzki, 2013) as well as solving spatial conflicts (Mergler, 2008). We may also stipulate that the need for involvement in the city future is a sign of raising social awareness concerning the importance of active participation in local politics and as such a part of wider transformation from post-communistic to fully democratic society. Although for many years the "home is my castle" rule would apply to Polish society, we can now witness how the semi-private (stairways, halls, common yards) and semi-public space (neighborhood parks, gardens, buildings surrounding, back alleys, playgrounds, etc.) invoke more sense of ownership and willingness to involve among residents (Lewicka, 2012).

Polish Urban Context

Poland has been shifting from rural to urban, and with more and more people living in the cities, the issue of quality of life in urban environment recently became one of the main social and political challenges. For the last 25 years, urban context in Poland has been transforming rapidly, catching up with modern trends in urban development. During transformation, the all-encompassing state started to move out from the field of urban policy, and the remaining gap was filled by the private investors and developers seizing opportunity to turn cities into profit-making machines. The speed of the changes and its focus on investors' rather than residents' interests ignited a series of local conflicts both around general plans as well as specific investments. Angry residents' groups mobilized against the possible threat to their quality of life, claiming their "right to the city" and reaching out to media, elites and public bodies to support their claims. Due to successful coalition building, some of those protests were successful enough to lead the way for a bigger change in terms of norms and rules of managing urban development (Domaradzka, 2015, 2017; Domaradzka & Wijkström, 2016).

The influx of trans-national capital has resulted in dynamic growth of some of the cities in Poland, with Warsaw being framed as a main growth machine. The shift from a centrally regulated communist regime to a proto-neoliberal state has resulted in a withdrawal of the "welfare city" as a main actor of urban development policy (Swyngedouw et al., 2002). The neoliberalization of public space management or housing sector affected the ordinary residents as well as previously marginalized groups, allowing for new coalitions breaching the ordinary class divide (Polanska & Piotrowski, 2015).

The intensification of negative social processes brought the residents' increased awareness, stemming from the growing discontent and leading to mobilization in many urban areas (Domaradzka 2015, 2017; Polanska 2015; Piotrowski & Lundstedt, 2016). Specifically, both large- and middle-sized cities in Poland became the arena for grassroots urban movements activism raging from neighborhood initiatives to local and national networks and coalitions (Nawratek, 2012; Erbel, 2014; Diani, 2015).

All over the country, local urban movements entered the scene with new postulates, demanding their right to the city: to social dignity; to participation; and to access to information, services and goods; but mainly the right to have a "good life" in the city. In practical terms, those movements usually opposed investments or plans that would lead to building over green spaces or public space, creating highways or other big-scale investments in the vicinity of housing districts, closing up spaces and places where the community used to gather (Mergler, 2010; Mergler et al., 2013).

In 2010, the first Congress of Urban Movements was organized to announce those postulates in the more general form of "Nine Urban Theses" (2011),[2] which included issues of residents' right to the city, social justice, revitalization, spatial order, urban democracy, sustainable development of metropolitan areas, decentralization and integration of public transport system. Three years later, in 2013, the second thesis about participative budgeting was already being implemented in many cities across Poland. What for a long time was considered as an exotic Brazilian idea quickly become a standard instrument of urban governance, allowing residents to define the most important livability goals for their communities (through projects) as well as encourage democratic redistribution of resources (Sikora, 2013). This new tool of voicing the needs and preferences of citizens is in no way perfect; however, it is now treated a one of the basic rights, proving how efficient can residents be in terms of lobbying (Erbel, 2014).

The efforts of grassroots activists, reflecting the growing frustration of urban residents, created a necessary push for the issue of livability to emerge as important part of public debates. Although the livability as a concept is not present in different actors' narrative (mainly because it's untranslatable to Polish), its different facets—from quality of life to well-being—are very much present in the public discussion right now. One of the visible results of this pressure is the central position of quality of life issue in the National Urban Policy, recently adopted by the government. On the meso level, the main reason for introducing different aspects of livability into a political debate is the constant pressure exerted by urban activists on the local and national governments. In the wider context, European Union's priorities expressed in Leipzig charter, as well as in the new structure of financing the urban development projects, are important factors facilitating this change in narrative. In this way, Polish livability policy is being shaped between the bottom-up pressure of citizens and top-down EU policies and structural funds' priorities.

Following Fligstein and McAdam (2011, 2012) theoretical approach, we can point out how urban grassroots movements entered the strategic action field of Polish urban policy, introducing new values, narratives and measures concerning livability. In their approach, Fligstein and McAdam (2012) place emphasis on various types of collective actors and the dynamics of how different fields change as well as on the broader inter-field environment and the importance of overlapping or adjacent fields. As a result, we can suggest that urban policy field in Poland is in the stage of formation, which is very much influenced by new civil society actors transforming the field from within. This situation creates what Tilly (1978) defines as "opportunity structure", combined with "threat" as distinct catalysts of challengers' mobilization. This mobilization is strengthened by the creation of institutional platforms (mainly Congress of Urban Movements) promoting new norm of livability. After the first stage of norm emergence, when norm entrepreneurs introduced the idea of livability in the public debate, urban activists used organizational platforms (Finnemore & Sikkink, 1998) to promote the new norm and to persuade others (governments or other public sector actors) to adopt them. Once enough actors were convinced, the stage of norm cascade began, during which actors were motivated to adopt a norm in order to enhance legitimacy or reputation of their institution or group. For example, as a result of a three-year process of negotiating National Urban Policy, a group of architects, academics and civil servants adopted the livability framework as a guiding concept to be included in all urban programs. According to Finnemore and Sikkink (1998), the final stage is internalization, where the bureaucratic procedures, the legal system and professional training should incorporate the norm so it becomes part of common knowledge. This is the next stage that livability as a norm if facing in Poland right now.

The chapter focuses on the case of Warsaw, the biggest city in Poland and also the most impacted by urban processes such as globalization, suburbanization and chaotic development as well as demographic changes linked to migration and aging of the population. On the basis of a number of newspaper critiques, it is clear that the local government was not coping well with problems arising from these issues (Siemieńska et al., 2011). This, in turn, led to growing discontent among Warsaw residents, which resulted in migration from the center toward the suburbs or in local social movements aimed at improvement of quality of life of local community. Such initiatives are increasingly needed in Warsaw, which has over 400 gated communities, and where social activity used to be limited to few enclaves (Gądecki, 2009; Polanska, 2013).

Livability in Polish Context

Until recently, the issue of livability was not properly recognized in official policies, on neither local nor national level. Polish municipal governments did not offer residents many possibilities for participation, leaving them a passive role of "consumers of the city services" (interview with one of the urban leaders, July 2013). The period between 2012 and 2016, however, has brought changes in this area, mainly related to the introduction of social development strategies and new mechanisms involving citizens in decision making (such as participatory budgeting or social consultation of revitalization programs) plus several improvements of existing mechanisms of participation (consultation of the zoning plans, social dialogue councils, referendums on local issues). This process was partly facilitated by the need to comply with European Union requirements with regard to implementation of the structural funds programs and the subsidiarity rule introduced in Leipzig Charter (2007).[3] However, the growing political power of grassroots groups demanding greater participation enabled the EU-forced measures to become real tools of opening up cities' management to the livable city idea.

The period between 2012 and 2015 was also when National Urban Policy 2023 was being drafted at the government level. Contrary to similar processes in the past, this document was built with wide engagement of activists and experts, allowing for creating a comprehensive set of goals and priorities for the upcoming years. As we read in the document:

> The main element of the strategic goal of urban policy is to improve the quality of life of the residents. It is a derivative of a number of determinants, including the sustainable development of a city offering high quality jobs. Looking from the same perspective on the National Urban Policy as a whole, it should be stated that any action taken at central level and at the level of particular local government (especially municipal authorities) needs to be considered and judged by the prism of human needs and the quality of life. (. . .) The model of the city the National Urban Policy is aiming at can be described with another name: liveable city—the city of "good life", which places its residents in the center. This high quality of life must be shared by all groups of city users—primarily their permanent residents, but also those who work and visit for business and leisure purposes.
>
> (National Urban Policy, 2015, 15–16)

Recently, the issue of livability gained a lot of traction in context of urban revitalization projects. The notion of city revitalization is one of the main topics and lines of investments in urban public policy in Poland, mainly due to EU-funded projects. Revitalization is also perceived as means for counteracting the increasing city fragmentation and urban sprawl that results in empty downtowns, growing suburbs and roads full of cars in between. The process is focused on the recovery of degraded urban districts, which aims to bring new life to the area through quality as well as function change. This is especially important in areas that became degraded due to deindustrialization or are deprived of equal access to services and infrastructure while they are populated by less affluent and marginalized groups of citizens.

The documents programming the urban revival projects usually follow the technical guidelines focusing on the build environment quality, aesthetics and attractiveness. The issue of quality of life is often replaced by residential attractiveness, which can be translated into real estate prices and potential to bring new (affluent) residents and businesses into area. Tourists also become an important target group of new investments as more and more cities make effort to re-brand themselves as attractive tourist destinations. Only recently the issue of livability, social revitalization or quality of life of existing residents is becoming a part of the concept too (Brzozowy et al., 2016; Ogrodowski, Gill-Piątek, & Kłosowski, 2016).

The existing urban sociology literature identifies three major factors that affect quality of life of cities' inhabitants. On one hand, this is the accessibility to various goods, services and institutions that people need in their everyday life. The second factor is the quality and extent of the social network, based both on family ties and relations with friends and on neighbor interactions within local community (Antonucci, 1985). Finally, the third factor concerns the quality of the urban space in which people spend they everyday life (Znaniecki, 1932). Specifically, whether it is friendly, aesthetic and safe, so it encourages people to spend more time outside and to engage in everyday interactions with others. Understanding the relations between these three factors and their impact on the well-being of the city dwellers allows for identification of the specific elements determining their quality of life, that then can be locally implemented through the city-run or grassroots revitalization processes.

To capture the most important factors of livability and the residents' well-being in the context of the changing urban environment, we should analyze the impact of different types of urban revitalization initiatives on the well-being of people living within the affected areas. Apart from the standard quality of life measures, one should point out the importance of frequency and quality of interactions that play out in transforming urban environment, influencing the quality of local residents' social life. Therefore, it is important to investigate how, through planning the pro-social public space or reshaping the existing space into friendlier one, we can create potential for greater livability and the city social life to flourish.

To better describe the way livability is defined and put into practice as part of local administration effort, this part analyzes one of the ongoing projects implemented in Warsaw since 2015. Its different stages illustrate the merging of "livability" and "lovability" frameworks, with more focus placed on residents' needs and preferences in the effort to develop more livable communities.

Between Livable and Lovable—Warsaw Local Centers Project

In 2015, the City of Warsaw together with Warsaw Charter of Polish Association of Architects launched the project aiming at selecting ten locations, where investments will be made to develop them into Warsaw's local centers. The Warsaw Local Centers program addressed the problems stemming from the diversity of the urban fabric characteristic for Warsaw, where many intercity areas lack well-developed local centers. As authors underlined in initial documents, this undertaking was in line with wider trend to make European cities more livable through investing in polycentric development:

> Currently, urban development in Europe takes place mainly through improving the internal structure of cities. Instead of expanding territorially, cities transform internally,

thus increasing the standard of living. This European trend to improve the quality of life includes Warsaw, which is also a city of very uneven spatial and social structure.
(Domaradzki et al., 2015, 7)

The project defined local centers as areas of concentration of goods, services and daily exchange between members of local communities. Initially, the project was focusing on selecting and designing ten non-central areas that would be (1) aesthetically attractive, and (2) allow residents' easy access to goods and services. More specifically, at the initial meetings, the discussion concentrated on how to make sure those areas become attractive in terms of design and infrastructure, in other words how to make them "beautiful" and therefore attractive for residents and passersby alike. Another issue was to design the "functional program" for the area, to serve most of local residents' activities and needs, so they wouldn't need to travel long distances to city center.

So defined local activity hubs were supposed to be the embodiment of livability idea—the spatial arrangement that allows for better, more comfortable and enriching life, where the daily interaction patterns thicken, with easy access to various goods and services. As the authors of the project underlined, both the spatial as well as social factors contribute to the wholesome life of the city and its friendliness toward the residents (Domaradzki et al., 2015).

More importantly, the project underlined the importance of developing the city on both a metropolitan and a local level, to achieve the synergy effect resulting in higher quality of life, more dynamic economy and stimulating environment. Consequently, the transformations of the city internal structure should include the city center on the one hand, and the local centers, used daily by residents, on the other. The initial diagnosis showed that local nodes, already existing in the network of public spaces, generally lack an attractive urban form and usually offers only incomplete services. Moreover, the team of experts pointed out how some places' unrealized potential hinders the development of local social life or fulfillment of the basic needs of the residents. Therefore, the project assumed the crucial role of local-level development for the general improvement of the quality of life in the city in general, addressing the existing "investment gap" in peripheral city areas. Although many investments in the previous years were carried out on the metropolitan level, catering to the needs of the 2 million inhabitant metropolis, much less has been done on the local level to render the city more livable and friendly in terms of the everyday routines of each districts residents.

The project's first objective was to define the concept of a local center in the context of Warsaw structure and according to the residents' needs. The second objective was to identify the potential local center areas, based on their location, spatial configuration and the potential to develop into lively centers of social life. Another important factor was whether the discussed areas already exist in the minds of residents as local centers and if they host more or less spontaneous meetings and grassroots activities that would confirm the informal role. In that case, the project aimed at strengthening those nodes by supplementing lacking services and organizing more friendly public space.

During the initial discussion, experts and city representatives agreed to make the process participatory and consult with local residents the definitions, the criteria for choosing the location, and the planned investments. To this effect, a series of workshops and project meetings was scheduled, during which participants were involved in defining important functions that local center should have as well as indicating potential locations on the city map.

The project consisted of several stages, starting with analyses of the spatial layout of the city and examining the functioning of diverse areas within its structure. Then the team consulted different definitions and functions of local centers with potential users to come up with the final selection of ten locations. In the first phase, the network of public spaces in Warsaw was analyzed to identify "node areas", taking into account their position in the city structure and the spatial formation of individual sites. The list consisted of center-forming areas, where natural social interactions occur, like intersections, areas surrounding public transport stops and those with desirable services attracting the residents, including marketplaces, small shops, culture and recreation spots. To pass to the second stage of selection, those sites were required to have a defined urban form or a potential for transforming into an organized public space. In this, the team was following urban literature (Lynch, 1960; Sitte, 1965; Krier, 2009) showing that people feel comfortable in clearly formed spaces with defined boundaries, hence improving the quality of social life calls for creating urban spaces in the form of urban interiors. The first stage ended with a list of over 200 node areas having an important role in the citywide network of public spaces and with potential to increase their appeal.

During the second stage, the team examined the ways in which residents define a local center, asking the participants of the workshops and social media followers to fill the open-ended questionnaire. On the basis of information gathered from questionnaire, during the meetings with residents and city activists, as well as through social media, a list of places perceived as current or potential local centers was created. During this process, the team discovered that according to residents' feelings and experiences, what makes a certain place a local center is not only the attractive design or access to services, but most importantly the presence of other people and space for diverse social activities, affordable to anyone. Workshops also proved how important the issue of local identity is in creating a truly inviting local center.

Participants usually defined local centers as open space, a place for social gatherings as well as everyday tasks that should combine cultural, social, recreational and commercial services. The metaphor of the local center as the "heart of the district" or "magnet" attracting different users was a recurring theme:

> The heart of the district, perceived by the residents as a place to spend free time, where you can find information and support in various areas of life. A place with tradition, but open to new activity and people who want to work in this place for others. Friendly space that attracts like a magnet.
>
> (quote from a questionnaire)

Linking the results of the first and second stage showed a clear correlation between the technical (spatial analysis) and the social criteria. In many cases, the conclusions from the first and second stages overlapped with each other, although, at times, residents also suggested the areas subjectively essential to them, even though these places did not have the characteristics of the local center according to the city planning criteria. The conclusions from spatial analyses and activists' opinions, together with the discussion during the workshop, served to further clarify the criteria to be met by the local centers. As a result, the following criteria defining the concept of the local center were adopted:

Local Centers

- contain an element of generally accessible public space;
- are multifunctional (allowing interchangeability of functions, depending on the season, weather, time of day);
- are within walking distance for a substantial group of residents (10- to15-minute walk);

- facilitate trade, intellectual and social interaction;
- have a program for different age and social groups;
- connect people, build the local community;
- have a pleasant and good looking urban form;
- have their own unique characters, supporting the development of local identity.

(Domaradzki et al., 2015, 8)

During several workshops with local activists and civil servants, the project team discussed the issue of specific needs that should be taken into account when planning local centers. Among groups whose needs should be included in the plan, they listed seniors, disabled persons, parents of small children, youth, and local entrepreneurs as well as activists. The participants also pointed out that poor residents' as well as affluent residents' needs should be addressed. Other specific focus groups included women, foreigners, students and dog owners. In other words, to create a well-functioning local center, it has to correspond to the needs of both younger and older users, as one of discussants put it: "It should be an intergenerational space—not excluding nor dividing people based on age". Local centers should be a multigenerational open public space; there, grassroots initiatives can be realized.

In terms of existing tools to introduce the livability measures, participants mentioned the preferential rents for local entrepreneurs offering missing services, restricted parking and car access in public areas, getting rid of architectural barriers. To raise the aesthetics and functionality of local centers, new measures introducing spatial order should be implemented, including accessible places of rest and play (benches, green squares, playgrounds, game boards and tables, etc.). When asked about most important elements local centers should include to meet the needs of the residents, the participants frequently mentioned open spaces, seating areas and neighborhood clubs. On the second place were issues of public transport, children's playground, restaurants and open markets. The most needed local services were groceries stores, libraries, post offices and pharmacies, along with sport facilities.

The list of all locations was collected by experts and reported on the meetings, on the shared map, as well as by mail or Facebook page. In the third stage, all 253 places picked according to the selected criteria underwent the on-site verification combined with spatial audit. The idea was to identify places where, with the use of the available means and in the foreseeable future, it will be possible to achieve the desired effects translating to a definite improvement in the spatial standard. The on-site verification examined the transformation capacity of the area, including the involved expenditures versus effects. After the spatial audit, the team identified 167 locations with highly diverse potential, showing the characteristics of the local centers. The on-site visits result together with land ownership data, conducted in the last phase, allowed for selecting 32 locations which, after taking into account all the criteria, were most likely to improve significantly after planned investments. An additional selection criteria was improving the network of local centers (in terms of land area and the number of residents they serve), so priority was given to those places that can clearly improve the quality of social life in less central areas of the city. The goal of the team was to maintain both local and citywide perspective, choosing the places that would not only suit the needs of the pilot local investment projects, but also strengthen the network of local centers throughout the city.

The sites itself were very different. Some lacked well-developed infrastructure, but could become a local center through improving the quality of public space. Others were serving as "hubs" on the daily routes of the residents, but were lacking in terms of sociocultural offer. Some mainly served as daily recreation areas, with high-quality space, but with no other attractors.

Finally, the proposed locations were verified for ownership issues as well as possible conflicts with planned investments (existing claims, formal and legal liabilities), to pick the first ten places where the necessary investments will be carried out. Among these were places with well-shaped urban form, but of poor functionality, those lying on communication routes, but offering unattractive public space and those offering attractive commercial functions, but little else. Important also were places of recreational values, where sociocultural programs could add to their usefulness. Therefore, all planned activities, aimed at strengthening or developing the local centers, require an individual approach and adaptation to the specific local needs, as their scope must be relevant to the situation and site-specific expectations. Therefore, all design activities are to be consulted with local communities from the starting phase of programming to preparing the final investment project.

The selection procedure showed how active residents are, especially in some neighborhoods, and how much they are involved in shaping the surrounding space. As authors of the project point out (Domaradzki et al., 2015), the project itself helped to uncover layers of a social capital and nudged residents into action, which should benefit the functioning of local centers in the future. They are not created in a vacuum now, but in response to the very specific needs of the residents.

Livability and the Neighborhood Effect of Revitalization Projects

The approach developed during Warsaw Local Centers project was informed by initial results of the neighborhood effect study, conducted in Warsaw in 2015. It attempted to measure the residents' response of ten investments in different parts of Warsaw that were aiming at scaling up the area though new buildings and revitalization of green areas or streets. Quantitative research was conducted in the framework of the project "City revival—from urban planning to grassroots initiatives" funded by Polish National Science Centre (research grant DEC-2013/09/D/HS6/02968). The main goal was to study residents' attitudes toward investments/revitalization initiatives that were conducted in their neighborhood. Fieldwork was conducted in ten Warsaw locations (total $N = 1,000$, random route sampling, with quotas according to education level and length of residency) and included residents, who were directly impacted by the change, in terms of everyday use of the "revitalized" area.

The results showed that in all locations, the majority of respondents expressed a positive opinion about the changes resulting from the investment (between 61% and 93% responded they are positive or very positive about it), which suggests that in the city like Warsaw every attempt to revitalize is usually perceived as a change for better. However, in the two poorest neighborhoods, the rate of residents unhappy with investments was the highest (17%), which suggests that those changes did not properly address the needs of less affluent neighborhoods. Interestingly, the evaluation of changes was not dependent of demographic variables like age, gender, employment, length of residency and so forth, but was positively correlated with household income and having children. Positive correlation between income and having children and opinion about the investment suggests that some of the projects may result in gentrification.

Also, one of the main benefits coming from investments was the possibility of spending free time in the neighborhood, especially in open public spaces. The investments that were most highly evaluated were those concerning the revitalization of green spaces, involving use of water (streams, ponds, fountains) and adding new functionalities like playgrounds, benches, outdoor gyms, skate parks and so forth. Some of the investments concerned creating modern cultural institutions (new museums, science center, local house of culture) in underdeveloped neighborhoods and were usually perceived as having a positive spillover effect on the neighborhood, leading new investments and general revival of the area. Much less attractive were investments renovating the streets and squares without added greenery or new functions. It suggests that design itself is not enough to create the positive neighborhood effect.

Interestingly, the results prove that top-down investments, especially in poorer districts, were generally less successful in terms of how residents perceive them. This means that social consultations may have an important role in shaping the attitudes toward investments as well as in creating opportunities for interaction and mobilization of neighbors involved in response to planned investment.

Conclusions

Florian Znaniecki, who initiated the Polish school of urban thought (Znaniecki, 1932), identified the city not just as a random set of streets, buildings and parks, but as a functional space perceived by its inhabitants. According to Znaniecki, only the overlap between the city plan and the functional map perceived by the individuals allows for identification of the true organization of the city. His reflection remains highly valid in discussions concerning ways in which the city should be studied and—as a result—changed to become a better living environment.

The discussion concerning the livability leads a sociologist to the premise that the organization of the urban built environment is intimately connected with the density and quality of the social networks and interactions, which in turn influence the quality of life of urban residents. New studies concerning livability should, therefore, not only concern the issues of health, happiness, access to jobs or education and quality of natural environment, but also should address the following questions: (1) Does the architectural organization of the urban space affect quality of social network? and conversely, (2) Does the quality of social network lead to social engagement, that in turn may improve urban space? and finally, (3) What does the success of city intervention depend on, in context of improvement of city residents' well-being?

This notion is supported by the works of Edward T. Hall (1966); William Whyte (1980, 1988); Jane Jacobs (1961); and Jan Gehl (1987, 2010), who identified the links between the type of urban space and the forms of interactions happening within it. At the same time, in order to investigate how the place of residence affects people interactions with others, Convoy Model of Social Relations can be used. The model focuses on personal social network and its role in well-being of the individuals through their lifetime. Thus, the proposed approach to livability study connects in a novel way proximity theory (Hall, 1966) with the convoy model of social relations (Antonucci, 1995; Antonucci & Akiyama, 1995) to identify the characteristics of urban interventions that lead to their success in terms of raising well-being of its inhabitants and livability of whole communities.

The ongoing process of creating Warsaw Local Centers illustrates how the issues of livability and lovability are intertwined and should be both examined when planning city investments. In terms of planning urban change, we can refer to lovability as a rule guiding the design (urban form) and livability as a rule guiding the functionalities (urban substance). The aesthetics can be a good starting point, leading to creation of the eye-pleasing urban form and enabling the transformation of certain locality. This form, however, has to be filled with livability measures, guiding specific solutions for human comfort, safety and dignity (Sadowy, 2014). Those measures are often difficult to design, as the process should include different voices and needs of end users. At this stage, the form has to be negotiated to cater to most important functions and allowing for synergy of what's beautiful with what's essential for quality of life. On the one hand, the design should not be guided by basic needs and functions only, as it leads to creation of spaces that do not involve positive emotions and evoke neither the sense of pride nor identity. On the other hand, the search for beauty and positive emotions should not ignore the practical use of the space, as the designed experience should be both pleasing and useful. The aesthetic order is often based on bigger scale solutions—creation of axis and symmetries, linking public spaces in one fluid chain. In these terms, creation of lovability effect should always involve thinking on a higher level that allows for creating the complex of urban forms, instead of just one local square.

If cities are about people and their quality of life, as contemporary literature increasingly suggests, we need to understand what factors are involved in "the city experience": how people use, emotionally connect and identify with cities in which they live, work and play. Despite great academic as well as administrative efforts to distill a measurable set of empirical indicators of what makes the city or the neighborhood great, it inevitably misses important elements of humans' interactions with places: perception and attachment. As authors of the Lovability index (Garduño Freeman & Gray, 2015, Novacevski et al., 2017) underline, the concept can be used to balance the rationalist approach to the quality of urban life. Lovability responds to the idea that there are elements of city life that can't be measured directly, as they relate to more intangible qualities that define how people experience cities and neighborhoods.

The notion of lovability allows for re-engaging with people and communities to understand the nuances of their interaction with urban space and build better recommendation for city planning. Combined with other data, lovability measures can provide more direct, relevant information to guide urban planning and place-making by identifying peoples' needs and local assets. It also underlines the importance of qualitative factors in creating more livable cities and raising their residential attractiveness without excluding less affluent members of urban community. As authors put it:

> Lovability emphasizes the importance of the "vibe" of a place—its character, diversity, uniqueness and connection with people. Above all, it points to the fact that connections to place are subjective and worthy of further analysis.
>
> (Garduño Freeman et al., 2016: no page)

Lovability is not intended to replace livability, but it can help develop a more humane approach to it, exploring and defining the elements that form meaningful links between people and particular places. Fused with other data, this presents a world of new opportunities for policymaking, planning and city ranking. Adding lovability measures to the procedures guiding the cities development allows us to look beyond infrastructure and economics, to tell a full story of the experience of living in a particular city. As the example of Warsaw Local Centers projects show, through harnessing the sentiments and perceptions that inform people and place interactions, lovability provides an important addition to traditional livability measures, allowing urban planners and policymakers to engage with the qualitative aspects of city diagnostics. This "new form of urban analysis" refocuses on understanding livability of cities, districts and neighborhoods, instead of creating new rankings and competitive measures.

Notes

1. Data were gathered in the framework of the project "City revival—from urban planning to grassroots initiatives", financed by National Science Centre, DEC-2013/09/D/HS6/02968.

2. In 2015, Nine Urban Theses were developed into Fifteen Urban Theses, widening the scope of urban movements postulates as well as describing them in more details, see: http://kongresruchowmiejskich.pl/tezy-miejskie/
3. The "Leipzig Charter on Sustainable European Cities" is a document of the European Union member states in which national agencies responsible for urban development agreed upon common principles and strategies for urban development policy through European Union. Its provisions relate to the "policy of integrated urban development"—a process of coordination of key areas of urban policy, involving "business entities, stakeholders and the general public" (Leipzig Charter, 2007, 2–3).

References

Antonucci, T. C. (1985). Personal characteristics, social networks and social behavior. In R. H. Binstock & E. Shanas (Eds.), *Handbook of aging and the social sciences* (pp. 94–128). New York: Van Nostrand Reinhold.
Antonucci, T. C., & Akiyama, H. (1995). Convoys of social relations: Family and friendships within a life span context. In R. Blieszner & V. H. Bedford (Eds.), *Handbook of aging and the family* (pp. 355–372). Westport, CT: Greenwood Press.
Antonucci, T. C., Birditt, K. S., & Ajrouch, K. (2011). Convoys of social relations: Past, present, and future. In K. L. Fingerman, C. A. Berg, J. Smith, & T. C. Antonucci (Eds.), *Handbook of lifespan development* (pp. 161–182). New York: Springer Publishing Company.
Brzozowy, A., Górecki, R., Hołdys, M., Kędzierska, A., Krystek-Kucewicz, B., Niemczyk, J., Pawlak, P., Popławska, Z., Ryś, R., Siłuszek, A., Thel, K., & Tomczyk, E. (2016). *Ludzie—Przestrzeń—Zmiana. Dobre praktyki w rewitalizacji polskich miast*. Warszawa: Ministerstwo Rozwoju. Retrieved July 11, 2017, from www.mr.gov.pl/media/22237/dobre_praktyjki_rewitalizacja.pdf
Diani, M. (2015). *The cement of civil society: Studying networks in localities*. New York: Cambridge University Press.
Domaradzka, A. (2015). Changing the rules of the game: Impact of the urban movement on the public administration practices. In M. Freise, F. Paulsen, & A. Walter (Eds.), *Civil society and innovative public administration* (pp. 188–217). Baden-Baden: Nomos.
Domaradzka, A. (2017). Leveling the playfield: Urban movement in the strategic action field of urban policy in Poland. In J. Hou & S. Knierbein (Eds.), *City unsilenced: Urban resistance and public space in the age of shrinking democracy*. Abingdon, UK: Routledge.
Domaradzka, A., & Matysiak, I. (2015). Pushing for innovation: The role of citizens in local housing and childcare policies in Warsaw. In M. Freise, F. Paulsen, & A. Walter (Eds.), *Civil society and innovative public administration* (pp. 302–324). Baden-Baden: Nomos.
Domaradzka, A., & Wijkström, F. (2016). Game of the city re-negotiated: The Polish urban regeneration movement as an emerging actor in a Strategic Action Field. *Polish Sociological Review*, 3, 291–308.
Domaradzki, K. (2013). *Przestrzeń Warszawy—tożsamość miasta a urbanistyka*. Warszawa: Oficyna Wydawnicza Politechniki Warszawskiej.
Domaradzki, K., Domaradzka, A., Happach, M., Sadowy, K., & Wasilewska, A. (Eds.). (2015). *Warszawskie centra lokalne. Warsaw Local Centers*. Warsaw: Wydawnictwo SARP.
Erbel, J. (2014). Ruchy miejskie jako nowa forma zaangażowania społecznego. *Władza Sądzenia*, 4, 37–47.
Fifteen Urban Theses. (2015). Retrieved July 11, 2017, from http://kongresruchowmiejskich.pl/15-tez-o-miescie-kongresu-ruchow-miejskich/
Finnemore, M., & Sikkink, K. (1998). International norm dynamics and political change. *International Organization*, 52(4), 887–917.
Fligstein, N., & McAdam, D. (2011, March). Toward a general theory of strategic action fields. *Sociological Theory*, 29(1), 1–26.
Fligstein, N., & McAdam, D. (2012). *A theory of fields*. New York: Oxford University Press.
Gądecki, J. (2009). *Za murami. Osiedla grodzone w Polsce—analiza dyskursu*. Wrocław: Wydawnictwo Uniwersytetu Wrocławskiego.

Garduño Freeman, C., & Gray, F. (2015). *The Melbourne lovability index 2015: Findings report.* Committee for Melbourne Future Focus Group in collaboration with Deakin University. Melbourne, VIC: Deakin University.

Garduño Freeman, C., Gray, F., & Novacevski, M. (2016). Lovability: Restoring liveability's human face. Retrieved July 11, 2017, from https://theconversation.com/lovability-restoring-liveabilitys-human-face-67627

Gehl, J. (1987). *Life between buildings: Using public space.* Washington, DC: Island Press.

Gehl, J. (2010). *Cities for people.* Washington, DC: Island Press.

Grzegorczyk, J. (2009). Jak powstają polskie metropolie? *Le Monde Diplomatique.* Retrieved July 11, 2017, from http://monde-diplomatique.pl/LMD39/index.php?id=3

Hall, E. T. (1966). *The hidden dimension.* Garden City, New York: Doubleday.

Jacobs, J. (1961). *The death and life of great American cities.* New York: Vintage.

Jacobsson, K. (2015). *Urban grassroots movements in Central and Eastern Europe.* Farnham: Ashgate.

Krier, L. (2009). *The architecture of community.* Washington: Island Press.

Leipzig charter on sustainable European cities. (2007). Retrieved July 11, 2017, from http://ec.europa.eu/regional_policy/archive/themes/urban/leipzig_charter.pdf

Lewicka, M. (2012). *Psychologia miejsca.* Warsawa: Scholar.

Lynch, K. (1960). *The image of the city.* Cambridge: Harvard University Press.

Mergler, L. (2008). *Poznań Konfliktów.* Poznań: Wydawnictwo Lepszy Świat.

Mergler, L., & Pobłocki, K. (2010). Nic o nas bez nas: polityka skali a demokracja miejska. *Res Publica Nowa, 201–202,* 9.

Mergler, L., Pobłocki, K., & Wudarski, M. (2013). *Anty-Bezradnik przestrzenny: prawo do miasta w działaniu.* Warsaw: Res Publica Nowa.

National Urban Policy. (2015). *Krajowa Polityka Miejska.* Warsaw: Ministry of Infrastructure and Development.

Nawratek, K. (2012). *Holes in the whole: Introduction to the urban revolutions.* Winchester, UK: Zero Books.

Nine Urban Theses. (2011). Retrieved July 11, 2017, from http://kongresruchowmiejskich.pl/tezy-miejskie/

Novacevski, M., Gray, F., & Garduño Freeman, C. (2017). Lovability: Putting people at the centre of city performance. *Planning News, 43*(1), 22–23.

Ogrodowski, J., Gill-Piątek, H., & Kłosowski, W. (2016). *Partycypacja społeczna i partnerstwo w rewitalizacji.* Retrieved July 11, 2017, from http://docplayer.pl/14405418-Partycypacja-spoleczna-i-partnerstwo-w-rewitalizacji-jaroslaw-ogrodowski-hanna-gill-piatek-wojciech-klosowski.html

Piotrowski, G., & Lundstedt, M. (2016). Right-to-the-city movements in Poland: A new opening for grassroots mobilizations? In I. N. Sava & G. Pleyers (Eds.), *Social movements in central and Eastern Europe: A renewal of protests and democracy* (pp. 199–212). Bucharest: Editura Universităţii din Bucureşti.

Polanska, D. V. (2013). Gated housing as a reflection of public-private divide: On the popularity of gated communities in Poland. *Polish Sociological Review, 181,* 87–102.

Polanska, D. V. (2015). Alliance-building and brokerage in contentious politics: The case of the polish tenants' movement. In K. Jacobsson (Ed.), *Urban grassroots movements in Central and Eastern Europe* (pp. 195–218). Farnham: Ashgate.

Polanska, D. V., & Piotrowski, G. (2015). The transformative power of cooperation between social movements: Squatting and tenants' movements in Poland. *City: Analysis of Urban Trends, Culture, Theory, Policy, Action, 19*(2–3), 274–296.

Sadowy, K. (2014). Godność życia jako miernik rozwoju społeczno-gospodarczego miast. *Studia Regionalne i Lokalne, 1*(55).

Siemieńska, R., Domaradzka, A., & Matysiak, I. (2011). *Local welfare in Poland from a historical and institutional perspective.* WILCO Publication no. 09. Retrieved March 11, 2017, from www.wilcoproject.eu/wordpress/wp-content/uploads/WILCO_WP2_reports_09_PL1.pdf

Sikora, K. (2013, March 14). Brazylijski wynalazek podbija Polskę. Budżet partycypacyjny uczy nas dbania o swoje miasto. *Na Temat.* Retrieved July 11, 2017, from http://natemat.pl/54079,brazylijski-wynalazek-podbija-polske-budzet-partycypacyjny-uczy-nas-dbania-o-swoje-miasto

Sitte, C. (1965). *City planning according to artistic principles*. New York: Random House.
Swyngedouw, E., Moulaert, F., & Rodriguez, A. (2002). Neoliberal urbanism in Europe: Large-scale urban development projects and the new urban policy. *Antipode, 34*(3), 542–577.
Tilly, C. (1978). *From mobilization to revolution*. New York: Random House.
Wagner, F., & Caves, R. (2012). *Community livability: Issues and approaches to sustaining the wellbeing of people and communities*. Abingdon, UK: Routledge.
Whyte, W. (1980). *The social life of small urban spaces*. Washington, DC: The Conservation Foundation.
Whyte, W. (1988). *City: Rediscovering the center*. New York: Doubleday.
Znaniecki, F. (1932). *Miasto w świadomości jego obywateli*. Poznań: Polski Instytut Socjologiczny

7 Pune Metropolis
Unlivable Cities Within a Livable Metropolis

Christopher Benninger

First Society Versus the Second Society

Pune provides an excellent setting in India to understand the potentials of applying the concept of livable cities to South Asia. It has a highly educated population and an established high-tech manufacturing base and is a center of information technology. It enjoys an open press and a lively civil society, with many NGOs active in urban issues ranging from pedestrian rights and riverfront rehabilitation to heritage issues. English is the language of youngsters who are seen fashionably dressed, moving about in the city's numerous malls, fancy restaurants, or walking along 'high streets.' This is the superficial image welcoming visitors from abroad, and they immediately feel at ease making subconscious 'connects' here, as they check into any of the city's twenty-five luxury hotels. Large industrial satellite towns surround the metropolis, providing employment for the continuous flow of newly educated youth, graduating from any of the fourteen universities and over 800 colleges found in the metropolis. Lying 160 kilometers to the south-east of Mumbai, in the Sahyadri Mountains, the metropolis enjoys a salubrious climate. The metropolis' highly visible middle class and large slum population mirror scenarios in similar metropolitan cities like Hyderabad, Ahmedabad, Bengaluru, Mumbai and New Delhi, making it a good laboratory to study urban processes. Although in these other metropolitan areas, urban development authorities were established over a half century ago, the Pune Metropolitan Region Development Authority, covering a population of 10 million people, was formed only in April 2015, limiting reliable data and information on the metropolis. Thus, one often draws from information culled from the Pune Municipal Corporation with a population of 6 million, the Pimpri-Chinchwad Municipal Corporation with a population of 2 million, or takes references from Mumbai and New Delhi hard data, as a comparison, and extrapolates that onto the Pune metropolitan scenario. There are obvious limitations to such a notional use of information. Thus, in this chapter, data and information references are minimal.

Pune projects an image of a well-to-do, middle-class modern city. Countering this image are studies indicating that a large proportion of city dwellers do not have access to any form of legal dwelling ownership.[1] A study of the Mumbai Metropolitan Region (see Figure 7.1) would also reflect Pune's crises of access to shelter. Only 3 percent of the households can afford the equated monthly installments (EMI) required by financial institutions to buy dwellings in the elite inner core of the city, only an additional 6 percent can afford the EMIs for new dwellings within the inner suburbs that form a high-income belt around the inner city, and only 17 percent more households can afford the EMIs for dwellings from the edge of the high-income belt, on out to the edge of the metropolitan region, which is about 60 kilometers in diameter. So, only 26 percent of the households living in the metropolis can afford a 'right to the city,' in terms of access to legally owned habitat. It is this 26 percent of people who are showcased with smiling faces in promotional media

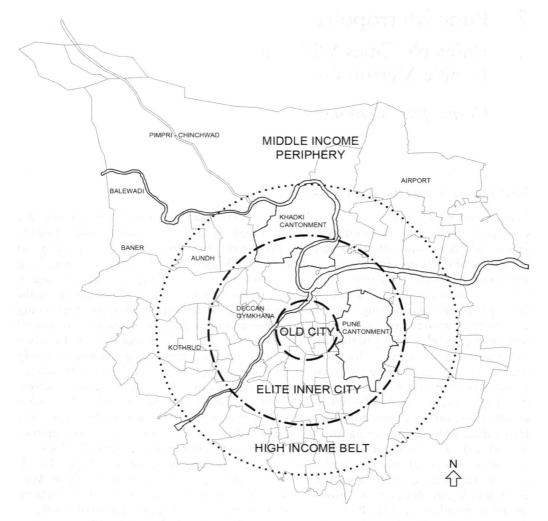

Figure 7.1 Map of Pune Metropolitan Region
Source: Christopher Benninger, CCBA Design

of the city. The other 74 percent are left out of the picture. In this conundrum, a question arises: who has access to what amenities, public spaces, services and shelter?

Beginning with this image of a growing, contemporary Indian metropolis, this chapter will argue that there are contradictions between the superficial image of the city and the city that dwells largely out of sight. The Pune Metropolitan Region is composed of two municipal corporations, several military cantonments, small and many government-sponsored industrial estates and information technology parks, each having their own systems of governance, building controls and administration.

Across India, the Pune region is thought to be one of the well-managed systems of urban governance. It is seen to be administered by well-educated city officials and technical professionals, honestly, through a seamless and transparent system of modern governance. Yet behind its image of modern urban management is an informal system driven by favoritism and political influence. The urban land regime is largely controlled by a nexus between land agents, builders and revenue officials, backed up by a pliable revenue bureaucracy, police officials and street gangs. So, there are two contradictory images and realities of the metropolis: a corporate branding image of how things should be and a grassroots reality of how things are (see Figure 7.2).

The elite national press highlights the city's corporate entities, IT and automobile industries, art and fashion shows, club life, horse races, cricket matches, high-tech economy and cutting edge governance, pioneering the Smart Cities movement in India and initiating 'best practices.' The media is crowded with advertisements of high-end, gated residential communities nestled around tropical swimming pools. These give scant evidence of the people who make up most of the city's fabric, who have never entered an air-conditioned mall or cinema multiplex. One Pune speaks English at work, and the other Pune speaks Marathi and Hindi. A 2008 survey of Pune's slum population revealed that 32.5 percent of the Pune Municipal Corporation's population live in 477 slum pockets, crammed into only 2.34 percent of the city's total land area.[2]

Urban policy documents, the chambers of commerce and city strategy papers see the city as a highly corporatized system in terms of its growth sectors, occupational structures, urban development plans, management and decision-making processes. Yet the city's reality is that of a highly informal economy, occupational structure and manner of government functioning.

India is adept at legislating modern statutory systems, presenting attractive organizational charts and inventing catchy sounding programs of action. High-profile management

Figure 7.2 Balewadi High Street
Source: Deepak Kaw

firms from the US prepare well-illustrated and insightful position papers on urban areas, looking at their opportunities and potentials, highlighting the bright future that surely lies ahead. Yet behind the corporate branding and media hype is a system of loopholes, special interest groups, misuse of discretionary decisions, unethical bureaucrats, with personal relationships working around the system.

In India, barely 1.5 percent of the population pays income tax, raising the question, 'Where is everyone else?' Most non-payers are just too poor to fall within the income tax net, and others fall within exempt social categories.[3]

In India, the rural population is growing at a rate of 2 percent annually, whereas the urban population is growing at 3 percent a year; the Pune Metropolitan Region is growing by 4 percent, and the slums within the Pune region are growing at 5 percent annually.[4] A Pew Research Center analysis carried out in 2015 illustrated that 19.8 percent of Indians fall in the poor income group, and 76.9 percent in the low-income group, with only 2.6 percent in the middle income, and 0.6 percent in the upper-middle income. The high-income group in India made up only 0.1 percent.[5] The study termed as poor people who lived on $2 a day or less, and people of low income who lived on incomes between $2 and $10. An interesting conclusion of the Pew study is that India's middle class grew only from 2.6 percent in 2001 to 3 percent in 2011. A large majority of these new middle-class people are youngsters who have moved into cities like Pune, fetching jobs in growing corporate sectors of the economy (see Figure 7.3).

Behind the streets congested with shiny imported cars, and past one's views of gated communities, classy shopfronts and malls, lie large squatter settlements, congested old city lanes, workers' colonies and urban villages engulfed within the sprawling city. Here is

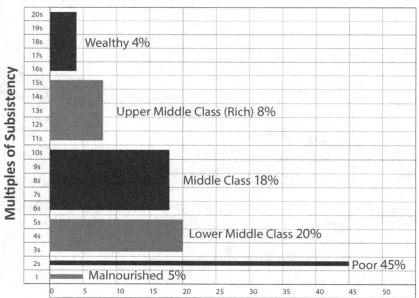

Figure 7.3 Consumption Distribution by Multipliers of Subsistency

where around 70 percent of the population lives and survives in an undocumented informal second society.

So when we hear the discussions on smart cities, sustainable cities and livable cities, these dialogues largely take place in the elite English press, within the air-conditioned offices of corporate governments and businesses, and amongst the NGOs run by people who drive automobiles and complain of congestion. This is the anomaly that challenges urban planners and managers who wish to reach outside of corporate Indian, go beyond the first society, planning for the underclass who dream of a better life and future for their children. If the cities of India are to become more 'livable,' this population is the community that must be reached and provided with the fundamental necessities of an urban existence.

Ironically, the formal first society, and the informal second society, share a strong sense of social and cultural bonding, strengthened by cultural threads, knitted together through a shared fabric of meaning and knowledge systems that weave all the seemingly disjointed and conflicting pieces into one holistic tapestry. The second informal society and the first corporate society are economically interdependent and socially intertwined through their daily work and interdependent behavioral patterns. The drivers, cooks, nursemaids, houseboys, guards, office attendants, priests in temples, repairmen, tailors and barbers all come from the second society, and these are the people with whom the first corporate society interact with on a personal level daily. All the workers in one's business, and most of the ancillary suppliers, are from the second society. Pune citizens celebrate large Hindu festivals together, with non-Hindus joining in the festivities. All the citizens of Pune sit spellbound at their television sets during major cricket matches, sit together and watch Bollywood films, hum and sing Hindi playback songs, and have the same sports and film heroes. People of all classes belong to the same political parties, observing the ups and downs of politicians as a national pastime. Across income groups, Pune families send their children to school, most of whom will sit together for the tenth standard Secondary School Certificate Board exams, in the same examination halls. Beginning in their early teens, Pune's youngsters are hooked onto smartphones. Most secondary school children have mobile phones, whether expensive iPhones for the well-to-do students, or cheap Chinese and local brands from the gray market for the lower income groups. Pune has the highest rate of mobile phone ownership of any city in India, and on peak days, Indians initiate more than 1 billion calls and text messages, linking people together through social networks, for a myriad of personal and public interests. WhatsApp has become the new street corner society, and its where everyone meets their friends, gossips with work colleagues, orders vegetables or voices their political opinions. Young Pune males cherish their motorcycles, chatting with strangers at stoplights or sitting on them sipping tea in front of street vendor shops.

The concept of livability is being introduced into this unique cultural context. The livable cities movement emerged from the English-speaking world, at a time when post-industrial societies were emerging, with large service sectors, shrinking family sizes, and with new household characteristics. New concerns related to lifestyles, to the qualities of life itself, in terms of health, clean environments and sustainable energy, became major urban issues. These concerns, along with concerns about institutional integrity and economic justice, became essential to the urban dialogue everywhere. In India, there are rising concerns about urban rights, catalyzing a dialogue on the 'rights to the city.' A growing disenfranchised class of people is emerging parallel with the Livability Index.

Livability in Pune Through History

Understanding this ethos and mentality becomes easier knowing the city as the erstwhile capital of the Maratha Empire that ruled indigenous Hindu India from the late seventeenth century through the early nineteenth century, unifying a large portion of the nation that had been invaded, divided and colonized by alien states for over five centuries. A literate elite of Chitpavan brahmins, in partnership with an elite of Maratha warriors, ruled the Maratha Empire and the lands across India, from the Shaniwar Wada citadel in the heart of Pune[6] (see Figure 7.4). The names of these elite brahmin and Maratha clans still sway social influence and political power in the region. Government structures and official titles are evolved variants from the Maratha system. Tax collecting and judicial representatives of the Peshwas (emperors), known as 'deshmukhs,' morphed into the British colonial administration, emerging as English District Collectors who were officers of the British Indian Civil Service (ICS). Toward the end of the British Raj, Indians from educated families were admitted into the ICS, and Post-Independence, they emerged as the indigenous administrative elite, as members of the Indian Administrative Service (IAS). These are the officers who hold the top administrative positions within the Pune Metropolitan Region, and across India.

From Independence, in 1947, Pune began to evolve slowly from a military, educational and trading center into a modern industrial metropolis, and then with the opening of the economy in the early 1990s, rapidly grew into a global information technology center. This process was given a fillip in the early 1960s when policy steps were taken to restrict industrial development in the Mumbai metropolitan region and to create industrial parks and incentives for manufacturing in the Pune area. At present, Pune hosts multinational companies like Mercedes Benz, General Motors, Sandvik Asia, Cummins India, and Volkswagen. Parsis from Mumbai, like the House of Tatas, established major industries, including TELCO the truck manufacturer and rail locomotive giant, and Tata Consulting Services, India's largest software and information technology exporter. After purchasing the Jaguar and Land Rover companies in Britain, manufacturing units opened in Pune.

Figure 7.4 Shaniwar Wada Citadel
Source: Deepak Kaw

Forbes Marshall, a leading Parsi family of the city, produces high-technology industrial measuring equipment, boilers, valves and steam systems. Thermax, another Parsi enterprise, is an international player in environmental engineering and energy.

Early on, Pune became the automotive hub of India, with indigenous global players like Bajaj manufacturing scooters, motorcycles, and 'auto rickshaws' that are seen on the streets from Indonesia to East Africa. At one time, more two wheelers were produced daily in Pune than in any other place in the world, and even today, Pune has more two-wheeler vehicles on its roads than any other city in India. After the opening of the Indian economy in the early 1990s, Pune flourished as a global information technology center and educational center. Hundreds of international players like IBM, Google, Oracle, Accenture, Cognizant, Veritas and Microsoft, along with Indian information technology giants WIPRO, Infosys, Mahindra Technologies, KPIT and Tata Consulting Services set up shop in the city. New private universities and colleges sprouted and flourished, attracting a large international student population to the city.

Since the days of the Marathas and the British, Pune has been the military nerve center of central India, hosting the National Defense Academy, the College of Military Engineering, the Armed Forces Medical College, the Controller General of Defence Accounts, the Southern Command Headquarters, an air force base and major defense research laboratories. Colleges date back to the middle of the nineteenth century, like the Deccan College (1851) and the College of Engineering at Pune (1854). In fact, the Deccan College finds its roots in the Maratha era Dakshina Fund (1700) that propagated Sanskrit studies and morphed into the Hindoo College in 1821. This long history of progress and modernization has tempered the peoples' sense of importance, leadership and civility.

Like other past royal cities of central India, the old city of Pune was created under guidelines laid out by its rulers, with clear development rules, that guided Sheth Mahajans, or city development managers who laid out planned areas, called peths, having potable water supply, cultural and religious public domains, including bathing places, gymnasia and wrestling clubs. Major roads clearly defined neighborhoods, with interior lanes giving access to 'kattas,' which are well-defined neighborhood meeting places, in a larger system of open gardens, hosting temples and lotus pools, all fed by aqueducts and reservoirs created above the city.[7]

In the early nineteenth century when the East India Company defeated the Marathas, deposing the Peshwa emperor, the British set out creating idyllic English settlements around Pune called cantonments, separating the Europeans from the Indian population, the English staff from their Indian subordinate staff, all higher officials from their lower subordinates and the men from the women. The only place these people crossed one another was in the bazaar. This class-, gender- and position-based model persists in the organization of Pune's modern universities, contemporary government enclaves and new company towns in the metropolitan region. In fact, in the traditional fabric of Pune, each peth, or traditional ward, had a pluralistic mix of various castes and communities, working symbiotically as integrated communities. Under British Rule these wards slowly evolved into ghettoized, less pluralistic social communities, with many wards, or peths, becoming Brahmin peths or Maratha peths, and lower caste areas to the east of the city.

With urbanization, catalyzed by the arrival of the railway from Mumbai in 1864 and the designation of Pune as the Monsoon Capital of the Bombay Presidency, Pune became a major trading and administrative center, where a large urban underclass gradually emerged, often as refugees from rural famine and drought. Poverty and its causes became central to economic and social debates amongst Pune's intelligentsia resulting in well know texts on poverty, malnutrition and their causes. Pune's social leaders like Jyotirao and Savitribai Phule, Gopal Krishna Gokhale, M. G. Ranade and Lokmanya Tilak molded modern social thinking in India, from the rights of women to the equality of all castes. The Tilak Maharashtra University (1921) and the Gokhale Institute of Politics and Economics (1930) became national centers of social and political thinking, playing major roles in social movements and in creating empirical models of development. Modes of production, the economic system, exploitation of labor and of women became thematic in the discussion of the quality of life and the emerging dialogue on livability in India. Though livable cities may appear as an imported Western concept in Pune, it fits neatly into the intellectual tradition of the city, where identifiable goals and objectives were set, to be achieved and measured comparing, the development of different spatial areas and groups under stress. This trend has drifted from comparisons between the Indian states, with the Gadgil Formula initiated in Pune, to the present rankings of Indian cities, raising a proposition that having comparative indices between cities will spur competition, generating more livable cities.[8] This proposition is a useful one but raises questions as to the inclusiveness of such approaches. The Pune case study throws light on the rising debate.

Comparing one Asian city with another raises the problem of complex socioeconomic structural differences, even within a single human settlement, much less between two or more cities. Using indices to compare Western cities with each other is perhaps a rational tool to set measurable standards and goals of urban development, as these cities possibly share common employment patterns, similar household income structures and consumer expenditure levels and enjoy similar urban infrastructure and comparable ideals of governance. Bringing Indian cities into this arena raises the question of the concept's applicability across income groups that inhabit the same urban space. Moreover, unlike the founding cities of the livability movement in post-industrial societies, where new lifestyles were emerging and creating local demands for livability, in India, the Livability Index is a top-down strategy to make the national system of city administration more accountable. Improved city livability for the citizens will be a by-product of the program, as managers try to increase their city's livability rankings for a better scorecard. In the West, a growing understanding of the importance of sustainability and urban health also triggered an interest in livability. The introduction of the Livability Index into the lexicon of urban administrative jargon will add support to the growing voices in India that understand these issues and the related crises of inhumane human habitats.

An investigation into the Pune Metropolitan Region's livability elucidates the fact that within one metropolitan region, and indeed within one city, there are variant frameworks of livability, reflecting different vectors of stresses tempering the lives of different household types (see Table 7.1).

In applying livability indexes, one must be cautious of simplistic paradigms of human and city development that may conceal the complexity of required city strategies. Paradigms that espouse optimums, against which livability can be evaluated, are fraught with the possibility of excluding large segments of the population. An early study by the author of habitat mobility models constructed at the Joint Center for Urban Studies in America, showed that the popular Turner Model of self-help housing was not a representation

Table 7.1 Percentage of Income Expended on Basic Needs

Food %	Clothes %	Shelter %	Transport %	Health %	Education %	Research %	Saving/Debt %	Total %	Target Groups
35	10	22	12	7	4	7	3	100	Lower Middle Class
50	12	14	8	5	2	6	3	100	Poor
85	5	3	5	5	1	6	−10	100	Subsistence

Source: Centre for Development Studies and Activities (CDSA) estimates based on National Sample Survey Office (NSSO) and CDSA definitions of Subsidies

of Asian urbanization processes, yet was a good policy voice tempering governments to respect people's self-help efforts.[9]

There are two structural aspects of South Asian cities that emerge as complexities that need to be addressed. Analysts of urbanization in Asia have noted that there are 'cities within cities'.[10] These are not just ghettoized geographical enclaves, but different historical periods coexisting in one physical space, and for analytical clarity, appearing like separate pieces of paper, floating one over the other. These are not mere historical references, but living cultural systems of behaviors, values and mores, all active, intermixed with one another, somehow in harmony, yet each holding very different cultural territories. Added to this complexity is the rapid growth of low-income groups that accompanied economic growth. Over the past two decades, the population of the metropolitan area more than doubled, and the number of people living in illegal, substandard and unhygienic habitats more than tripled.

Dotted across the metropolis, lie hundreds of squatter settlements, illegally organized on government and private lands, housing a growing underclass of citizens (see Figure 7.5). A recent survey of the Delhi metropolis reveals that 75% of the capital region lives in poor and low-income settlements, and a study by the National Sample Survey Office reports that the informal, unorganized sector's workers' earning grew at 86%, from $ 2.20 per day five years ago, to $4 per day in the year 2015–2016, with 20% of the enterprises owned by women.[11] Multiple, small-scale ancillary manufacturing units operate within Pune slums, densified villages and illegal layouts. Essential ancillary production takes place within these settlements, forming the base of a complex chain of ancillary inputs moving forward for assemblage into larger and larger fabrications, often finding their way into complex, high-technology machinery and products. Machine parts, garments, traditional Indian

Figure 7.5 Slum on Parvati Hill, Pune
Source: MASHAL

cigarettes (bidis) and utensils are manufactured in Pune's slums and shanties. Carpentry shops, metal fabricators, tailors and craftspeople work within these informal settlements. The old villages that once surrounded Pune city were engulfed and densified in a haphazard manner as the metropolis grew. About 10 percent of the metropolitan population lives in crowded, four to five storied, walk-up dwellings, often illegally built within these uncontrolled settlements. Along with these slums and urbanized villages are illegal layouts, large workers' camps, old workers' tenements and low-income neighborhoods in sub-divided old houses in the city center. Nearly 70 percent of the households in the metropolis live in unhygienic, overcrowded settlements! Herein lies yet the most challenging puzzle of livable cities: what is livable to the inhabitants of these settlements? What are their priorities and essential unmet needs?

Pune's Leap Into the Livability World

Early development initiatives in post-Independent India focused on rural development and agriculture productivity, along with the Community Development Programme and Integrated Area Planning that employed central place theory, with the objective of converging services and economic facilities to centrally located settlements. Only after half a century of Independence did urban development and major infrastructure projects begin to attract the attention of the central government. Following the opening of the economy, India saw two decades (1992–2012) of many new large urban infrastructure projects, mainly with the objective of bringing India into the global economic framework, and thus attracting Foreign Direct Investment (FDI), and igniting economic growth. Airports in major cities, port facility improvements, express highways and Special Economic Zones were facilitated, through vast land acquisitions and incentives for private enterprises to create modern industrial estates and economic infrastructure. State governments created many industrial estates on the peripheries of cities. Thus, surrounding Pune lie vast, mono-functional industrial satellite townships catering to large-scale industries.

Be that as it may, the 'regulation raj' of public administration crippled much of that progress through a myriad requirement of permissions, complicated by an endemic culture of corruption. A telling indicator is India's poor position of 85 in the 2015–2016 rankings of Best Countries to Do Business In.[12] In the search for effective development policies, a realization emerged that India's future development lay in a framework of urban development where private enterprises, guided by good governance practices, become fillips to rapid investment and growth. The previous government had initiated the Jawaharlal Nehru National Urban Renewal Mission (JNNURM) in 2005, meant to improve the quality of life and urban infrastructure. It had specific approaches to address problems of the urban poor through the provision of Basic Services to Urban Poor (BSUP), including wide-ranging urban sector reforms. Slum improvements and new strategies for rapid urban bus transit were notable outcomes. The ruling Bharatiya Janata Party set out positioning cities as the engines of growth and examining means to make these engines more effective and efficient. There is an emphasis is on strengthening the manufacturing and export sectors. The new government inherited a corruption-riddled government framework. Much needed to be done to clean up and reorganize a large, inept system headed in the wrong direction. Smart Cities, Demonetization, the Livability Index and the Goods and Services Tax are amongst the reorganization strategies.

The new government initiated techno-managerial approaches, with urban-led transformational strategies involving cities like Pune. An early focus of this initiative envisioned capital accumulation and foreign investment employed to link urban development, industrialization and a technological culture, wherein urban restructuring becomes a key element of the nation building process. Pune was identified as an excellent laboratory through which to explore the intervention of global models, such as the Smart Cities movement and very recently, Livability Indexes, into the evolution of large urban agglomerations. Even before liberalization in 1991, Pune had most of the components in place to be a forceful lead city and model for other cities in India. It had a lively free press and active non-government organizations focused on urban environment, sustainability, heritage, biodiversity, encouraging cycling, facilitating pedestrians and employing rights to information legislation. Several approaches tempered Pune's early Smart Cities discussion, including kick-starting investments in the manufacturing and information technology sectors, by creating incentives for investment. Another was to bring empirical and transparent management practices into its development administration, and still another was to make urban governance a digital, web-based system of development, participation and management.

After the 2014 national general election, the Prime Minister immediately initiated the vision of the One Hundred New Cities Programme and the Urban Corridors strategy between major metropolises. These grand strategies were quickly tempered into more participatory and achievable strategies, like the Smart Cities program, where major cities would define and fashion their own set of core priorities and action plans. Pune became the first city to set in motion its Smart City program of action, with key strategies that included:

- Green building strategies;
- A strategy to intelligently light city streets;
- Sustainable transport initiatives;
- A potable water supply strategy;
- An approach to overcome storm drainage problems;
- A river conservation project;
- A solid waste management strategy;
- A Pune cycle path plan;
- Vehicle movement tracking project;
- Converting waste to energy;
- Bio-gas from food wastes;
- A mobile application for mass transit information;
- Maximize solar energy project; and,
- The Quantified Cities Movement.[13]

When this shelf of schemes was finalized, the Pune Smart Cities program was refined into six key themes, namely:

- Improving hard infrastructure, like sewerage lines;
- Improving social infrastructure, increasing women's security;
- Improving livability quotients;
- Creating socially inclusive growth;
- Improving sustainability quotients;
- Putting in place information and communication technology (ICT).

It was in the process of refining hundreds of possible initiatives into a program that the concept of livability entered the national discussion on improving life in Indian cities! It offered senior officials an empirical handle to measure activities and progress in numerous large cities.

In Pune, the Smart City projects were based on local citizen and non-government organization proposals, with the Pune Municipal Corporation supporting some of the initiatives through grants in aid. The Quantified Cities Movement (QCM), an initiative of the Centre for Development Studies and Activities, sparked the most response, with the United Nations supporting the project through UNICEF. UNICEF saw a huge potential in the QCM Application, through its school training component, where children are taught to use their mobile phones to note city stresses and actively participate in building an urban stress map! Microsoft soon came forward donating server space, hosting the QCM Application globally.

QCM holds the potential of bringing all citizens onto a system of observing, reporting and mapping stresses. With the QCM application on their smartphones, citizens' locations are marked within a 5-meter radius upon opening the app. Citizens find themselves located on a map where they are standing and they can then click icons for urban stresses observed, like sewerage overflowing! Clicking this Sewerage Stress Icon immediately sends an email notification to the concerned city official in charge of sewerage maintenance. The citizen can add a photo image of the sewerage overflow. This immediately creates a pin mark on the city stress map, and at the neighborhood level stress map, indicating that there is sewerage overflow at this point. All the stresses in the city can be seen on one map that lights up pins indicating high-density stress areas! This stress image is like global images of urban night lights across global regions, highlighting through satellite imagery high-density regions in the world. But in the QCM case, high urban stress areas are highlighted in one's own city and neighborhood. Alternatively, one can see all the stress pin points in their neighborhood, or one can see the stress map of the city only illustrating the concerned sewerage stress pin points across the city! This allows citizens to SEE their city's situation and possibly to think of the livability of their neighborhood compared with others, or to see where stresses are more, and accordingly the city is less livable! QCM has icons for sewerage, solid waste heaping up, street lights out, potholes in roads and sidewalks, and so forth. A unique, participatory aspect of this smartphone-based livability tool is its training of trainers' program wherein about 5,000 secondary school teachers are being trained, through instructions on how to teach QCM methods to their students. Then they will teach their students how to 'own their city!'

The Livability Index Enters Pune

Over the two years since the inauguration of the Smart Cities movement in Pune, by the Prime Minister, the Central government proposed a larger, centrally managed canvas of urban management employing empirical measuring of the livability of each city, comparing the achievement of targets by competing local bodies. This new approach was first articulated in March 2017 under the banner of Livability Indexes. Accordingly, the Ministry of Urban Development, Government of India, released its Livability Index,[14] by which the ranking all the 100 cities under the Smart Cities program will be compared on 77 parameters, including education, traffic surveillance systems, pollution, availability of water and power, online citizen services, grievance redressal of citizens, upkeep of historical buildings, increase in tourist footfalls, crime rate, extent of crimes against women recorded and care of children and the elderly. Using these indexes, 'points' will be accumulated by each city, whereby they can then be ranked and compared. The new Livability Index would chart a city's progress against various standards under four categories, with each category holding a weightage in terms of the percentage of points it will finally represent: institutional (25 percent weightage), social (25 percent weightage), economic (5 percent weightage) and physical (45 percent weightage). The concept holds potential for a transparent framework, dealing with the needs and expectations of city dwellers in an empirical manner. A major objective of this system is the sensitization of local city managers to take proactive steps to improve the governance and deliverables of their cities. The main component indicators of this program are:

- Under the Institutional Theme (25 percent) is a Governance Index;
- Under the Social Theme (25 percent) are a Health Index, Education Index, Identity and Culture Index and a Security Index;
- Under the Economic Theme (5 percent) is the Economic Index;
- Under the Physical Theme (45 percent) are the Compact Development Index, Water Index, Energy Index, Waste Water Index, Solid Waste Index, Housing Index, Open Space Index, Mobility Index, and Pollution Index.

Through this program, benchmarks of achievement are set for each of the 77 indicators. Some indicators are 'core,' and some are 'supporting.' For example, under Assured Water Supply, one could achieve full marks if the household level coverage of direct water supply connections reach all the city's households. Then the benchmark on this 'core' indicator would be 100 percent. Proportionate points would be awarded on the level of achievement. A 'supporting' indicator in the area is 'percentage of water connections covered through smart meters.' In each Category Index, 0.7 proportion points go to 'core' indicators, and 0.3 proportion points go to 'supporting' indicators.

So the first step of this process is the analysis of a city's progress in each indicator and converting each situation into a score. For example, if half of the households in the city have direct potable water connections, then the score would be 50 percent. In the second step, the levels of achievement in all Core and Supporting Indicators will be calculated in detail and adjusted between 0.7 weightage for core indicators, as to 0.3 weightage for supporting indicators. Next, in the third step, the percentage of weight adjustments will be applied as proportioned between the four themes (i.e., as above: 25 percent, 25 percent, 5 percent and 45 percent). In the fourth step, the City Livability Index will be calculated. And in the fifth step, cities will be ranked against each other.

Livability as Integrating the First and the Second Societies

If this system is based on enumerated households of all types, legal and illegal, it will indeed be a major achievement in employing the formal system to objectify the informal system and bring poor and low-income settlements within the ambit of formal governance. If all slums, urbanized villages, labor camps, overcrowded city center houses and illegal layouts are brought within the Livability Index purview, this will indeed be a milestone in integrating the first and the second societies of Pune into a cohesive urban management system.

A major lacuna of both the Smart Cities and Livability Index programs is that they see change taking place through formal governance, driven by corporate public and private sector actions, through elite segments of the society. For example, in Pune, the Smart City program selected a pilot area that includes three of the wealthiest new areas of the city, with a goal of raising the level of development in this Smart Cities Pilot Area to levels matching global standards. To begin with, this pilot area is one of the socially and economically elite areas of the city, housing highly paid IT technologists, executives, business owners and professionals. Not more than 6 percent of the city's population could afford the equated monthly installments required to buy an apartment in this area. Very likely, the purchasing power per capita of the inhabitants of this pilot zone is higher than the average personal purchasing power per capita of the citizens in the very global cities whose standards the program hopes to emulate and to reach! Clearly, the selection of the pilot area was based on creating a good showpiece, rather than demonstrating dramatic improvements in the livability of a low-income community. This echoes the initial discussion in this chapter, that the proposed metropolitan area is focused on the formal, corporate society, and not on the informal, poor and low-income sections of society.

There is a risk that such top-down programs, expanding the existing ill-performing governance system, will overlook the critical need to reform the failing system. Clearly, any new and successful strategy must walk a tight rope between an entrenched system of formal governance while addressing the basic needs and livability levels of a voiceless underclass of city dwellers, who make up a larger and larger share of the electorate year by year.

Some Concluding Thoughts

Livability means different things to different people and to different urban households. In the Pune Metropolitan Region, a household's occupation, earnings and ability to pay for basic goods and services will dramatically impact on the kinds of public interventions that improve the livability of their city. Their view of improved livability will surely begin with access to potable water, with the security of tenure for their simple shelter, with clean and private toilets, and with neighborhoods free of crime. Storm drainage, paved pathways to their shelters, street lights and solid waste management mean a lot to them. These are very simple and obvious livability indicators for the urban poor. They will sense a right to their city once they see that these urban inputs are in the pipeline and are being realized. But their city is not the city envisioned by the elite planners, managers and city engineers. Cutting across these layers of 'cities within cities' are some common areas where constructive action is required. Perhaps, starting with more elemental changes would be an appropriate strategy prior to intervening in specific components. What are the critical livability actions?

Foremost, **institutional integrity** through Pune's Livability Institutional Theme is the most critical action area. Under Pune's Governance Index, a new independent and transparent structure must replace the opaque, discretionary and corrupt character of our urban management systems. Activities like clearing new land layouts and approving building plans need to be removed from the local bodies' functional purview, put on the Internet, and then subcontracted to respected management consulting firms with track records of honest and professional performance. If one cannot ameliorate a malfunctioning system, one must terminate it, and bypass it! Our cities involved well-known management firms to create media hype through position papers emphasizing potentials and opportunities. Now these same firms should be called in to work on the ground fixing the system and making it work!

City Commissioners know that their three-year term of duty as the senior official in a city can turn sour, ending in their unceremonious transfer to a lower post, or it can be a highlight of their career if they play their cards carefully, not stepping on the toes of special interest groups. A good term in office is ensured by initiating new programs popular with the state and central political leadership, showcasing these and then disappearing up the ladder to a higher post! The new focus on livability must thrust the responsibility of clean governance on the City Commissioner, where a benchmark measuring citizen's perceptions of municipal corruption is given a high percentage under the Governance Index.

Likewise, the Ward Officers, who are on the ground and turn their eyes the other way by not reporting encroachments on open lands, river fronts or in roads, are subordinates of the Municipal Commissioner. They must be benchmarked and rated too. They are the weak end of a malfunctioning system of urban development based on bribes, not livability.

Urban development statutory mechanisms need reconceptualization as tools to facilitate and empower citizens, not to restrict and penalize them. Pune's development plans, re-planned, often after decades of neglect, address only land uses, floor area ratios, infrastructure corridors and mega-projects. Along with Development Control Regulations, they are automobile owner oriented and suited to the needs of developers, not the people of the city. Such urban planning makes cities unlivable, not more livable! There is nothing in the new Pune Development Plan that will enhance the lives of the people living in low-income human settlements. There is no hint of creating humane human habitats.

The protection of public open spaces, river fronts, biodiversity zones, hill sides and any form of public asset or domain is under continuous threat of collusion between city officials and land developers for illegal conversion into buildable zones. In this manner, about a third of the declared non-buildable "flood zones" along the 44 kilometers of riverfront in the city of Pune has been illegally built upon. Plots in the development plans reserved for amenities and gardens are under continuous threat for a change of use to favor developers, who want to develop profitable, commercial assets on these reserved lands.

Under the Pune Livability Governance Index, there must be capability building for **visionary imaging and planning** for the region, its local bodies and their components. The local bodies have no operational urban planning and urban design capabilities. The Pune Metropolitan Region was the last urban agglomeration in India to institute a metropolitan planning authority, as recently as 2015. This nascent body lacks any semblance of a professional urban planning, urban design, investment planning, socioeconomic analysis, infrastructure engineering design, or any other institutional capability that can deliver the inputs that will make the Pune region more livable.

Given the conundrum of the Pune metropolis, it seems appropriate for the leadership to identify key interventions that will make the urban environment more livable for everyone as first steps. A critical step for the livability of all citizens is their access to pedestrian areas, including sidewalks, recreation areas, gardens and parks. A major new intervention under active planning is comprehensive riverfront development that would open large water's edge park lands to the people of Pune, necessitating major improvements in the sewerage treatment system that presently dumps a large percentage of the urban regions' raw sewerage into the rivers that cut through the metropolis.

A major improvement in Pune's livability can be achieved by integrating humane habitat programs into ongoing large Special Economic Zones, Information Technology Parks and industrial townships created by the Maharashtra Industrial Development Corporation. These vast land development initiatives have no space allocated for small-scale, informal industries, or allocation of any space for shelter and community services. These large, urban development initiatives must be re-conceptualized from Special Economic Zones into holistic Special Socioeconomic Zones, introducing large areas for site and services, self-help housing land development, healthcare facilities, education, skill development and recreational uses. The objectives of these large infrastructural schemes must shift from attracting investment and exporting manufactured goods to developing and constructively employing the human resources of India's youth.

Cities around the world can benefit from Pune's experience by employing the Quantitative Cities Movement as a cutting-edge urban participation, planning and management tool that eases urban management while improving citizen participation and transparency (www.qcmweb.org). It went live globally in early Spring 2018.

Notes

1. Refer to Jain, V., Chennuri, S., & Karamchandani, A. (2016). *Informal housing, inadequate property rights: Understanding the needs of India's Informal Housing Dwellers.* Mumbai: FSG Mumbai. Retrieved from www.citiesalliance.org/sites/citiesalliance.org/files/Informal%20 Housing,%20Inadequate%20Property%20Rights.pdf

2. Refer to *The Times of India* Report. (2011). *32.5% population of city lives in slums*. Pune. Retrieved from http://timesofindia.indiatimes.com/city/pune/32-5-population-of-city-lives-in-slums/articleshow/7315211.cms
3. Refer to *The Economic Times* Report. (2017). *Why income tax payers in India are a small and shrinking breed*. Retrieved from http://economictimes.indiatimes.com/news/economy/policy/why-income-tax-payers-in-india-are-a-small-and-shrinking-breed/articleshow/56929550.cms
4. Refer to MASHAL. (2009–2010). *Housing study for Pune municipal corporation*. Pune: Pune Municipal Corporation. Retrieved from https://pmc.gov.in/informpdf/City%20Engineer%20office/Housing%20Report%20Final.pdf
5. Refer to Kochhar, R. (2015). *China's middle class surges, while India's lags behind*. Washington, DC: Pew Research Center study. Retrieved from www.pewresearch.org/fact-tank/2015/07/15/china-india-middle-class/
6. Refer to Gordon, S. (1993). *The Marathas 1600–1818*. New York: Cambridge University Press.
7. Refer to Eaton, R., & Wagoner, P. (2014). *Power, memory, architecture: Contested sites on India's Deccan Plateau 1300–1600*. Oxford: Oxford University Press.
8. Refer to Gadgil, D. R. (1945). *Poona: A socio-economic survey*. Pune: Gokhale Institute of Politics and Economics.
9. Refer to Benninger, C. C. (1970). Models of habitat mobility in transitional economies. *Ekistics*, 29, 124–127.
10. Refer to Mehrotra, R., & Dwivedi, S. (1995). *Bombay: The cities within*. Mumbai: Eminence Designs.
11. Refer to National Sample Survey Office Report. (2017). *Key indicators of unincorporated non-agricultural enterprises in India*. Retrieved from www.mospi.gov.in/sites/default/files/publication_reports/NSS_KI_73_2.34.pdf
12. Refer to *Forbes* Ranking for Best Countries to Do Business In. (2017). Retrieved from www.forbes.com/best-countries-for-business/list/#tab:place_search:india
13. Refer to Pune Smart City Projects. Retrieved from www.punesmartcity.in/?wicket:bookmarkablePage=:Com.SmartCity.Page.frmsmartcityproject
14. Refer to Smart Cities Mission, Ministry of Housing and Urban Affairs, Government of India. (2017). *Liveability Standards in Cities*. Retrieved from http://www.smartcities.gov.in/upload/files/files/LiveabilityStandards.pdf

Further Reading

B. D. Karve Research and Consultancy Cell. (2008–2009). *Socio-economic survey of Pune city*. Pune: Karve Institute of Social Service. (A socioeconomic survey of Pune).

Diddee, J., & Gupta, S. (2000). *Pune: Queen of the deccan*. Pune: Elephant Design. (The most comprehensive book on the history of Pune).

Future Institute. (2012). *Towards more livable Indian cities: Decoding livability for a city*. New Delhi: Future Institute. (An introductory review of possible goals and objectives of livable cities in India).

Mashal. (2009–2010). *Housing study for Pune Municipal Corporation*. Pune: Mashal. (A NGO's report on shelter in Pune).

Shaw, A. (2012). *Indian cities*. New Delhi: Oxford University Press. (A review of possible strategies for Indian Cities).

Sivaramakrishnan, K. C. (2015). *Governance of megacities, fractured thinking, fragmented setup*. New Delhi: Oxford University Press. (A detailed analysis of the governance of Indian metropolitan cities in India).

Voyants Partnering Visions. (2013). *Revising/updating the city development plan of Pune city-2041*. Pune: Pune Municipal Corporation. (Consultant report on environmental issues and strategies for the Pune City Development Plan).

Part III
Livability and Equity Concerns

Introduction

One of the most important issues facing areas striving for livability involves the issue of equity. Do all citizens share in or benefit from an area's livability efforts? Does everyone have opportunities for economic prosperity? Is affordable housing and quality schools available to all residents or only some of the residents? These equity concerns are the focus of Part III. Because developing livability policies and actions should be a total community effort, it only makes sense that everyone benefits from the various policies and actions.

Chapter 8 examines equity concerns in livability efforts in Sydney, Australia. Being another city typically found in the top ten lists of livable cities, the authors investigated the issue of livability from a spatial geography perspective. They found that by examining various issues, disadvantages and inequalities exist within Sydney. As such, there are winners and losers in regards to livability by area.

Chapter 9 focuses on how Tokyo has responded to the issue of livability. The city continues to expand outward to essentially form a multi-core urban area. Suburbs continue to stretch outward. As other areas around the globe experienced, Tokyo felt the collapse of the real estate bubble. The chosen course of action was to renew the urban areas while the suburban areas declined in popularity and suffered. As such, with the younger population moving to the urban area, the question became what to do with the suburbs. This was complicated, with almost a third of the area's population being elderly. The challenge facing Tokyo is to increase the livability of the suburban areas, especially with an aging society. The challenge is also how to gain the collaboration of multiple stakeholders in such a large area.

Chapter 10 discusses livability for whom in Vancouver, Canada. The author wants to know if livability is extended to all residents. Although Vancouver ranks high in livability ranking, it is not without problems like homelessness, housing insecurity, economic inequities, and an increasing poverty rate. High-quality developments have been constructed over the years. Sound planning and design principles have been followed. Density has increased, with many citizens resisting densification with calls of gentrification be voiced by various groups. Incomes have not kept pace with core essentials like housing, utilities, and food costs. Ultimately, is Vancouver a victim or casualty of its own success? A dichotomy has been seen among the haves and have nots. Prosperity should be shared between various population groups and not the privilege of certain groups.

8 Livable Sydney
Livable for Whom?

Roberta Ryan and Yvette Selim

Introduction

The top ten cities in global livability indices are often dominated by European, Australasian and Canadian cities, with Sydney frequently in the top ten. Today, "livability" has become a buzzword in public discourse and planning (Ruth & Franklin, 2014, 8), and the number of livability indices are proliferating; yet, despite this growing popularity, questions remain about what livability actually entails. How do we measure livability? How are indicators chosen and what weight are they assigned? Are they value free? Do the indicators remain static? What does a livable city look like, and what is its highest pursuit? And, the focus of this chapter: livable for whom?

This chapter uses Sydney as a case study to demonstrate that when a spatial geography[1] perspective is adopted, particular features bring into question the notion of livability. We argue that although the notion of livability, and the related livability rankings, have some utility, they do not adequately illuminate the spatial disadvantages and inequalities *within* cities. Social disadvantage and inequalities (such as income, education levels and employment status) are worsening in Sydney and of particular note is their spatial distribution. Spatial disadvantage has been explored since the 1960s (see Beer, 1994; Bill, 2005; Baum et al., 2006) where "spatial disadvantage" is generally considered to be "the tendency for disadvantaged people to be clustered in particular localities" (Cheshire et al., 2014, 6). Gleeson and Randolph (2002, 102) describe these disadvantages as being "manifested in enclaves afflicted by distinct combinations of social exclusion, transport poverty, environmental blight and locational inaccessibility". Other scholars, such as Stilwell and Jordan (2007), have shifted this to locational disadvantage, which "focuses on the ability to gain access to resources and encompasses income factors, as well as the cost of travelling to health care, shops or work" (Beer, 1994, 182).

Although disadvantages and inequalities have been explored at a city level, greater attention is being paid to regions and suburbs within cities. With regard to Sydney, Bill (2005, 4) claims:

> The key change is that the inner cities are no longer the location of urban disadvantage in Sydney (Randolph & Holloway, 2005, 52). Instead there has been a "suburbanisation of disadvantage" (Randolph, 2003) and middle suburbs (suburbs between the east-west divide) are the new locations of relative social and economic decline.

Echoing this view, Irvine (2015) suggests that "Sydney is the epicentre of a 'crisis of suburbia', as new figures reveal inner city postcodes enjoyed the fastest income gains over the past decade, while the poorer outer suburbs went backwards after inflation."

Inequalities and disadvantages in Sydney can be situated within Lefebvre's notion of the "right to city", as this notion assists to *reframe* and *counteract* approaches to urban policies (Attoh, 2011, 675). Lefebvre (1996, 173–174) describes the right to the city

> as a superior form of rights: right to freedom, to individualization in socialization, to habitat and to inhabit. The right to the *oeuvre*, to participation and *appropriation* (clearly distinct to the right to property), are implied in the right to the city

Purcell (2005, 14) conceives of this right as an individual right for those who "live in the city, who contribute to the body of lived experience and lived space". For Purcell (2002, 103), Lefebvre's conception of the right to the city is "one of radical transformation of urban social and spatial relations" whereby

> users [are not] claiming more access to and control over the existing capitalist city, a bigger slice of the existing pie. Instead it is a movement to go beyond the existing city, to cultivate the urban so that it can grow and spread.
>
> (Purcell, 2013, 150)

In contrast, David Harvey conceives of the right to the city as a collective right to have "some command over both the use and distribution of urban surpluses" (Attoh, 2011, 676), which "depends on the exercise of collective power to reshape the process of urbanization" (Harvey, 2008, 23).

Lefebvre conceives of the right to the city to be voiced "from the directly oppressed, the aspiration from the alienated" (Marcuse, 2009, 191) and his notion has been increasingly considered along with the rise of neoliberalism (O'Loghlen, 2015, 7). For example, according to Purcell (2002, 101), Lefebvre's notion and his broader "ideas for social and political relations in cities" has "potential for resisting the anti-democratic trends of neoliberal urbanization" and "offers a radical alternative that directly challenges and rethinks the current structure of both capitalism and liberal-democratic citizenship" (2002, 100). This is significant, because neoliberal urban development results in a fragmentation of space, in which government (at all levels) "facilitates and promotes [fragmentation] . . . through the creation of insular and isolated spaces in our urban and metropolitan geographies by private sector developers" (Beatty, 2014, 44, 45). Today, these rights are "exclusively wielded by private interests and in which an increasingly small urban elite produces and manages surpluses for their own ends" (see Attoh, 2011, 676). Further, this fragmentation results in "the creation of insular and isolated spaces in our urban and metropolitan geographies" (see Mele, 2011 in Beatty, 2014, 45); put simply, socio-spatial exclusion. This neoliberal project can be constituted and reconstituted by policy-makers who design and implement urban policies (Beatty, 2014, 48). When considering spatial inequality, there are implications for individual life chances resulting from poorer access to critical supports and services as well the power and control over everyday lived experiences, the very nature of how cities are reconstituted and in whose interests. The use and application of global livability indices reflect the exercise of collective power in the ongoing narrative about the processes of urbanisation and the implications for citizens to control them.

Livability

The roots of livability can be found in quality of life literature. In earlier debates, the quality of life literature juxtaposed livability theory and comparison theory (Scerri, 2008): "In recent years, researchers have attempted to coalesce the two theories by proposing the view that persons' judgments about quality of life implicate both absolute standards and recent changes in quality of life" (Scerri, 2008, 3641). Today, the urban livability literature emphasises "the subjective nature of the concept, urging planners to consider the city not only in its form and function, but in the mind" (Zeisel, 1981 in Teo, 2014, 921–922; see also Ruth & Franklin, 2014). Also considered important to the experience of livability is a sense of place (Sell et al., 1984 in Teo, 2014, 922).

In 2007, *The Economist* utilised the term "liveability" to differentiate The Economist Intelligence Unit's (EIU) Global Liveability Ranking from existing quality of life rankings or hardship rankings (see Conger, 2015, 6). Jon Copestake, editor of *Liveability & Cost of Living* at the EIU, explains:

> Most liveable is not the same as being the best. Liveability measures the level of lifestyle that can be achieved in a location. Rather than defining itself by what is 'good' about a city [liveability] seeks to define itself by what is 'least challenging'. Therefore the most liveable city is not necessarily the 'best' simply the least challenging in which to live.
>
> (Copestake, 2014 cited in Conger, 2015, 6)

Despite the term's proliferation in planning and public discourse, few definitions of livability are provided. The academic and grey literature usually provides "an implicit definition of the concept" whereby the meaning of livability needs to be derived from "the context or choice of indicators" (Lowe et al., 2013, 11). It is apparent that in many respects "[l]iveability has come to mean all things to all people" (see Conger, 2015, 1).

Livability is usually captured by published indices or projects/studies.[2] Broadly speaking, there are three categories of indices that focus on decision making from the perspective of individual lifestyle preferences, the firm, and policy-makers (Conger, 2015, 1), and the most prominent indices are commercially developed. The livability indices vary in terms of the number of cities/countries selected; their purpose and methodology. For example, they include Economist Intelligence Unit's (EIU) Global Liveability Index, Mercer Quality of Life Survey, PricewaterhouseCoopers' Cities of Opportunity Quality of Life, Monocle's Quality of Life Survey, and Global Liveable Cities Index. The various indicators can be grouped into the ten policy areas (Lowe et al., 2013, 16).[3] There are significant differences in the types of data used and weight assigned to various indicators (Conger, 2015, 3–4; see, for example, EIU Liveability Ranking, 2016; Mercer Quality of Living Survey, 2016; PwC, 2016a; Monocle, 2016; Numbeo, 2017).

However, there are critical factors that these indices overlook. In relation to EIU Global Livability Index, Davies (2015) says, "[w]hatever its usefulness for companies sending executives on assignment might be, the Index has little relevance for permanent residents of a city or for urban policy-makers." Other critiques include that many indices are developed for specific commercial purposes, the number of cities is limited and too selective, the data are misinterpreted and some indices vary from year to year, making yearly comparisons more difficult. Also by simplifying livability to an aggregate figure, they suffer from the same problems of all composite indices, in that a positive aspect and a negative aspect can simply cancel each other out in the overall assessment. We argue that arriving at a comprehensive definition of livability might be elusive, and not necessary for their stated purposes, but this does not negate the need for greater examination and interrogation of how these livability rankings *mask* the disadvantaged, marginalised and excluded *within* cities and how assessment of these issues should affect an overall city rating.

Sydney

Sydney frequently rates among the top ten cities on the leading livability indices (see Table 8.1).

In previous years, Sydney was often ranked more highly. In 2016, Sydney dropped from seventh to 11th for the EIU Global Livability Index 2016 due to heightened perceived threats of terrorism (and it was the sixth year in a row that Melbourne was ranked first in EIU's Global Liveability Index, see Chapter 1 of this volume). With headlines in *The Sydney Morning Herald* such as "Why The Economist says Sydney is no longer one of the world's 10 most liveable cities", it seems like at least part of the livability project is to remain in the top ten irrespective of the slight variations between these rankings. This highlights the extent to which these indices are being applied in a limited and instrumental manner and are indeed capable of accommodating new issues as they arise and are considered pertinent. In the context of Singapore, Teo (2014, 916) argues that "the concept of urban livability is used as a political tool by the Singaporean state to further its pursuit of global city status."

Taking livability a step further, Sydney suburbs have been ranked according to various livability indices. One example is the *Domain Liveable Sydney 2016* conducted by Tract Consultants and Deloitte Access Economics. Sixteen indicators were measured: access to employment, train/light rail, bus, ferry, culture, main road congestion, education, shopping, open space, tree cover, topographic variation, cafes and restaurants, crime, telecommunications, views and beach access. The suburbs that top this list are in Sydney's eastern and northern suburbs, which are exclusive locations. The index is owned by Domain, a property company, and it is apparent that livability is closely linked to suburbs that are also *commercially* desirable. Another example is the *Urban Living Index* by McCrindle Research and the Urban Taskforce Australia (a lobby group for the property sector). The index "explores the suburbs that are most equipped to deal with the densification of the population and cater for the needs of people living in high density housing" (Urban Taskforce Australia & McCrindle Research, 2016, 6). It measures 20 indicators across five categories: affordability, community, employability, amenity and accessibility. A component

Table 8.1 Top Ten Ranking Cities From Selected Livability Indices and Surveys

	EIU Global Livability Index 2016	Mercer Quality of Living Survey 2016	PWC Cities of Opportunity: Quality of Living 2016	Monocle Quality of Life Survey 2015	Numbeo Quality of Life Index 2017
Number of cities	140	230	30	25	177
	1. Melbourne 2. Vienna 3. Vancouver 4. Toronto 5. Calgary 6. Adelaide 7. Perth 8. Auckland 9. Helsinki 10. Hamburg 11. Sydney	1. Vienna 2. Zurich 3. Auckland 4. Munich 5. Vancouver 6. Dusseldorf 7. Frankfurt 8. Geneva 9. Copenhagen 10. Sydney	1. London 2. Singapore 3. Toronto 4. Paris 5. Amsterdam 6. New York 7. Stockholm 8. San Francisco 9. Hong Kong 10. Sydney	1. Tokyo 2. Berlin 3. Vienna 4. Copenhagen 5. Munich 6. Melbourne 7. Fukouka 8. Sydney 9. Kyoto 10. Stockholm	1. Canberra 2. Raleigh 3. Wellington 4. Victoria 5. Edinburgh 6. Adelaide 7. Eindhoven 8. Vienna 9. San Diego 10. Melbourne 39. Sydney

Source: EIU Liveability Ranking (2016); Mercer Quality of Living Survey (2016); PwC (2016a); Monocle (2016); Numbeo (2017)

of this index includes survey responses from residents, and for the majority of respondents, housing affordability was a significant challenge. These respective indices tell a particular story about Sydney; however, this is only a partial picture, and none of the new approaches consider the implications of inequality within cities.

Livability and Inequality

Although Sydney fares pretty well in terms of the current measures of livability, as we have noted, livability indices tend to homogenise, simplify and disregard crucial factors. When viewed through the lens of spatial geography, it is apparent that Sydney's (global) ranking as a livable city requires greater acknowledgement of the ways in which some Sydneysiders experience inequality and disadvantage and the broader implications of this for control of urban futures. Despite the strong economic growth in the 1990s, there is a "clear dichotomy" between eastern and western Sydney (Bill, 2005, 1).

Here we demonstrate this through a limited selection of only four issues: income, unemployment, travel to work and housing tenure. Although others could have been selected, these examples provide sufficient demonstration of our argument. We compare the data from 1991 or 2001 with the data from 2011[4] from Australian Bureau of Statistics, Census of Population and Housing.

The total number of people employed in Greater Sydney slightly increased (94% in 2001 compared with 94.3% in 2011) and the number of unemployed decreased (6% in 2001 compared with 5.7% in 2011). People in full-time employment decreased, whereas the number of people working part time increased, bringing it almost on par to the Australian figure.

However, these data do not reveal the disparities in people's incomes according to where they live. When viewed spatially, it is evident that people who live in the city, inner east and inner west, and the north shore of Sydney have higher weekly incomes than those living in the western parts of Sydney (see Figure 8.1).

There are also spatial disparities in the way people commute to work. Driving remained the main method of travel (49.2% in 1991 compared with 53.8% in 2011), demonstrating the continued automobile dependence in Sydney. Train travel remained second (13.8% in 2011). The number of people who travelled by bus decreased, whereas the proportion of people who travelled by tram or ferry remained constant.

The disparity between east and west is evident in people's opinions and preferences about travel (see Table 8.2). People in eastern Sydney felt more able to live close to where they work (72% compared with 62% in western Sydney). People in western Sydney were less likely to feel they had the transport they needed (86% compared with 91% in eastern Sydney) but interestingly they also felt that transport was less important than eastern Sydney residents.

Gleeson and Randolph (2002, 102) refer to the disparity in relation to transport as "[t]ransport poverty", which they explain "occurs when a household is forced to consume more travel costs than it can reasonably afford, especially costs relating to motor car ownership and usage". Additionally, research by the Grattan Institute (Kelly & Mares, 2013a, 32; see also 2013b) has found that "[i]f outer-suburban residents have to own more cars due to lack of other options, this imposes additional costs of up to thousands of dollars a year. These households are particularly vulnerable to increases in petrol prices".

In relation to housing tenure, over a 20-year period, the level of homeownership fell by almost 10% (see Table 8.3). The proportion of people with mortgages increased (26.6% in 1991 compared with 33.2% in 2011) as did the number of people renting (28% in 1991 compared with 30.4% in 2011).

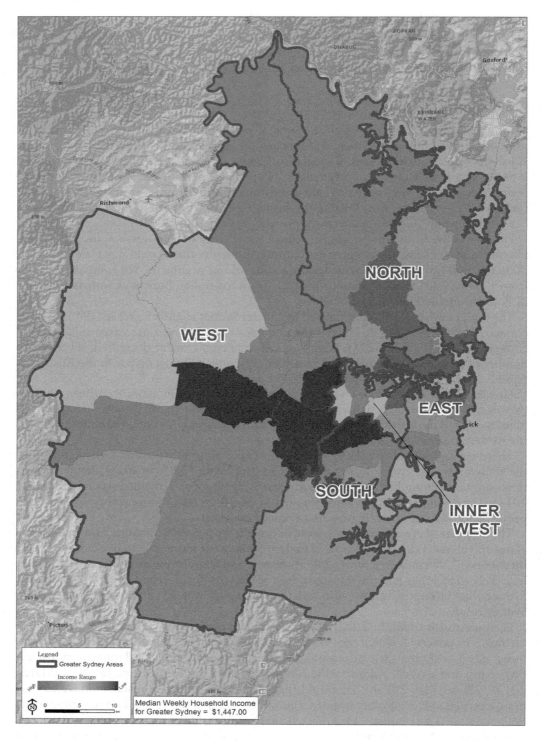

Figure 8.1 Income Levels in Sydney
Source: Australian Bureau of Statistics, 2011

Table 8.2 What Matters to People in NSW in Relation to Transport

	Do they feel they have the transport they need?	Overall, how important is it to them?	How important is access to public transport for their local area?	How important is having good public transport for the future?
Overall	Yes—89% No—11%	17%	84%	91%
Eastern Sydney	↔Yes—91% No—9%	↔18%	↔88%	↔93%
Western Sydney	↓Yes—86% No—14%	↔16%	↔80%	↔88%

Source: Ryan and Lawrie (2015)

Table 8.3 Comparison of the Housing Tenure in Sydney in 1991 and 2011

Housing tenure							
Greater Sydney	2011			1991			Change
Tenure type	Number	2011 (%)	Australia %	Number	1991 (%)	Australia %	1991 to 2011
Fully owned	465,347	29.1	31	467,025	38.8	40.6	−1,678
Mortgage	532,100	33.2	33.3	319,372	26.6	26.5	212,728
Renting	487,404	30.4	28.7	336,919	28	26.6	150,485
Renting—Social housing	79,540	5	4.5	82,875	6.9	6.8	−3,335
Renting—Private	400,071	25	23.5	242,962	20.2	18.9	157,109
Renting—Not stated	7,793	0.5	0.7	11,082	0.9	0.9	−3,289
Other tenure type	12,158	0.8	0.9	78,997	6.6	6.3	−66,839
Not stated	104,517	6.5	6.1	0	0	0	104,517
Total households	1,601,526	100	100	1,202,313	100	100	399,213

Source: Australian Bureau of Statistics, Census of Population and Housing 1991 and 2011

In a statistically representative survey of NSW (Ryan & Lawrie, 2015), "the type of housing" was the most important feature of the local area identified by those with low household incomes, followed by living close to friends and family. Respondents with low household incomes (61%) were more likely to disagree that they have the type of housing they need than those with high household incomes (39%). The spatial distribution of housing tenure between Sydney regions is illustrated in Figure 8.2.

An explanation for this disparity in housing tenure is given that house prices have increased most quickly in inner and middle suburbs, many people can afford to live only in suburbs on the outer fringes of Sydney. However, living on the fringe cuts households off from opportunities, particularly easy access to employment, and exacerbates the growing divide in our cities between where people live and where they work. Also, there are wealth implications of homeownership rates in Sydney. The number of property investors has ballooned from 1.3 million at the end of last decade to more than 1.8 million in 2010–2011.[5] What has also ballooned is the subsidy these taxpayers claim from the public purse: from posting rental profits of $700 million in 1998–1999, investors now claim rental losses of almost $8 billion on their income tax returns.

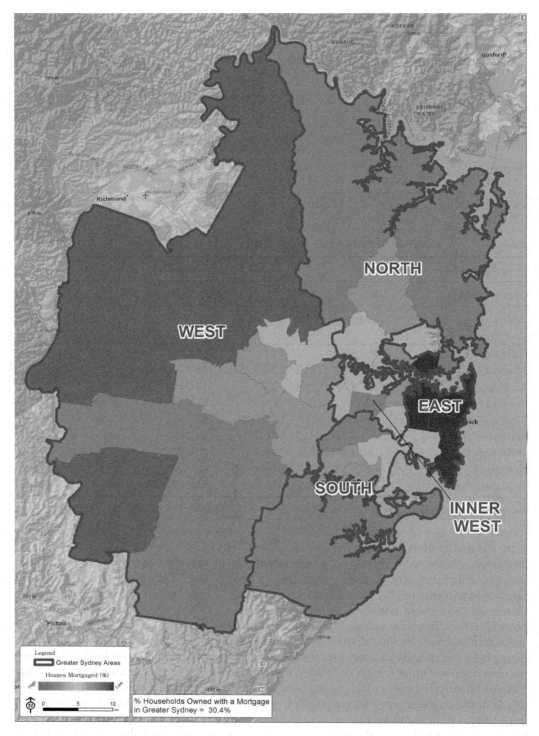

Figure 8.2 Housing Tenure in Sydney
Source: Australian Bureau of Statistics, 2011

Livable Sydney 119

These data indicate there are clear "winners" and "losers" in Sydney. The winners: live in the city, inner east, inner west and parts of northern suburbs; have relatively easy access to well-paid work; own their homes; and are well-educated professionals. The losers: live further from the concentrations of economic activity (jobs) and have higher job insecurity, longer travel to work times, poorer transport choices and connections, lower incomes, more rental stress, less time with families, and poorer reported well-being.

The analysis of this data aligns with others. The Grattan Institute's 2015 book *City Limits: Why Australia's Cities Are Broken and How We Can Fix Them* shows that more than half of recent population growth in large Australian cities has occurred in outer suburbs more than 20 km from city centres. By contrast, more than half of the new jobs are in inner suburbs within 10 km of city centres. *City Limits* reveals that the costs of this divide include fewer job opportunities, heavy traffic congestion, long commute times and a big drop for many city residents in the quality of family and social life. In large outer areas of Australia's biggest cities, fewer than 10% of all jobs in the city can be reached in a 45-minute drive. People living in fast-growing outer suburbs spend 20% longer commuting than people in inner suburbs. Many face higher living costs of thousands of dollars a year due to dependence on long commutes by car. And because long commutes make life harder for families, there is a bigger gap between male and female workforce participation in the outer suburbs.[6]

Concerns about disparities have also been raised about Melbourne, which has generally outperformed Sydney in recent years. According to research conducted by the University of Melbourne's Faculty of Architecture, Building and Planning and the McCaughey VicHealth Centre for Community Wellbeing (School of Population and Global Health, Faculty of Medicine, Dentistry and Health Sciences) in Victoria, as part of The Place, Health and Liveability Research Program:

> There are concerns about growing disparities *within* cities in Australia and internationally. Some communities are experiencing significant problems with regards to liveability, such as a lack of affordable housing, marginalisation of lower income populations, poor education, social and health infrastructure, limited access between homes, workplaces and shops, and related dependence on cars, with low rates of walking, cycling and public transport use. Growth areas in Australian cities are a key concern, particularly new low-density outer suburban growth areas. Some growth areas are experiencing such rapid growth in their populations that it is difficult for essential services and infrastructure provision, let alone employment, to keep up.
> (Lowe et al., 2013, 7)

The Australian Housing Urban Research Institute conducted a multiyear research project on addressing concentrations of disadvantage in Australia's major cities. Spatial disadvantages were taken to comprise three aspects: poverty concentration, disadvantage of resource access and spatial concentration of social problems; the relationship between these different forms is illustrated in Figure 8.3.

The 2015 report concludes that "spatial disadvantage in Australian cities is now increasingly an outer-suburban problem" and

> the lines that much of Australia's historic spatial disadvantage has been more about concentration of poverty rather than concentration of social problems, with disadvantage of resource access emerging as a relatively recent form, and perhaps the most problematic form in terms of policy interventions.
> (Burke & Hulse, 2015, 2, 5)

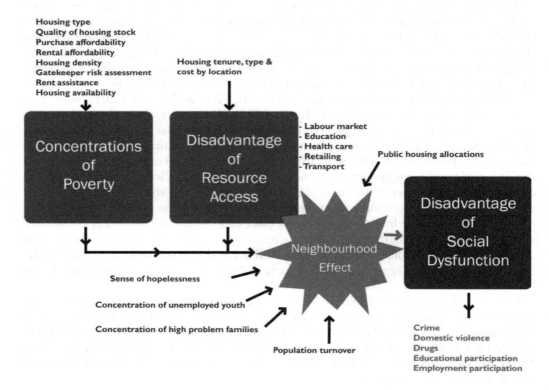

Figure 8.3 Relationship Between Different Forms of Spatial Disadvantage
Source: Burke and Hulse, 2015

These findings have been bolstered by a number of key government reports. For example, various Australian Department of Infrastructure and Regional Development reports (2015a, 2015b) have noted the disparities within Sydney, stating:

- From 2001 to 2011, Sydney's "clusters of social disadvantage [were] increasingly being pushed further towards city periphery".
- Workforce participation rates declined in South West Sydney, which has some of Sydney's lowest workforce participation rates.
- From 2001 to 2011 in Greater Sydney, real household weekly income grew by $150 (from $1,300 in 2001 to approximately $1,450 in 2011), "while in South West Sydney, real weekly household income grew by less than $50 over the same period".
- South West Sydney is the second lowest region in terms of levels of growth in people with vocational or higher educational qualifications.
- The outer suburbs of Sydney and South West areas had "the largest share of commuters by private vehicle (up to 80%)".

It is evident that spatial inequality and disadvantage remain a key problem in Sydney. How then do the various livability indices account for this?

In 2012 the EIU, in partnership with BuzzData, had a competition to encourage people to improve their Global Liveability Index. The winner, architect Filippo Lovato, produced an additional category based on "spatial adjustments", which included seven new indicators; these were green space, lack of sprawl, natural assets, cultural assets, connectivity, lack of isolation and pollution (The Economist Intelligence Unit, 2012). The Spatial Adjusted Liveability Index now makes up 25% of the score with the remainder calculated; according to the EIU Global Liveability Index, in so doing the Spatial Adjusted Liveability Index "complement[s] the existing EIU Liveability index with an awareness of cities' spatial characteristics" (The Economist Intelligence Unit, 2012, 7). In 2012, Sydney's EIU ranking was second place, but its Spatially Adjusted Liveability Index fell three places to fifth place.

In the same year the Property Council Australia (the peak property lobby group) adopted an interesting approach to measuring livability whereby "[t]he 'liveability index' is accordingly a function of both: the importance that residents place on particular attributes of a city [and] the performance of their city on each of these attributes" (Department of Infrastructure and Transport, 2012, 214). Australian city residents rank their city against the 17 attributes (e.g., accessibility, affordability, health, diversity of social, safety, cultural and recreational opportunities, congeniality, environmental sustainability and quality of urban design and amenity). The two attributes that were highest in the ten cities were the range of outdoor recreational facilities and the attractiveness of the natural environment. Although these approaches indicate promising attempts to find new approaches for measuring livability, they still do not, however, adequately account for spatial inequality.

There have been various policies to address livability in Sydney. The Liveable Cities Program, a funding initiative by the Australian Federal Government in 2011, was created to support local, state and territory governments to improve the quality of life in city capitals and major regional cities. Grants were awarded to projects that were aimed to make cities more liveable by:

- encouraging "residential developments that were affordable, adaptable and accessible, with good access to services and public transport";
- creating/enhancing "mixed-use precincts that optimise public transport use";
- developing "strategic plans for major regional cities with populations greater than 100,000" people.

(Department of Infrastructure and Transport, 2012, 217)

More recently, in 2016, a discussion paper was launched by the City of Sydney as part of its development of Sydney's Social Sustainability Policy. The paper highlights some of Sydney's strengths (e.g., "social and cultural diversity . . . safety and security . . . and opportunities for democratic civic participation") but it also recognises the various challenges including that one third of Sydney's residents experience housing stress, there is increased homelessness, 40% of residents live alone and the majority of households live in high-density housing and some residents experience food insecurity and financial stress (City of Sydney, 2016, 19).

Four interrelated strategic directions were identified for Sydney to be: an inclusive city (social justice and opportunity), a connected city (diverse, cohesive communities), *a livable city* (quality places and spaces) and an engaged city (good governance and active participation) (our emphasis). In terms of livability, the discussion paper notes:

> A liveable city has great quality places and spaces that are planned and designed for people of all ages and abilities. Residents, workers and visitors can access jobs, services and facilities in vibrant local centres and distinctive neighbourhoods through well-connected transport networks. People can live healthy, active and safe lives, with ample quality green open spaces in harmony with the natural environment.
>
> (City of Sydney, 2016, 14)

The City of Sydney's Roadmap for a Liveable City includes "People focused urban design and planning", "Accessible places and spaces", "Quality natural environment and climate", "Healthy active living" and "Safe and secure communities" (see also Direction 3—A liveable city: quality places and spaces).[7]

Conclusion

Without finding an acceptable definition of livability, then, "its use for planning and policymaking is considerably curtailed" (Ruth & Franklin, 2014, 22). Given the limitations of the different livability indices (e.g., commercial orientation and methodological weaknesses) there are clear dangers of utilising livability indices for decision making and planning in their current form. Spatial inequality and locational disadvantage, as Beer (1994, 183) argued over 20 years ago, "are still important because they have substantial implications for urban development strategies and the distribution of resources".

Approaches to livability need to be integrated (both place based and people based) (see Cheshire et al., 2014). In a similar vein to the initiatives taken in Victoria, New South Wales could undertake projects that "have a strong interest in developing indicators that are evidence-based, specific and quantifiable, relevant to the Australian policy context, and able to be measured at both city-wide and neighbourhood-level scales" (Lowe et al., 2013, 5). Projects such as these, which are interdisciplinary, can take into account the multifaceted nature of livability and, in turn, be sensitive to the differences within cities and suburbs. A key starting point is to ensure that reform in urban governance, public transit, housing affordability, universal access to public goods and genuine participation in Sydney, and Australian cities more broadly.

In light of the previous statements and influenced by notions of the right to the city, we make the following recommendations. As one of the consequences of spatial inequality is differential access to resources and power, *cities need cooperative governance* whereby citizens can affect decision making through legitimate involvement. According to Gleeson and Randolph (2002, 102)

> [g]iven Sydney's complex and multiply constituted governance, solutions to social and other problems must necessarily involve "policy coalitions" that seek to integrate a range of institutional forces—public, private, NGO, community—at a variety of policy scales: local, regional, metropolitan, state and federal.

And more than that, institutions need to *decrease fragmented responses* in order to be effective (see Kübler, 2005; Blakely & Hu, 2007) and recognize the exercise of power and privilege by self-interested and self-serving coalitions of property interests. They also need to have the capacity to respond to local variations and to do so in speedy manner while protecting quality/standards/amenity. There is the need for shared language for institutional change (e.g., housing costs and travel times).

Greater Social Inclusion Is Vital

This includes participatory approaches to planning and equitable access to jobs and services and amenity. People should be included at the strategic (city shaping) stage to ensure there is a broad-based balance between general and specific interests which, in turn, provides greater legitimacy to decision making. Returning to Lefebvre, who advocates for participation among activated citizens, which encompasses:

> inhabitants increasingly coming to manage the production of urban space themselves. As they engage in real and active participation, their own collective power is revealed

to them, and they increasingly understand themselves as capable stewards of the urban and its collective life . . . As inhabitants become activated and come to manage the city themselves, they are effectively appropriating the city and the production of its space. They are taking control of the conditions of their own existence. They are making the city their own again.

(Purcell, 2013, 150)

Notes

1. Spatial geography in general terms refers to the physical or spatial distribution of resources, activities and demographics.
2. Other indices that measure well-being include the OECD Better Life Index and the World Happiness Report. Also, the ISO standard for city indicators (ISO 37120:2014) was "developed as part of an integrated suite of standards for sustainable development in communities". The 17 indicators are Economy, Education, Energy, Environment, Finance, Fire and emergency response, Governance, Health, Recreation, Safety, Shelter, Solid waste, Telecommunications and innovation, Transportation, Urban planning, Wastewater, Water and sanitation.
3. These policy areas are Crime and Safety; Housing; Education; Employment and Income; Health and Social Services; Transport; Public Open Space; Social cohesion and Local Democracy; Leisure and Culture; Food and other local goods; and Natural Environment. For further information about indices and their indicators see Lowe (2013, Ch. 5); Giap et al. (2012); and Conger (2015).
4. At the time of writing, the 2011 Australian Census data were the most recently available.
5. This research utilised existing data from a range of available sources (e.g., statistical information from Australian Bureau of Statistics, Census of Population and Housing).
6. In 2015, the Dropping off the Edge report, published by Catholic Social Services and Jesuit Social Services, analysed 621 NSW postcodes using 21 indicators "of disadvantage, including internet access, incomes, education level, literacy and numeracy, long-term unemployment, unskilled workers, juvenile offending and criminal convictions . . . [found that] more than half of the 40 most disadvantaged postcodes were in the same category in a similar 2007 study, with many also repeating the result in 2004 and 1999 studies" (Ireland, 2015). Also the Committee for Economic Development of Australia (CEDA) 2015 report found that "deprivation is highest among sole parent households" and "those who are most at risk of long-term disadvantage or of falling back into poverty are older people, less-educated people, jobless households, people with low socioeconomic status, Indigenous Australians and those with chronic health problems" (CEDA, 2015, 9–10).
7. In the remainder of 2016, there were community and stakeholder engagements and a Social Sustainability Policy was adopted; in 2017, a Social Sustainability Action Plan is due to be drafted for consultation.

References

Arlington, K. (2016, August 18). Why the Economist says Sydney is no longer one of the world's 10 most liveable cities. *Sydney Morning Herald*. Retrieved January 12, 2017, from www.smh.com.au/nsw/the-heightened-perceived-threat-of-terrorism-affects-sydneys-liveability-20160817-gqv8kf.html

Attoh, K. A. (2011). What kind of right is the right to the city? *Progress in Human Geography*, 35(5), 669–685.

Australian Bureau of Statistics. (1991). Census of Population and Housing (1991). Canberra: Australian Bureau of Statistics.

Australian Bureau of Statistics. (2001). Census of Population and Housing (2001). Canberra: Australian Bureau of Statistics.

Australian Bureau of Statistics. (2011). Census of Population and Housing (2011). Canberra: Australian Bureau of Statistics.

Baum, S., Haynes, M., van Gellecum, & Han, J.H. (2006). Advantage and disadvantage across Australia's extended metropolitan regions: A typology of socioeconomic outcomes. *Urban Studies*, 43(9), 1549–1579.

Beatty, R. (2014). Neoliberal urbanism: Socio-spatial fragmentation & exclusion. *New Visions for Public Affairs*, 6, 41–49.

Beer, A. (1994). Spatial inequality and locational disadvantage: New perspectives on an old debate. *Urban Policy and Research*, 12(3), 180–184.

Bill, A. (2005). *Neighbourhood inequality: Do small area interactions influence economic outcomes?* Working Paper No. 05-11. Newcastle: Centre of Full Employment and Equity, The University of Newcastle.

Blakely, E. J., & Hu, R. Y. (2007). *Sydney first who's governing Sydney.* Sydney: Sydney Chamber of Commerce.

Burke, T., & Hulse, K. (2015). *Spatial disadvantage: Why is Australia different?* Melbourne: Australian Housing and Urban Research Institute. Retrieved from www.ahuri.edu.au/publications/download/ahuri_myrp704_rp5

Cheshire, L., Pawson, H., Easthope, H., & Stone, W. (2014). Living with place disadvantage: Community, practice and policy. *AHURI Final Report No. 228.* Melbourne: Australian Housing and Urban Research Institute. Retrieved January 12, 2017, from www.ahuri.edu.au/publications/projects/myrp704

City of Sydney. (2016, March). A city for all: Towards a socially just and resilient Sydney social sustainability. *Discussion Paper.* Retrieved January 12, 2017, from www.cityofsydney.nsw.gov.au/__data/assets/word_doc/0020/262343/A-City-for-All-social-sustainbility-discussion-paper-accessible-word.docx

Committee for Economic Development of Australia. (2015). *Addressing entrenched disadvantage in Australia entrenched disadvantage in Australia.* Sydney: CEDA.

Conger, B. W. (2015). On livability, liveability and the limited utility of quality-of-life rankings. *SPP Communiqués*, 7(4), 1–8. Retrieved from www.policyschool.ca/wp-content/uploads/2016/03/livability-conger.pdf

Copestake, J. (2014, June 16) "Measuring liveability." Presentation at the International Festival of Business in Liverpool, UK, slide 3.

Davies, A. (2015). Is being 'the world's most liveable city' such a big deal? *Crickey.* Retrieved January 12, 2017, from https://blogs.crikey.com.au/theurbanist/2015/08/19/is-being-the-worlds-most-liveable-city-such-a-big-deal/

Department of Infrastructure and Regional Development. (2015a). *Fact sheet Sydney, state of Australian cities 2014–15.* Canberra: Commonwealth of Australia. Retrieved January 12, 2017, from https://infrastructure.gov.au/infrastructure/pab/soac/files/factsheets_2014/Sydney_Factsheet_2014.pdf

Department of Infrastructure and Regional Development. (2015b). *State of Australian cities 2014–15.* Canberra: Commonwealth of Australia. Retrieved January 12, 2017, from https://infrastructure.gov.au/infrastructure/pab/soac/files/2015_SoAC_full_report.pdf

Department of Infrastructure and Transport. (2012). Liveability. In *State of Australian Cities* (pp. 203–278). Canberra: Commonwealth of Australia, Chapter 5. Retrieved January 12, 2017, from https://infrastructure.gov.au/infrastructure/pab/soac/files/2012_08_INFRA1360_MCU_SOAC_CHAPTER_5_WEB_FA.pdf

The Economist Intelligence Unit. (2012). Best cities ranking and report: A special report from the Economist Intelligence Unit. *The Economist.* Retrieved January 12, 2017, from http://pages.eiu.com/rs/eiu2/images/EIU_BestCities.pdf

Economist Intelligence Unit. (2016). *Global liveability ranking 2016.* Retrieved January 12, 2017, from www.eiu.com/public/topical_report.aspx?campaignid=liveability2016

Giap, T. K., Thye, W. W., Yam, T. K., Low, L., & Aw, E. L. G. (2012). *Ranking the liveability of the world's major cities: The Global Liveable Cities Index (GLCI).* Singapore: World Scientific Publishing Company. (A useful comparison of the different indices).

Gleeson, B., & Randolph, B. (2002). Social disadvantage and planning in the Sydney context. *Urban Policy and Research.* Retrieved January 12, 2017, from http://ezproxy.uws.edu.au/login?url=http://dx.doi.org/10.1080/08111140220131636

Harvey, D. (2008, September–October). The right to the city. *New Left Review*, 53, 23–40.

Ireland, J. (2015). Most disadvantaged communities in NSW not showing improvement: Report. *Sydney Morning Herald*, 1–2. Retrieved January 12, 2017, from www.smh.com.au/action/printArticle?id=998443637

Irvine, J. (2015). Sydney is turning into a ghetto as poor are trapped by fewer jobs and rising housing costs. *Sydney Morning Herald*. Retrieved January 12, 2017, from www.smh.com.au/nsw/sydney-is-turning-into-a-ghetto-as-poor-are-trapped-by-fewer-jobs-and-rising-housing-costs-20150508-ggwyj0.html

ISO. (2014). *How does your city compare to others? New ISO standard to measure up (2014–05–14)—ISO*. Retrieved January 12, 2017, www.iso.org/iso/news.htm?refid=Ref1848

Kelly, J.-F., & Mares, P. (2013a). *Productive cities opportunity in a changing economy*. Grattan Institute. Retrieved January 12, 2017, from www.grattan.edu.au/publications/reports/post/productive-cities-opportunity-in-a-changing-economy/

Kelly, J.-F., & Mares, P. (2013b). *Who lives where: Sydney productive cities: Supplementary maps*. Melbourne: Grattan Institute.

Kübler, D. (2005). *Problems and prospects of metropolitan governance in Sydney: Towards "old" or "new" regionalism?* Sydney: City Futures Research Centre,

Lefebvre, H. (1996 [1968]). Writings on cities, edited and translated by E. Kofman & E. Lebas. Oxford: Blackwell.Lowe, M., Whitzman, C., Badland, H., Davern, M., Hes, D., Aye, L., Butterworth, I., & Giles-Corti, B. (2013). Liveable, healthy, sustainable: What are the key indicators for Melbourne neighbourhoods. *Research Paper 1, Place, Health and Liveability Research Program*, University of Melbourne. Retrieved January 12, 2017, from http://mccaugheycentre.unimelb.edu.au/research/health_and_liveability

Marcuse, P. (2009). From critical urban theory to the right to the city. *City, 13*(2–3), 185–197.

Mele, C. (2011). Casinos, prisons, incinerators, and other fragments of neoliberal urban development. *Social Science History, 35*(3), 423–452.

Mercer, M. (2016). *Quality of living rankings*. Retrieved from www.imercer.com/content/mobility/quality-of-living-city-rankings.html#list

Monocle. (2016, July–August). Top 25 liveable cities. *Monocle, 10*(95), 42–65.

Numbeo, Quality of Life Index by City. (2017). Retrieved January 12, 2017, from www.numbeo.com/quality-of-life/rankings.jsp

O'Loghlen, A. (2015). *Neoliberalism and the right to the city: The challenge for the Urban Slum Dweller*. Retrieved from www.rc21.org/en/wp-content/uploads/2014/12/D4-OLoghlen.pdf

Price Waterhouse Coopers. (2016a). *Cities of opportunity 7*. PwC. Retrieved January 12, 2017, www.pwc.com/us/en/cities-of-opportunity/2016/cities-of-opportunity-7-report.pdf

Price Waterhouse Coopers. (2016b). *Reader's guide cities of opportunity 7: Performance and scoring basics*. PwC. Retrieved from www.pwc.com/us/en/cities-of-opportunity/2016/cities-user-guide.pdf

Purcell, M. (2002). Excavating Lefebvre: The right to the city and its urban politics of the inhabitant. *Geo Journal, 58*(2–3), 99–108.

Purcell, M. (2005). Globalization, urban enfranchisement, and the right to the city: Towards an urban politics of the inhabitant. In D. Wastl-Walter, L. Staeheli, & L. Dowler (Eds.), *Rights to the city*. International Geographical Union, Home of Geography Publication Series (Volume III; 11–25). Rome: Società Geografica Italiana.

Purcell, M. (2013). Possible worlds: Henri Lefebvre and the right to the city. *Journal of Urban Affairs, 36*(1), 141–154.

Randolph, B. (2003, December 3–5). *Overview: Changing spatial structure*. State of Australian Cities National Conference, Carlton Hotel, Parramatta.

Randolph, B., & Holloway, D. (2005). The suburbanization of disadvantage in Sydney: New problems, new policies. *Opolis: An International Journal of Suburban and Metropolitan Studies, 1*(1), 49–64.

Ruth, M., & Franklin, R. S. (2014). Livability for all? Conceptual limits and practical implications. *Applied Geography, 49*, 18–23. (A critical review of livability).

Ryan, R., & Lawrie, A. (2015). Survey research into community views spatial planning issues (unpublished). UTS, Institute of Public Policy and Governance, Sydney.

Scerri, A. (2008). Livability index. In A. Michalos. (Ed.), *Encyclopedia of quality of life and well-being research* (pp. 3640–3645). Dordrecht: Springer.

Sell, J. L., Taylor, J. G., & Zube, E. H. (1984). Toward a theoretical framework for landscape perception. In T. F. Saarinen, D. Seamon, & J. L. Sell (Eds.), *Environmental perception and behaviour:*

An inventory and prospect, research paper no. 209. Chicago, IL: Department of Geography, University of Chicago.

Stilwell, F., & Jordan, K. (2007). *Who gets what? Analysing urban inequality in Australia*. Cambridge: Cambridge University Press.

Teo, S. (2014). Political tool or quality experience? Urban livability and the Singaporean state's global city aspirations. *Urban Geography*, *35*(6), 916–937.Urban Taskforce Australia & McCrindle Research. (2016). *Urban living index*. Urban Taskforce Australia. Retrieved January 12, 2017, from http://mccrindle.com.au/resources/UrbanTaskforce_The-Urban-Living-Index_McCrindle.pdf

Zeisel, J. (1981). *Inquiry by design*. Monterey: Brooks, Cole.

9 Making Tokyo Livable for a Super-Aging Society

Hideki Koizumi

Introduction

In this chapter, the process of formation and transformation of Tokyo or Tokyo metropolitan area from after World War II until recent years is reviewed. The author clarifies why the problem of low birthrate and aging in suburbs residential areas, which is the biggest problem of the Tokyo metropolitan area including Tokyo and surrounding prefectures, has occurred, from the process of historical formation and transition. Furthermore, the direction of response to the problem of low birthrate and aging population in suburban residential areas is described and models presented. In the final thoughts section, issues to be addressed in the future in Tokyo or Tokyo metropolitan area are presented.

"Tokyo" as discussed in this chapter does not necessarily refer to the single municipality of Tokyo Metropolitan Government, but rather to different entities of different sizes depending on the topics under discussion (e.g., the Tokyo Metropolitan Area, downtown Tokyo).

Expansion and Changes in the Tokyo Metropolitan Area in Post-War Japan

Formation of the World's Largest Metropolitan Area—Spatial Expansion of Urban Areas From Post-WWII to the 1990s

Tokyo has continued to expand in area ever since its name was changed from Edo, the city's predecessor. Today, Tokyo is one of the largest metropolitan areas in the world, with a population around 40 million spread over an area ranging in radius from 50 to 100 km (see Table 9.1). Ahead, the author briefly recounts what led to its formation, focusing on the sequence of events after World War II.

The Formation of a Multi-Core Urban Area

Post-war reconstruction efforts in Tokyo included a growth management plan that provided for vegetative "green zones" as city limits on the perimeter of Tokyo's 23 constituent special wards to restrict its population size to around 3.5 million. However, few of the green zones seen in the plan were actually implemented, and so Tokyo started to see sprawling housing developments, primarily small, low-rise, detached houses.

Within the city limits and around the Yamanote Line, a circular railway line that circumscribes central Tokyo, on the other hand, land readjustment projects in response to war damage were restricted to a handful of areas, including around Tokyo's modern-day urban subcenters, such as Shinjuku, Shibuya, and Ikebukuro.

128 Hideki Koizumi

Table 9.1 Population Change in Tokyo Metropolitan Area

	1945	1955	1965	1975	1985	1995	2005	2015
TMA	9,368.1	15,424.3	21,016.7	27,041.8	30,273.2	32,576.6	34,478.9	36,130.7
		39%	27%	22%	11%	7%	6%	5%
23 wards	2,777.0	6,969.1	8,893.1	8,646.5	8,354.6	7,967.6	8,489.7	9,272.7
		60%	22%	−3%	−3%	−5%	6%	8%
Downtown 3	217.2	548.7	462.6	361.2	325.1	243.6	326.0	333.6
		60%	−19%	−28%	−11%	−33%	25%	2%
DSW	539.4	2,023.2	2,288.1	1,982.1	1,845.2	1,621.4	1,766.4	2,228.3
		73%	12%	−15%	−7%	−14%	8%	21%
Suburban	6,521.7	8,375.1	12,046.0	18,313.8	21,828.9	24,515.7	25,901.2	26,773.1
		22%	30%	34%	16%	11%	5%	3%

Source: Census Data

Note: The upper row shows number of population in thousands.
The lower row shows the rate of change from 10 years ago.
TMA: Tokyo Metropolitan Area (Prefectures of Tokyo, Kanagawa, Saitama, Chiba)
Downtown 3: Three Wards of Chiyoda, Chuo, Minato
DSW: Downtown Surrounding Seven Wards (Koto, Sumida, Taito, Bunkyo, Shinjuku, Shibuya, Tosima)
Suburban: Tokyo Metropolitan Area Without 23 Wards

Previously concentrated in urban centers such as Marunouchi, Yurakucho, and Shinbashi, the city's office functions expanded into areas surrounding the major rail stations on the Yamanote Line (e.g., Shinjuku, Shibuya, Ikebukuro). From Japan's high-growth era until the 1990s, these stations were also terminal stations for private railways and had been equipped with the foundations for urban infrastructure by the country's war damage reconstruction efforts. Japan started to adopt policies to spur growth in these subcenters, building them up as hubs of economic activity (Ishida, 2004).

Furthermore, as the suburban residential areas described ahead stretched outside the city limits, the Japanese government turned its efforts, from 1970 onwards, to designate core cities in neighboring prefectures (i.e., Kanagawa, Chiba, Saitama) and develop office districts in them to ensure serious policy developments.

The Formation of Dense Urban Areas Within Tokyo 23 Special Wards and Residential Areas on Its Perimeter

After World War II, affordable apartments aimed at (primarily blue-collar and young) workers and students were constructed in the areas around the Yamanote Line, while urban infrastructure such as roads and parks remained undeveloped. This trend led to the formation of dense urban areas consisting predominantly of low-rise wooden housing.

Additionally, from the late 1960s to the start of the 1980s, railway-adjacent housing developments, in other words, transportation-oriented developments, were built on the margins of the city, in the residential areas where workers lived, extending the spatial range of the metropolitan area outward. Many of their inhabitants were "Baby Boomers" who immigrated to the Tokyo area from other regions (i.e., the post-war Baby Boomer generation, born between 1945 and 1950).

Consequently, while the residential population density of central Tokyo was kept lower than in other cities, the widespread detached housing throughout the periphery of the metropolitan area resulted in these areas having a relatively high population density compared with many foreign countries (Tokyo Metropolitan Government, 1991). An extensive metropolitan area was thus formed wherein the region's city centers, subcenters, and core cities were connected to suburban residential areas by railway networks.

Further Expansion of the Perimeter and Damage to Urban Communities Due to the Bubble Economy

Prime Minister Yasuhiro Nakasone's administration worked on driving up domestic demand in the late 1980s within the framework of the Plaza Accord. The agreement included important measures such as relaxing urban planning regulations and injecting capital into real estate development, which were supported by loose monetary policy. Their actions caused land prices to start to rise dramatically in downtown Tokyo, with ripple effects causing sharp jumps in the suburbs and provincial cities as well. This was the birth of Japan's bubble economy.

Land prices occasionally soared in the midst of the bubble economy: residential areas for (primarily white-collar) workers seeking affordable housing were built in locations more than 50 km from the city center, a distance that requires a commute time to central Tokyo of close to 2 hours. In addition, anticipating that the price of land in downtown Tokyo would rise, many buyers engaged in land speculation, driving out residents with the large sums of money involved. With the economic downturn, much of this land turned into vacant lots or parking lots, and the sharp decline in population delivered a major blow to the traditional communities who had continued their livelihoods in these areas since the Edo feudal period.

Effects of Urban Housing and Urban Renewal Policies Since the Late 1990s

After the collapse of the bubble economy, financial institutions were saddled with large quantities of significant real estate debt, which greatly affected their operations. For a time thereafter, Japan and Tokyo experienced a period of continuous stable or low growth. With land prices in a slump, the bad debt was almost intractable, and so the government adopted new policies to deal with these problems: namely, the promotion of urban housing and urban renewal.

Urban Living as a Commodity

Demand for office developments in downtown Tokyo and surrounding areas had fallen due to the heavy investment and completion of major office developments during the bubble era and the economic downturn after its collapse. After the bubble's collapse, major real estate operators, iron and steel industry players, and electronics manufacturers began to consider high-rise and ultra-high-rise apartments located in city centers as a way to stimulate new consumer demand.

While some economists made political entreaties, the Japanese government prepared various deregulatory frameworks for driving up the housing supply in downtown Tokyo and surrounding areas. These systems were actively used in both the central area and its surrounding wards that had experienced rapid depopulation since the 1970s. Major real estate database companies and advertising agencies also promoted the new properties with extensive public relations, turning "Urban Living" into a new commodity in Tokyo and in other major cities in Japan. Their efforts rapidly increased the housing supply in three central wards and its surrounding wards (Suzuki et al., 2011).

However, the large numbers of high-rise and ultra-high-rise apartments in downtown Tokyo and the surrounding areas caused an outbreak of construction-related disputes with residents, who began to stand up in response to the problems of destruction of scenery and loss of natural light.

Promotion of Urban Renewal

In 2002, Prime Minister Jun'ichiro Koizumi's administration enacted the *Act on Special Measures Concerning Urban Reconstruction*, aiming to provide aid to major financial institutions and developers who struggled with bad real estate debt. The Japanese government would accomplish this by directly designating those areas in urgent need of urban renewal, and then extensively deregulated these so-called "Special Districts for Urban Regeneration". The policies were aimed at resolving the bad debt by generating "mini-bubbles" in urban centers in Tokyo and other major metropolises.

The initiative was a success, and redevelopment was soon underway in downtown Tokyo, primarily focused on office districts. However, the large-scale redevelopment caused by these urban renewal policies led to an over-concentration of office space development in downtown Tokyo.

In parallel with this trend, the relative status fell not only on provincial cities, but also on core cities that had been growing until then (e.g., Yokohama). This was one factor that made the suburban housing decline even more severe, as discussed ahead.

A Variety of Area-Based Activities, Mainly in Downtown Tokyo and Surrounding Residential Areas

Several of the areas targeted by the large-scale redevelopment have experienced an increase in so-called area-based management activities, even after the original redevelopment projects have concluded. These were activities performed by real estate developers in attempts to raise the value of an area. (Examples include Mitsubishi Estate in Otemachi, Marunouchi and Yurakucho; Mitsui Fudosan in Nihonbashi; Mori Building Roppongi and Toranomon; and Yasuda Real Estate in Awajicho.)

In addition, there was an increase in community-based town-planning activities that utilized each area's unique history and culture, in opposition to the large-scale redevelopment and the construction of high-rise apartments ("tower mansions") to serve as receptacles for urban residences. These were pursued primarily in downtown Tokyo and some remaining historical urban areas: representative examples include Yanaka and Kagurazaka (Sorensen et al., 2008).

On the other hand, many so-called white zones also exist in Tokyo that have not been particularly affected by these trends. No community-based movements are actively attempting to determine the direction of Machizukuri, community-based town-planning approaches in these white zones, and government efforts have been insufficient. However, downtown Tokyo and its surrounding residential-type areas are actually made up of an aggregate of diverse towns. These communities have each accumulated a unique set of not only historical and cultural resources, but also human and organizational resources, handed down from the Edo period to the present day. These communities are in need of development strategies to be built that utilize these diverse historical, cultural, human, and organizational resources as well as designs for specific actions they can take.

Decreased Relative Attractiveness of Suburban Residential Areas

As seen previously, the collaborative efforts of industry and government to promote urban living have established it as a commodity in Tokyo. In addition, Japan's national urban renewal policies drove employment to become even more concentrated in the Tokyo area.

However, these policies resulted in a decline in the relative status of suburban residential areas. They no longer appeared attractive to the youth market and had a limited influx of new residents. Consequently, these areas are now populated predominantly by left-behind Baby Boomers. This trend is particularly apparent in the so-called "Baby Boomer Juniors", the generation born between 1970 and 1975. It was expected to constitute a major home buyer demographic in 2000–2010. Although the boomer juniors were expected to re-enter suburban areas after leaving their parental household, they instead tended to select tower mansions constructed around urban centers and railway stations, with many in later generations following suit.

The Baby Boomer generation in suburban residential areas is approaching their late 1960s, and aging is expected to progress ever further in these areas. We take up this issue in the next section and discuss it in detail.

Merits and Demerits of the 2020 Tokyo Olympics

In 2013, Tokyo was invited to hold the 2020 Summer Olympics. Tokyo's Olympic bid was successful thanks to its emphasis on two concepts: the event's symbolization of Japan's recovery after the Great East Japan Earthquake and its environmental friendliness due to the compact, urban setting. In reality, however, the Olympics seem to have many negative aspects, attributable to the land development and expansion of the Tokyo region involved.

One issue is that hosting the Olympics has intensified is the concentration of people, things and money into Tokyo. Large-scale real estate developments are being built in great numbers, particularly along the waterfront lines connecting downtown Tokyo (around Shinagawa Station) with Haneda Airport. In addition, the Olympics have spurred the new construction of large-scale sports facilities in downtown areas across Tokyo.

These developments have led to a sharp increase in construction costs, exacerbated by their timing overlapping with reconstruction projects following the Great East Japan Earthquake. This has led the various reconstruction projects in the affected areas to be reconsidered from the viewpoint of profitability, slowing their progress and lowering their quality.

It is not inevitable that the urban planning and land development prompted by this Olympics will be any more environmental friendly, have a smaller footprint, or be more socially inclusive than before. Many find it difficult to imagine the legacy the event will leave for later generations; rather, there are fears it will saddle them with debt. However, Governor Yuriko Koike, elected in the summer 2016 Tokyo gubernatorial election, may be able to reverse this trend.

Suburban Residential Areas With Predominantly Left-Behind Elderly and Renewal Efforts

The discussion earlier has begun to suggest that the biggest current challenge for the Tokyo Metropolitan Area is to renew the vast suburban residential areas on its margins, which are predominantly inhabited by left-behind elderly (LBE) primarily from the Baby Boomer generation.

Aging in the Tokyo Metropolitan Area Today

Household Trends and Aging in the Tokyo Metropolitan Area

The household dynamics of Tokyo Metropolitan Area from 2000 to 2010 show a notable concentration in downtown areas of districts that have experienced continuous population

132 Hideki Koizumi

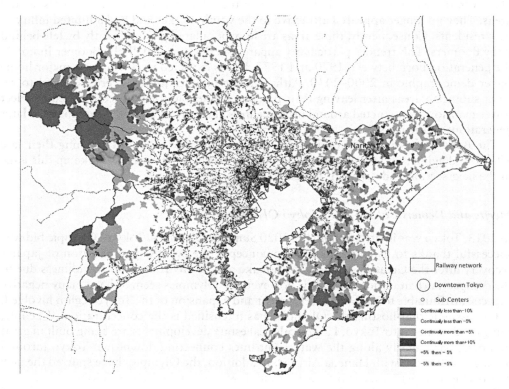

Figure 9.1 Changes of the Number of Households in Tokyo Metropolitan Area 2000–2005 and 2005–2010
Source: Census Data

increases. There are also noteworthy increases in sectors southwest of the area: for example, Hachioji, Tama, and Aoba ward of Yokohama city along the JR Chuo Line and other private rural lines. These are areas where households are increasing even in Narita city near Narita International Airport. Other than these, areas where households are increasing are distributed along the waterfront line from Tokyo to Chiba and the railway network throughout the Tokyo metropolitan area, and such areas are located near the station (see Figure 9.1). Some citizens are relocating from suburban areas to regions around railway stations or closer to downtown or the international airport. In the other parts of the suburbs, the population has declined continuously or intermittently in many places (Miyake et al., 2012).

However, these trends do not imply that all households have moved to city centers or around railway stations. In Japan, households have low mobility following the purchase of a residence, and many elderly people choose to remain in suburban residential areas. Analyzing population census data with respect to age demographics, we can see that most of the depopulated areas have high numbers of elderly residents belonging to the Baby Boomers or earlier generations.

Increased Vacant Houses and Vacant Lots, and Left-Behind Elderly Households Today

Let's make clear the state of suburban residential areas in more detail. Figure 9.2 takes a given residential area in Sakura City in which both the population and number of

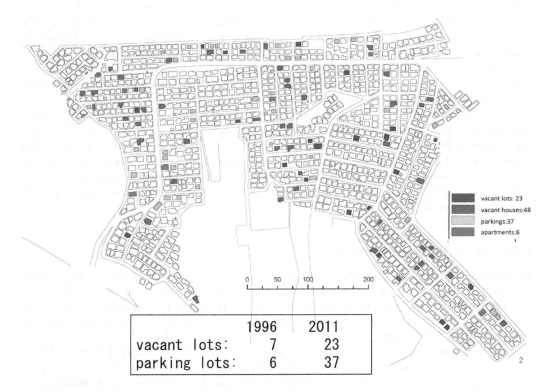

Figure 9.2 Distribution of Vacant Lots and Houses in Sennari-danchi, Sakura City, Chiba Prefecture
Source: Koizumi, based on interview with leader of neighborhood organization

households have decreased, taking care to exclude low-use and unused land such as vacant houses, vacant lots, and parking lots. The elderly makes up 32% of the population of this residential area.

The ratio of vacant houses, vacant lots and parking lots in this area is approximately 10%. Although approximately 60% of vacant houses and vacant lots are managed by the owner or housing management companies, the remainder of properties create nuisances for neighboring residences: for example, in the form of overgrown weeds (Miyake et al., 2014).

Key Points of the Sustainable Renewal of Suburban Residential Areas Facing Declining Birthrates and Aging Populations

Renewal initiatives in suburban residential areas is a multifaceted issue. Following are some key points that should guide renewal initiatives in suburban residential areas of the Tokyo Metropolitan Area facing declining birthrates and aging populations (Koizumi, 2015).

Comprehensive Community Care Systems

The Ministry of Health, Labour and Welfare considers the construction of comprehensive community care systems throughout Japan to accommodate population aging to be an important policy issue. Such systems are constructed at the community level and include each of the following elements: housing in which residents, even elderly residents, can live continuously; promotion of preventative care and health-promotion activities; livelihood support and nursing-care businesses provided at home or at a neighborhood facility to which residents commute; and medical care systems that permit home care. Moreover, they reduce, as much as possible, long-term convalescence at hospitals and elderly relocation to assisted living facilities.

However, tangible measures to develop such systems have not been sufficiently implemented in Tokyo Metropolitan Area. Current policies designed to help the elderly are short-sighted because they are subjected to rolling review every 3 years, meaning that medium- to long-term strategies cannot be accommodated in these systems. In addition, although spatial development strategies are indispensable to the various services involved in accommodating seniors in residential areas, but the policies of the Ministry of Health fall greatly short in this regard.

Providing a Child-Rearing Environment

If suburban residential areas are to be sustainable, it is essential that they attract child-rearing families. It is thus necessary that any facilities built are combined with a good child-rearing environment. Households with children make up a minority of suburban households today, and moreover female staff turnover due to childbirth and childcare continues to rapidly decrease in the Tokyo region. Ensuring the availability of nursery schools and childcare facilities is a given. It is also necessary to make Tokyo's suburbs attractive to child-rearing individuals, as a place where they can begin a new stage in their life. Commute time in particular can be a decisive factor in choosing a residence for working women. Challenges will impede the renewal of suburban residential areas as long as these women assume that their workplace and residence could be in different locations in the metropolitan area at large (i.e., that they would have to commute downtown from the suburbs).

Problems With Mobility

Most suburban residential areas are located in hilly land, which creates problems for households with elderly or children who need to visit train stations, hospitals or childcare facilities. Elderly with diminished capabilities (in both physical and cognitive terms) are of particular concern, as driving a personal vehicle may not be feasible for their ability level. This makes it necessary for city planners to ensure these denizens have the means to go out to facilities in and around their neighborhood of residence.

Community Living

As discussed earlier, future suburban residential areas will be required to satisfy a variety of conditions in a comprehensive manner. The ideal suburbs are a "live/work space", furnished with satellite offices, shared offices, and co-working spaces, and with options for teleworking; they are a place where retired elderly and child-rearing families can create a new lifestyle for themselves. In addition, the facilities and housing built in residential areas in various locations in the ideal suburbs are connected to train stations, hospitals, and other facilities outside the neighborhood by new transportation modes such as community transport schemes and ride-sharing.

Calling this new spatial image "Community Living", the authors are endeavoring to put it in practice in a trial attempt at renewing a suburban residential area. We briefly introduce the trial study's details ahead.

Leading Initiatives Aimed at the Sustainable Renewal of Suburban Residential Areas—Next Generation Suburban Machizukuri in the Tama Plaza Area

Collaborative Efforts Between Private Business, Government, Academia, and Citizens

Next-Generation Suburban Machizukuri[1] is a project currently underway for creating a model of the area around Tama Plaza Station (on the Tokyu Den-en-toshi Line). Originally based on a joint agreement between Yokohama City and Tokyu Corporation, the professors of Institute of Gerontology, the University of Tokyo including the author are also collaborating in this project. This project is being conducted through resident collaboration with the local government, private businesses, and the university. It aims to solve creatively a wide range of social issues confronting urban and rural communities in Japan related to the advent of Japan's "low-birthrate, aging society" and the high level of environmental constraints. In the preliminary investigation stage of the project, we called on businesses in necessary fields to cooperate and participate, such as medicine and nursing, environmental science and energy, transportation (mobility), and information and community technology (ICT).

Community Living as a Concept for the Project

The Essential concepts of the grand design for *Next-Generation Suburban Machizukuri* include the reconstruction of "walk-able living areas" and public transportation networks, with an emphasis on the concept of "community living". In addition to the reconstruction of "walk-able living areas" and public transportation networks, the design involves the construction of social infrastructure for home-based health-care and welfare services. These measures are aimed at stimulating residents to engage in various activities, even in suburban residential areas where population aging is accelerating, to endow them with sustained vitality.[2]

Neighborhood centers and other community places utilizing vacant rooms and houses, pedestrian paths, and parks serve as the setting of residents' livelihoods and of their various activities and interactions. These are connected through a community information infrastructure, consisting of information and communications technologies and traffic networks (route buses, on-demand transportation, car sharing, private mobility, etc.). We envision that the reconstruction of the suburbs will thus position the community itself as the "livelihood sphere" of the residents, covering both their immediate whereabouts and their place of residence.

Of course, this grand design cannot be totally realized in a short time. When local residents, government, and businesses check for themselves what form their unique machizukuri should take, responsible community members should be educated at the same time as they are provided with implementation systems for concrete projects whereby local communities can be renewed in a collaborative way and at an accelerated pace.

Settling on a Vision for Next Generation Machizukuri

In June 2012, Yokohama City selected the area north of Tama Plaza Station, spanning Utsukushigaoka districts 1, 2, and 3 in Aoba Ward, as the first model area for *Next-Generation*

Suburban Machizukuri. A kick-off event in the model area was held on July 14th of the same year. As next step Tokyu Corporation, Yokohama city and the University of Tokyo conducted a survey investigation of all households in the area with the aim of understanding the attitudes and needs of area residents. Furthermore, they held a series of workshops for residents starting in September 2012 and established our vision for *Next-Generation Machizukuri* in the model area in July 2013.

Promoting Co-Creative Projects Between Residents and Businesses

After formulating the project vision, we supported organizational formation and planning processes and encouraged area residents to participate in activities in order to extract suitable collaborative activities and projects aimed at solving specific problems. In this regard, the novelty of our attempt lay in our provision of planning support by encouraging collaboration with external companies. In total, 28 community projects were carried out with the objectives of problem-solving and realizing the project vision of *Next-Generation Suburban Machizukuri*. Moreover, by encouraging crowd funding, we attempted to cultivate community projects during the implementation process, by encouraging residents to explore crowd funding and other opportunities to gain financial support.[3]

Moving Towards a Tokyo That Can Accommodate Japan's Super-Aging Society

In recent years, the population of the Greater Tokyo Metropolitan Area (consisting of Tokyo and its neighboring municipalities) has begun to concentrate in its central wards and to its southwest. It seems fair to say that this outcome is the result of the urban renewal policies pursued by Japanese government. As a result, declines have been experienced by nearly all suburban residential areas. Community planning efforts must take particular care to ensure that the vast numbers of the "left-behind elderly" (LBE) can continue to live in the region. Regaining lost value and achieving sustainability are also necessary components of sustainable renewal. For younger generations, something must be done to restore the value of living in the suburbs: to rehabilitate them as a so-called "live/work space". Several advanced initiatives are being implemented at present: although they have only just begun, they must nonetheless be fostered, developed, and spread.

Also, in order to realize such initiatives, the following two points are important. One is to set up a framework of collaboration among the government sector, citizens and local communities, nonprofit organizations, and private businesses to solve problems. In particular, positive engagement by private enterprises is becoming important. In the next decade, it is anticipated that issues accompanying the declining birthrate and the aging of the population will become more serious, and the government sector is facing the problem of decrease in tax revenue and human resources. For this reason, the role that the government sector can play in solving issues has become limited. Also, as the community is rapidly aging, the time it takes to demonstrate its power is limited. For these reasons, it is becoming indispensable to build a collaborative framework including private enterprises at each local community level.

The second is to build a multilevel governance mechanism. At present, the local municipalities are working on regenerating suburban residential areas in the Tokyo metropolitan area. However, there are limits to this. For example, in order to disseminate the comprehensive care system efficiently, it is necessary to take more extensive measures by prefectural governments. In addition, regarding measures such as more dispersing employment, efforts involving mutual cooperation among prefectures in the Tokyo metropolitan area are also necessary. In addition, measures such as act revision such as amendment of the zoning system and provision of subsidies by Japanese government are required. By coordinating governance at each level of local governments, prefectures, Tokyo metropolitan area, and the country, it is possible to effectively promote the regeneration of suburban residential areas. Thus construction of a multilevel governance mechanism is the key to comprehensively promoting the regeneration of suburban residential areas in the Tokyo metropolitan area.

Notes

1. See the following link of next generation suburban machizukuri website for further information. Retrieved June 2017, from http://jisedaikogai.jp
2. See the following link of press release presentation material on next generation suburban machizukuri for further information. Retrieved June 2017, from www.city.yokohama.lg.jp/kenchiku/housing/jizokukanoupj/toukyuwll.pdf
3. See the following link of co-creative community projects (jumin sohatsu projects) website for further information. Retrieved June 2017, from http://jisedaikogai.jp/sohatsu/

References

Ishida, Y. (2004). Nippon Kingendai Toshi Keikaku no Tenkai, Tokyo, Japan: jichitai kenkyū-sha 石田頼房、『日本近現代都市計画の展開』自治体研究社、2004年.

Koizumi, H. (2015). Strategic and communicative planning toward sustainable communities through intergenerational co-creation. *Planning and Public Management*, 38(4), 3–8.

Miyake, R., Koizumi, H., & Okata, J. (2012). A basic study on the stable maintenance of vacant lands and houses in detached housing estates in a suburban area: A case study of housing estate in Sakura city, Chiba prefecture. *Papers on City Planning*, 47(3), 493–498.

Miyake, R., Koizumi, H., & Okata, J. (2014). Research on the distribution of the households-decreasing districts and district characteristics in the Tokyo metropolitan area. *Papers on City Planning*, 49(3), 1029–1034.

Sorensen, A., Koizum, H., & Miyamoto, A. (2008). Machizukuri, civil society, and community space in Japan. In M. Douglass (Ed.), *The politics of civic space in Asia: Building urban communities*. Abingdon, UK: Routledge.

Suzuki, A., Koizumi, H., & Okata, J. (2011). Housing change on population recovery in Tokyo wards from 2000 to 2006. *Papers on City Planning*, 46(3), 439–444.

Tokyo Metropolitan Government. (1991). Tokyo Toshi Hakusho. 東京都都市計画局総合計画部都市整備室編 (1991) 東京都市白書.

10 Livability for Whom?
Vancouver's Conundrum

Penny Gurstein

Introduction

Consistently ranked one of the most livable cities in the world, internationally acclaimed as a model of good urbanism, and lauded for a series of planning policies and practices that have resulted in a dynamic and diverse metropolis, Vancouver's luster is starting to diminish, as unaffordability, and deep divides between rich and poor, are reshaping the urban realm. Although being extolled for urban livability and ecological sustainability, Vancouver faces unprecedented levels of homelessness, housing insecurity, and economic inequities. Significant investments over many decades in public realm infrastructure—green spaces, public schools, community centers, and libraries—has made the city a highly desirable place to live. At the same time, Vancouver has been marked by real estate speculation, cyclical housing prices, and global investment in land creating a city of haves and have-nots. What can Vancouver's world ranking tell us about the kind of city that is prioritized in these rankings, and what are other ways to evaluate a city's success?

The conundrum facing Vancouver is that livability is not extended to all of its citizens. High housing costs for both homeowners and renters have resulted in people living in inadequate, insecure housing with often long commutes. It also means that a significant portion of the population is spending a large percentage of their income on housing. This chapter addresses the factors that have made the City of Vancouver livable, and the forces that are precipitating a decline in the quality of life for a large percentage of the population. It concludes with thoughts on how a holistic understanding of city building could shape policies that address inequities and make Vancouver a city for all citizens.

Livability and Quality of Life Rankings

Livability, defined as suitable for living in or habitable, has been used as the main measure to rank cities. Although different surveys have used different criteria to assess livability, generally, the social, political, and natural environment; education; infrastructure; and health are part of these assessments. Recognizing that all cities have challenges, when rankings are developed, what is looked for is not the best, but the least challenging, place in which to live (Conger, 2015; Okulicz-Kozaryn, 2013). Although other cities may have a more vibrant economy, and cultural opportunities, Vancouver is highly ranked in the Mercer Quality of Living Survey[1] and the Economist Intelligence Unit (EIU) Global Liveability Survey[2] on political stability, lack of violence, and quality of social services and education. It is also a mid-sized city in a relatively wealthy country, as are the other two highly ranked cities, Melbourne and Vienna.

Of the top ten most livable cities ranked in 2016, 70% are located in either Australia or Canada. Vancouver has been in the top three for a number of years but has fallen to third place from first since 2011, with Toronto just after Vancouver in fourth place and Calgary tying for fifth with Adelaide, Australia. As well, there is less than one full rating point between Calgary and Melbourne, which is in first place. However, increased instability has caused a drop in the scores of nearly a one fifth of the cities surveyed including those from the EU and the US, making Vancouver (and Canada, generally) relatively safe in an increasingly more unstable world. Vancouver rankings portray an urban environment that is the least dangerous, and the least lacking in a social safety net. This, however, does not portray the whole story, as the stability that Vancouver offers is not evenly distributed.

Vancouver in Context

Vancouver is the third largest city in Canada. Although other cities have larger, more robust economies, the desirability of its social and physical assets is a significant factor in drawing residents from other provinces and internationally, as well as its temperate climate. It is known as a city with a relatively good education system and a strong network of parks, community centers, and neighborhood houses, all publicly financed. The citizens also have publicly funded medical care, as do all residents of Canada.

Because of its attributes, and the political stability of Canada, Vancouver has become a "hedge city": a safe place for the wealthy to park money in real estate.[3] Corresponding with global capital's investment in Vancouver housing has been a sharp increase in housing prices that has affected a large portion of the population. In 2016, out of 406 cities surveyed, Vancouver was ranked as the third worst city in the world for homeownership affordability, behind Hong Kong and Sydney, Australia.[4] It takes 11.8 times the median household income of $76,040 to afford the average home price of $897,158. Single family homes in Vancouver are typically over $2 million. The decoupling between housing values and household incomes in Vancouver and its region, Metro Vancouver, is an extreme example of the pattern that is occurring in Canadian cities as well as in other countries. As is shown in Table 10.1, whereas median household incomes have stagnated, housing prices have exploded.

More than half of Vancouver residents are renters, a significantly higher percentage than other Canadian cities. Rental vacancy rates in Vancouver are among the lowest in Canada at 0.7% and have consistently been low for the last twenty years. This is mainly due to the lack of new purpose-built rental housing being built. The cost of renting in Vancouver is also high, and Vancouver renters pay the highest rents in Canada in what is one of the country's tightest rental markets. A one-bedroom apartment is renting for an average of $1,900 per month and a two-bedroom is $3,130, the highest in Canada.[6] These rates have more than doubled since 2006 and tripled since 1996.[7]

Table 10.1 Median Household Incomes and Average Home Prices in Greater Vancouver[5]

Year	Median Household Income	Average Home Price	Home Price to Income Ratio
2001	$49,940	$295,978	5.9
2006	$55,231	$483,822	8.7
2011	$63,347	$661,919	10.4
2016	$76,040	$897,158	11.8

Sources: http://data.cid-bdc.ca/ and Canadian Real Estate Association, 2014: These data are for the whole metropolitan region of Vancouver. For the city of Vancouver, the average home price is much higher.

British Columbia also has one of the highest percentages in Canada of people in core housing need.[8] In a survey of housing experiences in Metro Vancouver,[9] the majority of respondents reported spending more than 30% of their household income on housing, with one quarter spending more than 50%. Renters reported substandard housing with mold, rot, and bedbugs. These findings attest to a tough housing climate, with many forced to live in substandard, unhealthy, unaffordable, and inadequate housing.

For those who cannot get into the tight housing market, Vancouver has an acute homelessness and housing insecurity problem. A March 2017 homeless count found that 3,605 people in the Metro Vancouver region identified as homeless, a 30% increase since 2014.[10] Of those, 2,138 homeless were in the City of Vancouver. Current numbers (widely acknowledged to be underreported) are the highest ever recorded.

The increase in homelessness has been directly attributed to the federal government's disengagement with the provision of affordable housing since the mid-1990s. This has left the provinces, and more critically, cities such as Vancouver, which have the most limited in financial resources, to deal with this problem. Recognizing that the solutions to homelessness are affordable housing, support services, and adequate income, government agencies, and nonprofit and faith-based organizations, provide services and temporary and permanent shelter but given limited resources that are inadequate to meet the demand.

High housing costs in Vancouver have resulted in residents seeking housing they can afford in the Metro Vancouver region, resulting in long commutes as they navigate the work-home nexus. This has resulted in a heavy reliance on automobiles. Vancouver is the most congested city in Canada (and 34th worldwide).[11]

A Bifurcated City

Wilkinson and Pickett (2009) argue that societies with more equal distribution of incomes have better health outcomes and fewer societal problems. Although Canada has a social safety net that includes medical care and social services, intended to ensure benefits throughout the society, there are still inequities. British Columbia's overall poverty rate is at 13.4%, the second highest in Canada. The rate has steadily increased since the late 1980s.[12] For children under 18 years of age, it is 15.3%,[13] and those in single mother households, it is 49%. Fifty-two percent of on-reserve Indigenous children live in poverty and, in Vancouver, the poverty rate for Indigenous children is 33%.[14] Metro Vancouver has the second highest rate of working poor in Canada at 8.7%, just after Greater Toronto at 9.1%.[15] The last increase in social assistance benefits occurred in 2007. For a single person on basic assistance, the benefit rate remains $610 per month, and for a single parent with one child, it is $946 a month.

Vancouver is more unequal that any other Canadian city and has the largest and fastest growing income gap between rich and poor. Disproportionately represented among the poor are single parent families, Indigenous people, people with disabilities and mental illness, recent immigrants and refugees, single female seniors, and the LBGTQ community. In Vancouver, the price of core essentials like housing, childcare, utilities, and food have increased much faster than incomes. The decoupling of incomes from essentials such as housing, and escalating prices of these essentials, are placing additional stress on the already-tight budgets of low-income families.

Though Vancouver is considered relatively safe, there is a major problem with substance use and the consequences of people using and dealing drugs.[16] Crimes associated with these activities are high, and Vancouver is in the middle of an opiate crisis with the number of overdose deaths increasing every year.

Unreported and untaxed economic activity (the underground economy) is more prevalent in British Columbia than in the country as a whole, accounting for estimates of 10%

of GDP.[17] Money laundering is highly correlated with real estate transactions in Vancouver, where nearly half of the most expensive properties do not report their owners on their titles and one third are owned through shell companies.[18]

Though poverty and affordable housing are critical issues facing residents, a 2011 study found that the top concern among residents was isolation and disconnection[19]—the factor of "friendliness" not evaluated in livability rankings. Positive social relationships are powerful predictors of human health and well-being (Schwanan & Wang, 2014), whereas isolation and loneliness have been highly correlated with decreased longevity and a host of mental and physical risks. The built environment affects our physical and social well-being if it is designed to provide opportunities to interact in neighborhoods (Stevenson et al., 2016). However, cities, generally, are perceived as lonely venues, and Vancouver, in particular, has factors precipitating an environment of social isolation.

The alleviation of poverty requires actions plans by the provincial and federal governments that would increase social assistance benefits, invest in affordable housing and create a public childcare program. Vancouver has limited ability to address this except in the coordinated efforts that are being done through partnering with nonprofit agencies to provide needed services. The city is, however, providing community supports and services to new immigrants and vulnerable populations through an extensive network of Community Centres and Neighbourhood Houses.

Nevertheless, the city is hollowing out. Unoccupied units in Vancouver are at 8.2% of the total housing stock, contributing to uninhabited neighborhoods.[20] Neighborhoods are densifying but not with a full spectrum of households. Units being developed are studio, one- and two-bedrooms, which are not conducive for young growing families who contribute to the life of a community. What is increasingly being identified in Vancouver, and other North American cities, is the "missing middle,[21] middle-income households who no longer can find suitable accommodation in these cities, or afford those that are available. The range of multi-unit or clustered housing types compatible in scale with single family homes that can help meet the demand from this segment of the population, and create walkable neighborhoods, is missing. Vancouver, however, is trying to address this trend by encouraging medium density housing of four- to five-story apartment buildings along transportation corridors, and townhouses and infill housing in neighborhoods where there is predominately detached housing, though often with resistance from neighborhood residents.

The growth in Metro Vancouver is in its outer suburbs, not in Vancouver.[22] School-age children's enrollment in public schools has decreased in Vancouver, attributed to an aging population, fewer children per household, and families of school-age children seeking homes elsewhere in the Metro Vancouver region. The 2016 census also revealed baby boomers, after selling their homes, are leaving the region entirely, resulting in a loss in the volunteerism and support of arts and cultural institutions associated with this cohort.

Vancouver is becoming a bifurcated city of haves and have-nots, with expensive market housing for the wealthy encircling the remaining social and affordable private sector rental housing for those living in abject poverty. Low- and middle-income households must seek housing in the suburban communities, which has put pressure on communities in the Metro Vancouver region to provide rental housing and small units for ownership.

What Makes Vancouver Livable?

Notwithstanding the bleak picture painted previously, Vancouver still stands out as an exemplary city mainly due to the planning decisions that have provided high-quality developments that have enhanced its setting and an extensive and accessible public realm of seaside walkways and bicycle paths, parks, and social, cultural, and recreational facilities (Grant, 2009). Vancouver has a network of city-financed and city-operated community centers and neighborhood houses that are widely used, help to provide social cohesion in neighborhoods, and opportunities for new residents to integrate into their communities. It has lively arts and cultural communities, strong neighborhood associations, and citizen involvement.

Punter (2003) analyzes the successes of Vancouver in two broad categories: high standard of design that has allowed urban intensification to be negotiated successfully, and the bridging of the gap between discretionary versus administrative planning systems. Starting in the 1970s, Vancouver has promoted neighborhood rehabilitation and redevelopment of industrial lands into dense residential neighborhoods and made the waterfront publicly accessible. In the late 1960s, a highly effective protest movement stopped the building of a freeway that was to demolish Vancouver's historic inner core, thereby allowing for the gradual revitalization of inner-city neighborhoods. In the 1970s, Vancouver's planners, emboldened by a city council that respected their advice and a federal government that provided funding for rehabilitation projects, undertook neighborhood planning processes that strengthened neighborhood characters.

Also in the 1970s, a partnership between municipal, provincial, and federal governments allowed the redevelopment of former industrial lands fronting an inner waterway, the south side of False Creek, into low- and medium-rise mixed-income and mixed-tenure residential neighborhoods anchored by arts, culture, and commercial precincts. After the highly successful Expo '86, a World Exposition on Transportation and Communication, the north side of False Creek, where the Expo was located, was sold to a private developer who has been developing it into high-density, high-rise neighborhoods. Planners worked with these developers, and others, to provide a framework for large-scale redevelopment of industrial lands. From these planning decisions came "Vancouverism", which is characterized by a dense city center residential population, mixed-use developments of high-rise towers and medium-height podiums fronting streets, park spaces, and preservation of view corridors (see Figure 10.1).

The City of Vancouver is one of the most livable cities in the world because, aside from the setting, a structure of sound planning and urban design principles was laid in place in the 1970s and 1980s that provided a framework when Vancouver began to grow after Expo '86. Citizen engagement was further refined by the CityPlan process in the 1990s. During that time, the negotiation process that evolved between developers of large tracts of land and city planners provided many of the public amenities.

Of particular note is the Community Amenity Contributions (CACs), a growth financing charge negotiated with developers during rezonings that is used to partially fund public goods like parks, libraries, childcare centers, community spaces, and affordable housing. CACs were initially implemented in the 1990s in response to a series of major development projects requiring rezoning from industrial uses to residential and mixed-use sites around the downtown core. CACs have recently come under scrutiny for several reasons, including their impact on market housing prices in Vancouver and lack of transparency in the rezoning process, but they continue to be a critical source of revenue for the City of Vancouver's efforts to lessen negative impacts of development on communities. The city is now de facto being planned by rezonings, with each rezoning allowing greater density for the proliferation of high-rise condominium developments in the city's hope of extracting some community benefits in the form of amenities and affordable housing units. The city is becoming a patchwork of developments with little relation to the nuanced public realm that has made us an exemplar of urbanism and doing little to address the affordability crisis.

Livability for Whom? 143

Figure 10.1 View of Development in North and South False Creek From South Side
Source: author

Vancouver's planning reputation, and livability profile, was created by the successful redevelopment of large parcels of waterfront land ringing the city center. It has been less successful in densifying existing low-density neighborhoods. The Bartholomew Plans of 1928 and 1945,[23] though never adopted, were the source code for the city, as they set the pattern for the large tracts of low-density, single family housing that still predominates in many neighborhoods. This pattern has been resistant to change and adaptation. Zoning as a tool for exclusion has reinforced this pattern. Although CityPlan,[24] in 1995, was successful in reinforcing and encouraging the development of strong distinctive neighborhoods, decisions on densification have been resisted in many of the neighborhoods that could most benefit from growth.

Lauster (2016) found that 80% of Vancouver's land base is devoted to single family homes (though of those, over half have secondary suites). Thirty-five percent of Vancouver's residents live on the 80% of the land zoned for detached and duplex houses, whereas the remaining 65% of residents live on the 19% of the land base devoted to multifamily housing. Though low-density neighborhoods are unsustainable because they use more energy and encourage more driving, they are protected through city zoning laws that prohibit denser housing to be built on much of Vancouver's land base, except by lengthy spot rezoning processes.

Although Vancouver has many attributes that make it a highly livable city, it has become a casualty of its own success. Because of its desirability, and limited development potential, property values have escalated, making it a place that only the wealthy can afford. This is a pattern in other highly desirable locales. Displacement and gentrification is rampant. The neighborhoods that Jacobs (1961) sought to preserve and replicate have lost their diversity and vitality because of the limited resident base who can afford to live there and high property taxes that have forced out small businesses.

Vancouver's economic development strategy (besides real estate) is focused on attracting the creative and technology sectors such as the film and television industry, design, software development and engineering. Although British Columbia is known historically for resource extraction industries such as forestry, mining, and fishing, since 2006, employment in the technology section has surpassed these industries, and in 2009, it surpassed resource extraction industries in overall contribution to the provincial GDP.[25] However, real estate transactions, and the accompanying activities such as the construction industry, far surpass any other economic activity in the metropolitan Vancouver region, representing 25% of British Columbia's GDP.

Like many other cities searching for a way to diversify their economic base, Vancouver's policies were adapted from Florida (2005), who postulated that providing amenities in the urban environment to attract the "creative class" would generate a high level of economic development. Among the many critics of Florida's theories, Florida, himself, in 2017 acknowledged that cities are facing a crisis point with increasing inequality, segregation, and the loss of middle-class households.

What Besides Livability?

Given these conditions, the question is not whether livability is what should be sought but, instead, should the aims of cities such as Vancouver be reframed from livability to allow diversity, resiliency, and sustainability to be re-introduced? How can we make cities that are more convivial, that nurture the spirit through inclusive, democratic systems, and restore a sense of local citizenship? How can urban citizens learn to live within the finite realities of ecological systems, economic imperatives and human needs?

Healthy communities are shaped by the determinants of health—social, economic, and environmental choices—that are constrained by economic and social opportunities, income, education, and quality of environmental experiences. Resilient communities are healthy communities that are capable of withstanding adverse situations and actively anticipate, influence, and accommodate economic, social, and environmental change. These are communities that welcome diversity and innovation as means of expanding their socioeconomic and cultural base.

Looking at Vienna, as an example, can provide a framework to develop such a city. Although Vienna does not have as beautiful setting as Vancouver, it does have low crime, relatively low pollution, good public health policies, good city services, and relatively high wages. It is very pedestrian friendly, with good public transport, and a well-maintained public realm. Of particular note, is that the public realm is at a human scale—most developments are medium-rise—allowing for a mix of uses.

It also has an extensive and innovative public housing program that has succeeded in meeting critical housing shortages, preventing housing prices from escalating, and encouraging social cohesion by creating housing as a permanent solution for the majority of residents (Reinprecht, 2007). The majority of Vienna's residents (60%) live in subsidized apartments, including both city-owned flats and limited profit housing associations. Vienna's Municipal Department 50 owns more than one quarter of the city's entire housing stock. Starting with the premise that housing is a basic human need, the Viennese government recognizes that housing should not be subject to free market mechanisms, but, instead, it is up to government to ensure that a sufficient supply is available.

Vienna leads the Mercer Quality of Life ranking for the eighth year in a row. It has been ranked the most prosperous city by UN Human Settlements Programme,[26] the city with the best reputation by the Reputation Institute,[27] and highly ranked in innovation[28] and within global smart cities.[29] The heavy expenditure in its social and physical infrastructure has not impeded its success, but has been attributed to it.

An excellent quality of life need not be attributed to only those few with financial means. Two fifths of Vienna's population are migrants from other parts of Europe and the Middle East, and the population has grown by 10% from 2005 to 2015, making it the fastest growing city in Europe.[30] Careful city planning that links its work to socioeconomic imperatives has allowed the city to flourish.

Comparing Vancouver in this light, we see deep divisions and inequities. Vancouver's prosperity is not being shared equally between population groups (notably, Aboriginal groups, low-income families, and new immigrants in low-wage jobs). Affordability is a key issue and risks driving away talented individuals who could contribute economically. This growing economic divergence undermines productivity, increases household debt, reduces the tax base to pay for government services, and puts the brakes on consumer consumption as a driver of growth.

Conclusion

Although there are many aspects of urban planning that Vancouver is doing right, without a reframing of how to address the inequities in the city, Vancouver's reputation will increasingly become tarnished. This cannot be done alone. Municipalities in Canada have very limited funding compared with provincial and federal governments. Their mandates are set and regulated by provinces. In addition, there has been limited federal funding to address woefully deteriorating physical infrastructure such as roads and bridges in cities, and even less funding to address housing affordability.

Along with other countries in Europe and North America, neoliberal restructuring has meant the lessening of government involvement in social and physical infrastructure spending and the devolution of responsibilities to more local levels of governments. We are now at a point where we need to rethink these relationships if cities are to survive as viable entities.

Vancouver, so famous for planning, stands at the verge of a precipice. The collective actions of previous generations of citizens and their elected and appointed officials produced a city that is the envy of the world. The irony is that Vancouver's attractions have served as a magnet to those who would capitalize on those previous efforts without ensuring that this tradition of good planning is continued. Without a citywide framework in place, and agreed-upon guiding principles, planners are losing their ability to guide development, maintain the integrity of neighborhoods, address complex issues such as climate change, and provide a home for future generations.

Planning is ultimately a political process. A plan is the manifestation of the collective will of the citizens. It is the most important tool that citizens have to resist the global forces of capital that presently threaten to overwhelm and transform Vancouver, making it impossible for further generations of citizens to live and work in the city. Although recent planning efforts have focused on the greening of our city to become more environmentally sustainable, far fewer efforts have been focused on ensuring social sustainability—a fair and just community—for all of its citizens. That is the direction that is needed.

Notes

1. *Mercer quality of life rankings*. Retrieved May 15, 2017, from www.imercer.com/content/mobility/quality-of-living-city-rankings.html

2. *Economist Intelligence Unit (EIU) liveability rankings.* Retrieved May 25, 2017, from www.eiu.com/Handlers/WhitepaperHandler.ashx?fi=Liveability+Ranking+Summary+Report+-+August+2016.pdf&mode=wp&campaignid=Liveability2016
3. *What are hedge cities and why is Vancouver considered one of them?* Retrieved May 20, 2014, from www.theglobeandmail.com/news/british-columbia/the-unusual-nature-of-vancouvers-real-estate-market-gets-the-new-yorker-treatment/article18768027/
4. *13th annual demographia international housing affordability survey rating middle-income housing affordability* (2017 Edition: Data from 3rd Quarter 2016). Retrieved from www.demographia.com/dhi.pdf
5. These data are for the whole metropolitan region of Vancouver. For the city of Vancouver, the average home price is much higher.
6. Business Vancouver. *Average Vancouver one-bedroom rent reaches record high: PadMapper.* Retrieved February 16, 2017, from www.biv.com/article/2017/2/average-vancouver-one-bedroom-rent-reaches-record-/
7. *Canada mortgage and housing corporation rental market.* Retrieved from http://data.cid-bdc.ca/TableViewer/document.aspx?ReportId=109&IF_Language=eng&BR_CSD_CODE=5915020
8. A household is said to be in core housing need if its housing falls below at least one of the adequacy, affordability or suitability, standards **and** it would have to spend 30% or more of its total before-tax income to pay the median rent.
9. See Metro Vancouver Housing Affordability Survey. (2014). Retrieved August 18, 2014, from http://housingjustice.ca/wp-content/uploads/2012/02/HJP-Affordable-Housing-Survey-Results.pdf
10. *2017 homeless count in Metro Vancouver.* Retrieved May 19, 2017, www.metrovancouver.org/services/regional-planning/homelessness/HomelessnessPublications/2017MetroVancouverHomelessCountPreliminaryData.pdf
11. *Tomtom Travel Index: Vancouver, Canada.* Retrieved April 20, 2017, www.tomtom.com/en_gb/trafficindex/city/vancouver
12. BC Poverty Reduction Coalition. (2013). *5 things you should know about poverty in BC.* Retrieved from http://bcpovertyreduction.ca/wp-content/uploads/2013/10/2013_prc_5-things-to-know.pdf
13. Statistics Canada, CANSIM Table 206–0041.
14. Klein, S., Ivanova, I., & Leyland, A. (2017). *Long overdue: Why BC needs a poverty reduction plan.* Vancouver: CCPA. Retrieved from www.policyalternatives.ca/sites/default/files/uploads/publications/BC%20Office/2017/01/ccpa-bc_long-overdue-poverty-plan_web.pdf
15. *UNICEF report card 10: Measuring child poverty.* Retrieved from www.unicef.ca/en/our-work/article/unicef-report-card-10
16. *Crime rates in Vancouver.* Retrieved May 25, 2017, from www.numbeo.com/crime/in/Vancouver
17. *B.C.'s underground economy likely leads all other provinces, Vancouver Sun.* Retrieved June 17, 2015, from www.vancouversun.com/news/barbara+yaffe+underground+economy+likely+leads+other+provinces/11144811/story.html
18. Doors wide open: Corruption and real estate in four key markets, transparency international. Retrieved March 29, 2017, from www.transparency.org/whatwedo/publication/doors_wide_open_corruption_and_real_estate_in_four_key_markets
19. Vancouver Foundation. *Connections and engagement.* Retrieved May 25, 2017, from www.vancouverfoundation.ca/sites/default/files/documents/VanFdn-SurveyResults-Report.pdf
20. Unoccupied units are mainly attributed to speculators buying units and leaving the empty until they are flipped or buyers who have several homes and use their unit in Vancouver only occasionally.
21. Black, I. (2017, April 17). Housing affordability in search of the missing middle. *Vancouver Sun.* Retrieved from http://vancouversun.com/opinion/op-ed/opinion-housing-affordability-in-search-of-the-missing-middle
22. From 2011 to 2016, Vancouver grew by 4.6%; Langley Township, an outer suburb, grew by 12.6%. Census 2016, Statistics Canada.
23. *How did Harland Bartholomew's plans shape Vancouver?* (2011, April 18). Retrieved from www.vancouverarchives.ca/2011/04/18/how-did-harland-bartholomew's-ideas-shape-vancouver/
24. *Cityplan.* Retrieved May 25, 2017, from http://former.vancouver.ca/commsvcs/planning/cityplan/Visions/
25. BC Tech Association. (2016). *2016 TechTalentBC report.* Retrieved from www.wearebctech.com/advocacy/publications/publication/techtalentbc/techtalent-bc-report-2016

26. "State of the world's cities" (PDF). UN Habitat. Retrieved October 15, 2016, from https://sustainabledevelopment.un.org/content/documents/745habitat.pdf
27. Most reputable cities in the world. (2014). Reputation Institute. Retrieved January 20, 2017, from www.reputationinstitute.com/Resources/Registered/PDF-Resources/2016-City-RepTrak.aspx
28. Innovation cities index 2014. (2014). 2thinknow. Retrieved May 25, 2001, from www.innovation-cities.com/innovation-cities-index-2014-global/8889
29. The 10 smartest cities in Europe. Boyd Cohen. Retrieved May 25, 2017, from www.fastcompany.com/3024721/the-10-smartest-cities-in-europe
30. "Vienna in figures 2012, Vienna city administration municipal department 23 economic affairs, labor and statistics. (PDF). Retrieved May 25, 2017, from www.wien.gv.at/statistik/pdf/viennainfigures.pdf

References

Conger, B. (2015). *On livability, liveability, and the limited utility of quality-of-life rankings*. University of Calgary. Retrieved February 15, 2017, from www.policyschool.ca/wp-content/uploads/2016/03/livability-conger.pdf

Grant, J. (2009). Experiential planning: A practitioner's account of Vancouver's success. *Journal of the American Planning Association, 75*(3), 358–370.

Florida, R. (2005). *Cities and the creative class*. London: Routledge.

Florida, R. (2017). *The new urban crisis: How our cities are increasing inequality, deepening segregation, and failing the middle class: And what we can do about it*. New York: Basic Books.

Jacobs, J. (1961). *The death and life of great American cities*. New York, NY: Random House.

Lauster, N. (2016). *The death and life of the single-family house: Lessons from Vancouver on building a livable city*. Philadelphia, PA: Temple University Press.

Okulicz-Kozaryn, A. (2013). City life: Rankings (livability) versus perceptions (satisfaction). *Social Indicators Research, 110*(2), 433–451.

Punter, J. (2003). *The Vancouver achievement: Urban planning and design*. Vancouver, BC: UBC Press.

Reinprecht, C. (2007). Social housing in Austria. In C. Whitehead & K. Scanlon (Eds.), *Social housing in Europe* (pp. 35–43). London: London School of Economics.

Schwanan, T., & Wang, D. (2014). Well-being, context, and everyday activities in space and time. *Annals of the Association of American Geographers, 104*(4), 833–851.

Stevenson, M., Thompson, J., De Sa, T. H., Ewing, R., Mohan, D., McClure, R., & Woodcock, J. (2016). Land use, transport and population health: Estimating the health benefits of compact cities. *The Lancet, 388*(10062), 2925–2935.

Wilkinson, R., & Pickett, K. (2009). *The spirit level: Why more equal societies almost always do better*. London: Allen Lane.

Part IV
Livability and Metrics

Introduction

How do we go about measuring or assessing the performance of what cities are trying to accomplish in regards to livability? This represents a constant challenge any city faces when it attempts to meet the livability needs of its residents. Cities are not static entities. They must adapt to changes and make any necessary policy changes in their quest for city livability.

Chapter 11 examines the livability and transformation of the global city-state of Singapore. The authors discuss the key policy principles that Singapore has chosen to meet livability by identifying the desired livability outcomes of social concerns, environmental regulations, and economic interests and the means to achieve them. Singapore recognizes that any outcome could affect an outcome in another policy area. Moreover, it acknowledges that changes will be needed over time and that, once again, collaboration and coordination is critically important with multiple stakeholders in the city-state.

Chapter 12 explores livability issues in Salt Lake City, Utah. Salt Lake City saw livability as a means of organizing and framing issues and as a means of determining the success of various policies and programs. Key components of a livable city were identified, and the means used to measure livability initiatives was developed. A key issue was how to reactivate the downtown area that had suffered over the years so that it could become a vibrant downtown. The chapter identifies policies and metrics for success and offers reflections on their progress in Salt Lake City.

Melbourne, Australia, consistently ranks high in livability. This may be due, in part, to its long-standing concern with livability. Chapter 13 examines how livability is operationalized in Melbourne. It discusses what counts as livability and how the various components of livability are measured. This is done with the acknowledgment that livability is a subjective concept. The chapter investigates the use of indicators and spatial analysis tools such as the Community Indicators Victoria and the Spatial Indicators project based at the University of Melbourne.

11 A Global Perspective on Building a Livable City

Singapore's Framework

Teng Chye Khoo and Hwee Jane Chong

Introduction

A small Southeast Asian global city-state, Singapore has been consistently ranked in livability indexes such as Mercer's 2017 Quality of Living Survey as one of the most livable cities in Asia and in the world.[1] Singapore stands out in maintaining high standards of living within a high-density context (see Figure 11.1). Its model of livability is also remarkable for the city's transformation from a landscape of slums and squatters to a modern and green metropolis of 5.3 million inhabitants within 50 years.

This chapter presents the Singapore Liveability Framework (first published in 2012) that describes Singapore's principles for achieving livability. According to this framework, livability is defined in the following outcomes: a competitive economy, a sustainable environment and a high quality of life. The framework distills key processes and policies that have developed Singapore's various urban systems—systemic components that make up a

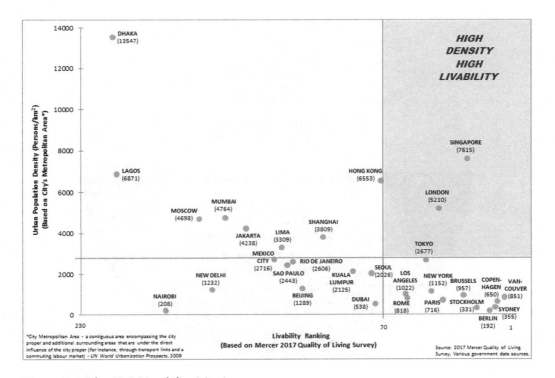

Figure 11.1 The CLC Liveability Matrix

Source: CLC

Note: The matrix measures the livability of cities according to Mercer's 2017 Quality of Life survey against city population density.

city—contributing to its success as a livable city today. Even though Singapore's case might be considered as more of an outlier in the area of urban development, this chapter discusses how the principles of the Liveability Framework also apply to other cases of successful cities in the world. The Singapore Liveability Framework thus invites urban practitioners from around the world to take into account strategic, managerial and political perspectives in planning for a livable city, instead of just technical ones.

The Singapore Liveability Framework

Singapore is a city-state with a landmass of just 719.1 km². Its urban development has been defined by geographical limitations that have called for the implementation of highly dense urban structures. Nonetheless, its residents enjoy a high standard of living that has made it widely regarded as a livable city.

The factors that have contributed to Singapore's success in balancing density and livability were the focus of the Centre for Liveable Cities (CLC)'s study from 2010, and its findings were reflected and distilled into the Singapore Liveability Framework, which was published by CLC in the book *Liveable & Sustainable Cities: A Framework* in 2014. In this study, key policies on various urban systems such as water and transport were analyzed, and interviews with Singapore's leaders in urban planning and governance were conducted in order to understand firsthand how the development of key urban systems had contributed to Singapore's growth. Singapore's principles of urban development and desired outcomes were inductively derived from these studies to form the basis of the Singapore Liveability Framework (see Figure 11.2). These desired livable city outcomes—a

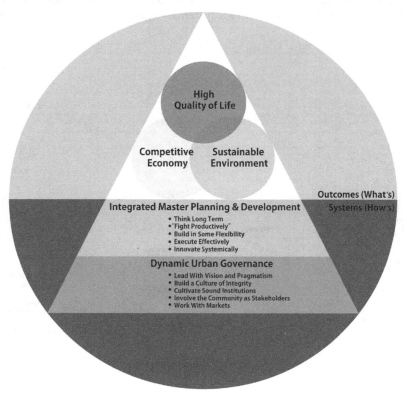

Figure 11.2 The Singapore Liveability Framework
Source: CLC

competitive economy, a sustainable environment and a high quality of life—constitute Singapore's principles of livability.

Besides identifying desired outcomes of urban development, CLC also looked into how Singapore became livable by examining the processes and mechanisms that enabled the city-state to achieve and sustain those desired outcomes. These processes and mechanisms could be summarized into two key elements: (1) an Integrated Master Planning system, and (2) a Dynamic Urban Governance approach.

Livable City Outcomes: Defining Livability With the Singapore Liveability Framework

Singapore's principles of livability are reflected in the following three livable city outcomes:

A Competitive Economy in Order to Attract Investments and Provide Jobs

Singapore's competitive economy has provided economic security to its residents, thus contributing to Singapore's livability. The importance of having a competitive economy becomes increasingly apparent as cities vie for global investment and talent. Singapore's urban systems have been a crucial factor in maintaining the competitive edge of its economy. The urban infrastructure that was built in the 1960s and 1970s for economic development (Lee & Tan, 2011) gave Singapore the element of connectivity, which, as former Prime Minister Lee Kuan Yew noted (2012), was an advantage in the region.

A Sustainable Environment Because the City Has to Survive With Limited Natural Resources, Especially in Terms of Land and Water

Given the natural limits of the island city-state, Singapore's leaders have always been aware of the need to preserve the availability of Singapore's natural resources for the long term. Environmental sustainability was a key concern for them, with environmental protection deemed as important as economic development. This was further demonstrated when the government did not compromise on mandated environmental controls, even in the face of potential loss of investment. In the mid-1970s, Japanese company Sumitomo had threatened to pull out of building a petrochemical plant in Singapore, citing the imposed government pollution controls as extra cost. When the Ministry of Environment did not back down on its stance, Sumitomo finally acquiesced to the necessary environmental requirements (Dhanabalan, 2011). Singapore's regard for environment protection and its public campaign to become a "clean and green" city further contributed to its early economic development by distinguishing Singapore from its neighbors and demonstrating to foreign investors that it was a sound place for investment.

A High Quality of Life, Including the Social and Psychological Well-Being of the Population

In this study, CLC has more specifically focused on the economic, social and environmental aspects of daily life as indicators of a high quality of life. The primary concerns of livability also evolve according to the city's various developmental stages. For instance, a higher quality of life during Singapore's earlier stage of development meant the provision of safe and secure housing, sanitation infrastructure and basic public health services, which were a considerable improvement over the pervasive slums and poor living conditions of that time. But as these provisions became more established as Singapore matured over the decades, greater consideration was given to addressing the less tangible aspects of the lived experience, such as social and psychological well-being.

Beyond basic housing provisions, recreational outlets in housing estates were designed to create a greater sense of space and to help foster a sense of community among residents. City planning also increasingly focused on balancing development with the natural landscape as well as culture. For instance, the Urban Redevelopment Authority's 2013 draft Master Plan unveiled initiatives to encourage citizens to remain engaged with the physical landscape within an increasingly built-up environment, with plans to open up 100 km of waterways and 360 km of park connectors by 2030. In spite of Singapore's land scarcity, conservation of our architectural heritage has also been actively pursued since the late 1980s, thereby enhancing the city-state's identity and enriching its character and soul.

These three livable city outcomes described earlier have been consistently set as policy goals over the last five decades of Singapore's development. The assessment of each outcome as well as its performance indicators depends on the developmental stage of the city-state. CLC suggests that for other cities to measure livability, they should take into account city-specific factors, such as geography and demographics. Livability is not an absolute standard—it is enacted at the point where trade-offs are optimized between the three outcomes.

Achieving Livability by Balancing Outcomes

For the Singapore government, livability is achieved by balancing the three livable city outcomes that are directly linked to Singapore's national-level outcome indicators, which are published in the Ministry of Finance's Revenue and Expenditure Estimates for each financial year. Available to the public, these indicators align individual agencies within the government with the three overarching outcomes of urban development, affirming the government's commitment toward making Singapore a livable city.

The main challenge for the government in maintaining Singapore as a livable city-state is balancing social concerns, environmental regulation and Singapore's economic interests. If one outcome is overemphasized at the expense of other outcomes, there could be negative consequences.

CLC's study has also revealed that in some cases, in achieving one livability outcome through creating solutions to an urban challenge, the Singapore government also generated business opportunities in areas connected to another outcome. For instance, Singapore's significant research and technology investments in its mission to attain water self-sufficiency has given rise to a thriving sector of Singapore-based companies that specialize in providing services along the value chain for the reclamation of used water and desalination. The government has identified this as a profitable niche and is investing in it to achieve $2.85 billion of annual value-added contribution and 15,000 jobs by 2020 (PUB, 2016).

The Active, Beautiful and Clean Waters (ABC Waters) Programme demonstrates how the government's emphasis on water management coalesces social, economic and environmental benefits. Under the program, areas with existing drainage infrastructure were transformed into naturalistic streams and rivers that beautified residential environments and became focal areas where residents could engage in community activities (see Figure 11.3). Although the focus of the ABC Waters Programme was environmental sustainability, the waterways also added aesthetic, economic and social value to the residential areas.

Figure 11.3 Under the ABC Waters Programme, the Kallang River at Bishan-Ang Mo Kio Park Was Transformed From a Concrete Canal to a Naturalistic River for the Community to Enjoy

Source: Thinesh Kumar Paramasilvam

How Singapore Became Livable: Systems of Urban Planning and Governance

While the three livable city outcomes reflect Singapore's urban leaders' definition of the notion of livability, Singapore achieved such standards of livability through the processes and mechanisms of an **integrated master planning** system and a **dynamic urban governance** approach. CLC has identified ten principles from these two systems that underpin Singapore's development as a livable city.

Integrated Master Planning and Development

Singapore's comprehensive integrated master planning system aims to optimize planning decisions that balance outcomes for the economy, environment and quality of life, so as to address both short-term and long-term priorities in a dynamic environment, especially in situations where there are competing uses for the same resources (see Figure 11.4).

The key aspect of the Integrated Master Planning system is the Concept Plan, which projects Singapore's land use over a time horizon of up to 50 years, and is generally reviewed every 10 years. It is created between more than twenty government ministries and agencies so that all the city's important land-use functions are accounted for, especially when limited land requires the government to prioritize between competing needs. It integrates

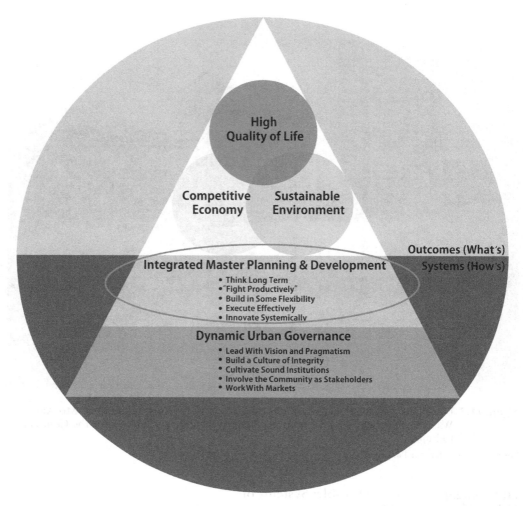

Figure 11.4 Implicit Principles of Integrated Master Planning and Development
Source: CLC

individual urban systems such as transport, water and infrastructure planning with housing estates to facilitate employment, services and recreation for the city's residents.

Singapore's land limitations require agencies to be careful about how plans are implemented to reduce the likelihood of disastrous or irrevocable consequences. The other key component of the Integrated Master Planning system is the Master Plan, Singapore's statutory land-use plan. This is where the strategies of the Concept Plan are translated into finer operational details, such as land-use zoning, gross plot ratios and building height controls that help align developers from both the public and private sectors with land-use requirements.

How Do We Plan for the Long Term?

The 50-year time frame of the Concept Plan reflects the importance Singaporean planners had placed on planning with a long-term view. Long-term planning enabled Singapore planners to project a more efficient use of space in anticipation of larger populations. It also allowed planners to balance between the three livability outcomes at the planning and implementation stages. Planners could engage in projects that did not meet immediate needs but would have significant future impact, such as greenery, which was only deeply appreciated by the public years after its initial implementation.

Long-term planning also enabled the government to identify and preempt potential problems in the future as well as to keep in view technological developments ahead of their time to develop innovative solutions in the future. The development of Marina Bay is one such example, with planning and reclamation of the area having begun as early as in the 1970s in anticipation of future needs to grow Singapore's city center. The Master Plan for Marina Bay, first drawn up in 1983, already included detailed urban design guidelines such as safeguards for public access to the waterfront. Strategic infrastructure such as the Common Services Tunnel (CST), which consolidated all underground services within an integrated network of underground tunnels, was also implemented within Marina Bay ahead of other developments, thus facilitating maintenance of underground services while also freeing up land set aside for such services (Centre for Liveable Cities, 2016).

How Do We Ensure That 'Fights' Are Productive?

Government agencies in Singapore have their own specific domains of expertise and targets to meet, which may be at odds with each other due to the competing demands for limited resources. An interagency structure has been instrumental in bringing different parties together to have productive "fights". All options have to be weighed critically and collectively, so that when a consensus is reached, it is with a clear understanding and agreement on the trade-offs and implications of such a decision on all involved.

Singapore's former Deputy Prime Minister Goh Keng Swee was known to intentionally spark debates to encourage critical thinking, such as the debate on the need for a Mass Rapid Transit (MRT) system in Singapore. Former Head of Civil Service Lim Siong Guan explained,

> [He] objected to the MRT because the case for having the MRT was that "you had no alternative". You can run an all-bus system so we should not be giving the argument that we need the MRT simply because there is no alternative . . . that's not to say that he objected to the MRT, but he objected to the logic, which is not a frivolous matter. He objected to people who don't think deeply enough and argue deeply enough.
> (2012)

The debate compelled all parties involved to rigorously weigh the costs, benefits and feasibility of an MRT system versus an all-bus system, and the decision was eventually made to proceed with an MRT system despite the $5 billion investment involved, which was an extremely large sum at the time.

Leaving Room for Change in the Future

Even though the Master Plan fixes details for land-use implementation, the Singapore government also remains open to allowing necessary changes to the schedule or the form of projected development. A key example of this is Singapore's Sungei Buloh Wetland Reserve. Originally slated to become an agro-technology park, the area was retained as a nature park in 1989 after civil society groups proposed for it to be preserved and managed as an educational site. Then-Minister of National Development S. Dhanabalan recognized the proposal as aligned with the government's commitment to preserve the environment (2011) and felt that Singapore could "afford" to leave Sungei Buloh undeveloped at that time. Sungei Buloh was eventually gazetted as a Nature Reserve in 2002 and designated as Singapore's first ASEAN Heritage Park in 2003, an accolade that would not have been achieved if not for the change in the original plans for its development.

How Do We Implement Plans Effectively?

As former Minister for National Development Mah Bow Tan succinctly explains, "A plan is only as good as how well you implement it" (2011). The Singapore government places great importance on the effective execution of plans, and much credit goes to strong action-oriented government agencies who were professional and developed effective policies and programs to translate plans into reality. Such plans involved much effort in preparatory work even before implementation. In planning Singapore's "new town," Liu Thai Ker spent more than half a year looking for a definition of a concept that had no precedent. He notes,

> I interviewed a lot of people . . . industries and so on . . . Basically, the question is how many people do you need to sustain an emporium, to sustain a supermarket, to sustain a polyclinic, etc. And the number came to 250,000.
>
> (2011, September 16)

The effective execution of plans is supported by extensive and rigorous development of programs and policies to ensure that plans effectively meet the needs of the city.

Effective interagency collaboration and coordination also ensure that plans are well executed and achieve broader national objectives even when agencies differ on certain issues or projects. As Aline Wong, former Chairman of the Housing & Development Board, bluntly puts it,

> You can have all kinds of plans but if the finance people don't give you the budget, you can't move . . . the fact that you have a cooperative bureaucracy is important . . . Government policies have t[o] be implemented by capable civil servants
>
> (2011)

Thinking Outside the Box

Although limited resources might pose obstacles to urban development, these challenges can be overcome by technological and policy innovations. The challenge of Singapore's urban problems motivated its urban leaders to think outside the box and ambitiously pursue possibilities beyond conventional solutions. To address Singapore's need to dispose an increasing amount of waste, policy makers looked beyond Singapore's limited land and created the world's first man-made offshore landfill—the Semakau landfill—in 1999 to meet the city's waste disposal needs beyond 2040. Pulau Semakau also subverts conventional expectations of landfills by serving as an ecological haven that is home to more than 700 types of plants, animals and several endangered species (Ministry of the Environment and Water Resources, 2016). Another example of innovation can be seen in the development of linear greenways known as the Park Connector Network. Developed on drainage reserves next to canals that were otherwise left unoccupied, park connectors not only creatively optimized the use of space, but also created a green network around Singapore that gave even more Singaporeans access to green spaces, which played a key role in building Singapore's identity as a City in a Garden.

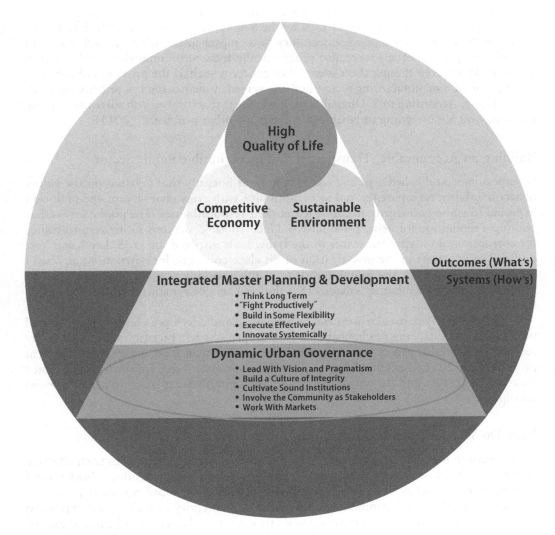

Figure 11.5 Implicit Principles of Dynamic Urban Governance
Source: CLC

Dynamic Urban Governance

CLC defines urban governance as the manner in which public leadership interacts with citizens and other stakeholders to make decisions on and have oversight of how a city plans, develops, utilizes and manages its physical and environmental resources. Given Singapore's geographical limitations and lack of resources, a sound dynamic urban governance approach is needed to allow its leaders to be responsive to a complex and ever-changing external environment in their decision making processes (see Figure 11.5).

Leading With Vision and Pragmatism

Singapore has managed to effectively plan and implement its urban projects due to the presence of leaders with vision and political will and who demonstrated commitment to their vision. This is especially the case for unpopular and politically difficult projects that were deemed by the government to have long-term benefit for the people. One key example of this is the land acquisitions conducted by the Singapore government in the late 1960s, which might seem drastic but were necessary for comprehensive urban redevelopment in the city. Singapore's leaders were also pragmatically focused on immediate and practical issues. In 1959, even though there were other concerns such as the provision of jobs and the creation of a manufacturing sector, housing was identified as the key priority for land-use planning. According to S. Dhanabalan, it was clear that "unless you solve the housing problem, you are not going to be able to solve many other problems" (2011).

Building an Accountable, Transparent and Incorruptible Public Sector

Singapore has established a public sector culture of integrity that is based on the values of accountability, transparency and incorruptibility, with every civil servant and politician expected to embody integrity in carrying out their responsibilities. The public service has built up a reputation for being principled and incorruptible, demonstrating zero tolerance for corruption, no matter the status of the individuals involved. In 1986, Lee Kuan Yew declined to intervene in the investigation of his close colleague for corruption, as "had I made an exception . . . the moral authority of the government would have dissipated" (2009). A culture of integrity ensures that the civil service remains credible and builds legitimacy.

Accountability is particularly crucial in proposing and developing large infrastructural projects. Sound financing mechanisms ensure that projects remain sustainable and fiscally solvent. One notable aspect is that the Singapore government funds its own development projects (Lim, 2012). Accountability in city planning was also enacted through public key outcome indicators and formal systems and public punishments put in place to prevent corruption.

How Do We Cultivate Robust Institutions and Processes?

Good decision making is dependent on the existence of strong institutions with effective systems and processes as well as sound professional leadership. Besides robust formal institutional structures, informal institutions such as governance norms that include respect for professional competence, the culture of integrity and the commitment to incorruptibility, enable government agencies to work together effectively. In the case of Singapore, professional bureaucrats who were technical experts worked separately from political leaders in their agencies in handling professional and technical issues. This separation of duties, facilitated by a culture of mutual respect between the political leadership and the bureaucracy, ultimately led to greater accountability and responsibility (Liu, 2011, June 29). The 1977 Singapore River cleanup that spanned over a decade was a clear example of the effectiveness of such an organizational arrangement. According to Lee Ek Tieng, who led the project, the experts could deal with the technical engineering problems without interference from politicians telling them what to do (Lee & Tan, 2011).

How Can the Government Work Better With the Community?

While the government is responsible for policy and planning decisions, these policies and plans cannot succeed without the public's desire and support. There is a greater chance for the public, people and private sectors to mutually benefit from working together when the community has a stake in the city. The Singapore government has increasingly engaged the public in their decision making and policy outcomes and has encouraged

Figure 11.6 Today, Chek Jawa Is a Popular Spot for Nature Lovers to Gather and Observe Wildlife
Source: Lim Swee Keng

public participation in land-use planning since the 1990s. The Chek Jawa Wetlands is a key example of how government and community stakeholders worked together to create a space that Singaporeans could enjoy. Initially earmarked for development, the Nature Society of Singapore[2] eventually worked with the government to preserve Chek Jawa for its rich biodiversity, and today Chek Jawa is a popular site for Singaporeans to draw closer to nature and appreciate our natural heritage (see Figure 11.6).

How Can the Government Work Better With the Private Sector?

In Singapore, the government engages the private sector to provide services that the government cannot provide by itself, or deem as not as important. The government also mobilizes market forces in specific areas to incentivize behavior and increase productivity. Although some public services have been privatized, such as power generation and some elements of public transportation, not all public services have been administered by the private sector. Water remains under the purview of the government, as well as Singapore's Changi Airport, as too many regulations would have to be changed for the airport to become a private company. As S. Dhanabalan noted, "Competition is good [but] it is good up to a point. And then we have got to ask ourselves also—is private sector operation the best way to run a public utility and should a public utility be subsidized?" (2011). The role that the private sector plays in the supply of public services is carefully calibrated according to the government's overall goals.

The Singapore Liveability Framework in Global Practice

Although the Singapore Liveability Framework abstracts the principles of livability from the city-state of Singapore, these principles are also applicable in explaining elements of other successful livable cities. This section highlights how various cities manifest the principles of the Singapore Liveability Framework in aspects of their respective governance structure and practices.[3] These insights illustrate the universality of the Singapore Liveability Framework principles, which could form the basis of a developmental framework for a successful livable city.

Systemic Innovation to Turn Constraints Into Opportunities

As previously mentioned, Singapore's approach of systemic innovation has encouraged its leaders to look beyond conventional solutions through technological and policy innovations. Bilbao is a city whose leaders had demonstrated great enterprise when they turned Bilbao's economic and physical decline into an opportunity for dramatic regeneration. Due to the delocalization of heavy steel and shipbuilding industries in the 1980s, the city had experienced record rates of unemployment and also physical degradation. The city's national, regional, provincial and municipal governments and civil stakeholders drafted the Strategic Plan for the Revitalization of Metropolitan Bilbao that was adopted in 1991. Based on eight long-term pillars that included aspects such as the development of human capital, environmental regeneration and social inclusion, the plan reflected a holistic and ambitious approach to regenerating the city. It identified Bilbao's competitive advantage as an international cultural center—the Frank Gehry-designed Guggenheim Museum established in 1997 has become an icon of Bilbao's success, with the building itself recognized as a landmark of architectural innovation (see Figure 11.7).

Other cities that have set their policy standards high are Suzhou and Copenhagen. Suzhou's provision of free compulsory education for its residents and increased healthcare benefits especially for migrant workers (Urban Redevelopment Authority, 2016), along

Figure 11.7 View of the Guggenheim Museum, an Icon of Bilbao's Transformation Into an International Cultural Center, From the Iberdrola Tower, the Tallest Building in Bilbao

Source: Nisha Sharda

with the conservation of its historic gardens and city areas such as Pingjiang Historic District in the face of pressures from urban growth, have greatly contributed to its livability. Copenhagen aims to be the world's first Carbon Neutral Capital by 2025, with its adoption of the 2009 Copenhagen Climate Plan that lists fifty interrelated initiatives that would reduce motorized transport, phase out fossil fuel energy and adopt green building standards. Placing climate consciousness as central to everything that the city initiates, the plan ambitiously sets an example for other cities to follow (City of Copenhagen Technical and Environmental Administration, 2009).

The Need for a Long-Term, Integrated, and Dynamic Planning Approach

The creation of livable cities calls for strategic planning that keeps in view the different aspects and sectors of society as an integrative dynamic whole. The nature of a livable city is necessarily complex and coordination is required between agencies to ensure the city's maintenance. Long-term planning allows city administrators to anticipate the city's challenges, and an adaptive approach to the plan keeps agencies aligned through the constant establishment of tangible realistic goals.

In 2006, New York City, under Mayor Michael Bloomberg, established the Mayor's Office of Long-Term Planning and Sustainability and in 2007, released PlaNYC, a plan that adopts a 30-year time frame and is reviewed every 4 years. Recognizing the need to integrate environmental sustainability with economic sustainability, PlaNYC demonstrated the municipality's commitment to responding to issues of population growth, climate change, economic performance and quality of life, underpinned by public engagement and civic ownership through stakeholder input from nongovernmental organizations (NGOs) and experts in various fields. PlaNYC has evolved to become "OneNYC" under Mayor Bill de Blasio in 2015 and has included economic inequity to its list of identified challenges in tackling the city's high poverty rates. Some of the plan's achievements in 2016 include having tripled solar energy installations citywide since 2014, the phasing out of the dirtiest heating oil in city buildings, as well as a record establishment of nearly 4.3 million jobs (City of New York, 2016).

Melbourne is another city that is widely regarded as one of the most livable cities in the world today, and its success could be attributed to its various urban plans and studies that strive to make the city livable. Plan Melbourne is the strategic plan setting out the government's vision for Melbourne to 2050, whereas Future Melbourne 2026 engages the citizen community in coming up with visions and goals for the city that serves as a planning resource. Architect Jan Gehl's "Places for People" study, first launched in 1994, is a complementary study to these plans. Charting urban developments over time by documenting changes in urban form and their subsequent social impact (City of Melbourne, 2016), "Places for People" has helped Melbourne set targets over 10 years for attracting people into the city center (Hayter, 2006), which was presented by *The Age* in 1978 as "empty, useless". There was a reported increase of 275% in the number of cafes (1993–2004) and an 830% increase in residents in the inner city (1992–2002) in the course of 10 years (Vaggione & Ludher, 2014).

Sound Urban Governance for the Effective Execution of Plans

As illustrated by Singapore's experience, a visionary leader, sound government agencies and organizations and programs that connect the grassroots sectors to the city administration are elements of a sound urban governance system that provide the necessary conditions for cities to achieve livability objectives. Mayor Tri Rismaharini of Surabaya is an exemplary leader who has transformed Indonesia's second largest city into an environmental award-winning city, increasing its green cover to 20%. Leading by example in picking litter off the streets, Rismaharini also implemented Indonesia's first transparent, e-procurement system in 2003, which saved approximately 20% of the city government's budget (Jasin, 2008). Sound government agencies promote a culture of transparency and integrity that enable governments to win citizens' trust and to attract business and investment. The 1974 Independent Commission Against Corruption (ICAC) was an initiative that saw government syndicates in Hong Kong eradicated in three years, along with 247 government officers charged with corruption (Kwok, 2000).

A city cannot be made livable without the community's engagement in processes of urban governance. Bogotá's Cómo Vamos (BCV) ("Bogotá, how are we doing") is a program formed in 1997 that aims to improve the quality of life in the city through the analysis of public perception and technical survey indicators (Bogotá Cómo Vamos, 2016). BCV also works in monitoring and evaluating the work of the Bogotá District Council, which keeps the city government accountable to their plans and the community informed.

Conclusion

The definition of urban livability can be wide ranging, especially when contexts differ from city to city. However, there are particular factors of livability that are commonly acknowledged across cities across the world as important and desirable. Singapore is an example of a highly dense global city that has been recognized as one of the most livable cities in the world. Its status as a developmental city-state also provides a model for cities of varying developmental stages to achieve livability.

In Singapore's case, as identified under the Singapore Liveability Framework, livability is defined by three outcomes: (1) a competitive economy, (2) a sustainable environment and (3) a high quality of life. These outcomes have been reached in 50 years, and much of Singapore's success as a livable city can be attributed to the systemic processes and mechanisms undergirding its development. This chapter has explained the principles behind how livability has been attained in the case of Singapore. At CLC, we have found that these principles are also relevant in explaining how other livable cities in the world have maintained their high standards of livability. We recognize that livability can be achieved through constantly reviewed and adjusted mechanisms and systems pertaining to institutional, strategic and cultural factors. Given the global applicability of the Singapore Liveability framework, its principles and outcomes could be incorporated into the creation of other livable cities, attuned to their particular contexts.

Acknowledgments

The authors would like to thank Ms. Serena Wong and Ms. Wong May-Ee for their contributions to the chapter.

Notes

1. Singapore was ranked 25th in the World in Mercer's 2017 Quality of Living survey, and first in the world in Mercer's inaugural city infrastructural ranking.
2. Formerly known as the Singapore branch of the Malayan Nature Society, the Nature Society (Singapore) is a nongovernmental nonprofit organization dedicated to the appreciation, conservation, study and enjoyment of the natural heritage in Singapore, Malaysia, and the surrounding region.
3. This section incorporates the insights of Pablo Vaggione and Elyssa Ludher's "What Lies Behind Successful, Liveable Cities?" (2014).

References

Bogotá Cómo Vamos. (2016). *About Bogotá Cómo Vamos*. Retrieved from www.bogotacomovamos.org/acerca/

Centre for Liveable Cities. (2016). *Urban Redevelopment: From Urban Squalor to Global City*. Singapore Urban Systems Studies Series. Singapore: Ministry of National Development.

City of Copenhagen Technical and Environmental Administration. (2009). *Copenhagen climate plan: The short version*. Retrieved from www.energycommunity.org/documents/copenhagen.pdf

City of Melbourne. (2016). *Places for people* 2015. Retrieved from www.melbourne.vic.gov.au/SiteCollectionDocuments/places-for-people-2015.pdf

City of New York. (2016). *OneNYC progress report*. Retrieved from www1.nyc.gov/html/onenyc/downloads/pdf/publications/OneNYC-2016-Progress-Report.pdf

Dhanabalan, S. (2011). Interviewed by the Centre for Liveable Cities (unpublished transcript), Singapore, December 20.

Hayter, J. A. (2006). Places for people 2004-Melbourne, Australia by Gehl architects and the city of Melbourne (EDRA/Places Awards 2006-Research). *Places, 18*(3), 28–32.

Jasin, M. (2008). *The Indonesian Experience in Addressing Corruption in Public Procurement*. Presentation at the Second Regional Seminar on Good Governance for Southeast Asian Countries, Bangkok, Thailand. Retrieved from http://www.unafei.or.jp/english/pdf/2nd_Regional_Seminar.pdf

Kwok, T. M. W. (2000). *Making Hong Kong an ideal place to do business – ICAC's fight against corruption*. Retrieved from http://www.kwokmanwai.com/Speeches/Making_HK_an_ideal_place_to_do_business.html Lee, E. K., & Tan, G. P. (2011). Interviewed by Asit Biswas and Cecilia Tortajada (unpublished transcript), February 9.

Lee, K. Y. (2009). Interviewed by Asit Biswas and Cecilia Tortajada (unpublished transcript), February 11.

Lee, K. Y. (2012). Interviewed by the Centre for Liveable Cities (unpublished transcript), August 31.

Lim, S. G. (2012). Interviewed by the Centre for Liveable Cities (unpublished transcript), November 26.

Liu, T. K. (2011). Interviewed by the Centre for Liveable Cities (unpublished transcript), June 29.

Liu, T. K. (2011). Interviewed by the Centre for Liveable Cities (unpublished transcript), September 16.

Mah, B. T. (2011). Interviewed by the Centre for Liveable Cities (unpublished transcript), November 30.

Ministry of the Environment and Water Resources. (2016). *Managing our waste: Landfill*. Retrieved from www.mewr.gov.sg/topic/landfill.

Jasin, M. (2008). *The Indonesian Experience in Addressing Corruption in Public Procurement*. Presentation at the Second Regional Seminar on Good Governance for Southeast Asian Countries, Bangkok, Thailand. Retrieved from http://www.unafei.or.jp/english/pdf/2nd_Regional_Seminar.pdf

PUB. (2016, July 11). *$200 million funding boost for Singapore's water industry over the next five years*. Retrieved from www.pub.gov.sg/news/pressreleases/s$200millionfundingboostforsingaporeswaterindustryoverthenextfiveyears

Urban Redevelopment Authority. (2016). *2014 prize laureate: City of Suzhou, Jiangsu province*. Retrieved from www.leekuanyewworldcityprize.com.sg/laureate_suzhou.htm

Vaggione, P., & Ludher, E. (2014). What lies behind successful, liveable cities. *Urban Solutions, 5*, 68–75.

Wong, A. (2011). Interviewed by the Centre for Liveable Cities (unpublished transcript), September 21.

12 Livability in Salt Lake City

Holly Lopez and Ralph Becker

In his 2012–2016 Mayoral Agenda: Livability in Salt Lake City, and the 2012 State of the City Address, Salt Lake City Mayor Ralph Becker proposed livability as a way to organize discussions and frame policy decisions and to determine the success of policies and programs:

> Livability has emerged as a unifying theme for framing our priorities. What makes one city more livable than another? It's not one factor, and a livable city means many different things to different people. We focused on making our City one of the greenest, most accessible, most inclusive and most economically viable municipalities in the country.
>
> (Becker, 2012, 5)

For the Becker administration, he concluded that achieving livability meant looking comprehensively and holistically at all aspect of Salt Lake City. Many areas were identified as key pieces to a livable city, including energy sources and use, a healthy downtown, ease of mobility, social equality, access to and protection of natural areas and recreational opportunities, urban agricultural opportunities, recycling and re-use, and diverse arts and cultural offerings. This chapter will look at key initiatives for each of these areas as defined in the Mayoral Agenda, identify the metrics used to measure these initiatives, and look at the data to see if Salt Lake City has been successful. The Becker administration created an online dashboard to measure metrics for more than 80 elements of a Livable City Agenda over time.

Creating the financial resources to devote necessary City personnel and leverage private sector participation in the Livability Agenda was a special challenge in the heart of the Great Recession. The Becker administration found a new City funding stream so that stretched public dollars for other necessary functions wouldn't be impacted. The City was co-owner of the County of the regional landfill. The landfill generated a small surplus every year, and a closure study concluded that the set-aside to cover closure costs could be reduced with a one-time financial return to the landfill owners. The Becker administration took the $300,000/year to create a segregated account for a new Sustainability Division and the City's share of the one-time payment to invest in sustainability practices, particularly recycling programs. In the next few years, glass and organics recycling were added to the City's recycling program, taking Salt Lake City from 12% of waste recycling and re-use to almost 50%.

In 2016, a new administration took office as Mayor Jackie Biskupski began her term as Salt Lake City mayor. This chapter will also list livability goals the new administration has identified, along with progress updates to the original metrics.

Vibrant Downtown and a 24-Hour Population

The downtown piece is critical for livability; any successful city has a vibrant downtown. Conventions and tourism are beneficial to a capital city, but they do not replace people living in and inhabiting the urban core. Salt Lake City lost core activation when people left for the suburbs in the suburbanization common across the United States after World War II. This community development pattern resulted in Salt Lake City's population going from almost 190,000 in 1960 to 180,000 in the 1980s without a material change in its geographic boundaries. The population of Salt Lake City remained relatively stagnant through the early 2000s.

The 1970s were the tail end of a vibrant downtown for the City. At this point, residents were no longer living in the downtown area, and people predominately came to downtown to shop in the many department stores. These had street-facing storefronts that were mixed in along Main Street and promoted small business, as hundreds of little shops were mixed in among the larger department stores giving people additional reasons to visit downtown. The creation of two malls in the downtown core, Crossroads Plaza in 1980 and the ZCMI Center in 1975, began pulling customers inside off the main streets, and the small businesses began to disappear.

The 1990s were the bottom for vibrancy in downtown Salt Lake City. The population was roughly 160,000 for the entire city, with no more than a couple thousand people living in the downtown area (ucdp.utah.edu, 2013). To prepare for hosting the Olympics in 2002, the building of the light rail/TRAX line with a complete rebuild of Main Street killed the rest of the existing businesses in the downtown core, adding to the decline of vibrancy in the urban core. After 1.5–2 years of construction, the downtown core was nearly dead.

In the early 2000s, the two remaining malls in downtown Salt Lake City closed. The Gateway, a new outdoor mall, was built west of the downtown core. This led to the remaining stores in the downtown area moving out of the core. Losing the last of the retail areas that drew in suburban populations drained the remaining life in the downtown area.

The Becker administration took office after the completion of the Gateway and campaigned on bringing life back into the City core. With Salt Lake City's large city blocks and a patchwork of retail and entertainment sites, the City was not connected, making it difficult to support a 24-hour population. The administration worked to reactivate the core. They focused on projects and policies that provide for multi-use and promoted circulation and multimodal transportation throughout the City.

The timing was right for reactivating the urban core. The Church of Jesus Christ of Latter-Day Saints (LDS) had presented a plan to replace the two malls in the downtown core by combining them into the new City Creek Center. The initial plans did little for Main Street reactivation, including a sky bridge that would keep shoppers from leaving the mall when going from one half to the other. And there was no residential use. After negotiations with the City, the LDS Church came back with a completely redesigned plan that allowed for main street activation and included a residential component.

The recession also provided an ironic opportunity for core reactivation; with low interest rates and construction costs, it was a good time to invest in property for public buildings. Land was purchased to build a new Public Safety Building, and the residents approved a property tax increase to fund the construction to replace the existing building that was falling apart and had long been inadequate to meet public safety needs. The site was selected to be in the heart of downtown and provided for an expanded civic campus which included City Hall, the Salt Lake City Public Library, and a new Leonardo museum, converting an abandoned City Library. Annually, several festivals are held on the City Hall and Library grounds such as the Arts Festival, the Living Traditions Festival, Pride Festival, and music festivals. The addition of the Public Safety Building in the space allowed for expansion of these festivals and promoted a festival atmosphere for the civic center.

The Becker administration also undertook development of a new performing arts center in a central block on Main Street that had several boarded-up buildings. Land was also purchased for a touring Broadway-style, 2,500-seat theater. In the middle of the Great Recession, the performing arts organizations were concerned about impinging on their customer base, and taxpayers questioned a large capital expenditure for an arts facility. Over 5 years, the mayor worked with the business community, arts organizations, and the City Council, finally gaining approval for bonding for the new theater and a black box theater, in 2013. It was a $125 million dollar project, with $30 million of private funding. As the project unfolded, a mid-block street (Regent Street) was added to the project, bringing a festival street with connecting walkways and new art and retail establishments. The new Eccles Theater opened in 2016 on time and budget and has contributed to a new vibrancy in the downtown core and been a catalyst for hundreds of millions of dollars in development.

Mobility

Transportation was a large component of the Becker administration's plan for revitalizing downtown. Light rail/TRAX lines had been installed to downtown from southern suburbs and to the University of Utah east of downtown in preparation for the 2002 Olympics. The Becker administration wanted to take advantage of this existing asset by expanding it to provide service to the Salt Lake City International Airport. This project involved the reconstruction of the North Temple viaduct in an attempt to make the TRAX line more open and accessible. To fund the project, the City worked to pass legislation to increase funding to Salt Lake City from the State roads fund, created a special assessment area with the Salt Lake Redevelopment Agency, and aggressively sought federal funding through the Obama administration. North Temple Street, an arterial street previously lined a series of strip malls and decaying motels and establishments, was redeveloped as part of the Airport TRAX line to beautify the corridor and develop a form-based, Transit-Oriented Development land-use ordinance to provide for a mixed-use redevelopment of the west side of Salt Lake City.

With federal grants the administration was also able to build the first streetcar line in Salt Lake City since 1945. The Sugar House Streetcar line project was selected because the City and Utah Transit Authority took advantage of an abandoned freight railroad line to create a streetcar line and greenway bike and pedestrian path. The project was funded with a $26 million federal grant. Unlike traditional streetcars, the Sugar House streetcar, completed in December of 2013, ran on a segregated corridor that was formerly a Union Pacific train corridor. The line ended at the existing TRAX light rail line on its west terminus and extended into the heart of the Sugar House neighborhood and commercial area on the east. (Slcrda.com, 2012). The greenway was a critical link in a bike and pedestrian trail connecting the Wasatch Mountains at Parleys Canyon with the Jordan River and the center of the Salt Lake Valley.

Bike infrastructure was also added to the City's transportation network. Bike lanes were added to many of the City's roadways, and bike lanes separated from traffic with parking or a cement barrier were included on key routes to increase safety for cyclists and promote cycling as a form of transportation. GREENbike, the City's bike sharing program, was launched in August of 2013. Bike sharing along with increased bike lanes have increased mobility for alternative transit in the downtown core and throughout the City.

To be successful at expanding mobility, the Becker administration focused on working on an integrated plan as to increase livability rather than picking projects. Initiatives for mobility include deliver transportation services that result in a zero carbon footprint; develop a sustainable, high-performance transportation system that supports a robust economy; and enhance quality of life by integrating transportation with the built environment (Slcgov.com, 2015).

One metric for mobility included the number of streetcars. The target was to have two streetcars: the Sugar House streetcar (discussed earlier) and a Downtown Streetcar to be funded and/or under construction by 2015. The Downtown Streetcar Study and requirements for federal funding requests was completed in 2015. The project has been put on hold by the Biskupski mayoral administration.

Another measure was late night light rail TRAX service. In 2011, there was no late night TRAX service. By 2015, TRAX was running every 15 minutes until midnight Monday through Saturday, with service ending by 9:00 p.m. on Sundays.

Bike lane miles, mixed-use trail miles, and the creation of a bike sharing program were additional measures. The number of bike lanes nearly doubled during the Becker administration, with 207 total miles by 2015. There were 29 miles of paved shared use trails, and by 2015, GREENbike was in place with a total of 25 stations (Slcgov.com, 2015).

Affordable Housing

Affordable housing is increasingly more important the more successful a city becomes. As such, the Becker administration began to turn attention to maintaining affordable housing. A study was conducted that suggested leveraging City tools with the private sector. Out of this study, the 5000 Doors Initiative was born. This initiative had a goal of providing 5,000 affordable housing units in 5 years by offering developers incentives including federal tax credits, impact fee waivers, and low-interest loans (Salt Lake Tribune, 2015). At the time Becker lost re-election, the initiative was ahead of schedule.

In addition to the 5000 Doors Initiative, the City worked to remove stigmas from neighborhoods with existing affordable housing. These were cohesive, diverse neighborhoods adjacent to downtown Salt Lake City. They worked toward of goal of providing every neighborhood the qualities and infrastructure needed to make it successful.

Additional housing goals, indicators, and success measurements include (Slcgov.com, 2015):

> Cultivate urban living by supporting renovation and creative reuse of historic structures and non-residential units for residential use. This is measured by the number of multi-family rental housing rehabilitation projects. Between 2005 and 2011 350 units had been completed. In 2014 that number rose from 350 to 437 units.

Another goal was to provide affordable housing to promote a diverse community. Metrics included the number of affordable rental units, the number of First Time Home Buyer loans, and number of Downpayment Assistance Projects. By 2011, 321 affordable units were available. The goal for 2015 was to add 30–40 units, but by 2014, the number of affordable rental units had dropped to 204. One hundred First Time Home Buyer loans were given between 2005 and 2011, with an additional 78 loans by 2014. Between 2005 and 2011, 50 Downpayment Assistance Projects were completed. In 2017, there were an additional 17 projects.

Mayor Biskupski created a Blue Ribbon Commission on Affordable Housing and is working on an affordable housing plan. On May 2, 2017, Salt Lake City Council declared an affordable housing crisis in Salt Lake City: "According to a five-year plan presented to the council, more than half of city residents already pay more than 30% of their income toward housing. Incomes have risen slowly in the city, but rents have gone up faster" (Winslow, 2017).

Access to and Protection of Natural Areas and Recreation Opportunities

Salt Lake City is nestled in the spectacular Wasatch Mountains, rising 7,000' above the floor of the Salt Lake Valley. Residents and visitors are 45 minutes away from access to world-class mountain resorts for skiing, hiking, and biking. The City also has a network of mountain biking and hiking trails less than 15 minutes away in City Creek Canyon, directly behind the State Capitol or along the foothills. This provides a connection to nature that is distinct from other cities and is a major draw for people and businesses looking to relocate here. In addition to recreation, the Wasatch Mountains watershed provides clean water to the residents of the Salt Lake Valley requiring little treatment. Protecting the natural elements surrounding the valley is critical to the success of the City and region.

The Wasatch Mountains are also intensively used and competed for by Salt Lake City residents and international visitors. There are more visitors to the Wasatch Mountains east of Salt Lake City than Yellowstone National Park. Over the decades as use and competition for the area has increased and the watershed protection has been given high priority, numerous development proposals have come forward. One proposal, SkiLink in 2011, would have sold federal land by Congressional action to a ski resort for area expansion across dispersed recreation areas and sensitive watershed. It resulted in a firestorm of protest. The response included a proposal by Mayor Becker to comprehensively settle the long-term uses of the Central Wasatch Mountains with all parties, including local government, state government, the US Forest Service, ski resorts, and the environmental community.

This planning process became known as the Mountain Accord. "The Mountain Accord was established in February 2014 to benefit current and future generations by establishing an integrated, comprehensive, landscape-scale framework for the future of the Central Wasatch Mountains," (Mountain Accord, 2016).

Identified initiatives for access to and protection of nature and recreation, metrics for success, and status include the following (Slcgov.com, 2015):

> Place a conservation easement overlay on our City watershed and agricultural lands. The conservation overlay easement was measured by the number of Wasatch watershed lands preserved in perpetuity. The starting point was 26,000 acres in 2012, and by 2015, 28,500 acres had been preserved.

Engage all parties in a specific plan to comprehensively address the Wasatch Canyons. The metric was a comprehensive plan to address environmental protection, transportation, wilderness, and other uses of the Wasatch Canyons. The starting point included the City working with a coalition of stakeholders on the planning process, and in 2015, the Mountain Accord agreement was signed. Congressional Legislation was introduced in 2016, and implementation of the Agreement is underway on transportation, trail development, resource protection, and land exchanges to consolidate private land and public land in appropriate hands.

Continue improvements along and protection of the Jordan River corridor. The indicator for this initiative was the number of riparian improvement projects completed on the Jordan River and city creeks. The corridor assessments were completed in 2011, and the 2015 goal was a complete Jordan River assessment and implementation of 15 projects on the river or city creeks. As of 2014, several projects were under construction.

Engage citizens in conservation, park development, and open space stewardship. One metric included the ration of acreage of parks, natural lands, and golf courses per 1,000 residents. In 2012, there were 10.3 acres per 1,000 residents, and by 2014, there were 17.9 acres per 1,000 residents. Another indicator was the acres of natural lands restored. In 2012, two acres had been restored. In 2015, 11 acres were slated for restoration, with an additional 63 acres planned for 2016–2017.

Urban Agricultural Opportunities

Framed in the Livability Agenda as a method for combating poverty, increasing urban agricultural opportunities and ensuring access to quality food was included in the 2015 goals. A food desert analysis was performed and two large deserts, as defined by the United States Department of Agriculture (USDA), were determined in 2011. The USDA defines a food desert as a low-income census tract where at least 20 percent of residents have income at or below 80 percent poverty levels for family size or medium family income is at or below 80 percent of the surrounding area's median income, and at least 500 residents or 33 percent of the population live more than a mile from a supermarket or large grocery store (USDA, 2017). The goal was to eliminate those deserts by 2015, and at last update, strategies had been identified for increasing access to healthy food including healthy retail incentives, mobile farm stands, and new grocery store development (Slcgov.com, 2015).

Community gardens were also expanded in the City to promote sustainability and access to healthy foods. City properties were used for community gardens as well as prime Redevelopment Agency lands for temporary gardens while the land was waiting to be redeveloped. Between 2010 and 2015, the number of community gardens in Salt Lake City increased from nine to 37, with a goal of 50 by year 2016 (Slcgov.com, 2015).

In 2016, the City identified an additional eight City-owned or managed properties ideal for community gardens (see Figure 12.1). An additional garden is currently in the

Figure 12.1 9-Line Community Garden: Salt Lake Partnered With Wasatch Community Gardens to Provide Gardening Opportunities on City-Owned Lands

Source: Holly Lopez

application process. The City partners with Wasatch Community Gardens for the application process as well as development and coordination of the gardens.

Another metric for measuring urban agricultural opportunities was the number of farmers' markets in the City. In 2007, there was only one farmers' market in Salt Lake City. By 2014, there were seven markets dispersed throughout the City. The number of food hub/local food centers in the city was looked at. Initially there was no coordination for this effort, and the target for 2015 was to have identified a size, type, and property location and development for a food hub underway. In 2015, a $350,000 culinary incubator kitchen grant was created to help fund an incubator kitchen to be located within City limits (Slgcov.com, 2015).

In 2016, the Square Kitchen incubator kitchen was awarded the grant. The kitchen will provide an affordable, licensed, inspected commercial kitchen facility to help anyone interested in starting a food business try their ideas to determine if they can be successful without spending the usual startup costs. "The whole purpose of this is for businesses to become successful," says Ana Valdermos, Square Kitchen owner (Wiren, 2016).

This year, Salt Lake City announced a grant program to promote local sustainable farming efforts. The $85,000 Local Food Microgrant program encourages farmers to apply for technology, education, tools, and equipment funds to grow more organic, local produce. These funds can be used for sustainable farming techniques including purchasing of organic seed, installing hoop houses and green houses, and continuing education (Slcgreen.com, 2017).

Social Equality

One goal to improve social equality was improved communication with ethnically linguistically diverse communities. Metrics include foster stronger relationships with non-English media, expand the City's efforts to reach specific ethnic groups, create guidelines for all City departments to use when designing outreach materials so that English-language learners may understand the materials and feel included, identify bilingual employees within City services and market their availability to the specific communities that could benefit accordingly, and develop an outreach strategy for recruiting and retaining ethnic minority board and commission members.

Another goal was addressing hate crimes through work with the Human Rights Commission and other appropriate stakeholders to create a response contingency plan in the instance a hate crime occurs. Indicators included a Hate Crimes ordinance and a Hate Crime Response Plan. A Hate Crimes Ordinance was drafted but was found by legal counsel to be in conflict with State law. A policy and procedure are in place for investigating alleged hate crimes (Peterson, 2012).

The Becker administration also accomplished a domestic partnership registry and the first nondiscrimination ordinance that would protect against housing and employment discrimination based on sexual orientation in Utah. In order to accomplish this campaign promise, the administration worked closely with the LDS Church and the State Legislature to avoid pushback from the two entities.

The nondiscrimination ordinance, which was supported by the LDS Church, established a process for tenants and employees to file complaints of discrimination based on sexual orientation. "The church supports these ordinances because they are fair and reasonable and do not do violence to the institution of marriage," says Michael Otterson, spokesman for the LDS Church. There were concerns that the State Legislature would overturn the ordinance, but ultimately, they did not. Within 5 months of Salt Lake City passing the ordinance, six additional municipalities and counties in the state were considering similar protections for their communities.

Diverse Arts and Cultural Offerings

"More than any other factor, artistic and cultural offerings define a sophisticated, cosmopolitan city. They create the physical and emotional spaces that become a "sense of place" for residents and for visitors from the region and throughout the world," (Becker, 2012, 40). As such, arts and culture offerings play a major role in revitalizing the urban core and substantially contribute to the livability of a City.

Salt Lake City underwent a study to evaluate consumer demand, market comparisons, and growth projections as well as current facilities to identify the areas for expansion, which resulted in the Cultural Facilities Master Plan. The study produced a list of 15 priority projects for a future expansion and development of theaters, performance space, and cultural centers in the City (Raymond, 2008).

Additionally, the sustainability dashboard lists the following initiatives and indices the Becker administration pursued for increasing diverse arts and culture (Slcgov.com, 2015):

- Creation of a Utah Performing Arts Center: the goal was to have the Utah Performing Arts Center constructed by 2015 and operational in 2016. The arts center was named the George S. and Dolores Dore Eccles Theatre and held its grand opening in October of 2016.
- Audience development prioritization for funding programs: the audience development metric is now included on all grant applications and evaluations and considered prior to a project or program receiving funding.
- Cultural core plan completed and adopted: the Cultural Core Plan was completed and adopted in 2016 under Mayor Biskupski. It provides recommendations for creative place-making and marketing and promotion. These include increase the visibility, quality and quantity of art; improve wayfinding; activate underutilized places and spaces; provide opportunities to advance and showcase the work of Salt Lake's creative community; encourage and support culturally inclusive programs; develop a marketing platform; develop new promotion and ticket strategies; and develop metrics to measure program effectiveness and inform improvements (Slcdocs. com, 2016).

Sustainability Efforts—Energy Use

In a 2015 presentation, Mayor Becker equated sustainability with livability. The agenda became Sustainable Salt Lake: Ensuring the Future of Livability of Our Community. In addition to the goals under the Livability Agenda, new focus areas were added: air quality and climate change, waste reduction, and energy.

At times, Salt Lake City faces some of the worst air quality in the US. In winter months, the inversion caused by the mountains that bring so much beauty and quality of life to the area traps pollution. Policies and programs that help air pollution and air quality are the same things that make cities be a better place to live. Transportation and buildings make up two thirds to three quarters of our air pollution problems. By promoting circulation, walkability and alternative modes of transportation, Salt Lake City is working to reduce air pollution. The City is also working to reduce its carbon footprint and has focused on buildings, fleet, and regulations to accomplish this.

"We should be modeling best behavior, let's make net zero the goal," Ralph Becker said in reference to building the new Public Safety Building (Becker, 2017). When the City looked to relocate the Public Safety Building to the Civic Campus, they focused on making the building net zero, and it became the first net zero Public Safety Building in the US. To accomplish this, the city cut energy needs throughout the building and developed on- and off-site renewables to offset the energy use they could not cut. The City was able to use incentives and achieve the net zero status at no additional cost.

To encourage the private sector to also look to energy reductions for their buildings, the City used a mix of incentives and regulations. For example, if a proposed building would be LEED certified, the developer would move to the front of the line in the permitting process, saving valuable time. Goldman Sachs built a new building at 111 S. Main Street. The requirement was a LEED Silver building; however, they finished with a LEED Gold building when they realized they could do additional projects at minimal cost.

Waste was also addressed under the sustainability goals, with a goal of 50% waste reduction by 2015 and zero waste by 2040. At that point, Salt Lake City was recycling only 12% of the waste stream. A landfill analysis was done, and it was determined that the current landfill did not need to be capped as soon as expected. With the $7 million in savings due to not needing to locate a new site, or needing to cap the existing facility, Salt Lake City was able to use the money to expand the recycling program. This, in turn, could push the need for a new facility even further into the future. Salt Lake was able to add glass as an opt-in recycling service, where residents paid a small fee for a monthly pick up. The City also introduced the "pay as you throw" waste containers, where the 60-gallon garbage can is now 30% higher than the 40-gallon can. This increased the percentage of the waste stream being diverted from 12% to 20%. Sorting of organic brown waste for composting reuse became a mandatory program, and pushed diversion from 20% to 40% of the waste stream.

To further sustainability goals, Salt Lake City created the Sustainability Division. One of the first tasks of the new division was a complete review of all city codes to identify and remove barriers that inhibit sustainable practices. This review identified regulations that prohibited solar and wind power generation, prohibited green houses and hoop houses, prohibited beekeeping, did not allow residents to keep chickens, and forbade gardening in park strips. These codes were all revised to allow for these practices when certain requirements are met.

In 2016, the Biskupski administration elevated the Sustainability Division from the Public Services Department to its own department, with a primary goal of improving air quality. Mayor Biskupski said, "This elevation from a division to a department puts sustainability on equal footing—both real and perceived—with every other function of city government," (McKellar, 2016).

Sustainability to Livability to Sustainability

In 2015, the focus of sustainability shifted to livability, with the definition of both being closely tied. The current focus has shifted back to sustainability; however, many of the key areas and metrics identified under the Livability Agenda continue to frame the discussion for how Salt Lake City moves forward, and how it continues to measure success.

References

Becker, R. (2012).*Mayoral agenda: Livability in Salt Lake City*. Salt Lake City: Salt Lake City Corporation. Retrieved May 9, 2017, from www.slcdocs.com/mayor/livability.pdf

McKellar, K. (2016). Biskupski commits to cleaner, safer Salt Lake in first State of the City address. *Deseret News*. Retrieved May 30, 2017, from www.deseretnews.com/article/865646269/Biskupski-commits-to-cleaner-safer-Salt-Lake-in-first-State-of-the-City-address.html

Mountain Accord. (2016). *Mountain accord: The facts*. Retrieved June 2, 2017, from http://mountainaccord.com/

Peterson, E. (2012). SLC plan bias ordinance. *Salt Lake City Weekly*. Retrieved May 15, 2017, from www.cityweekly.net/utah/slc-plans-bias-ordinance/Content?oid=2284371

Raymond, A. (2008). Study evaluates cultural facilities. *Deseret News*. Retrieved May 15, 2017, from www.deseretnews.com/article/705270964/Study-evaluates-cultural-facilities.html?pg=all

Salt Lake Tribune. (2015). *Becker unveils plan to build 5,000 units of affordable housing in Salt Lake City*. Retrieved May 15, 2017, from www.sltrib.com/news/2117119-155/becker-unveils-plan-to-build-5000

Slcdocs.com. (2016). *Cultural core SLC action plan*. Retrieved May 15, 2017, from www.slcdocs.com/culcore/CCAPF.pdf

Slcgov.com. (2015). *Sustainable city dashboard*. Retrieved May 9, 2017, from http://dotnet0.slcgov.com/PublicServices/Sustainability/Topic/Metric/a2533d25-184a-4375-8dfa-ce9b62311249/200096#sthash.sXpKucZC.dpbs

SLCgreen.com. (2017). *Local food microgrant fund*. Retrieved May 28, 2017, from www.slcgreen.com/local-food-microgrant-fund

Slcrda.com. (2012). *Bringing back the streetcar*. Retrieved May 19, 2017, from www.slcrda.com/streetcar.htm

ucdp.utah.edu. (2013). *Salt Lake City basic population & household demographic trends, 1990–2010*. Retrieved May 19, 2017, from http://ucdp.utah.edu/reports/Place/Demographic_Trends/Demographics_Trends_Salt_Lake_City_city_67000.pdf

usda.gov. (2017). *Food desert locator*. Retrieved July 1, 2017, from www.fns.usda.gov/tags/food-desert-locator

Winslow, B. (2017). *Affordable housing 'crisis' declared in Salt Lake City*. Retrieved May 23, 2017, from http://fox13now.com/2017/05/02/affordable-housing-crisis-declared-in-salt-lake-city/

Wiren, P. (2016). Square Kitchen. *Utah Stories*. Retrieved May 28, 2017, from http://utahstories.com/2016/09/square-kitchen/

13 Livability and Access to Urban Goods in Melbourne

Heather MacDonald

Livability is difficult to reject as a planning goal—who would go on record as arguing for the unlivable city? The concept is both inclusive and vague; it is measured (and used) in widely varying and often subjective ways. Gough (2015) argues for the following definition of the concept:

> Community livability is constructed by the sum of the physical and social characteristics experienced in places—including the natural environment and a walkable and mixed-use built environment, economic potential near diverse housing options, and access to a broad range of services, facilities, and amenities—that add up to a community's quality of life.
>
> (Gough, 2015, 147)

Livability can be distinguished from the closely related concept of sustainability by its focus on the here and now, in contrast to sustainability's focus on future generations and global contexts (Ruth & Franklin, 2013). The tension between livability indicators as measures of what we do for present generations in specific places, and sustainability indicators that evaluate what we do for future as well as current generations, not just in particular places but also globally, underpins many intense debates about urban policy and planning. Thus, the concept of livability can be described as "laced with power" (Holden & Scerri, 2013, 445). It can be used to justify almost any policy agenda: "The contest over its meaning reveals much about the various publics who have competed for the power to define the quality of urban life" (Ley, 1996, 34).

Melbourne was named the Economist Intelligence Unit's (EIU) "most livable city" in 2016 for the sixth year in a row; it ranked high in the 2016 Monocle Quality of Life Survey, at six, but lower in the 2017 Mercer Quality of Living ranking, at 16. The city offers an interesting lens through which we can understand alternative ways in which livability indices can be constructed and how they might inform urban policy and planning. This chapter examines the evolution of livability indicators in Melbourne. Melbourne's lead position in international livability ranking rests on a definition of livability that speaks to corporate competitiveness—Melbourne as a "brand" that positions it on the global economic stage, competing for affluent tourists, skilled creative labor, investment capital, and corporate headquarters. But this is a limited definition of livability. Developed in 2006, Community Indicators Victoria (CIV) aims to capture how livability varies across the metropolitan area, how it varies for people of different socioeconomic or demographic positions, and to explore how more disaggregated measures of the concept might better inform public policy. The CIV includes 70 indicators that have remained consistent since its establishment in 2007, with an additional ten indicators under development. But the CIV measures are limited because they lack spatial specificity and cannot easily be related across categories of concern. A new generation of spatially enabled indicators (accompanied by analytic tools) aims to overcome these limitations.

The chapter explores how livability is operationalized in each of these approaches—what counts as livability, and how are these component parts measured? How does each approach deal with the complexities of geographic difference, socioeconomic and demographic diversity, and the problem of integrating measures to capture holistic outcomes? The final section examines how these alternative approaches have shaped urban policy and planning in metropolitan Melbourne, and how they are likely to do so in the future. The remainder of this introduction provides a brief history of the evolution of livability in Melbourne.

A Brief History of Livable Melbourne

Melbourne, incorporated in 1837, grew from a town to a large city during the gold rush of the 1850s, eclipsing Sydney in size by 1865 (temporarily). Melbourne soon became the financial center of the country, with the establishment of the first stock exchange. The city's first rail line opened in 1854 and continued infrastructure investment ensured its growth as a center for agricultural exports, once the gold rush had subsided. Rail lines also contributed to booming land prices in subsequent decades, with Melbourne ranked as the wealthiest city in the world during the 1880s, with a population approaching half a million (May, 2005). Growth stagnated after the financial crash of 1891, although Melbourne's role as national capital (from 1901 to 1927) resulted in strong public sector employment. Post Second World War immigration diversified Melbourne's population and its economy, and agricultural commodity prices and infrastructure investment stimulated a new era of prosperity.

Melbourne's twentieth century planning history demonstrates a long-standing concern with livability. The city's first metropolitan strategic plan, prepared in 1929 (but never implemented), focused on traffic congestion and the need to protect property values by regulating land use mix, and also identified an open space and recreational network. The 1954 Melbourne Metropolitan Planning Scheme built on this recognition:

> The people of Melbourne spend many of their leisure hours in the open air. The reservation of space sufficient to permit all sections of the community, whatever their age and inclination, to indulge in such healthy pastimes is therefore a very important function of a planning scheme.
> (Melbourne Metropolitan Board of Works, 1954, 77)

The plan proposed concentrating growth in corridors separated by green wedges, to ensure all neighborhoods had easy access to open space. It also designated district centers to decentralize some services, retail and employment from the central city. The growth corridors, green wedges, and district centers continued to shape metropolitan development, aided by an urban growth boundary introduced in the 1971 metropolitan plan. That plan reflected a growing concern with environmental quality, and the urban growth boundary (UGB) was an important conservation tool. In 2003, the UGB shifted from being a statutorily enforced policy to a legislatively enforced one, with the Planning and Environment (Green Wedge Protection) Act (Buxton & Taylor, 2011). Melbourne's growth boundary has been blamed for creating a rigidly regulated development environment that exacerbated housing affordability problems, and imposed a vision of "the compact city" that many residents believed undermined livability (Cox, 2005; Buxton & Taylor, 2011).

Melbourne has added significantly more high-density housing in recent years and rental affordability has benefited, with an average income renter household paying 24%

of their income in rent (compared with 28% in Sydney) (SGS Economics and Planning, 2015). Low-income households, however, face a severe affordability problem, although the poorest households are somewhat protected from the consequences of high housing prices by the Commonwealth Rental Assistance subsidy, which covers part of the cost of private rental housing for all eligible very low-income households. Public and social housing (the latter provided by nonprofit Community Housing Associations) makes up only a small proportion of the housing stock (approximately 5.5% in Victoria). But housing affordability problems extend beyond the lower 40% of the income distribution when we consider homeownership. Melbourne's median house price in late 2016 was AU$740,000, but there is a significant gap between median prices in inner suburbs (AU$1,336,500) compared with the suburban fringe (AU$572,000). Although homeownership rates in the Greater Melbourne region have remained steady at 69.5% in 2011, compared with 70% in 2001, the proportion of households with a mortgage has increased sharply from 28.1% to 36.8%. Although Melbourne's public transport network serves the inner suburbs effectively, Scheurer et al. (2005) argue that declining investment in transit has reduced connectivity (and thus livability) in much of suburban Melbourne.

A recent comparison of livability in Melbourne and Vancouver (Holden & Scerri, 2013) concluded that despite the former's efforts to increase density and reduce sprawl, Vancouver has achieved far more sustainable outcomes, offering better livability prospects for future generations. Holden and Scerri argue that local democratic engagement in planning issues is far stronger in Vancouver, where metropolitan government works with local governments to ensure a regional approach to sustainability (and thus a commitment to livability for future generations). For Melbourne, the state of Victoria plays the dominant role in metropolitan planning (as is typical in Australia). The state has taken an actively deregulatory approach to development, in a majority of cases overruling local governments' rejections of applications for higher density developments (Woodcock et al., 2011).

Melbourne overshadows Vancouver however because it "offers an exciting notion of what living in the city is for and a sociability in public life that benefits from an intact equity argument at the national scale" (Holden & Scerri, 2013, 444). For those who are less well off, Holden and Scerri (2013) conclude that Melbourne offers better prospects for livability, with lower rates of homelessness, better access to healthcare, education, public safety, and a living minimum wage. Public attitudes toward social equity ensure that minimum standards of livability are bipartisan policies in Australia more generally.

But despite Melbourne's comparatively high levels of social equity, the metropolitan area is spatially divided. An analysis of the spatial location of areas of advantage and disadvantage throughout the metropolitan area and its hinterland is presented in Figure 13.1.

The map shows the distribution of postal codes along a continuum from the most disadvantaged to the most advantaged locations. The Index of Relative Socio-Economic Advantage and Disadvantage (IRSAD) is constructed by the Australian Bureau of Statistics, based on Census of Population and Housing data. The IRSAD score is the weighted sum of 25 variables, with the weights assigned based on a Principle Component Analysis. Variables include household income, level of educational achievement, proportions of people who are unemployed or who have a disability, and many other dimensions of advantage and disadvantage (Pink, 2011). IRSAD scores are used to rank places throughout Australia, and that ranking is translated into quintile bands in Figure 13.1. Places ranked "most disadvantaged" are more likely to have high proportions of disadvantaged residents but are not necessarily homogenously disadvantaged.

In contrast to many US cities, Melbourne is notable for the absence of anything suggesting a "donut": inner-city neighborhoods are as likely to accommodate high proportions of

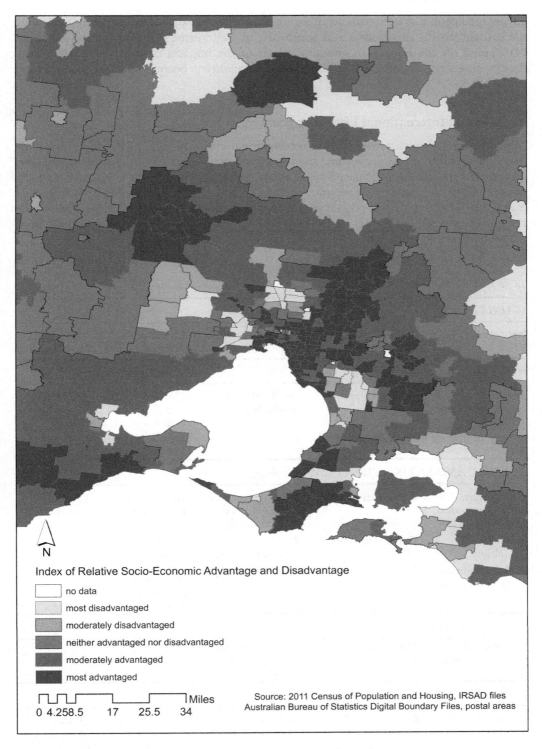

Figure 13.1 Index of Relative Socio-Economic Advantage and Disadvantage

advantaged people as suburban neighborhoods are. But pockets of suburban disadvantage are evident, to the north-west and south-east of Melbourne's central business district. "Dropping off the Edge," an annual analysis of the impacts of consistent community disadvantage, concluded in 2015 that spatial inequality is becoming entrenched (Vinson et al., 2015).

Melbourne's International Livability Rankings

Melbourne rates consistently high in international city rankings, in the top ten for the Monocle Quality of Life Survey and the top 20 for the Mercer Quality of Living ranking. As mentioned earlier, for the past 6 years, it has ranked first in one of the most high-profile quality of life rankings, the Economic Intelligence Unit (EIU). But what exactly does that mean, and what implications do these rankings have for urban policy? A closer look at the categories reflected in the EIU index (see Table 13.1) raises several questions about what livability means in this context.

Table 13.1 Components of the Economist Intelligence Unit City Ranking

STABILITY (25% weighting)				
Petty crime	Violent crime	Threat of terrorism	Threat of military conflict	Threat of civil unrest/conflict
HEALTHCARE (20% weighting)				
Availability of private healthcare	Quality of private healthcare	Availability of public healthcare	Quality of public healthcare	Availability of over-the-counter drugs
General healthcare indicators (World Bank)				
CULTURE AND ENVIRONMENT (25% weighting)				
Temperature rating (from local weather records)	Climate discomfort	Level of corruption (Transparency International)	Social/religious restrictions	Level of censorship
Sporting availability (EIU rating based on three indicators)	Cultural availability (EIU rating based on four indicators)	Food and drink (EIU rating based on four indicators)	Consumer goods and services (EIU rating of product availability)	
EDUCATION (10% weighting)				
Availability of private education	Quality of private education	Public education indicators (World Bank)		
INFRASTRUCTURE (20% weighting)				
Quality of road network	Quality of public transport	Quality of international links	Availability of good quality housing	Quality of energy provision
Quality of water provision	Quality of telecommunications			

Source: Components of the EIU City Ranking

Clearly, the majority of the components of the index are subjective, in the sense that they are rated by "the judgement of in-house expert country analysts and a field correspondent based in each city" (EIU, 2016, 8). A few components are based on external sources. Corruption is measured on the basis of an indicator of perceptions of corruption developed by Transparency International (Transparency International, 2015); the methodology is carefully documented, using at least three sources of valid data for each (interestingly, Australia was one of a small group of countries registering a significant increase in perceptions of corruption between 2012 and 2015). The World Bank is clearly a reputable source of comparable statistics on healthcare and education.

But many of the indicators are likely to be quite subjective, and comparability across cities is an issue. For example, in 2016, Sydney's EIU ranking dropped to 11, largely on the basis of an "increased threat of terrorism." Although that city had experienced two separate violent events (in each case, the work of an individual acting alone) in the previous two years, little about its level of public security, demographic profile, or overall levels of violence is significantly different to Melbourne's profile. It is unclear why Sydney should be judged significantly more vulnerable to terrorism than Melbourne, compared with its ranking in 2015.

Weightings of categories are another area where the subjective judgment of the indicator authors can make a substantial difference to ranking—what if Education in the EIU were ranked equivalently to Healthcare (at 20%), whereas infrastructure was scaled back to 10%? Relatively arbitrary decisions may have significant impacts on a city's perceived performance. One defensible source of subjective judgments would be actual residents, but whereas the EIU uses (at best) small groups of expatriate residents to evaluate several dimensions of quality of life, no international rankings rely on judgments about livability from the people with the most insight into it. The expatriates who ranked Melbourne's livability focused on a small number of affluent inner-city neighborhoods, rather than the typical suburbs where most residents live and work (City of Melbourne, 2011).

A second significant set of issues with these measures is whether city governments have any control over the elements that make up judgments about livability (Woolcock, 2009). Indicators such as political stability, or the threat of war, are clearly determined at the national rather than the city scale. For other groups of measures, scores may reflect what the national government does rather than what city government does: cities in countries with a functioning national public healthcare system (such as Australia or Canada) may be systematically advantaged over countries that do not (such as the US). Education too may be a national or a strictly local responsibility, with widely varying implications for rankings. National policies may have a far more significant effect on some elements than city governments ever could—policies such as gun control, and broader social policy approaches to poverty and inequality, may be much more important factors underpinning scores on crime and political stability than city policing resources or local governance.

The extent to which a high score on a particular indicator (e.g., healthcare) results in an outcome we would see as indicating quality of life (e.g., a community's improved health and well-being) is also questionable. Although Melbourne scores a perfect 100 on healthcare in the EIU rankings (and does indeed have an excellent healthcare system, based in part on a working national health scheme), some communities and cohorts of residents face significant health and well-being challenges, including some very high rates of obesity-related diseases (Giles-Corti et al., 2014). Similarly, although indicators might show suitable housing is available, recent analyses of homeownership trends suggest a very limited supply of affordable rental housing sufficient for younger households (Wilkins, 2016). For many indicators, the causal link to outcomes that we would all agree are necessary to a decent quality of life is quite thin. A related point is the lack of any reflection of the ranges of indicator scores. Are petty crime rates equivalent in all parts of the city, or are they sharply higher in a few locations? Is public transport easily available on average, but very scarce in lower density suburbs? Is an equivalent level of recreation activities available to people of all ages, incomes, and levels of physical ability?

Most international city livability rankings have a clear purpose: to offer corporations a way to benchmark remuneration to employees posted in particular locations (Woolcock, 2009). The measures are well designed for these purposes, within the bounds of what is possible. But this brief review highlights the gaps in what are popularly thought of as the major livability indicators:

- the data they summarize are often subjective and might not be comparable;
- many datapoints are not particularly relevant to anything cities can do;
- the causal link with livability outcomes is unclear;
- they are not disaggregated (by space, age group, income level, or other relevant differentiator).

As the City of Melbourne argues in a recent evaluation of its performance on international rankings, "[t]here are some good reputation management reasons why City of Melbourne notes the outcomes of liveability studies as they are released" but that "[a]nalysts and policy makers should avoid the temptation to treat them all as progress indicators or public policy tools" (City of Melbourne, 2011). The following section of the chapter explores an alternative approach to livability indicators, aimed not at comparing cities but at improving urban policy and planning.

Creating Livability Indicators to Improve Planning

An alternative approach is represented in the development of increasingly sophisticated indicators and spatial analysis tools in the State of Victoria. They are intended to provide the evidence needed to design and evaluate policies based on broader concepts of well-being, beyond the narrowly defined economic measures that underpin traditional policy development processes (Wiseman et al., 2006). Two indicator development projects are examined in detail in this section: Community Indicators Victoria, and the Spatial Indicators project based at the University of Melbourne. Previous to the establishment of these indicator portals, indicators were, of course, widely used in evidence-based planning and urban policy, but their use was uneven: larger local governments had the resources to maintain and update databases, but smaller governments did not. Typical indicators were based on widely available secondary data (such as the Census) and administrative records (such as road safety statistics), but even larger local governments did not always have the resources to update indicators frequently or to develop new indicators that would reflect new sorts of policy concerns.

Community Indicators Victoria was initiated to resolve this problem, by providing a consistent and evenly applicable data infrastructure, alongside some new specialized survey data. The first round of Community Indicators Victoria (CIV) was released in 2007. The 70 current indicators are organized around five policy domains:

- Healthy, safe, inclusive communities: this domain addresses policy issues related to personal health and well-being, community connectedness, early childhood development, personal and community safety, lifelong learning, and service availability.

- Dynamic, resilient local economies: policy issues included here are economic activity and employment, income and wealth, and work-life balance.
- Sustainable built and natural environments: access to open space, housing affordability, transport accessibility, sustainable energy use, air and water quality, biodiversity, and waste management make up the policy areas in this domain.
- Culturally rich and vibrant communities: policy areas in this domain include participation in arts and cultural activities, in recreational and leisure activities, and cultural diversity.
- Democratic and engaged communities: citizen engagement.

(Wiseman et al., 2006)

The indicators are available at the Local Government Area (LGA; the State of Victoria has 79, with 31 in metropolitan Melbourne). The indicators are based on a wide variety of data sources—some of these are fairly standard Census and service agency measures, but two crucial sources are the Victorian Public Health Survey (VPHS; which includes questions on social networks, social cohesion, and similar topics), and the Local Government Community Satisfaction Survey (LGCSS), which requires an opt-in from local councils (67 participated in 2014). Both are random digit dialed telephone surveys; the VPHS samples 450 people in each LGA, for a total sample size of around 35,000, whereas the LGCSS sampled 26,800 people (state-wide) most recently. The questions covered in these two surveys are far more directly related to measuring residents' quality of life than Census data and similar sources and begin to get at the causal links between policies and outcomes.

The CIV project provides qualitative subjective data based on the opinions of residents, rather than judgments by a small group of (unrepresentative) individuals. They use common sources of data that are comparable across the communities evaluated. In most cases, responses are disaggregated by major sub-populations (age and gender). But although they provide a broad-brush spatial disaggregation by local government, the CIV cannot provide spatially fine-grained data necessary for specific planning decisions. The CIV project has been a useful way to test out how indicators may be used for policy evaluation and improvement. They are also intended to empower residents to identify issues and track outcomes. They are available on a website that provides instruction on how to use and interpret the indicators and includes links to research based on the indicators (Community Indicators Victoria, n.d.).

A recent evaluation of the Victorian experience with indicators explored a number of the methodological and conceptual challenges with using livability indicators to inform policy (Lowe et al., 2015). The study concludes that, to be most relevant to policy, livability indicators need to focus on "*what* the problem is, and *why* the problem exists?" (Lowe et al., 2015, 138). One limitation identified with the CIV experience is the broad spatial scale of the data—many livability problems should be identified, and solved, at the neighborhood or even precinct scale. The effects of specific local improvements are unlikely to be evident in LGA-level data, with the result that policy outcomes are difficult to track, particularly for changes related to the built environment.

The other significant issue raised was the potential for indicators to inform holistic approaches, integrating several policy areas. Rather than formulating and implementing policy in silos, a focus on livability entailed a systems approach, for which indicators could be helpful tools to the extent that they were able to make links explicit (Lowe et al., 2015). For example, evaluating the role of the built environment in improving health would be best served by indicators linking data on cycle path development, walkability improvements, and rates of obesity.

Spatially Enabled Indicators

The need for geographically disaggregated measures of progress on complex, linked concepts of livability has driven a new round of indicator development, based on much more detailed spatial data at the property parcel and street level. The federally funded AURIN (Australian Urban Research Infrastructure Network) was developed between 2010 and 2015, with Demonstration data hubs launched in 2015. The initiative establishes a repository of spatial data available to researchers, with a metadata structure that manages disparate data sources, connecting them, cataloging them so they are easy to find, and ensuring that data are usable in many different sorts of applications (Kethers & Treloar, 2013).

A central aim of the Spatial Data Access project (a collaboration between University of Melbourne and several public agencies) is to develop indicators that can be linked spatially to reflect the holistic nature of real world policy problems. If livable communities are defined as those that are healthy, safe, and walkable, we need multidimensional indicators to capture that complex concept. The project aims to provide "an evidence base to understand the use of space, enabling analysis of connections and change based scenarios" (Rajabifard & Eagleson, 2013, 2). Overcoming the fragmentation of spatial information collected by different agencies, over different time periods, and for different purposes, is not simple. There are institutional, economic, and sometimes also political barriers to doing this. Information is, fundamentally, socially constructed—we measure outcomes with specific purposes in mind, and, as with the CIV data discussed earlier, the new generation of spatial data sits within a similarly fragmented policy context that means it is not necessarily suited to capturing livability outcomes. Connecting different sorts of data spatially poses technical challenges, but there are also conceptual challenges to be addressed.

First, spatially disaggregated information raises important ethical issues. This is particularly evident with data about health outcomes: although it would be very useful to be able to evaluate the link between proximity to parks or community centers and the incidence of mental health issues, obesity, or diabetes, identifying health outcomes at a fine-grained scale is unacceptable from an individual privacy perspective. Consequently, health data are not available at scales more detailed than Statistical Local Areas (and, in some cases, at the Local Government Area), and the causal links between investments in the built environment (such as new cycle ways) and the incidence of health problems can be traced only at an aggregated scale that makes policy implications very approximate.

Second, detailed comparable spatial data may not be available, particularly for the very local-level dimensions of urban form that may be most relevant to planning for greater livability. Geographic data availability is likely to vary on the basis of not just on the size and sophistication of a local government's planning office, but also on the relative priority assigned to particular issues. For instance, Badland et al. (2013) found that information on sidewalks was unevenly available through the North West Melbourne region, limiting planners' ability to evaluate walkability at a fine-grained scale, across the region.

Finally, information may not be collected in formats that are relevant to some aspects of livability. For instance, although most national censuses collect information about employment, it is usually not gathered in a form that is useful for assessing the employment options available to people in particular places. Estimating the job-shed for a community entails understanding the sorts of jobs for which residents are likely to be qualified, and the sorts of commuting trips those jobs are likely to justify (a part-time, low-paid food service job would have a much narrower commute-shed than a full-time, well-paid, professional job). Without a clear understanding of the mix of skills and experience of local residents, combined with an understanding of the commuting options available, it is challenging to use census and other workplace-based data to evaluate how economic development policy might, for instance, have altered an outcome that is quite central to concepts of quality of life: reasonable access to appropriate employment. In principle, this could be solved by providing greater ability to cross tabulate existing data, but in practice, the Australian Census (like many others) does not allow users to cross tabulate "place of work" and "place of residence" data, and the expense of special Census runs makes these sorts of analyses infeasible for small-scale projects.

Despite these challenges, the Spatial Data Access project developed a demonstration of how a set of integrated indicators and tools could offer a multidimensional perspective on real-world planning problems. Focusing on the need to improve livability in a gray-field industrial district in North West Melbourne, researchers analyzed multiple datasets to provide the evidence to inform a local livability strategy plan, aimed at achieving Melbourne's metropolitan-wide goal of a 20-minute city (one in which people are able to meet their daily needs for entertainment, food, services, and employment, within a 20-minute trip radius). The analysis brought together a variety of spatial analytic tools that estimated walkability (using agent-based modeling), the availability of sites that can be redeveloped, and the planning regulations associated with those sites. Property parcels with the potential to be redeveloped (based on an index that calculates the ratio of improved value to land value), and those within an 800 m (approximately half a mile) walking catchment of public transit, retail, and services were identified as highest priority for residential development. Local regulations were examined to determine how many of these sites could be redeveloped at densities high enough to offer relative affordability (Bishop et al., 2013, 92).

Other tools identified industrial clusters and the residential locations of workers employed in those clusters to provide insight into the sorts of employment strategies that would be most effective in improving livability. The study found that adding more local jobs may exacerbate traffic and parking problems without doing much to provide additional employment opportunities to local residents (Bishop et al., 2013, 89). Instead, improving residents' ability to commute to jobs elsewhere in the metro area might be more important for improving livability.

It is too soon to say how the new generation of spatially enabled indicators will inform actual strategic planning efforts in Melbourne. However, the project clearly has strong potential to improve decision support across several dimensions of livability. It grapples with some of the key challenges that limit the practical utility of livability indicators to inform and improve city planning. The project's key contributions are threefold:

- It integrates different sorts of data to enable a more holistic understanding of problems and potential solutions, which might stretch across several policy areas.
- It provides a spatially, socioeconomically, and demographically disaggregated way to analyze livability outcomes, at a scale appropriate to evaluate specific interventions.
- It enables simulations of proposed interventions, to understand what outcomes are likely.

One additional (potential) contribution may be to empower residents to use spatial analytic tools both to generate new data and to analyze existing data in new ways, to identify different sorts of problems than planners or policy makers might. Reframing problems in new terms has the potential to shift policy debates in new directions, and may alter Melbourne's historically top-down approach to not just metropolitan but also local-level planning (Woodcock et al., 2011).

Conclusions

The evolving experience with livability indicators in Melbourne highlights the lesson that what we measure is what we pay attention to. Although Melbourne's reputation as a business or tourist destination benefits from its consistently high rankings in the EIU and similar international indicators, the real business of understanding how livability plays out on the ground is clearly far more complex (as the City and State governments recognize). The first generation of indicators (CIV) significantly expanded the notion of livability and the ability of State policy makers to test out the association between specific policy issues, and broad-brush livability outcomes at the local government level. The second generation of indicators has gone far beyond this, enabling (given adequate data) much more spatially refined measures of livability across multiple dimensions. The potential of these fine-grained indicators to inform local planning is strong; perhaps even more promising is the potential for publicly accessible data and analytic tools to reshape the public debate around livability. This potential illustrates the sense in which the concept of livability is indeed explicitly "laced with power" (Holden & Scerri, 2013, 445). Livability is mismeasured when it is defined as how competitive a city is in the market for corporate headquarters and affluent tourists: evaluating livability outcomes should be the responsibility of local residents, rather than a small group of global elites, or even well-intentioned state and local government planners.

References

Badland, H., White, M., & MacAulay, G. (2013). Using agent-based modelling to inform neighbourhood walkability. In A. Rajabifard & S. Eagleson (Eds.), *Spatial data access and integration to support liveability: A case study in North and West Melbourne* (pp. 23–38). Melbourne, VIC: Centre for Spatial Data Infrastructures and Land Administration, The University of Melbourne.

Bishop, I., Eagleson, S., & Rajabifard, A. (2013). Demonstration projects applied: A case study in Footscray. In A. Rajabifard & S. Eagleson (Eds.), *Spatial data access and integration to support liveability: A case study in North and West Melbourne* (pp. 83–99). Melbourne, VIC: Centre for Spatial Data Infrastructures and Land Administration, The University of Melbourne.

Buxton, M., & Taylor, E. (2011). Urban land supply, governance and the pricing of land. *Urban Policy and Research*, 29(1), 5–22.

City of Melbourne. (2011). *International city comparisons*. Melbourne City Research, Retrieved December 9, 2016, from www.melbourne.vic.gov.au/SiteCollectionDocuments/international-city-comparisons.pdf

Community Indicators Victoria. (n.d.). Retrieved May 18, 2017, from www.communityindicators.net.au/

Cox, W. (2005). Destroying opportunity with 'smart growth'. *People and Place*, 13(4), 55–59.

Economist Intelligence Unit. (2016). *A summary of the liveability ranking and overview* (August). Retrieved December 8, 2017, from http://pages.eiu.com/rs/783-XMC-194/images/Liveability_August2016.pdf

Giles-Corti, B., Badland, H. M., Mavoa, S., Turrell, G., Bull, F., Boruff, B., Pettit, C., Bauman, A. E., Hooper, P., Villanueva, K., & Astell-Burt, T. (2014). Reconnecting urban planning with health: A protocol for the development and validation of national liveability indicators associated with noncommunicable disease risk behaviours and health outcomes. *Public Health Research and Practice*, 25(1), 1–5.

Gough, M. Z. (2015). Reconciling livability and sustainability: Conceptual and practical implications for planning. *Journal of Planning Education and Research*, 35(2), 145–160.

Holden, M., & Scerri, A. (2013). More than this: Liveable Melbourne meets liveable Vancouver. *Cities*, 31, 444–453.

Kethers, S., & Treloar, A. (2013). Perspective 2: Australian National Data Service (ANDS). In A. Rajabifard & S. Eagleson (Eds.), *Spatial data access and integration to support liveability: A case study in North and West Melbourne* (pp. 17–18). Melbourne, VIC: Centre for Spatial Data Infrastructures and Land Administration, The University of Melbourne.

Ley, D. (1996). Urban liveability in context. *Urban Geography*, *11*(1), 31–35.

Lowe, M., Whitzman, C., Badland, H., Davern, M., Aye, L., Hes, D., Butterworth, I., & Giles-Corti, B. (2015). Planning healthy, liveable and sustainable cities: How can indicators inform policy? *Urban Policy and Research*, *33*(2), 131–144.

May, A. (2005). Demography. *Encyclopedia of Melbourne*. Retrieved December 9, 2016, from www.emelbourne.net.au/about.html

Melbourne and Metropolitan Board of Works. (1954). *Melbourne metropolitan planning scheme 1954*. Retrieved December 9, 2016, from www.dtpli.vic.gov.au/planning/plans-and-policies/planning-for-melbourne/melbournes-strategic-planning-history/melbourne-metropolitan-planning-scheme-1954

Pink, B. (2011). *Socio-Economic Indexes for Areas (SEIFA): Technical paper*. Australian Bureau of Statistics. ABS Catalogue no. 2033.0.55.001.

Rajabifard, A., & Eagleson, S. (2013). Spatial enablement from an international context: A vision for the North and West Melbourne Corridor. In A. Rajabifard & S. Eagleson (Eds.), *Spatial data access and integration to support liveability: A case study in North and West Melbourne* (pp. 1–10). Melbourne, VIC: Centre for Spatial Data Infrastructures and Land Administration, The University of Melbourne.

Ruth, M., & Franklin, R. S. (2013). Livability for all? Conceptual limits and practical implications. *Applied Geography*, *49*, 18–23.

Scheurer, J., Kenworthy, J. R., & Newman, P. W. (2005). *Most liveable and best connected?: The economic benefits of investing in public transport in Melbourne: A policy document for the metropolitan transport forum*. Metropolitan Transport Forum. Retrieved December 9, 2016, from www.mtf.org.au/MTF-Reports/Most-Liveable-and-Best-Connected-The-Economic-Benefits-of-In.aspx

SGS Economics and Planning. (2015). *Rental affordability index (November)*. Retrieved November 15, 2016, from www.sgsep.com.au/assets/RAI-Release-Report-Final-231115.pdf

Transparency International. (2015). *Corruption perceptions index 2015*. Retrieved May 18, 2017, from www.transparency.org/cpi2015/

Vinson, T., Rawsthorne, M., Beavis, A., & Ericson, M. (2015). *Dropping off the edge 2015*. Retrieved May 18, 2017, from https://dote.org.au/

Wilkins, R. (2016). *The household, income and labour dynamics in Australia survey: Selected findings from waves 1 to 14*. Melbourne Institute of Applied Economic and Social Research, The University of Melbourne. Retrieved November 15, 2016, from www.melbourneinstitute.com/downloads/hilda/Stat_Report/statreport_2016.pdf

Wiseman, J., Heine, W., Langworthy, A., McLean, N., Pyke, J., Raysmith, H., & Salvaris, M. (2006). *Developing a community indicators framework for Victoria: The final report of the Victorian Community Indicators Project (VCIP)*. Melbourne, VIC: Institute of Community Engagement and Policy Alternatives (ICEPA), Victoria University, VicHealth Centre for the Promotion of Mental Health and Social Well Being, School of Population Health, University of Melbourne and the Centre for Regional Development, Swinburne University of Technology.

Woolcock, G. W. E. (2009). *Measuring up? Assessing the liveability of Australian cities*. Urban Research Program, Griffith University. Retrieved December 9, 2016, from www98.griffith.edu.au/dspace/bitstream/handle/10072/29808/?sequence=1

Woodcock, I., Dovey, K., Wollan, S., & Robertson, I. (2011). Speculation and resistance: Constraints on compact city policy implementation in Melbourne. *Urban Policy and Research*, *29*(4), 343–362.

Part V
Creating Livability

Introduction

How do cities create livability? There is certainly no cookie-cutter approach to doing so. It represents a broad topic that considers such topics as transportation, jobs, housing, open space, public health, public safety, and so forth. Cities must remember that their actions in one area can serve as catalysts for actions in one or more other areas. Resources must be used effectively and efficiently. Starting with a vision, areas need to work together in a transparent planning and decision-making process. The chapters in Part V discuss various means three cities have taken and the complications they have faced in their quest to create livability.

Chapter 14 examines the possibilities of overcoming inequalities in Rio de Janeiro, Brazil. The chapter discusses livability from a fragmented, hierarchical, and unequal city perspective. Rio remains a fast-growing area with many favelas. Their presence has shown the existence of inequalities in segregated cities. An issue facing the city is the impact of the global capitalism discussion on local communities. Is the entrepreneurial spirit heightening these inequalities? The authors explore how decisions affect different groups in the city by investigating port projects and initiatives dealing with the favelas.

Chapter 15 examines the concept of livability generally in South Africa and, more specifically, in Cape Town. The country is experiencing rapid growth and urbanization through natural increases and through in-migration from areas in the countryside. Growth represents some daunting challenges to urban planning in such areas as water, energy, climate change, sustainability, equity, and social justice. With high unemployment rates, families resort to generating their own livelihoods. Inequality levels are high and due, in part, the urban tradition in South African cities promoting separation in land uses, modes of transportation, race, and class. The chapter continues to discuss whether the area and country needs to rethink the way it plans. The author indicates that planning needs to be proactive, not reactive. Planning needs to think in more interdisciplinary terms and not to work in isolation from others.

Chapter 16 explores the issue of livability in Tehran, Iran, a city where the author declares the city "a sum of its political history and economy accented by cultural and social dynamics". The city has continued to experience a lot of growth and faces numerous challenges and contradictions. Nevertheless, according to one livability rankings service, its livability as improved over the past five years. The chapter also discusses what has contributed to this improvement and what has occasionally thwarted improvements in other areas. It is noted that more can be done to improve livability by planning for and accommodating change.

14 The Search for Livability in Third World Segregated Cities

The Entrepreneurial City and the Possibilities of Overcoming Historical Inequalities in Rio de Janeiro

Lucia Capanema-Alvares and Jorge Luiz Barbosa

Introduction

The urbanization of the territory is a significant mark of the modern world, making cities the central spaces of material and symbolic production processes in our existences. However, more than an expression of a social and cultural way of life, urbanization became a condition, means and product of capitalism realization. By expressing in specific ways the relationship between capital and labor, cities have become not only the shelter for factories, banks and commerce, where the labor force generates its surplus value and sees it appropriated; as the locus of production of goods and services, but urbanization has also become the mediation of goods circulation and consumption, of labor, and of money processes necessary for the reproduction of capital to an extended territory. Urbanization can be considered a capital product to the extent that it becomes a large "business" for the different fractions of capital (Harvey, 2008) and a machine of surplus value production and of socio-spatial inequalities.

In this sense, the concept of urbanization has to include social formats and issues that permeate the capitalist system itself in its geographical context. In Harvey, urbanization is a social process through which different actors with diverse goals and commitments interact through interpersonal socio-spatial practices, producing "built forms, produced spaces, and resource systems of particular qualities, organized into a distinctive spatial configuration" (Harvey, 2008, 168). It establishes specific institutional arrangements, political and administrative systems, and power hierarchies that provide objective qualities to the city. As such, it is imperative to consider the decisions, messages and codes that are expressed in the city and are related to groups and hegemonic corporations that act at different scales starting from the metropolises. Indeed, the entrepreneurial model, based on the accumulation of wealth centered on the investment of surplus capital in urbanization processes, has promoted economies of dispossession within cities (Harvey, 2012). This comes as a result of the overlays between financial capital and urban production systems that stretch inequalities by expropriating social groups, especially of their living spaces.

Ghettoes, urban peripheries and favelas have become places of exposure to the unequal and discretionary process of urbanization in all continents. It does not concern the speed of territory urbanization alone, but also its social, economic and political contradictions.

If urbanization is to mean not only decent housing, education and health services, transport infrastructures and access to cultural property, but also a right to better and collective imaginaries, and a right to reinvent urbanization itself, the livability concept, with its transactional perspective, its sense of community and belonging may become a key concept in order to realize the full humanistic potential of our cities.

As underlined in our brief discussion of capital production and reproduction in urbanization processes, this chapter seeks to identify and discuss the discourses and practices proposed by the global capital vis-à-vis local communities. It tries to look at livability from the perspective of a fragmented, hierarchical, or simply unequal city by building on the concepts presented in *Community Livability* (Wagner & Caves, 2012). In so doing, it adds discussions and principles of a few key authors and institutions and systematizes a conceptual framework against which we plan to develop our argument: the entrepreneurial city espoused by neoliberal administrations, fully embraces the livability ideal, but its practices only deepen inequalities in segregated cities, contributing to environmental, social and economic unsustainability. This seems to be specially the case in the developing and third worlds.

Working With the Livability Concept

The authors in *Community Livability* are very much in tune regarding the difficulty to establish measurable criteria or strict concepts on livability, but some patterns do emerge. As suggested by Whelan, "the concept involves the everyday physical environment and placemaking ideas" but also economic, ecological and equity sustainability at multiple scales expressed in public spaces, transportation systems and building and landscape design (Whelan, 2012, 1). Place-Making and place shaping to foster an engaging community is called for by most authors (in particular, see, Bright, 2012; Shaw et al., 2012; Howe, 2012).

Driving away from deterministic beliefs in designing environments and going along with the Congress for the New Urbanism principles,[1] Del Rio et al. argue that physical environments do not dictate quality of life; rather, the relationships that groups maintain with their environments will develop "perceived livability, (. . .) sense of community and thus (. . .) satisfaction with the place (people) live in"; they also see that livability and sense of community "might be different for lower-income and culturally diverse" (Del Rio et al., 2012, 99–100) populations and ask us

> If livability and sense of community are different for the poor, and specifically for the poor of a diverse social cultural context, (and) if residents of a poor community feel a stronger sense of community then those of a better-off community due to more intense environmental transactions.
>
> (Del Rio et al., 2012, 100)

"Quality of life" and "sustainability" come intertwined with the livability concept, for most authors of that volume. The Partners for Livable Communities also define livability as "the sum of the factors that add up to a community's quality of life".[2] That invites us to take a quick look at how these two concepts may, or may not, increase our understanding of livability. Bognar (2005) has found efforts to collect and systematically organize Quality of Life data since the 1960s. During seminars in the early 1970s and in a later book, Wilheim (1976) already discussed the concept under the planning perspective, proposing a number of variables to be considered including aspects such as feeling healthy and pleasure. From then on and to the current time, numerous indices have been developed including the UN's Human Development Index, probably the most used nowadays. Still, much like livability, it is a hard to define and measure concept, given the subjectivity of the widely accepted definitions; an example is the UN's World Health Organization: "the individuals' perception of their position in life in the context of the culture and value systems in which they live and in relation to their goals".[3]

Likewise, the sustainability idea gained social significance in the 1970s, reaching a peak in the 1990s at the RIO 92 Eco Summit. In order to address its multidisciplinary aspects, it has been framed within three interrelated and mutually interacting subsystems: the local relations, determined by the social, economic, cultural and environmental dimensions; the governmental organization of the local context; and the external relations dictated by the market and by global agents (Capanema Álvares & Carsalade, 2005). Given that all local relations are of a social nature, we can then state that the sustainability system is composed of local sociocultural, socioeconomic, and socio-environmental dimensions and their interactions with the governmental and the external forces (Capanema Álvares et al., 2014).

Secchi works with sustainability, taking from the discrepancies in the population growth and distribution processes throughout and inside our metropolises. According to the author, these processes enlarge the differences in all forms of capital securing (economic, social, cultural and spatial) among citizens of the same locality (Secchi, 2011, 2012). Drawing from Soja (2010), Secchi sees spatial capital as the opportunity given to the individual according to his or her capacity to reach and enjoy the various places in the city (Secchi, 2011). He, therefore, discusses access to the rich city or incarceration in the poor city and emphasizes isotropy (equality in the distribution of resources and flows within the city), mobility (thoroughly discussed by Steiner, 2012) and porosity (rate and distribution of environmentally qualified open spaces available and accessible through public transportation to varying flows of people, activities and demonstrations from different backgrounds)—all possible results of physical and social barriers that define enclaves and unsustainability (Secchi, 2014).

Some authors of *Community Livability* (2012) propose a look from different perspectives. Bright (2012) sees four broad categories composing quality of life: safety, shelter, services and social capital. Resourcing to Putnam (2000), Blanco also argues that social capital is an important aim of participatory neighborhood planning, and therefore implies that social capital should be an intrinsic part of livability. Still after Putnam, she differentiates between bonding Social Capital, which regards members of the same community, and bridging Social Capital which connects people from different communities, socioeconomic and cultural backgrounds; then she includes Woolcock's linking Social Capital, which connects individuals and communities to institutional resources to argue that participatory planning can booster all three towards the construction of livable communities.

Taking from Blanco (2012) and Secchi (2014), Putnam's bridging Social Capital and Soja's Spatial Capital seem to overlay to some extent. In any case, all four types of human capital should be taken under consideration towards sustainable, or livable, communities: economic, social, cultural and spatial (Secchi, 2014). Figure 14.1 summarizes desired livability aspects as proposed by the aforementioned authors and institutions.

We, therefore, should be looking at diverse contexts to compare and understand how and to what degree governments, institutions and communities are pursuing the desirable livability aspects under the sociocultural, socioeconomic and socio-environmental dimensions. At the other end, some highly undesirable factors, as pointed by most authors, are urban low-density sprawl, and exclusive and mono-functional neighborhoods filled with automobile-dependent citizens.

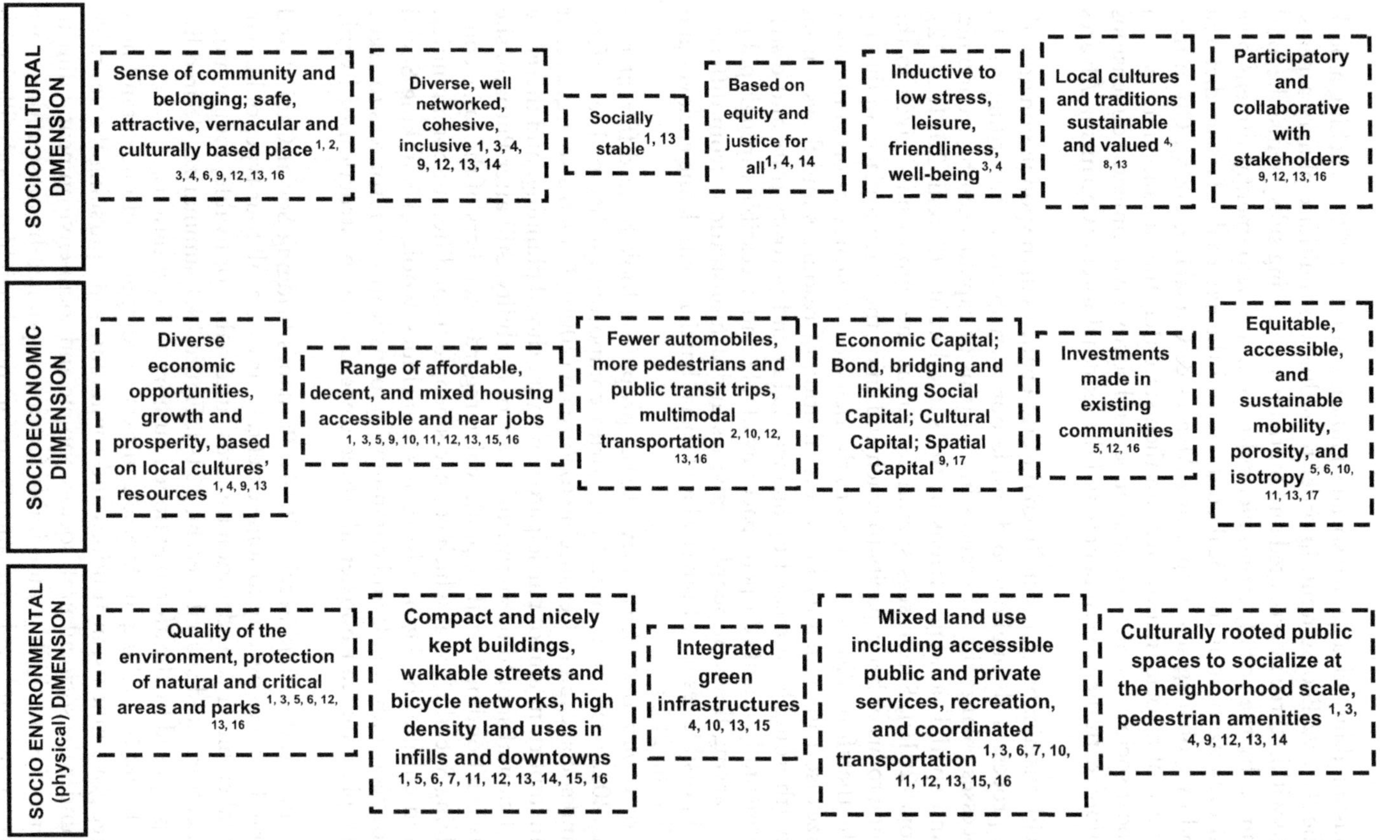

SOCIOCULTURAL DIMENSION

- Sense of community and belonging; safe, attractive, vernacular and culturally based place [1,2,3,4,6,9,12,13,16]
- Diverse, well networked, cohesive, inclusive [1,3,4,9,12,13,14]
- Socially stable [1,13]
- Based on equity and justice for all [1,4,14]
- Inductive to low stress, leisure, friendliness, well-being [3,4]
- Local cultures and traditions sustainable and valued [8,13]
- Participatory and collaborative with stakeholders [9,12,13,16]

SOCIOECONOMIC DIMENSION

- Diverse economic opportunities, growth and prosperity, based on local cultures' resources [1,4,9,13]
- Range of affordable, decent, and mixed housing accessible and near jobs [1,3,5,9,10,11,12,13,15,16]
- Fewer automobiles, more pedestrians and public transit trips, multimodal transportation [2,10,12,13,16]
- Economic Capital; Bond, bridging and linking Social Capital; Cultural Capital; Spatial Capital [9,17]
- Investments made in existing communities [5,12,16]
- Equitable, accessible, and sustainable mobility, porosity, and isotropy [5,6,10,11,13,17]

SOCIO ENVIRONMENTAL (physical) DIMENSION

- Quality of the environment, protection of natural and critical areas and parks [1,3,5,6,12,13,16]
- Compact and nicely kept buildings, walkable streets and bicycle networks, high density land uses in infills and downtowns [1,5,6,7,11,12,13,14,15,16]
- Integrated green infrastructures [4,10,13,15]
- Mixed land use including accessible public and private services, recreation, and coordinated transportation [1,3,6,7,10,11,12,13,15,16]
- Culturally rooted public spaces to socialize at the neighborhood scale, pedestrian amenities [1,3,4,9,12,13,14]

1 – WHELAN, 2012. 2 – MARTIN, 2012. 3 – BRIGHT, 2012. 4 – SHAW et al., 2012. 5 – HOWE, 2012. 6 – DEL RIO et al., 2012. 7 – BIRCH, 2012. 8 – BROOKS and HOUTMAN, 2012. 9 – BLANCO, 2012. 10 – ROTTLE and MARYMAN, 2012. 11 – STEINER, 2012. 12 – KENNEDY and DANNENBERG, 2012. 13 – CONGRESS FOR NEW URBANISM www.cnu.org/who-we-are/charter-new-urbanism. 14 – INTERNATIONAL MAKING CITIES LIVABLE www.livablecities.org/ 15 – LEED-ND www.usgbc.org/resources/leed-neighborhood-development 16 – THE SMART GROWTH NETWORK http://smartgrowth.org/smart-growth-principles. 17 – SECCHI, 2014.

Figure 14.1 Summary of Desirability Livability Aspects According to Authors and Institutions Under the Three Sustainability Dimensions

Source: Lucia Capanema-Alvares and Jorge Barbosa

Rio, the Fragmented City: A Portrait of Historical Urban Inequalities in Brazil

In 1950, the Brazilian urban population was only 36% of the total, and in five decades (up to 2000), that rate reached 81%. Currently, 84.5% of the population lives in cities accumulating a huge and unequal deficit of decent urban housing units. This process faced its decisive moment in the 1970s, when the urban population overcame the rural (56% against 44%). This phenomenon brought new dimensions to urban housing, especially in the main cities, which grew enormously due to the preferential location of industries; transportation, infrastructures and urban equipment investments; and concentration of services and technologies. Cities located in the Southeast Region (São Paulo, Rio de Janeiro, and Belo Horizonte) turned into metropolitan areas with high densities of capital, population and households.

In half a century, the number of urban housing units in Brazil went from 2 million to almost 40 million, fueled by the country's population growth and particularly by the urban population growth. From the total dwelling units somehow built in urban areas, only 20% were either constructed or financed by any State level or by development agencies (Silva & Barbosa, 2005) and most of the urban population had to build their houses with their own resources and efforts. The Brazilian scenario of slums, irregular occupations and settlements never ceased to grow and to be present in the landscape; between 1991 and 2010, the officially named *subnormal agglomerations* or *precarious settlements*—the favelas —doubled in number, going from 3.188 to 6.329 located in 323 cities. Eighty-eight percent of these favelas were concentrated in the major Brazilian cities.

We can, therefore, argue that the city of Rio entails not only Brazilian regional inequalities but also its intra-urban hierarchies and uneven income distribution. This chapter now turns to the discussion of the discourses and practices proposed by the global capital vis-à-vis those proposed by local communities, as the current and most prominent representatives of the antagonist (and highly unequal) powers in the city.

The Port Area Renovation Projects in Rio

Between 1983 and 2001, there were seven different plans focusing on the transformation of the port area as a whole. The SAGAS Project, encompassing all neighborhoods and slums in Rio's port area, was instituted in 1988 following the general aim of the Preservation Areas (APA) projects: "the maintenance of the important landscape and cultural characteristics of the area [. . .] and the preservation of typical cultural sites and their morphologies" (Soares & Moreira, 2007). City Hall planners became obsessive with ordering the "Portuguese heritage" site of Morro da Conceição, enforcing a cultural identity discourse that privileged the European heritage, what provoked a number of disturbances, since Morro da Conceição was highly heterogeneous, with centuries of African Brazilian influence. Mostly African descendants, residents found themselves threatened with mass removal and lobbied City Hall to incorporate their heritage into the Project. But the process of creating an imaginary historical site "when goods, streets and lifestyles are displaced of their polysemic contexts and idealized as authentic representations [of a chosen past, have impacted] residents' consciousness, creating not only different memories and identities but also new political, social and aesthetic processes", devaluing the local culture. (Guimarães, 2013, 49). Furthermore, the election of historic landmarks and preservation areas highlighted their opposite, the poor areas (and residents) chosen to be removed and forgotten.

From 1992 on, the official discourse in Rio de Janeiro emphasized the dangers of the rampant urban "crisis" (Vainer, 2000), calling for administrative efficiency, restoration of "urban order" and incentives to economic activities as a priority, inspired by Barcelona's experience.

From 1993 to 1997, the Conceição, Saúde, Livramento and Pinto hills—partly favelas, partly regular neighborhoods in the port area—had a number of properties designated as preservation sites; the SAGAS project promoted tourism and middle-class in-migration to these neighborhoods, rebuilt landmarks and squares and restricted a number of public spaces uses and activities such as sleeping under viaducts and street vending (Guimarães, 2013). In an opposite move, the other slums and brown fields in the area were left to rot.

The Entrepreneurial City and the Livability of Its Port Area: The Marvelous Port (*Porto Maravilha*) Mega-Project

The Sagas Project's objectives found a perfect match in the 2000s: following the neoliberal hegemonic canons and after the Barcelona model, the attraction of mega-events FIFA World Cup 2014 and Olympic Games 2016, together with the adoption of public-private partnerships, and new city marketing strategies, opened the doors to a number of changes in the urban structure of the port area under a single project (Capanema-Álvares et al., 2010).

As early as 2008, a redevelopment project was being designed inside a couple of private offices, the Odebrecht and the OAS construction companies, both under federal investigation for corruption. Between 2007 and 2009, the Federal Secretary of Cities led a project with the State of Rio and the City of Rio, which recommended the adoption of a Public Consortium including all three government levels and mandatory public participation in decision-making processes in order to manage the port area revitalization. By the end of 2009, through an unexpected and unexplained move, City Hall denied the three-year effort and engaged into the "New Port Public-Private Partnership" (PPP-PN), which adopted the very same plan privately designed to direct and manage the development project. The PPP-PN, composed exactly by Odebrecht, OAS, and two other construction companies, would report to City Hall through the recently created Port Region Development Company (Cdurp) and would receive a number of tax breaks and incentives for ten years.[4]

The highlighted Project principles are a) the prioritization of public transportation over the individual; b) the enhancement of the urban landscape, the urban environment and of the tangible and intangible cultural heritage; c) socioeconomic assistance to the population directly affected by the Project; d) the promotion of adequate use of vacant or underutilized plots; e) the integration of the area with its adjacent central area; f) the stimulation of residential occupancy, allowing a better use of the existing urban structure; g) transparency and control of the decision-making process with civil society representation; h) support to land regularization of social interest properties. The project website states that transportation choices prioritize those modes accessible to all citizens, non-motorized modes and foster the "idea of living close to work". All the streets of the Port Region were to receive new urban infrastructure, including drainage, water and sewage networks, natural gas, energy, street lighting and telecommunication cables by 2016. Last, solid waste should be stored underground, avoiding dirt in the streets and the proliferation of nuisances.[5] The Project also discursively abides to a number of economic, social and cultural sustainable principles, like keeping local people in the area and preserving their identity and heritage. A closer look at the ongoing activities, however, reveals carelessness with the project's financing, with local residents and with the newly built infrastructure.

The accomplishment of the Marvelous Port project required a new legal framework, constituting what Agamben (2004) would call exceptionalism. Taking from purposeful gaps stablished in the 1990 Municipal Organic Law (LOM) (Prefeitura, 2010), City Hall was able to enforce a "city of exception" in the port area: "Restrictions on existing buildings or activities that [did not] meet the conditions of the [area] where they are located" (art. 73) led to the expulsion of the area's negative externalities; the adoption of "Land Utilization Rates greater than those permitted [given] that the collective interest is justified in the Neighborhood Impact Report's terms", (art. 76) gave way to the location of skyscrapers in the historical area, without ever stablishing what the so-called collective interest would be.

In 2009, Complementary Law 101 (CL 101) modified the Master Plan and authorized the executive branch to institute an Urban Redevelopment Plan for the region, which enabled the construction of buildings of up to 50 floors at the seaside, overruling LOM art. 445—meant to preserve the UN-recognized heritage landscape with its views from the bay to the hills and vice versa—and destroying one of the most powerful image memories of Rio. CL 101 also foresaw social housing provision through residents' resettlement, opening the way to the forced eviction of residents, violating the LOM in its 6th precept, Article 6 of the Federal Constitution (on housing as a human right), Federal Law 11.124/2005 (on the mandatory prior use of public land to social housing projects) and international human rights treaties the country has signed.

When implementing mega-projects, local governments restructure the city in truly hygienist operations carried out in areas that have been left at the mercy of the real estate market without urban public investment or services as important as security; these areas are held as real estate stock, where the state can remove entire communities and industries, locate huge investments and pass the added value on to the private sector. The decaying port area in Rio, surrounded by communities left to drug trafficking and militias due to the state absence, also housed numerous positive externalities, as bay overviewing belvederes, proximity to city landmarks, availability of urban infrastructure, facilities, commerce, services and multimodal transportation. That is why City Hall strategic plans forged a "crisis" scenario in the port area, where abandonment became a trademark and the need for urban regeneration cried out. From the 2000s, the area and its big plots have been redeveloped and remarketed.

Together with the inclusion of new private actors in public management, the aforementioned acts of exception enabled City Hall to implement the region's "cleansing" operation and consequently a number of projects, with the insertion of off-scale architectural icons signed by internationally famous professionals and new exclusive transportation lines, creating what Marc Augé (1995) would call a "non-place", where local cultural references and histories are absent. As of 2013, 665 families had already been removed from that region and 1,142 families were under threat. Despite its historical importance as the first favela in Brazil and its rich cultural heritage mixing African and Northeastern Brazilian influences, 140 families of the "non-building" community of Morro da Providência— which houses almost 6,000 people—have been evicted and sent to live in housing projects some 64 kilometers away from their social networks, jobs, schools, health clinics, leisure and so forth. Back in 2011, the UN Human Rights Council Special Rapporteur on the right to adequate housing, Raquel Rolnik, already voiced her concerns about the tentative mass eviction in the area.[6] The "Housing Rio" program foresaw the eviction of 832 of its residences, partly due to questionable geotechnical risk allegations, partly aimed at preventing "high densities" within the community.

According to City Hall, as of 2010, about 93.3 % of the total Federal Social Housing Program "My house, my life" units were located in the far away Planning Area 5 (Veríssimo, 2010 *apud* Cardoso et al., 2011), a number of them built to receive evicted families that came from "non-building communities" (like Morro da Providência). Besides being in the western fringes of town, where perceived income is lower, this area presents the worst infrastructure indicators (water and sewage coverage, education, health and leisure facilities, etc.) as well as poor mobility. It also presents the highest formal employment deficit compared with the economically active population (EAP): only 17% of job offerings to the EAP, compared with 645% in the downtown area. Its increasing housing market worsens its livability, already presenting insufficient infrastructure, mobility and jobs to meet the demands (Cardoso et al., 2011).

Due to the US$1 billion tourist Light Rail Train implementation, 28 bus lines that served the port area residents were canceled and 21 were trimmed to give place to the rail lines. As far as finances go, the land use plan was 100% financed by the National Savings Bank (CEF), which used a US$3.7 billion fund composed of mandatory retirement savings pertaining to all Brazilian workers for the endeavor, expecting a fast return from the land sales, which never happened: by 2016, the debt had reached US$4.5 billion and the CEF had to inject another US$500 million.[7] From 2009 to 2024, the PPP-PN is to receive US$3.5 billion of public money to invest in garbage collection, lighting and transit operations in the area, aiming at a First World style refurbishment, as can be seen in picture 14.2.

Figure 14.2 First World Style Refurbishment in Rio's Port Area
Source: Rob Darwin

In order to abide to the "solid waste storage'" principle, the PPP-PN hired City Hall to operate the area's garbage collection for US$8.7 million per year[8] and installed a total of 34 "sustainable" bins in the whole area.[9] The legacy plan contract within the PPP-PN was amended with nine addenda up to January 2016, increasing public payments to the private partners in another US$250 million.

Currently, a City Council Commission of Inquiry is being organized in order to assist and deepen police investigations on the Marvelous Port Project, investigating among other aspects, the violation of social housing and environmental laws.

Popular Territories Answers to the Unequal and Discretionary Urbanization Processes

As already stated by Del Rio et al. (2012), a number of researchers on Third World slums, and especially Brazilian favelas, have pointed out that these popular territories are a solution to urban inequalities, where the poor are somehow able to settle their families and start their socio-spatial struggles towards minimum quality of life standards and security.

In this quest, they network with people of similar origins, interests, and objectives, finding social support and creating both a sense of place where they belong and ties to other communities (see Del Rio et al. discussions in Wagner & Caves, 2012). As a consequence, favelas may have not only an economic vibrant scene but also a life of their own, raising sustainability issues that question the middle classes' living standards based on high consumption levels:

> A favela is a good example of viewing livability from a transactional perspective [. . .]; it is a highly livable environment. [Results] show high levels of house satisfaction and perceived safety, a strong sense of community, a vibrant social system, and a sustainable lifestyle.
>
> (Del Rio et al., 2012, 121)

Sustainability and livability cannot be seen as a list of principles to create islands of well-being, detached from their socio-economic-cultural contexts. How favelas answer—as organized communities—to a pervasive and historical segregation process and how they insert themselves in the larger society become key to understand how their residents' "living-in-the-world" as subjects of rights, and to foresee their possibilities at a full-fledged, inclusive livability.

Working-class families, especially the poorest, understand that their presence in the city depends on their daily tactics in confronting the permanent process of material and symbolic dispossession of their existence. The concentration of private property and the real estate market domination of economic and spatial capital mean a daily effort for favela residents, not only when building their own shelters under unequal conditions but also by going beyond the housing unit and transforming the appropriation and usage of the territory into a possibility of living in the city.

Due to the reduced and insufficient offer of housing units through government public policies, slums and urban peripheries became socially necessary markets, fed both by family-based and intergenerational housing production, and by informal rents and sales of entire units or parts of them, like attics or rooftops. Altogether, they answer to the poor housing demands in Brazilian cities and metropolises and create vertical, high-density areas supported by a highly efficient use of the available infrastructure. The Rocinha slum in Rio de Janeiro is one of the main examples of slum verticalization: as the proximity to public services and job opportunities forged an active real estate market in the favela, it grew 23% in population between 2000 and 2010, despite losing 2.5% of its area (IBGE, 2000; IBGE, 2010).

The functions and activities spectra in the daily life of popular territories are much broader than simply residing: household socioeconomic activities multiply in an intimate association with job creation and income growth opportunities; these are intrinsic to their daily living. As a response to low wages, lack of formal employment opportunities and racial discrimination, residents of popular territories invent a socially necessary and diverse production and consumption of goods and services market in the territory. The slums of Maré and Rocinha, both located in Rio de Janeiro, had 3,500 and 6,500 commercial and services establishments, respectively, in 2014.[10] Because housing and job opportunities as well as education, healthcare, and recreation services provision are part of the urban life dynamics, they also are indicators of the distribution of symbolic and social capital in the city. Thus, popular housing is not just a random arrangement in the territory, but also a tenacious stand at the claim for livability and for the right to live a decent urban life.

Notwithstanding, this subaltern workers' combined efforts were never recognized by society in general, or by the State. Their territorialized constructions have always been seen and treated as illegal, irregular, clandestine, subnormal and precarious, especially for having been built without government approval, thus confronting the hegemonic order of the market and, most evidently, due to their social and racial origins (Barbosa, 2012). In a contradictory way, for a significant part of the working-class families, favelas mean both the most striking expression of a corporeal-territorial distinction of rights and the legitimation of their social struggles for living in the city.

The non-recognition of popular housing territories constitutes stereotypes of deprivation and stigmas of violence, which allow discretionary and authoritarian official policies to confront their residents' different and complex strategies. The brutal eviction of hundreds of families at once, the demolition of houses identified as irregular and the police abusive actions are all part of a long and dramatic history of the State's territorial violence against favelas in Rio. Local interventions and projects for urbanization and legalization of precarious settlements still are, in their majority, interventions that treat popular housing territories as mere objects of actions, disregarding not only their demands but also the solutions created by the residents.

The urbanization model that dictates which social subjects should or should not be integrated as subjects of rights is based on a perverse indifference to the other's life in his or her unequal condition. This territorial hierarchic distinction of rights has explicit ties with racial relations, has been defined by corporeal classifications of human superiority and inferiority and corresponds to non-recognition forms of urban citizenship and residents' fundamental rights. At the Cidade de Deus slum, for example, black residents compose 65% of the total, whereas in an upper-middle class neighborhood like Lagoa, this rate is 10% (IBGE, 2010).

Popular housing in Rio takes complex forms and can exhibit extreme differences beyond their particularities concerning morphology, location and history: they present unique compositions of work forms, levels of income and of insertion in the consumption of goods, and in the access to public services. Their intense social life sets the stage for a profusion of codes, pacts and sociability practices that constitute specific meanings and evidence unique sociocultural identities. Identifying the agreements, pacts and norms established in the experiences of these residents in their territory of existence takes overcoming the stereotypes and stigmas that mark the popular housing realm.

Even though the stigma of poverty and criminality still marks favelas, the richness of their artistic and cultural production is vital both to legitimate the presence of those territories in the city and to reassure residents of their belonging to a community. Although they are not defined by the hegemonic standards of production, the favelas' cultural repertoires generate art in networks of sociability that create dialectical relationships between society and space, integrate and renovate the sense of community and increase their cultural, social, and economic capital.

Cultural practices, be they institutional or freely organized, individual or collective, autonomous or group-linked, are concrete subjects' forms of manifestation that aim at signifying their lives and their ways of dealing with daily life, coming from multiple languages. New and radical expressions of citizenship emerge, with the ability to combine political struggles at global and local scales. New textures of relationships between concrete subjects are made possible, as these actors recognize themselves in the face of common demands and socio-spatial identities. They are able to establish, therefore, a sense of belonging by creating places of encounter and by distinguishing between what is a community and what is a territorial barricade or a ghetto that rises against the city. Culture can be, thus, a significant practice of appropriation and use of the territory, creating and updating the various ways the poor live in the world. Despite (or maybe because of) its potential, cultural activities in favelas are not favored by the ruling forces, as we shall see.

It can be hard to identify equipment of culture consumption—as museums, cinemas, libraries, theaters, and so forth, which are hegemonic emblems of a civilized culture—in a favela. This does not mean that slums are not spaces of cultural aesthetics inventions. Rather, their streets, squares, alleys and corners are filled with aesthetics repertoires bringing different ways of creating urban culture such as graffiti colors and videos that are self-portraits the slums and their residents as subject of rights, or as samba schools, carnival groups, *terreiros* of Umbanda and candomblé, funk dances, hip-hop parties and battles, with thousands of spectators, which affirm and consecrate Afro-Brazilian culture in the city. The recent art production in its visual, folk and technological aspects invents innovative territorial representations and reassure the favela as a part of the city. In so doing, favelas offer themselves as a locus of possible community construction within the city (see Figure 14.3).

Figure 14.3 Cultural Manifestations in Rio Favelas
Source: Francisco Valdean

Figure 14.3 (Continued)

In an investigation with 400 entities that promote cultural production, dissemination and communication activities in five slums (Rocinha, Cidade de Deus, Alemão, Penha and Manguinhos), we identified that they are formal organizations from civil societies in 25% of the cases, informal organizations in 22%, and run by single individuals in 20%. Private businesses run 18% of those organizations, whereas the State runs only 12% and religious institutions are responsible for 2% of the organizations.[11] That means a lot of community action and networking and a fragile state presence in actions that may have great significance not only to identity and sense of community processes but also in creating bonding, bridging, and linking social capital, and in fostering both cultural and economic capital. They are territories of sociability: in all five researched favelas, squares and streets (most of all), samba schools sheds, sports fields, bars, churches, ballrooms, schools and Internet cafes appear as the primary resources for sharing artistic experiences in the studied slums. These are, therefore, cultural scenarios that give art a socioeconomic dimension, especially because its embodiment has a necessary public and territorial dimension. In this perspective, cultures in permanent re-creation in favelas gain different meanings from those established by the consumer market of symbolic goods and services that differentiate and rank social classes and groups in the city. It is about political investments, which can be expressed in the construction of aesthetic repertoires and culture practices that promote the visibility of social subjects and a different project for the city.

Founded and coordinated by a group of residents, the Center for Studies and Solidarity Actions at the Favela da Maré created, among 15 educational and cultural projects, the innovative Maré Museum, dedicated to the registration, preservation and dissemination of its history and focusing on the social life of its residents (Abreu & Chagas, 2007, 4).

Assessing Livability Issues in the Marvelous Port and in Favelas Initiatives

Taking from the Marvelous Port project, it would be hard to say it has promoted much livability, both in the central area, where it is located, and in the urban fringes, where the project-evicted families have been sent to live. Considering the theoretical chart presented in the first section and looking at the social cultural dimension, it is possible to state that the existing communities in the port area have not been culturally recognized since at least 1998, when the Sagas project smashed the African-based local cultures and traditions; more than 600 families were actually evicted and, instead of promoting socially stable communities, the current project spread terror in favelas, threatening 1,142 families (as of 2013). Regarding the financing aspects, the project evidences that all Brazilian workers paid for the project using a mandatory national pension fund, thus eliminating any argument concerning equity and justice for all. The plan itself was designed by private agents who would later be the land developers, avoiding any participation and collaborative effort with other stakeholders.

Under the social economic dimension, we can see that the creation of diverse economic opportunities based on local cultural resources was avoided, street vendors were evicted and local undesirable land uses, namely the small community businesses, were shut down. No social housing has been financed or constructed in the area, violating local, national and international laws and treaties; the housing mix that existed in the area was radically disturbed by the evictions. Moreover, the project created a demand for low-income housing units in poor areas some 60 kilometers away from the incoming residents' jobs and social networks, diminishing residents' spatial capital and/or their bond, bridge and linking Social Capital forms. Worse yet, these new communities create the need for far away infrastructure and services. Regarding mobility issues, we can see that the exclusive transportation mode implemented to the detriment of bus routes harmed the existing neighborhoods, and the removal of families to the city fringes hinders the new residents' mobility.

Despite the environmental concerns expressed in the project and some of the new, intelligent, techniques adopted both in the infrastructure laying down and in the building designs, allowing skyscrapers that will entirely block the heritage landmark views to and from the historical bay goes not only against livability principles but also are unlawful, according to the municipal codes. Instead of encouraging high densities, the project designed urban voids surrounded by First World architectural references and icons, disrespecting and devaluing the local culturally based public spaces in their form, content and scale.

At the other end of the spectrum, Rio favelas do not count on public policies, projects or money. Favela residents endure physical, economic, social and cultural hardships in their everyday lives, as they struggle to exist in the city. Nevertheless, when considering the sociocultural and the socioeconomic dimensions, one can see that their networks and bottom-up ways of building their houses, their infrastructure and their job and consumers' markets can teach us some livability lessons.

They assure themselves of their own value as subjects of rights, and enhance their bonding, bridging and linking forms of social capital. The social stability of the community is one of their main quests, because they are constantly threatened with mass eviction. Their locational choices are based on complex symbolic and social capital arrangements in the territory, because opportunities, goods and services are mostly offered in more affluent areas of the city. Through their cultural entrepreneurship, they manage to claim for livability and for the right to live a decent urban life. Last, if both sets of actors—Rio governmental structure and favela residents—have not practiced many of the desirable socio-environmental aspects of livability, despite the humongous difference in assets and stablished capabilities, favelas have questioned the middle and high-income classes through their density standards, their efficient use of infrastructure and their mix of residential and commercial activities at the micro-level.

Concluding Remarks

We resort once again to Del Rio et al.: "While a favela has physical qualities that would probably not be recognized by new urbanists, it is able to create a [highly] livable environment without the qualities they say every city should have" (Del Rio et al., 2012, 122).

For those in a subaltern condition in the city—like favela residents—the intention and the act of ensuring their residence as an invention of urban forms contrasting with the power forces of the market and the state regulatory logic is, *per se*, a quest for livability. Popular territories represent a search for the creation of the human being (humanity) today, necessarily involving the material and symbolic conditions of living in the city. It is exactly in this sense that people build their tangible and intangible belonging relations and establish social horizons of the territory usage, considering that the territory combines social resources (schools, hospitals, daycare), emotional resources (love, affections, family relations, friendships) and symbolic resources (churches, bars, carnival groups, soccer fields, places of African American religion practices) mobilized and shared by individuals, families and peer groups in the process of giving meaning to their existences and to their struggle towards being in the city.

The popular fights for livable cities are expressions of social rights advances and take, in the current urban conditions, a historical and political significance for the construction of a transformative urbanization process.

Notes

1. The Charter of the New Urbanism. Retrieved March 9, 2017, from www.cnu.org/who-we-are/charter-new-urbanism
2. What is Livability? Retrieved March 9, 2017, from www.livable.org
3. WHOQOL: Measuring Quality of Life: Introducing the WHOQOL instruments. Retrieved March 8, 2017, from www.who.int/mental_health/publications/whoqol
4. A outra historia do Porto Maravilha. Retrieved November 4, 2016, from http://apublica.org/2016/08/a-outra-historia-do-porto-maravilha
5. Rio Prefeitura. (2015). *Porto Maravilha* [online]. Rio de Janeiro. Retrieved April 25, 2015, from www.portomaravilha.com.br
6. Rolnik, R. (2011). *Direito à moradia*. Retrieved November 3, 2016, from www.direitoamoradia.fau.usp.br/?regiao=brasil&paged=2
7. A outra historia do Porto Maravilha. Retrieved November 3, 2016, from http://apublica.org/2016/08/a-outra-historia-do-porto-maravilha
8. A outra historia do Porto Maravilha. Retrieved November 3, 2016, from http://apublica.org/2016/08/a-outra-historia-do-porto-maravilha
9. Rio Prefeitura. (2015). *Porto Maravilha* [online]. Rio de Janeiro. Retrieved April 25, 2015, from www.portomaravilha.com.br
10. Redes de Desenvolvimento da Maré/Observatório de Favelas. *Censo de empreendimentos da Maré, 2014*.
11. Observatório de Favelas. Projeto Solos Culturais, 2013.

References

Abreu, R., & Chagas, M. (2007). Museu da Favela da Maré: memórias e narrativas a favor da dignidade social. In *Revista Musas-IBRAM*, número 3. Retrieved July 8, 2015, from www.museus.gov.br/wp-content/uploads/2011/01/Musas3.pdf

Agamben, G. (2004). *Estado de Exceção*. São Paulo: Boitempo.

Augé, M. (1995). *Non-places: An introduction to anthropology of supermodernity*. London: Verso.

Barbosa, J. L. (2012). Da habitação como direito ao direito à Morada: um debate propositivo sobre a regularização fundiária das favelas na cidade do Rio de Janeiro. In J. L. Barbosa & E. Limonad (Eds.), *Ordenamento Territorial e Ambiental*. Niterói: POSGEO/Editora da UFF,

Birch, E. (2012). Living downtown in the twenty-first century: Past trends and future policy concerns. In F. Wagner & R. Caves (Eds.), *Community livability: Issues and approaches to sustaining the well-being of people and communities*. New York: Routledge.

Blanco, H. (2012). Public participation in neighborhood planning: A neglected aspect of community livability: The case of Seattle. In F. Wagner & R. Caves (Eds.), *Community livability: Issues and approaches to sustaining the well-being of people and communities*. New York: Routledge.

Bognar, G. (2005). The concept of quality of life. *Social Theory and Practice, 31*(4), 561–580.

Bright, E. (2012). Variations in regulatory factors affecting neighborhood livability: An international perspective. In F. Wagner & R. Caves (Eds.), *Community livability: Issues and approaches to sustaining the well-being of people and communities*. New York: Routledge.

Brooks, J., & Houtman, R. (2012). The cultural component of livability: Loss and recovery in post-Katrina New Orleans. In F. Wagner & R. Caves (Eds.), *Community livability: Issues and approaches to sustaining the well-being of people and communities*. New York: Routledge.

Capanema-Alvares, L., Bessa, A. S. M. & Benedicto, D. B. M. (2010). A Indústria do Turismo e as Transformações Urbanas no Mundo Globalizado: Críticas ao Modelo Estratégico baseadas no caso dos Jogos Pan Americanos do Rio de Janeiro (2007). *International Conference Mega-events and the City Annals*, Niterói. CD-Rom.

Capanema-Alvares, L., Câmara, B. P., Carvalho, G. M. P. P. & Santos, A. C. F. (2014). Megaevents and the construction of manifestations: Rio de Janeiro, 2013. *Anais do II Megaevents and the City*, Rio de Janeiro. CD-Rom.

Capanema-Álvares, L., & Carsalade, F. L. (2005). Planejamento e Gestão de Políticas Públicas para o Turismo Sustentável: O Caso do Programa Estrada Real. *Revista de Turismo*. Volume 1-No. 1. Retrieved December 12, 2005, from www.turismo.pucminas.br/revista

Cardoso, A. L., Aragão, T. A. & Araujo, F. S. (2011). Habitação De Interesse Social: Política ou Mercado? Reflexos Sobre a Construção do Espaço Metropolitano. *Anais do XIV Encontro Nacional da ANPUR*, Rio de Janeiro.

The Cities Alliance. (2007). *Liveable cities: The benefits of urban environmental planning*. Washington: York Graphic Services. Retrieved April 24, 2015, from www.unep.org/urban_environment/PDFs/LiveableCities.pdf

Congress for New Urbanism. (2017). *New urbanism charter*. Retrieved March 1, 2017, from www.cnu.org/who-we-are/charter-new-urbanism

Del Rio, V., Levi, D. & Duarte, D. R. (2012). Perceived livability and sense of community: Lessons for designers from a Favela in Rio de Janeiro, Brazil. In F. Wagner & R. Caves (Eds.), *Community livability: Issues and approaches to sustaining the well-being of people and communities*. New York: Routledge.

The EIU'S Liveability Ranking. (2014). Retrieved April 25, 2015, from http://en.wikipedia.org/wiki/World%27s_most_liveable_cities

Guimarães, R. S. (2013). O encontro mítico de Pereira Passos com a Pequena África. Narrativas de passado e formas de habitar na zona portuária carioca. In J. R. S. Gonçalves, N. P. Bitnar, & R. S. Guimarã (Eds.), *A alma das coisas: patrimônio, materialidade e ressonância*. Rio de Janeiro: Mauad/Faperj.

Harvey, D. (2008). The right to the city. *New Left Review, 2*(53).

Harvey, D. (2012). *Rebel cities: From the right to the city to the urban revolution*. London: Verso.
Howe, D. (2012). Aging as the foundation for livable communities. In F. Wagner & R. Caves (Eds.), *Community livability: Issues and approaches to sustaining the well-being of people and communities*. New York: Routledge.
IBGE – Instituto Brasileiro de Geografia e Estatística (2000). Censo 2000. Rio de Janeiro: Instituto Brasileiro de Geografia e Estatística. Retrieved April 14, 2017, from https://ww2.ibge.gov.br/home/
IBGE – Fundação Brasileira de Geografia e Estatística (2000). Censo 2010. Rio de Janeiro: Instituto Brasileiro de Geografia e Estatística. Retrieved April 14, 2017, from https://ww2.ibge.gov.br/home/
International Making Cities Livable. Retrieved March 1, 2017, from www.livablecities.org
Kennedy, S. H., & Dannenberg, A. L. (2012). Livability, health, and community design. In F. Wagner & Caves, R. (Eds.), *Community livability: Issues and approaches to sustaining the well-being of people and communities*. New York: Routledge.
LEED-ND. Retrieved March 1, 2017, from www.usgbc.org/resources/leed-neighborhood-development
Martin, J. A. (2012). Public policy promotion of livable communities. In F. Wagner & Caves, R. (Eds.), *Community livability: Issues and approaches to sustaining the well-being of people and communities*. New York: Routledge.
Partners for Livable Communities. Retrieved March 9, 2017, from http://livable.org/about-us/what-is-livability
Prefeitura Da Cidade Do Rio De Janeiro. (2010). *Lei Orgânica do Município 1990* (2nd ed.). Retrieved July 8, 2017, from http://www.rio.rj.gov.br/dlstatic/10112/4946719/4136646/Lei_Organica_MRJ_comaltdo205_2303.pdf
Publica. Agência de Reportagem e Jornalismo Investigativo. *A outra história do Porto Maravilha*. Retrieved November 4, 2016, from http://apublica.org/2016/08/a-outra-historia-do-porto-maravilha
Putnam, R. (2000). *Bowling alone: The collapse and revival of American community*. New York: Simon and Schuster.
Redes de Desenvolvimento da Maré/Observatório de Favelas. (2014). *Censo de empreendimentos da Maré*. Rio de Janeiro: Redes de Desenvolvimento da Maré/ SEBRAE.
Rio Prefeitura. (2015). *Porto Maravilha* [online]. Rio de Janeiro. Retrieved April 25, 2015, from www.portomaravilha.com.br
Rolnik, R. (2011). *Direito à moradia*. Retrieved November 3, 2016, from www.direitoamoradia.fau.usp.br/?regiao=brasil&paged=2
Rottle, N., & Maryman, B. (2012). Envisioning a city's green infrastructure for community livability. In F. Wagner & R. Caves (Eds.), *Community livability: Issues and approaches to sustaining the well-being of people and communities*. New York: Routledge.
Secchi, B. (2011). La nuova questione urbana: ambiente, mobilità e disuguaglianze sociali. *Crios*, 83(1).
Secchi, B. (2012). *A new urban question*. Oslo: City Council. (conference on 14 June 2012).
Secchi, B. (2014). *La città dei ricchi e la città dei poveri*. Bari: Editori Laterza.
Shaw, D., Pemberton, S., & Nurse, A. (2012). *Community livability: Issues and approaches to sustaining the well-being of people and communities*. F. Wagner & R. Caves (Eds.). New York: Routledge.
Silva, J. S. (2007). Um espaço em busca de seu lugar: as favelas para além dos estereótipos. In J. S. Silva & J. L. Barbosa (Eds.), *Favela: alegria e dor da cidade*. São Paulo/Rio de Janeiro: SENAC.
Soares, E. M. & Moreira, F. D. (2007). Preservação do patrimônio cultural e reabilitação urbana: o caso da zona portuária da cidade do Rio de Janeiro. *Da Vinci*, 4 (1).
Soja, E. W. (2010). *Seeking spatial justice*. Minneapolis: University of Minnesota Press.
Steiner, R. (2012). Does land use and transportation coordination really make a difference in creating livable communities? In F. Wagner & R. Caves (Eds.), *Community livability: Issues and approaches to sustaining the well-being of people and communities*. New York: Routledge.
Vainer, C. B. (2000). Pátria, empresa e mercadoria: notas sobre a estratégia discursiva do Planejamento Estratégico Urbano. In Arantes, O. et. al. *A cidade do pensamento único: desmanchando consensos*. Petrópolis: Vozes.

Veríssimo, A. A. (2010). Habitação, Emprego, Mobilidade: subsídios para o Plano Municipal de Habitação de Interesse Social. Trabalho apresentado na Reunião Pública e Oficina de Capacitação para o Plano de Reabilitação e Ocupação dos Imóveis do Estado situados na Área Central da Cidade do Rio de Janeiro, promovida pelo Ministério das Cidades, 14 de julho.

Wagner & R. Caves (2012) (Eds). Community livability: Issues and approaches to sustaining the well-being of people and communities. New York: Routledge.

Whelan, R. K. (2012). Introduction to community livability. In F. Wagner & R. Caves (Eds.), *Community livability: Issues and approaches to sustaining the well-being of people and communities*. New York: Routledge.

Wilheim, J. (1976). *Cidades: O Substantivo e o Adjetivo*. São Paulo: Perspectiva.

The World Health Organization Quality of Life (WHOQOL). Retrieved March 8, 2017, from www.who.int/mental_health/publications/whoqol

15 Livable Cities
The Case of Cape Town, South Africa
David Dewar

Introduction

The term "livable cities" is a directional one. It does not define an end-state, for cities are always in the process of becoming: there is always room for improvement. Positive change is a process, not a project. Rather, the term refers to the identification of the changes necessary to bring about significant improvements in the lives of inhabitants, particularly the urban poor, as they are the people with the least maneuverability and the ones who are most impacted by changes in material living conditions.

At any point in time, different cities have different baselines in terms of livability. It follows that priorities in terms of change will not be the same from place to place. In order to define these changes in any context, it is necessary to undertake three steps. The first is to identify the performance qualities which contribute to the concept of livability. The second is to evaluate the performance of the settlements in question, in terms of these qualities. The third is to identify the spatial principles which contribute to the achievement of these qualities.

This chapter seeks to address the issue of livability in terms of South African towns and cities. The chapter is structured in the following way. In Part 2, the performance qualities that should be informing urban decision making in South African towns and cities, in order to make them more livable, are identified and discussed. These are then synthesized to define clearly the urban model that decision makers should be moving towards in South Africa.

Part 3 is a brief assessment of the current performance of South African settlements through the lens of the model. It concludes that, in large part, they are performing poorly: for the majority of their inhabitants, they are highly unlivable.

Part 4 discusses a way forward. In it, the spatial principles that underpin the performance model identified in Part 3, and which, therefore, should inform all urban decision making in South Africa are discussed. Part 5 is a brief conclusion.

Performance Qualities Underpinning "Livability"

It is argued here that the performance qualities appropriate to South Africa should be derived from four main sources: emerging international tendencies, planning theory, the law and a contextually specific development filter.

Emerging International Tendencies

This refers to (complexly interrelated) global dynamics that have already taken root and that are likely to increase in importance in future years. Not all of these are equivalently relevant in all contexts, but spatial planning in all contexts needs to consider them.

Rapid Population Growth and Urbanization

Very different patterns of population growth and urbanization are occurring internationally. In more developed countries, both are slowing or even declining, bringing with them their own set of difficulties associated with ageing.

In developing countries, both remain high. In South Africa, population growth is still high (2.8% per annum), but declining and urbanization rates are very high. Only some 60% of the country is urbanized. The current flood of people to the towns and cities from the countryside and from the rest of Africa is likely to continue and even accelerate. The cities will be increasingly important stages where the development challenges of the country must be met. Bold and innovative urban planning is imperative.

Increasing Economic Globalization and Structural Unemployment

Economic globalization continues to grow apace, with a small number of large winners and an increasing number of losers. Inequality, both internationally and in South Africa, is increasing rapidly. Inevitably accompanying this is increasing structural unemployment in the formal economic sector. Developing countries, many of which have little global competitive advantage and a low skills base, are being particularly hard hit. South Africa is no exception to this. The national unemployment rate is conservatively estimated to be around 25%, but in many regions, it is far higher than this. Further, it is growing. There are no "big bang" solutions lying in the wings of the formal economy. The reality is that a large and increasing number of households will have no option but to generate their own livelihoods through their own ingenuity and energies, mainly in the informal economy. Increasingly, local economies will have to be more closed: it is necessary to meet local needs through local skills using, wherever possible, local resources (Dewar, 2015).

The central spatial planning issue that arises from this is how to create the pre-conditions for small businesses to flourish. There are two pre-conditions that are particularly important. The first one is to ensure vibrant local markets. One of the major problems with South African cities is that densities are so low that their generative capacity is dissipated—structural intensification and densification is essential (Dewar, 2015). A second pre-condition is to create viable locations for people to manufacture and trade with low or no overheads (Dewar & Watson, 1990).

Climate Change

There is growing evidence that global warming is occurring at a faster rate than previously projected. Cities are a major source of greenhouse gas emissions which, in turn, are a primary cause of warming. This makes climate change a city planning issue with numerous implications. (Seto et al., 2014).

One is that a primary source of greenhouse gas emissions is fossil fuel driven vehicular transport (Ewing & Rong, 2008; Newman & Kenworthy, 1989). This is particularly significant in South Africa, where the low-density nature of urban form makes public transport inefficient and expensive. Where vehicle kilometres travelled (VKT) are high, and where there is a high level of car dependence, the clear need is to move towards more compact, higher density urban forms that promote non-motorized transport (NMT) and that are based on efficient, viable public transportation (Jenks & Burgess, 2000). There are also significant co-benefits, such as improved public health, which will result from this (Seto et al., 2014).

A second implication is the increasing frequency of catastrophic natural events. This means that spatial planning must put nature first: natural constraints must be identified and strongly respected. The first design decision must be identifying where urban development should not go.

Food Security

A large and growing number of people globally have inadequate access to sufficient nutrition. This is certainly true in South African towns and cities. This is primarily a global distributional issue (where international dumping by developed countries leads to the subsidized flooding of markets in developing countries, undermining their agrarian economies), as opposed to a global production issue.

Further, the problem will almost certainly increase in many places because of climate change. The clear implication is that nutritional needs of local areas, including towns and cities, must be met locally to the greatest degree possible—urban agriculture must become a central concern of urban planning, particularly in the context of developing countries (Haysom & Battersby, 2016).

Water Scarcity

South Africa is already a semi-arid country, particularly in its interior. Further, all regional models of climate change predict that it will become warmer and dryer. Despite this, water usage is extremely wasteful. The dominant approach to water supply is a "big engineering approach": the creation of very large dams and piping water over hundreds of kilometres. Wastage is enormous: the very large water surfaces result in high levels of evaporation, and very large volumes are lost through leakage from ageing infrastructure. Additionally, little attention is paid to recycling: it is estimated, for example, that over 90% of the water entering Cape Town is returned to the sea after having been used only once (Gasson, 2000).

Perhaps most importantly, there is little awareness of the need for local water capture. A great deal of the rainfall that does occur is never captured: it simply exits towns and cities as storm water runoff. Local water capture needs to become an important part of the spatial planning agenda.

Fossil Fuel Dependence

Although the previously widely held view that fossil fuels were nearing a state of depletion no longer appears to be true (particularly with the discovery of large sources of natural gas and the growing use of fracking internationally), fossil fuel dependence remains a serious problem. There are three main reasons for this. First, it is still a finite resource that will eventually run out (Ewing & Rong, 2008). Second, it has very negative side effects (particularly in the form of air pollution and greenhouse gas emissions). Third, it significantly increases the economic risk for countries and regions that have to import these fuels: it is a non-controllable externality that can have very negative impacts on rates of inflation.

This has two main implications for urban planning. First, it is necessary to make much greater use of alternative, renewable sources of energy. Second, it is necessary to reduce the aggregate use of energy. In particular, it reinforces the need to move towards settlements that promote non-motorized and public transport (Dewar, 2015).

Planning Theory

The second informant of positive settlement performance is planning theory. Over the years, many planning theorists (e.g.,Crane, 1960; Dewar & Uytenbogaardt, 1977; Gutkind,

1956; Jacobs, 1962; Lynch, 1981; Mumford, 1961) have attempted to articulate the performance qualities that should be driving the planning and design of human settlements. Over time, a fairly high degree of consensus over the main qualities has emerged internationally. These include the following.

Efficiency

The term "efficiency" is an umbrella or meta-term. If all other performance qualities are met to a reasonable degree, a settlement could be described as "efficient". More narrowly, however, it refers to minimizing energy utilization (of which movement is a significant contributor) in carrying out human activities in settlements. This has a number of specific implications for urban structure and form.

One is achieving a satisfactory compromise between the potentially conflictive requirements for mobility (relatively rapid movement, particularly for freight traffic) and greater accessibility (reduced aggregate amounts of movement and the dominance of non-motorized and public transport over private vehicular use) (Dewar & Todeschini, 2004).

A second priority is to compact urban forms in order to reduce sprawl, to reduce aggregate amounts of movement, to increase densities, to reduce investments in utility infrastructure and to lower costs of waste collection.

A third is promoting greater activity-mix to encourage NMT movement and to increase convenience.

A fourth is, as settlements grow, to encourage the emergence of more polycentric structural forms to reduce aggregate amounts of movement and congestion (Dewar, 2015).

Sustainability

Sustainability is also a meta-term (and one which is overused). Nevertheless, it has great importance for settlement design. The term has ecological (respecting the systemic nature of natural systems and ecological principles), social (the idea of communities with easy access to livelihoods and urban support systems) and fiscal (ensuring a balance between capital and operational costs) meanings. At the most fundamental level, however, it recognizes that settlements themselves are like metabolisms, in the sense that they have inputs and outputs (Gasson, 2000). Sustainability requires that, in terms of inputs, maximum use is made of renewable resources and that both the hinterland (the area from which it draws its inputs) and the ecological footprint (the amount of land necessary to ensure healthy and enriching living) are kept as small as possible. In terms of throughputs, sustainability requires that energy and other resource flows are optimized (e.g., land, water, finance). In terms of outputs, it requires that wastes are disposed with minimum negative human and ecological impacts and, wherever possible, are recycled productively.

Finally, the term has implications for humans working harmoniously with nature. Contained in the concept of harmony are a number of different dimensions (McHarg, 1991):

- *Avoiding hazards and protecting resources*: the natural system may contain areas that are hazardous for human occupation (e.g., geological instability, areas prone to flooding or sea level rise). These conditions obviously should be avoided. Similarly, the landscape may contain potential resources (e.g., commercial minerals, clays suitable for brick making and so on) that need to be protected.
- *Recognizing ecological interdependencies*: certain parts of the landscape are of unique importance (e.g., unique habitats for flora and fauna, places of exceptional beauty) and human actions should not interfere or destroy that uniqueness.

- *Designing with nature* (McHarg, 1991): the particular natural context within which the settlement occurs should profoundly affect the form of that settlement. Central to this are issues of comfort, which affects the positioning of the settlement on the landscape; orientation (particularly in relation to the sun and wind); the tightness or looseness of the urban fabric in order to influence air flows; the optimization of sun and shade and so on. Part of this, too, relates to the sustainable use of resources within settlements. Nature potentially provides resources which can be used by people (e.g., agriculture, aquaculture, woodlots as supplementary sources of fuel and building materials and the use of local clay for brick making). Sometimes, these occur naturally. However, nature can and should be improved to provide reserves of these resources. Appropriate planning and management requires the creative and sustainable use of local resources. It also requires efficient and non-wasteful use of non-renewable resources such as land and water.
- *Respecting the interdependence of landscapes*: this has two interrelated forms. One is that, in environments of quality, there is a dynamic balance between the three landscapes of society: wilderness, rural and urban. Maintaining this balance, so that synergies are generated between all three, is one of the most fundamental spatial planning tasks. The other is that there is a fundamental interdependence between the landscape, the kinds of activities that take place upon the landscape and the technologies and practices which emerge over time in response to those activities and landscapes (Geddes, 1949). These factors, when moderated through generations of historical practices, underpin culture (e.g., they influence food tastes and folklore). It is this which Mumford calls the territorial basis of civilization (Mumford, 1961). Sensitive planning builds on this.

Equity and Social Justice

This is a critical issue in South Africa. A 2008 United Nations Review of World Cities found that South African cities are the most inequitable and (by implication, inefficient) in the world (UN Habitat, 2008; Dewar, 2015). Further, it is the urban poor who are the most disadvantaged by the structure and form of towns and cities. It is the poor who (by compulsion historically) primarily live on the urban peripheries furthest from urban opportunities.

Equity does not imply that all parts of settlements should be the same. This is not possible nor, arguably, desirable. It primarily relates to equity of access (particularly by the urban poor) to the opportunities of a settlement. It relates to convenience and reducing the costs of overcoming the friction of distance. It implies that all inhabitants should be able to conduct most of their daily activities quickly, easily and inexpensively. The most equitable situation pertains when people have access to most of their daily activities on foot or by NMT. When the cycle of movement on foot is broken, however, access by public transportation becomes a critical factor. It also requires subscription to principles of universal access.

Integration

This, too, is a critical factor in South African towns and cities where the overwhelmingly dominant spatial patterns are sprawl, fragmentation and separation. Almost everything is separate: land use, human activities, neighborhoods and, most problematically, race and class (there is a high correlation in South Africa between race and class). The term "integration" lies at the heart of holistic thinking. It represents a concern about making settlements in which different activities and elements find a natural, logical place and in which they "lean on" or reinforce each other.

The term has urban (integrating the elements of public structure-green space, movement of all nodes, public institutions, urban public spaces, utility services and emergency services), natural (integrating the landscapes of society), social (not marginalizing any person or group) and cultural (accommodating heterogeneity) meanings.

Dignity

The right to dignity is a basic human right. It is also the first constitutional right of all people of South Africa. It is essential to create environments in which all people have equivalent rights to dignity, regardless of their personal incomes.

In contexts where there is a high degree of inequality and in which there are high levels of poverty, such as South Africa, it is public spaces that are central to the achievement of spatial dignity, for these belong to all people. It is towards the public spatial environment that public investment should be directed.

Sense of Place

A concern with a sense of place and place-making reflects, in the first instance, a concern with uniqueness and memorability. It implies a rejection of uniformity and standardization. A number of factors contribute to the creation of a sense of place (Norberg-Schulz, 1980).

One is the appropriateness of the form of settlements to the landscape of which it is a part (climate, landform, the way in which surface water flows, the use of materials and so on). In this regard, it is useful to distinguish between two different types of landscape: romantic and cosmic.

In romantic landscapes, the positive qualities of the natural landscape tend to lead design: design is a sensitive and sympathetic response to the landscape. In cosmic landscapes, there are fewer and much weaker, natural informants: a sense of place needs to be created through processes of settlement formation.

A second contributing factor is the quality and coherence of the public spatial environment.

A third is the clarity and legibility of urban public structure and the creation of landmarks.

A fourth, related, factor is the creation of "special places". Not all parts of settlements can be special, but the inhabitants of all settlements should be entitled to have access to special places. In contexts of high levels of poverty and inequality, such as in South Africa, special places are of great importance: they are places where everybody, regardless of personal resources, is treated with equivalent respect and dignity. They are places of promenading. They are places of escape from intensity, routine and the struggle of daily life. In this respect, they belong to everyone.

Sociability and Privacy

In their essence, settlements are places of interaction, of face-to-face contacts, both formal and informal. How settlements are made can considerably enhance or hinder this interaction. The public environment within which the interaction takes place, and the forms of activity, through which these interactions are expressed, profoundly impact on the quality of life.

Although interaction and sociability are essential dimensions of humanness, so too is the need for privacy: the need to escape from the intensity of human interaction. The concept of privacy is clearly a hierarchical and zonal one: there are degrees of privacy. Indeed, a useful way of depicting settlements is as a continuum ranging from high levels of privacy to high levels of publicness or exposure. This conceptualization has considerable significance for the making of human settlements.

Safety and Security

Creating settlements that are safe and secure is a universal concern. The terms have broad ramifications (e.g., security of tenure, food security, safety from hazards, safety from accidents, particularly vehicular accidents, safety from attackers, security in terms of crime prevention and so on).

Although concerns with safety and security are obviously valid, they should not be pursued obsessively (as they have in many parts of South Africa): they can easily be pursued to a degree where vitality, spontaneity and room for uncertainty, which are essential dimensions of urban life, are destroyed.

Aesthetic Appeal

Human settlements should appeal to the senses of people: they should be attractive. Attractiveness is obviously a normative concept. One attempt to define it, with which many would agree, is from the London School of Life, founded by the philosopher and writer, Alain de Botton, which identifies six principles that govern the attractiveness of a city (November, 2015):

1. Order but not orderliness;
2. Visibility of life: people should be visibly engaged in life on the streets;
3. Compaction, as opposed to sprawl (this is key to walkability);
4. Orientation and mystery: one must be able to get lost but not too lost. A mixture of larger and smaller streets (and spaces) is the way to get it right (the use of landmarks is also an important part of this);
5. Scale: the ideal size is five stories, which is more humane than high-rise developments (scale also relates to the appropriateness of height to width in the definition of public spaces);
6. Local relevance and unique character.

The Law

The third source of direction is the law. South Africa is one of the few countries in the world where the law relating to land and land development is based on normative principles. The Spatial Planning and Land Use Management (Act 16 of 2013) requires that all land development decisions should further five normative principles:

1. The principle of social justice;
2. The principle of spatial sustainability;
3. The principle of efficiency;
4. The principle of spatial resilience;
5. The principle of good administration.

The first three of these have already been discussed. The principle of good administration is not a spatial principle. It relates to process and primarily calls for transparency and accountability in decision making. The principle of resilience is highly relevant in South Africa, where rapid urbanization and urban growth is occurring. It relates to the ability of a settlement to accommodate growth and change well. The principle has strong implications for urban structure and form.

A Context-Specific Developmental Filter

A fourth direction-informing source is the developmental characteristics of the particular context that is being considered. This provides a filter through which all urban actions should be viewed: it is this which defines the appropriateness of those actions. As a general principle, all urban actions should improve the developmental profile of that particular context. In this way, these actions should contribute to improving livability.

The main developmental characteristics of South African towns and cities include high and growing levels of poverty, unemployment and inequality; a deep correlation between race and class; a sluggish economy; low levels of literacy, education and skills; high levels of informality in both housing and the economy; high and increasing levels of air and water pollution, including greenhouse gas emissions; considerable food insecurity; periodic water shortages and a ubiquitously poor quality of open space.

The Performance Model

When these four sources of direction-setting are considered in combination, it is quite clear what urban professionals and decision makers should be seeking to achieve to make settlements more flexible, viable and appropriate to their context. South African towns and cities should:

- Maintain a dynamic balance with local wilderness and rural areas and not ride roughshod over them;
- Draw their inputs from as small a local area as possible;
- Engage in local food production and water capture;
- Make maximum use of renewable energy resources;
- Use all resources efficiently;
- Make productive use of wastes through recycling;
- Avoid hazardous conditions;
- Be compact and prevent sprawl;
- Be scaled by pedestrian and non-motorized transport;
- Promote efficient and viable public transportation;
- Be integrated and not fragmented;
- Be based on a legible order, but not be orderly;
- Be structured around high-quality public spaces (including streets) and institutions, not roads and houses;
- Promote mixed use;
- Promote maximum choice in terms of lifestyle from very public to very private living;
- Be sufficiently high density to create vibrant local markets, to make public transport viable and efficient and to generate adequate social services and facilities while taking primarily walk-up forms;
- Be unique and appropriate in form to their place;
- Be vibrant in the more public places;
- Be resilient.

A Brief Assessment of the Performance of Contemporary South African Towns and Cities: The Case of Cape Town)

Although the natural setting of Cape Town is unique, in terms of socioeconomic and spatial characteristics, it is fairly representative of other cities in South Africa. It will, therefore, be used as a case to assess livability.

The Case of Cape Town

The metropolitan area of Cape Town had 3 740 025 inhabitants in 2012 and is growing rapidly: it is now estimated to house some 4.5m people. In terms of race, the majority of people (some 42.4%) are classified as "colored" or mixed race; 38.6% are Black African; and 15.6% are white. Growth is being fueled both by natural increase (the rate of which is decreasing) and in-migration, both from the South African countryside and from the rest of Africa: the city is increasingly cosmopolitan.

The natural setting of the city is magnificent. It is a many-placed place. It is surrounded by sea, mountains, fertile winelands and fruit lands. It nestles at the foot of the iconic Table Mountain range, and Table Mountain itself provides timeless and dramatic orientation. It is part of the Cape Floral Kingdom, the smallest and, in terms of species, most diverse of the twelve global floral kingdoms. Its beauty, its diversity and its relatively weak currency makes it a highly rated international tourist destination and a highly popular place in which to live for those households that have adequate resources to experience its beauty and its recreational resources. Its Mediterranean climate, with rain in winter, is benign, although in the summer months it is frequently buffeted by high winds from the south and south-east.

Socioeconomically, however, the picture is bleak, for Cape Town is two cities: one is made up of a small minority of relatively wealthy households; for the rest (the vast majority), life is a hard struggle for survival.

Poverty is rife. Twenty-one point seven percent of households are officially classified as indigent by the metropolitan municipality, and many more live below the poverty datum line. Further, there is a strong correlation between class and race, with the vast majority of the poorest households being black African and colored. (Western Cape Government, 2016).

Unemployment, too, is high. The official estimate of unemployment is some 25%, but in parts of the city it is closer to 40%. An increasing number of households are dependent on the informal sector for survival. A major problem in terms of the economy is the lack of education and skills: only 15.6% of children of school-going age will complete secondary school education.

Levels of inequality are dangerously high. A 2008 United Nations Review of Global Cities found South African cities (excluding Cape Town) to be the most inequitable (and, by implication, inefficient) in the world (UN-Habitat, 2008).

Spatially, most of the urban growth of Cape Town has occurred subsequent to the Second World War. The implication of this is that the growth of the city has been strongly informed by two ideologies: the planning ideology of modernism, which promoted separation of uses, and the political ideology of "apartheid" or Separate Development, which grotesquely distorted the concept of separation and extended it to include race (Dewar, 2015). In terms of this policy, areas were reserved for exclusive use of particular race groups. Massive removals were undertaken at enormous cost to implement the policy. In the process, it was primarily the black African and colored households that were targeted for removals. As a consequence, it was the poorest households which were moved furthest from urban opportunities.

The dominant spatial patterns that have resulted from these ideologies, acting in combination, are sprawl, separation and fragmentation. The majority of poorer households are concentrated in the south-east of the city, on a flat, sandy plain known as the Cape Flats, which is prone to wind-driven sand and flooding. Access to formal housing is becoming increasingly difficult, and informal shacks, both in the form of free-standing and informal settlements or in the backyards of formal accommodation, are commonplace. In the order of 10% of accommodation takes the form of informal dwellings (Western Cape Government, 2016)).

An Evaluation in Terms of Livability

When these indicators of livability are applied to Cape Town (and thus the other contemporary South African towns and cities), it soon becomes apparent that almost the opposite applies on almost every count. Rather than being compact, a low-density sprawling form of development has driven, and continues to drive, roughshod over wilderness and rural landscapes, destroying potentially productive land and land of high amenity at an alarming rate. Although pockets of higher densities occur in places, on average, densities are below 20 units per hectare gross and are decreasing.

Inputs (food, potable water, power) are drawn from over hundreds of miles at great costs and with significant wastage. There is very little attention given to local water capture. Urban agriculture is not on the agenda of most local authorities. By far, the dominant source of energy derives from the burning of fossil fuels, with serious effects in terms of CO_2 and other greenhouse gas emissions. Recycling of urban wastes is very limited, and a considerable amount of settlement (particularly informal settlements) occurs on hazardous land, particularly areas prone to flooding. In general, the use of critical resources (land, water, energy, finance) is extremely wasteful.

Cities are scaled to the motor vehicle, not to non-motorized travel. The dominant form of travel is private, road-based vehicular movement. The system generates enormous amounts of movement at great cost on terms of household budgets (the structure and form of South African towns and cities significantly and negatively impacts on the primary societal problems of poverty, inequality and unemployment), congestion and production time, infrastructural investment, freight efficiency, air pollution and greenhouse gas emissions. Further, densities are too low to support viable, efficient pubic transport, vibrant local markets (a pre-condition for small-scale, self-generated economic activity) or adequate levels of social facilities and other forms of social back-up.

Together with sprawl, the dominant spatial patterns are fragmentation and separation. Settlements reflect a high degree of orderliness: evidence of the tyranny of the engineering handbook are everywhere to be seen, particularly in terms of transport (Dewar & Louw, 2012), but there is little apparent order (Dewar & Todeschini, 2017). Towns and cities are structured not by public space and public institutions, but by roads and houses. Limited access routes fragment the city into small "boxes" (ibid.).

The spatial quality of these areas is almost ubiquitously poor (Dewar & Louw, forthcoming). The open spaces that do exist are largely undefined, unscaled, residual spaces. The movement network reflects qualities of "road" as opposed to "street" (a multifunctional space which can accommodate many human activities, including movement of different modes). There is little evidence of urban design.

The overwhelming feel of larger parts of these cities is mind—numbing sterility. Two factors in particular contribute to this. One is uniformity resulting from state-funded, capital intensive, mass-housing programs in the form of single houses on single plots, and from large private developments that reflect the involvement of too few designers.

The second is mono-functionality. The urban tradition in South African cities over the last 70 years has been to promote separation. Everything is separated: land uses, urban activities, modes of movement, race and class. The result is huge swathes of mono-functional areas that are inherently sterile. Furthermore, within these, choice of lifestyle is limited. The dominant urban model of the single-story house on its own plot continues to dominate.

Finally, these settlements are far from being resilient. There are two main dimensions to this. First, there is no coherent public structure guiding new development, so that each new development contributes to an emerging, coherent and improving whole. Rather, growth is developer led (whether the developer is public or private)—each project is an isolated event. Public structure follows; it does not lead. The outcome is a pattern of fragmented pockets of development linked only by limited access roads.

Second, the dominant patterns of the movement networks are destination based. They largely take the form of radial systems focusing on the historic cores as opposed to more neutral, permeable geometries. The consequence is that they are extremely vulnerable. The blockage of a few routes would throw the entire system into turmoil. The system also promotes mono-centric as opposed to polycentric structural responses.

A Way Forward: Urban Planning and Spatial Principles

Historically, the discipline of urban planning in South Africa has been part of the problem, not the solution (Dewar & Louw, 2012). It has been firmly based on the rational-comprehensive model promoted by the modernists. Its focus is on land use and the central precepts upon which it is based, results almost precisely in the opposite performance qualities to those identified in Part 1 (Dewar, 2015). Two aspects of this are particularly significant. First, the dominant suburban model, upon which the system is based, is, as has been shown, simply non-sustainable and is the cause of many of the problems identified in Part 3. It is imposing enormous costs on both society (and its negative consequences impact most on the urban poor), on nature and on the economy.

Second, it results in settlements which are orderly but not ordered. They are overplanned at a small scale, but there is nothing that gives direction to the whole: growth and change are reactive, not proactive. Further, orderliness inevitably results in sterility and monotony—a hallmark of South African urban settlements.

Significant improvements in urban performance, therefore, require radical changes in two ways. The one is enthusiastically embracing an urban, as opposed to suburban, model of development. The other is changing the spatial planning focus away from land use (which is an urban management and not a forward-planning issue) towards the provision of public structure and public space (Dewar & Louw, forthcoming).

In structural-spatial approaches, the elements of public structure (green space, movement of all modes, public institutions, hard open space and utility infrastructure) are manipulated and coordinated to create a geometry of point, line and grid. The geometry generated by the way in which these elements are brought into association creates a logic to which all activities, large and small, formal and informal, respond in their own self-interests.

In the first instance, this logic is the logic of access. All activities have their own requirements in terms of the need for publicness and privacy (Dewar & Louw, forthcoming). Similarly, in the same way that it is possible to create a hierarchy of access, it is possible to create a hierarchy of public space. When these two hierarchies are coordinated and married, rich choices are offered, without imposing particular forms of lifestyle on everyone.

Minimalism is critical to this way of thinking. It is not possible, necessary or desirable to plan each square metre of land from the top down, as is advocated in the rational-comprehensive model of modernism. The search is for the minimum strong actions necessary to give direction to the settlement as a whole while allowing space for freedom of action by other designers at smaller scales.

In terms of this framework, positive urban settlements commonly reflect the following principles:

Order

They are ordered in the first instance by the relationship between public institutions and the public spaces which announce these, and not by roads and houses, as is the case with many contemporary settlements in South Africa and elsewhere.

Compaction

The footprint of settlements should be kept as small as possible. They should not sprawl. There are a large number of reasons for this: compaction protects rural and wilderness landscapes; it promotes walkability; it reduces public investment in infrastructure; it promotes adequately high densities; and it promotes convenience.

Human Scale

Settlements should be scaled to people, not motor vehicles. This has both horizontal and vertical dimensions. Horizontally, it means that settlements should be scaled to people on foot and other forms of non-motorized transport. Vertically, it means that the majority of buildings making up the urban fabric should not exceed walk-up forms (five stories) (Bliss, 2015). This is particularly true in developing countries where there are insufficient funds to provide and maintain elevators. High-rise forms are also more inefficient in terms of greenhouse gas emissions.

Adequate Densities

Densities must be relatively high to achieve qualities of urbanity. They are necessary to achieve vibrant local markets, which are a pre-condition for promoting self-generated, small-scale economic activity; to provide efficient, viable public transportation; and to achieve high levels of social support. It has been shown that it is possible to achieve relatively high densities (between 400 and 450 dwelling units net) in highly livable forms without exceeding four stories (Dewar & Louw, 2012).

Continuity

The spatial principle of continuity is central to achieving the performance quality of integration. These types of continuity are particularly important.

- *Continuity of movement*: Movement (represented by flows of people, finance and goods) is the lifeblood of urban systems. Movement lines define the energy flows of cities. They represent planes of higher accessibility and are therefore desirable locations for activities requiring the greater exposure. Activities requiring the greater public support will gravitate naturally towards the lines and points of greater accessibility. This locational tendency enables more continuous lines to integrate different local areas. These areas then collectively contribute to support of, and share, the more public facilities. This explains the common tendency for "activity corridors";

to emerge in all settlements where they are not prevented from doing so (as is the case in South Africa). It is a principle that can be used consciously to break down fragmentation in spatially highly fragmented settlements such as those in South Africa (Dewar, 2015).
- *Continuity of urban fabric*: This refers to the need to move away from situations in which settlements are simply a collection of parts to one where they operate as coherent systems.
- *Continuities of green space*: Achieving continuities of green space which is self-maintaining is important for natural regeneration, biodiversity and habitat selection for flora and fauna. It is also important in ensuring human access to nature.

Discontinuity

While achieving continuities of movement flows is important, if the routes are too long, they result in monotony and encourage speeding. Accordingly, it is important to interrupt them periodically. The design device most commonly used to achieve this is the insertion of urban public space (squares and so on) where traffic is diverted around the edges. These are places of pausing: they contribute to emerging nodes of intense activity.

Permeability

In positive urban environments, people should be able to change direction and modes of movement, quickly and easily. The ability to change direction quickly is particularly important for pedestrian and NMT movement, where the engine is human energy. The principle is central to convenience. This suggests the concept of "superblocks'": a number of shorter blocks (particularly but not exclusively pedestrian based), making up a superblock, which is scaled to the motor vehicle.

Mixed Use

Although there will always mono-functional pockets of land use within cities, as a general rule, urban settlements should be as mixed-use as possible. This is central to convenience and vibrancy, which are hallmarks of livable towns and cities.

Legibility

This refers to legibility of settlement structure. In particular, structure should create deep divisions between points and lines which are very visible and exposed and those which are very private and embedded. The most fundamental level of choice in settlement is choice of lifestyles, from very public to very private living. When public structure is clear and legible, it promotes resilience. Even though precise uses may change over time, uses requiring the greatest exposure will always gravitate towards the most accessible locations.

Surveillance

There is now a large body of evidence internationally showing that surveillance (human eyes over space) and exposure are the two most significant factors in promoting safety and security in urban settlements (Hillier, 1983). Despite this, an increasingly common response to safety and security in South Africa, where crime rates are high, is the phenomenon of gated communities (pockets of development surrounded by high walls or other forms of security fencing), which significantly increases fragmentation and decreases surveillance.

Generality and Generosity

These are both principles that contribute to resilience. Generality is a structural item. It refers to situations where the urban public structure of settlements is not so specific that it can work only under particular conditions or with particular technologies. In many cases, the dominant movement network in South African settlements is radial, focusing on the historic centres, as opposed to being more grid-like and permeable. This is a certain recipe for congestion and gridlock.

Generosity is a spatial term. It refers to spaces that are not designed to accommodate any particular activity, but which can positively accommodate a wide range of activities, albeit none perfectly. Most of the public space in South Africa is not defined. It is residual space which fails to contribute to the enjoyment of human activities.

Clarity of Thresholds

In positive settlements, the transition from public to private space is always clear. Problems arise when this transition is blurred, because no-one takes responsibility for these spaces. They frequently become dumping grounds for rubbish and sites of antisocial behavior.

Spaces of this kind are commonplace in South African cities, where a large amount of space is residual or leftover space.

Spatial Quality

The quality of the public spatial environment—the spaces between buildings (Gehl, 2010)—is a critical factor in determining high-performing settlements.

In well-performing settlements, all public space is seen as multifunctional social space (there is no residual space). When these spaces are properly made (when they are defined, enclosed, humanly- scaled, surveilled and landscaped), they significantly enhance the enjoyment of the activities that take place within them, and they impact significantly on the dignity of the entire environment.

Conversely, when these spaces are poor, the entire environment is miserable and even hostile, regardless of how much is invested in individual buildings. The primary role of buildings, therefore, is to define and scale public spaces.

Although being significant for everyone, public spaces are particularly important in contexts where large numbers of people are poor. By definition, poor households are unable to conduct all, or even most, of their daily activities in private space. Much of their lives is played out in public space. These are the places where people meet, children play, lovers court and scholars read when the houses are overcrowded.

Public space can take many forms. One of the most important (because it is one of the largest land uses in any city) is land related to movement. Here, the essential distinction is between "road" (an engineered conduit or "pipe" for motor vehicles) and "street'" (a linear space which accommodates many human activities, including movement, albeit none perfectly).

Conclusion

Apart from a limited number of pockets exhibiting qualities of urbanity, the levels of livability in South African cities, defined in terms of the indicators discussed in Part 1, are very low. The performance model which decision makers should be seeking to achieve is quite clear (Part 1) as are the spatial principles which underpin the achievement of these qualities (Part 4).

Despite this, there has been little improvement in the performance of these settlements since the attainment of a universal franchise in 1994: if anything, the situation has worsened. The question is, why is this so?

The problem is not a lack of awareness. The restructuring of towns and cities is rhetorically high on the reform agenda of the ruling party, the African National Congress. It is also not the national law: national planning legislation is progressive. It calls for significant changes to current planning practices.

At the heart of the problem are four factors. One is that the professions concerned with the built environment have failed to give a lead to society (Dewar & Louw, 2012). The dominant approach to planning is multidisciplinary, not interdisciplinary. Different professions work on the same problem but from entirely different perspectives. Very often, there is no common agreement about the problem, let alone about the best way forward. Frequently, the process is combative: it involves power struggles, and commonly, engineering perspectives prevail (Dewar & Louw, 2011).

A second factor is that, urban decisions in the local authority bureaucracies are often taken in silos: different professions make decisions about different elements of public structure, commonly without consultation. Although integrative spatial plans are required by law, they have little impact on actual public investment patterns.

Third, political decision makers, who have the final say, are more driven by party political concerns and political patronage than they are by a consistent, progressive program of reform. The influence of the officials who advise them is generally very weak.

Fourthly, although national legislation is normative and performance based, there has been little change in terms of local rules, regulations and bylaws. These remain prescriptive. They were originally drafted to support the failed modernist model with which the majority of bureaucrats are familiar and comfortable. There is no drive to change from within—from the bottom-up.

Until these factors are reversed, significant change is unlikely to be generated by city governments. Top-down initiatives are now required.

References

Bliss, L. (2015, February 27). What makes a city beautiful? *CityLab*. Retrieved from https://www.citylab.com/solutions/2015/02/what-makes-a-city-beautiful/386291/

Crane, D. (1960). The city syndrome. *American Institute of Planners Journal*, 26(4), 280–292.

Dewar, D. (2015). A transformational path for Cape Town, South Africa. In F. Wagner, R. Mahayi, & A. G. Piller (Eds.), *Transforming distressed global communities: Making inclusive, safe, resilient and sustainable cities* (pp. 231–244). Surrey, UK: Ashgate.

Dewar, D., & Louw, P. (2011). *An integrated curriculum design for the built environment professions*, UIA International competition for *Research Papers in Architecture and Urban Design* (Honorable Mention), Tokyo, Japan: International Union of Architects.

Dewar, D., & Louw, P. (2012). J'Accuse: The professions concerned with the built environment', *Architecture SA*, 57, September–October, Cape Town, 54–60.

Dewar, D., & Louw, P. (forthcoming). *Seeking urbanity through design*. Cape Town.

Dewar, D., & Todeschini, F. (2004). *Rethinking urban transformation after modernism: Lessons from South Africa*. London: Ashgate Publishers.

Dewar, D., & Todeschini, F. (2017). South Africa. In D. Pojani & D. Stead (Eds.), *The urban transportation crisis in developing countries* (pp. 221–246). New York: Springer Publishers.

Dewar, D., & Uytenbogaardt, R. S. (1977). *Housing: A comparative evaluation of urbanism in Cape Town*. Cape Town: Cape and Transvaal Printers.

Dewar, D., & Watson, V. (1990). *Urban markets: Developing informal retail*. London: Routledge.

Ewing, R., & Rong, F. (2008). The impact of urban form on U.S. residential energy use. *Housing Policy Debate*, 19(1), 1–29.

Gasson, B. (2000). *The urban metabolism of Cape Town, South Africa: Planning imperatives in an ecologically unstable Metropolis*, paper presented at the Association of European Planning Schools Campus, Beno, Czech Republic, July.
Geddes, P. (1949). *Cities in evolution*. London: William and Norgate.
Gehl, J. (2010). *Cities for people*. Washington, DC, USA: Island Press.
Gutkind, P. (1956). Our world from the air: Conflict and adaption. In W. C. Thomas (Ed.), *Mans' role in changing the face of the earth*. Chicago, USA: University of Chicago Press.
Haysom, G., & Battersby, J. (2016). Urban agriculture: The answer to Africa's food crisis? *Quest: Science for South Africa*, 12(2), 8–9.
Hillier, R., & Hanson, J. (1983). *The social logic of space*. Cambridge, UK: Cambridge University Press.
Jacobs, J. (1962). *The death and life of great American cities*. London: Jonathan Cape.
Jenks, M., & Burgess, R. (Eds.). (2000). *The compact city: A sustainable urban form for developing countries?* London: Spon Press.
Lynch, K. (1981). *A theory of good city form*. Cambridge, MA, USA: MIT Press.
McHarg, I. (1991). *Design with nature*. New York, USA: John Wiley and Sons.
Mumford, L. (1961). *The city in history: Its origins, its transformations and Its prospects*. New York: Mariner Brooks.
Newman, P. W. G., & Kenworthy, J. R. (1989). *Cities and automobile dependence: A source book*. London: Gower Technical.
Norberg-Schulz, R. (1980). *Genius Loci: Towards a phenomenology of architecture*. London: Academy Editions.
Republic of South Africa. (2013). *Spatial planning and urban management act* (Act 16 of 2013). Pretoria: Government Printer.
Seto, K. C., Dhakel, S., Bigio, A., Blanko, H., Delgado, G. C., Dewar, D., Huang, L., Inaba, A., Kansal, A., Lwasa, S., McMahon, J. E., Muller, D. B., Murakami, J., Nagendra, H., & Ramaswami, A. (2014). Human settlements, infrastructure and spatial planning. In Q. Edhover, R. Pichs-Madruga, Y. Sekona, E. Farahani, S. Kadner, K. Seyboth, A. Adler, I. Baum, S. Brunner, P. Eickemeier, B. Krieman, J. Savolainen, S. Schlomer, C. Von Stechow, T. Zwickel, & J. Minx (Eds.), *Climate change 2014: Mitigation of climate change*, Contribution of Working Group iii to the fifth assessment report of the Intergovernmental Panel on Climate Change. Cambridge, UK and New York, NY, USA: Cambridge University Press.
United Nations Habitat. (2008–2009). *State of the world cities report: Harmonious cities*. London: United Nations Human Settlements Programme, Earthscan Publishers.
Western Cape Government. (2016). 2016 Socio-Economic Profile: City of Cape Town. Cape Town: Western Province Government. Retrieved from https://www.westerncape./gov.za/general-publication/cape-metro

16 Livability and the Challenge of Planning in Tehran

Ali Modarres

After a revolution and a war, followed by a real estate boom, the city of Tehran has emerged as the embodiment of 21st century conflict planning, where no act, be it in service of livability or capital accumulation (as if the two are contradictory), is apolitical. Tehran, as in the case of every city, is the sum of its political history and economy, accented by cultural and social dynamics. However, during the last four decades, the city has discovered what it means to be the capital of the Islamic Republic while simultaneously maintaining its status as economic hub for a nation that grew from 38.7 million residents in 1980 to 79.1 million in 2015. Tehran itself expanded from 4.5 million on the eve of the revolution (1976)[1] to nearly 9 million (not including the conurbation area and extended commute zone). This phenomenal increase in population has acted as a magnifying glass highlighting the challenges of everyday existence in a city with crawling traffic, contrasted geographies of wealth, and tenacious inhabitants who eke out a living despite sanctions and economic challenges. Through its form and function, design and history, Tehran is a geography of contradictions in motion. This is a city with unaffordable housing and a polluted environment that is also home to luxury hotels, expensive restaurants, major shopping malls, and expansive public parks.

From a global perspective, Tehran's image conflates with that of Iran, and a discourse on the livability of the capital of the Islamic Republic may be the last thing a Western reader would expect. How can a country that appears on the news every other day as an international source of concern (albeit more often by only a few other nations) have any concern about the livability of its cities? Why would Iranians, scholars or otherwise, want to assess the livability of their cities when they should have more immediate existential concerns? Nothing about Iran, and by extension, its cities, sounds livable to a typical person who relies on Western mass media for international news. Yet to Iranians and urbanists who study Iranian cities, the reality is more complex. To a commuter sitting in rush hour traffic on a Tehran freeway, the true measure of happiness may be getting home a bit earlier and spending the evening with the family. If weather allows, dinner in a nearby park and playing with the kids in an ad hoc neighborhood soccer field may be the desired measure of livability (see Figure 16.1).

It is important to emphasize at the onset of this chapter that Tehran is generally a fun and lively city, regardless of the challenges it shares with other megacities. Its residents are not likely to worry about urban safety from armed conflicts; they are more apt to be deeply concerned about housing affordability, traffic, quality education and healthcare, air pollution, the state of the economy, and access to the most recent consumer goods at reasonable prices. A typical conversation with an expat easily lands on the income potential outside Iran and the dream of mass consumption in other places. For a good number of Iranians, particularly the residents of Tehran, livability is a desired space, not for the next generation alone, but for the here and now. This is by nature the space that separates livability

Figure 16.1 Nighttime at a Park at Chitgar Lake, Western Tehran
Source: author

from sustainability. If a major distinction between these two concepts is their temporality (Ruth & Franklin, 2014), where livability focuses on the needs of a current generation and sustainability on future generations, then Tehran is a great case study for understanding this difference. Furthermore, if livability begins with needs and arrives at desires, there is no better place to study livability than Tehran, a city haunted by generations of expectations and the promise of consumable modernity.

In this chapter, I will begin with a brief review of livability literature (which has been done often since at least 1990; e.g., see Pacione, 1990), laying the foundation for understanding some of the materials published about Iran. Although this is necessary for situating Tehran's experience within a larger international context, starting with perspectives from the west is somewhat uncomfortable, because it may appear that a particular voice is being privileged or used as a point of reference. However, my purpose here is not to evaluate Iranian scholars' and practitioners' approaches to livability vis-à-vis Western theories, but to highlight overall patterns of divergence and convergence, pointing to local urban politics, social geography, and economic dynamics as influential forces that have shaped and continue to shape the meaning and practice of livability within Iran, particularly Tehran.

Background

In its 2001 Charter, the City of Tehran adopted sustainability and democracy as its core principles. This decision was based on a collective agreement between city council members and nongovernmental organizations (Madanipour, 2006) during the "reform era" in Iran (1997–2005). Sustainability as a principle was used to guide various planning activities including transportation, economic development, and urban management. Under the reformist mayor at that time, a focus on sustainability manifested in additional park planning, an air pollution abatement program, transit planning, and various livable cities initiatives that loomed large in spatial planning. Following this period, consultants were hired and a team was assembled to develop plans for each of the city's 22 districts. Although this process was may have been viewed as less than perfect, the running narrative remained focused on sustainability and equity. Livability, translated as *zist-pazyri* in Persian, has become a buzzword in recent years and has often been used interchangeably with sustainability (e.g., Sasanpour et al., 2014). Of course, the mixing of these two concepts is not exclusive to Iran and Iranian scholars: recognizing their relationship, Leach et al. (2017) argue for the adoption of 'livable sustainability' when discussing the case of Birmingham, UK. The framework for this concept comes from Gough (2015), who attempts to reconcile livability and sustainability by highlighting their differences and commonalities as well as complementary areas. In doing so, the long-term sustainability goals are connected to a series of livability outcomes.

Locating Livability

Overall, as Ruth and Franklin (2014) argue, livability can be divided into two parts: needs (e.g., shelter, energy, food, water, etc.) and wants (e.g. economic prosperity, access to consumable goods, entertainment). This division resonates well with livability research (e.g., Mesimäki et al., 2017) and well-known livability indexes. Australia's *State of Australian Cities Report 2010* (Major Cities Unit, 2010) adopts a similar approach to measuring the livability of Australian cities. Embedded within this larger view of livability is a long list of needs and desires that cover the built environment, infrastructure, design, planning, urban services, environmental conditions, health and well-being, physical geography, climate, and urban governance, a list that could serve as a framework for selectively measuring how a specific city falls short or succeeds in achieving livability. As early as the 1990s, livability researchers have been aware of the behavioral/perceptual aspects of this concept (Couclelis, 1990; Ley, 1990; Pacione, 1990; Pacione, 2003): livability is both a state of mind and a physical manifestation of a particular interpretation of what a city needs and what a city has.

It is for that reason that some international measurements of livability use both objective and subjective indicators (e.g., the Economist Intelligence Unit's report includes "over 30 qualitative and quantitative factors, across five broad categories: stability, healthcare, culture and environment, education, and infrastructure"[2]). The *State of Australian Cities Report* concludes that "[w]hile opinions vary about the precise characteristics of liveability, liveable cities are widely perceived to be healthy, attractive and enjoyable places for people of all ages, physical abilities and backgrounds" (Major Cities Unit, 2010, 93). However, as livability has become a branding strategy and an important indicator for attracting capital that allows cities to jump scale, quantitative measurements have been deployed to easily communicate the quality of life in a city (for one of the earlier examples of focusing on quantitative measurements of urban quality of life, see Sufian, 1993). This has been the underlying theme in producing global lists of the best places to live, retire, work, and so forth. It is on these global measurements of livability that Tehran and other cities would like to compete, a point to which this chapter will return shortly.

Although a critical assessment of livability has remained important in academic research, a significant number of case studies have moved toward a contextualized assessment of livability, meaning that livability is analyzed from the perspective of a particular demographic group or a particular geography. For example, a large number of articles have focused on aging (Heatwole Shank & Cutchin, 2016), youth (Appleyard, 2017), or gender (Roberts, 2013). Transportation, including walkability and pedestrianization, has also been a significant thematic focus of livability research (Gehrke & Clifton, 2017; Marshall, 2013; Miller et al., 2013), as have safety (Kotus & Rzeszewski, 2013) and green spaces. From this standpoint, livability has moved from a mathematical assemblage of indexes to an understanding that cities and the neighborhoods within them are livable only if they match the needs and desires of their residents. This awareness connects livability to the spatial structure of our cities, as they manifest our social, cultural, demographic, and economic divides. Furthermore, livability has to be contextualized and further complicated by the dimension of time (Ruth & Franklin, 2014): a neighborhood that at one time houses families with children could become home to older empty nesters in a few short decades. As such, the context for livability shifts, resulting in a livable neighborhood becoming less livable, even for a population that opts to age in place.

This spatial and temporal understanding of livability indicates that it is permanently captured in a moving "now." Under such a proposition, planning solutions move from being fixed to being dynamic across time and space, but this proposition is hard to achieve under the current systems of planning practice. Instead, livability converges with ideological definitions of a good city, producing prescriptive urban forms that cater to particular demographics and tastes. At times, what is defined as livable can be similar to smart growth, new urbanism, creative class, or garden city concepts. This is what Eisinger (2004) suggested, when he wrote that although livability is not a social science concept, it is something that planners recognize when they see it. Kashef (2016) similarly highlights the inclusion of normative urban design concepts, such as transit-oriented development, smart growth, and urban transect (e.g., Calthorpe & Fulton, 2001) in defining livability. However, as one expands the scope of livability research, the diversity of related topics and disciplines engaged in this area of study suggest the complex nature of livability and why, despite its seemingly formulaic measurement, it may be difficult to achieve. Given the multidimensionality and multidisciplinary nature of livability, various attempts have been made to create a more macro-level definition for its operationalization. Kashef (2016) made one such attempt by focusing on architecture and planning literature, as well as some of the more well-known global livability ranking publications: the EIU livability ranking, Mercer Quality of Life Survey, and OECD BLI[3] (Better Life Index). He concludes by indicating that although a more perfect methodology for measuring livability could not be offered, "cities that strive to achieve livability must create a governance model that supports the civic ecology of participatory democracy" (Kashef, 2016, 252). In other words, without good governance, it is difficult to achieve and sustain livable cities.

Livable Tehran?

On August 18, 2016, the *Guardian* reported that "[A] period of relative stability has put the Iranian capital No. 1 on the list of world cities that have achieved biggest improvements in liveability over the past five years, as calculated by the Economist Intelligence Unit."[4] This simply meant that over a 5-year period, Tehran had moved from being ranked 132 among 140 world cities to 126. Although the photo in this story that illustrates Dubai, United Arab Emirates (which ranked second in the most improved cities in terms of livability, moving from 88th to 74th position), shows an overly opulent environment of tall buildings and an architecturally narrated city, Tehran's livability is illustrated by a picture of seven young men smoking water pipes, playing cards, and spending their national spring holiday in a park. The young man at the center is wearing a gray tee shirt, with the word "Brooklyn" shown prominently on his chest. Far on the photo's right side, there is a woman riding a bicycle. This photo depicts livability as an everyday experience, something Tehran and other cities in Iran have gradually attempted to elevate. The origin of this movement can be found in the 1990s reformist era. Under Karbaschi, the mayor of Tehran from 1990 to 1998, who was trained as an architect and planner, a large number of parks were created. He also initiated aggressive transportation policies, such as preventing the use of private cars in the center of the city. This pattern was continued by later city leaders, not only to improve the quality of life in an ever-expanding city, but also to attract public support for the electoral process. Under the current mayor, Dr. Ghalibaf (who holds a PhD in political geography and has a background as Iran's Chief of Police), Tehran has experienced additional gains in transportation management and urban governance. This was widely acknowledged in 2008, during the World Mayor Commendation review, when he was recognized as eighth among the top 11 world mayors.[5]

Although more parks have been added, including the controversial women-only park (Mothers' Paradise), there are some expressions of dismay at how various neighborhoods are treated differently in terms of the distribution and expansion of urban services and amenities.[6] This points clearly to the difference between livability at the city and neighborhood levels. Both in indicators and perceptions, or needs and desires, neighborhoods differ in how they see the state of livability in a city. While in 2012, Javaheri wrote about the *Four Changes That Made Tehran a More Liveable City*,[7] residents of Navab district may disagree with those in the northern neighborhoods about whether the city is more livable. Javaheri points to the growth of green space (i.e., parks), increased use of public transport (i.e., metro), reduced number of road accidents (through the use of various traffic control measures), and correction of parking policies as the measures that have made Tehran more livable. Given the distribution of parks and the focus of transportation mitigation policies, it may be a bit easier to understand the differing geographies of livability perception by reviewing the map of Tehran. A significant majority of the city's larger parks (perhaps due to availability of land parcels) are found north of Azadi, the street that divides northern and southern Tehran. Some of the most well-known parks in Tehran, including Mellat, Abo-Atash, Sa'ee, and Tabiat Bridge, which connects Taleghani Park with Abo-Atash and traverses a major freeway, are all built in the north. This pattern of urban amenities is not new; in fact, recent additions have simply accentuated an existing difference, as both Mellat and Sa'ee were built under the previous regime. Other parks, including the Nahjolbalagheh Park, a 35-hectare, 1.5-kilometer linear park bordering some of the newest residential developments, are by-products of the recent urban government. This park sits across from and visually connects with Pardisan Park, which is a 270-hectare urban park in Tehran's District 2, giving this area the largest green space in Tehran. The neighborhoods bordering over 300 acres of green space differ from those in Districts 10 and 11, which are separated by the Navab Expressway (an area with significant air pollution problems). After analyzing all 22 districts of Tehran, Sasanpour et al. (2015) concluded that the most livable districts were 1 and 3, located furthest north in the city. The city's least livable area was District 20, located furthest south. Earlier, Faryadi and Taheri (2009) illustrated the overall pattern of urban disparity by focusing on the availability of green space per capita in all districts, highlighting the urgent need for attention to this topic.

This north-south division in livability is not a shocking revelation, especially to those who have witnessed the development of the entire urban conurbation across multiple decades of uncontrolled growth. Although the increase in Tehran's livability ranking may be a promising moment in Iranian urbanism, the dilemma of global indicators becomes clearly obvious when one considers the patterns of uneven development in a city such as Tehran. This is a condition that is internally recognized by decision makers within urban government. In fall 2016, the Tehran Urban Planning Research Center published a report called Tehran's *Commitment Toward a New Urban Agenda*. The first full image in the front section is a nighttime picture of Tabiat Bridge (Nature Bridge), followed by a picture of Milad Tower after the table of contents. The first topic in the introduction is social inclusion and inclusive livable cities. In his foreword to the report, the mayor (Dr. Ghalibaf) refers to the importance of inclusive livable cities and writes: "Cities belong to all citizens and the rights of citizens must be respected. This axis seeks an answer to the following question: 'How to put an end to spatial exclusion, segregation, ghettoization and urban apartheid?'" (8). Given that the document was prepared in anticipation of Habitat III and positioned as a series of "issue papers," it is clear that the topics of livability and inclusivity should loom large. Under inclusivity, the report pointed to enhanced urban management, increased attention to women's empowerment, and retrofitted urban services, such as the metro, for persons with disabilities. Under "safer cities," the focus shifts to the 5-year strategic plan to improve urban health, the establishment of "health-oriented social centers" and other measures that deal with health issues such as obesity. "Urban culture and heritage" and "migration and refugees" are the next two topics. In this section of the report, Tehran Vision Plan 2025 is used as the guiding document for achieving inclusive livability. Given the existing body of research (some of which was highlighted earlier), inclusivity will continue to be a challenge, despite efforts made to ameliorate the existing condition. To highlight some of the additional complex issues facing the livability agenda in Iran, I will now turn to a review of some of the existing research published inside and outside Iran.

Examining Livability Through Academic Research on Tehran

Over the last decade, a number of articles have appeared in academic journals inside and outside Iran pointing to a native view of the topic. Because the conflation of sustainability and livability is a common problem, I have included a few publications that refer explicitly to sustainability but are equally applicable to livability, in order to provide a slightly wider view.

Overall, Iranian scholarship on this topic takes the position that cities happen to people, suggesting that deficiencies are externally caused by technology, modernism, politically motivated agents of change, and the perpetuation of Western ideas through planning and design. This view of livability is concerned mostly with equitable access to urban amenities, as well as identity and place-making with a certain reverence for a lost era, and it relies upon an assemblage of internationally recognized indicators, such as transportation, pollution, walkability, health, and so forth. As such, improving livability requires significant public investment in infrastructure projects, abatement programs, or expensive corrective measures to undo damages caused by past practices. The picture of seven young men smoking water pipes is hardly an image of livability to a typical critical academic. As such, it is fascinating that the *Guardian*, a Western media outlet, would imagine livability as a moment in the everyday experience of Tehran's citizens.

For some Iranian scholars, such as Riahifard (2013), cities were robbed of their livability. This author suggests that modern technology disrupted and disturbed the calm neighborhoods of an imagined bygone era, producing chaotic places lacking in human communication. Within this narrative, Iranian cities were the victims of Western-influenced governments, designers, architects, and urban planners who induced these changes and displaced the traditional social values. The way to create better open spaces, it is suggested, is a better method and, preferably a non-Western approach, to planning and urban design. However, in adopting a methodology or establishing a framework for measuring livability (Bandar Abad & Ahmadinejad, 2014; Golkar, 2007; Majedi & Bandar Abad, 2014; Riahifard, 2013; Sasanpour et al., 2014, 2015), a return to Western literature is apparent. For example, Mofidi and Kashani Jou (2010), in the spirit of smart growth and new urbanism, focus on the pedestrianization of Tehran. Their research recommends creating pedestrian-oriented areas in the city, highlighting some of the potential obstacles and the role local government could play in overcoming them. The obstacles presented by Mofidi and Kashani Jou are adopted from Living Streets, an advocacy group in UK. Using ten criteria listed by Living Streets, the authors conclude that it would take a long time to achieve them. However, they are optimistic, on the basis of a report from the Ministry of Housing and Urban Development that emphasized the importance of positive factors such as Tehran's high-density, mild climate, navigable topography, and young population, that improving the walkability of Tehran is a possibility. They conclude the paper by assessing some of the difficulties facing the city and listing possible policy solutions to fix them.

Safavi Sohi et al. (2014) equally rely on Western definitions of livability when discussing the Darake neighborhood of Tehran. To these authors, who cite Cities PLUS, a project of Vancouver, Canada, livability is a wide-ranging topic that includes the psychological, social, physical, and personal well-being of all residents. They also refer to the "livable streets" concept from Appleyard (which should be cited as Appleyard et al., 1981), with a nod to Jane Jacobs. On the basis of their synthesis of livability literature, they adopt a long list of factors (transportation, natural hazards, economy, housing, infrastructure, pollution and clean energy sources, community service, good governance, poverty and deprivation, security and comfort, neighborhood hygiene, social cohesion and public space, production of tangible and intangible heritage, place attachment, vision and urban perspective, and technological innovation and communication) as indicators of livability. This assemblage is not unlike a Western case study, and the conclusion would be highly familiar to scholars and practitioners outside Iran. The authors suggest that a better mix of land use would improve access to services such as libraries, post offices, and shopping centers. Transportation solutions that focus on traffic calming and improved roads for cycling and walking are additional recommendations. Although interesting as a case study, this paper exemplifies an approach in livability research that begins with an overview of Western literature, applies an intense subjective and objective analysis to a plethora of indictors, and concludes by putting the solutions at the doorstep of the public sector.

What appears to be common in the angst about Tehran's livability extends beyond the urban experience at the center to include concerns about the metropolitan area's rapid growth. This concern is best manifested by a number of studies that examine the pattern and rate of urban growth in Tehran. A number of highly quantitative articles have focused their attention on Iranian cities (e.g., Jokar et al., 2013a, 2013b, 2011; Rafiee et al., 2009; Sabet Sarvestani et al., 2011; Tayyebi et al., 2011). In the case of Jokar et al. (2013b), the focus turns to predicting future growth patterns, a significant portion of which will occur in the northwestern section of the city. This mainly covers District 22, which at this point enjoys better air quality, provides one of the largest per capita green spaces (Faryadi & Taheri, 2009), and according to Sasanpour et al. (2015), ranks third in livability among Tehran's 22 districts. The challenge for a livability agenda is clearly how to maintain the current quality of life and improve it where and when possible. In the case of western and eastern districts, lower housing values will attract a new population and those moving from other districts. In the case of the northwestern region, it might be the added presence of parks, good quality of air, and adequate local shopping opportunities that will attract more people to some of the newer neighborhoods. Urban growth in Iran, particularly Tehran, requires better urban planning approaches as well as management. As the Mayor of Tehran and the authors of *Commitment Toward a New Urban Agenda* are fully aware, the move forward on livability is an urban governance structure that fully embraces the principles of equity planning and provides an urban management approach that improves quality of life in Tehran and other cities in Iran.

Although concerns about urban growth have attracted the attention of Iranian scholars in a number of disciplines, including planning and geography, urban management and its relevance to successful urban development has also been explored in a number of articles (e.g., Rasoolimanesh et al., 2014; Zamani & Arefi, 2013). Inadequate attention to management issues could result in further exacerbation of illegal settlements (Zebardast, 2006) and a worsening of livability indicators, however they are defined and perceived.

Moving Toward a Conclusion

Seeing the city as a source of problems and not solutions is a favorite Western pastime. The persistence of urban problems (e.g., traffic, pollution, high cost of living, crime) may have reproduced a similar condition in Iran. The body of work on livability, at least those studies discussed in this chapter, seems to identify and measure a number of livability indicators about Iranian cities (objective or subjective). The result is rarely positive, requiring government investment in infrastructural projects or remediation activities. Meanwhile, migration and the economic development that instigates it move forward. Iranians may migrate to Tehran for its amenities, but they are also there for what they perceive (accurately or otherwise) as plentiful jobs and opportunities for amassing capital. The growth of the city, its crawling traffic (despite many miles of freeways that have been added over the last four decades and the new metro), air pollution, and high cost of living, combined with differentiated geographies of wealth, have generated that familiar western attitude about cities as the source of problems. This is nowhere more obvious than in those articles that carry an air of nostalgia about the loss of old communities (some mentioned earlier) or angst about the destruction of smaller villages on the periphery.

Khorasani and Zarghamfard (2017) exemplify the scholars whose deep concern about rural communities has translated to research that explicitly extends the challenge of livability to the peri-urban villages that surround Tehran. For them, livability is related to a greater sense of community and permanence. They see Tehran as negatively affecting these settlements and requiring intervention by planners. In this case, the agent is a by-product of defective urban planning and design that extends the unhealthy environment of the city to the neighboring villages. Negative outcomes include the imposition of high environmental costs, increasing pressure on the biophysical elements of the ecosystem, and the weakening of traditional ties. Khorasani and Zarghamfard (2017), although not incorrect in their assessments, join other Iranian and Western scholars who have come to see cities as the source of problems, requiring improved urban management and growth control or, in other words, spatial disciplining. Unconvinced that the very agents of change, that is, modern technologies, Western planning techniques, and modernist design tactics, can help, they hope for a local definition of livability (e.g., Khorasani et al., 2013, in addition to Riahifard, 2013).

This plea is cultural, but also somewhat political, because it attempts to decolonize Iranian society through a recursive act of delegitimizing Western narratives of "progress" and "development." In their reply to a commentary on an earlier article, Sintusingha and Mirgholami (2015) refer to livability in their explanation of the framework for understanding "indigenous modernity." They pose a question that is worth considering: "[T]he difficulty to establish an 'applicable' comparison framework poses the question of whether non-Western academia has been 'divided and ruled' (or self-divided and ruled)?"

(151). In an attempt to decolonize an intellectual framework, the language of colonizers is used. Undoing that linguistic framework, in this case, "livability," requires a significant change that goes beyond adopting differing indicators of livability. It should go back to what a native population needs and wants. The difficult question to ask is whether people in Iran and other non-Western places want something different from their counterparts in the West.

Conclusion

Being ranked 126 among 140 cities for livability is hardly a cause for celebration. In an interview with Iranian Students' News Agency (ISNA), Dr. Babak Negahdari (a medical doctor and the President of Tehran Urban Planning and Research Center, the organization that produced *Commitment Toward a New Urban Agenda* for Tehran), indicated that more could be done to improve livability in Tehran.[8] In this interview, he focused on the death rate due to air pollution and its economic impact. According to Dr. Negahdari, 30% of all Iran's annual deaths are due to air pollution occur in Tehran, which translates to a negative economic impact of close to 1 billion dollars (or 30.6 billion dollars at the national level, which equates to 2.48% of GDP).

Although air pollution is an important topic that should be confronted, the underlying forces that shape this problem appear to be land use, transportation, and economic development patterns. Monajem and Nosratian (2015) illustrate the geography of population and labor, which suggests some of the current and future challenges in achieving a job-housing balance. Tehran is both polycentric in its workplaces and expansive in terms of its population distribution. The city, however, has attained a significant density in most of its districts. Tehran's lack of attention to an effective job-housing balance means that although residents of District 22, in the northwestern section, may enjoy good air quality, numerous parks and green spaces, and a relatively reasonable density that makes urban services possible, they have to commute to neighborhoods in the central and southern regions where jobs are located. Despite traffic management approaches that reduce the number of cars in the central city and promote the use of public transit, particularly the new metro, high levels of traffic appear in almost every section of the metropolitan area. To reduce air pollution, land use planning becomes important, and urban/growth management becomes a priority.

It is no wonder that Iranian scholars find themselves perplexed by the complexity and depth of the challenges facing livability in Tehran. A complicated problem requires a multipronged approach, backed by an effective urban governance and a planning regime that remains committed to long term goals of improving an inclusive livability for all neighborhoods. For Tehran, equity planning is fundamentally urgent, as the *Guardian* article,[9] mentioned earlier, illustrates. For Tehran, livability cannot be a summative indicator but must account for how each of its neighborhoods fares. Both in indicators and perceptions, or needs and desires, neighborhoods differ in how they see the state of livability in a city. This is particularly important in Tehran, where the north-south divide persists. The solution, nonetheless, is neither a nostalgic response nor a technocratic remedy. Agency matters in the final definition of livability. After all, people perceive and experience livability. For them, none of the international rankings are a point of concern or a cause for rejoicing. For a city filled with vitality and exuberance, all sectors of the society need to feel that their voice matters. As such, the urban government's approach to inclusive livability is a welcome approach. What must be added is a communicative planning approach with a focus on equity. The agency of residents should be central to a local definition of livability, a plea that a number of Iranians have expressed in their articles.

Finally, as discussed earlier, in addition to the spatiality of livability and its differing manifestations and perceptions, temporality matters as well (Ruth & Franklin, 2014). This does not mean that a nostalgic trip to the past is warranted. What it does imply, however, is a major concern about livability measurements. Time will affect how we see livability, and the residents of Tehran are no exception to this rule. It should be clear that what Iranian grandparents would consider a good life is no longer fully relevant to their grandchildren. As urban experiences, needs, and desires shift, livability becomes a constant expression of a moving now. Although this is less a challenge for sustainability, which focuses mostly on the future, livability is an exercise in conflict planning across time and space. For Tehran and other rapidly growing cities, planning is an act of negotiation and fluid management that accommodates change instead of stopping it. After all, if cities are living entities, livability is an act of continuation, not a moment in time.

Notes

1. Online *Atlas of Tehran*, Mayoral Office. Retrieved from http://atlas.tehran.ir/Default.aspx?tabid=264
2. Retrieved from http://store.eiu.com/product.aspx?pid=435217628
3. Retrieved from www.oecdbetterlifeindex.org/
4. Retrieved June 26, 2017, from www.theguardian.com/cities/gallery/2016/aug/18/tehran-economist-intelligence-unit-global-liveability-ranking
5. Tann vom Hove, Editor. Retrieved June 26, 2017, from www.worldmayor.com/contest_2008/world-mayor-2008-results.html
6. Retrieved June 26, 2017, from www.theguardian.com/world/iran-blog/2013/oct/08/tehran-reacts-mayor-ghalibaf-third-term
7. Elyana Javehri. Retrieved June 26, 2017, from http://thisbigcity.net/four-changes-that-made-tehran-a-more-liveable-city/
8. Retrieved June 26, 2017, from www.isna.ir/news/96022718052/
9. Retrieved June 26, 2017, from www.theguardian.com/world/iran-blog/2013/oct/08/tehran-reacts-mayor-ghalibaf-third-term

References

Appleyard, B. (2017). The meaning of livable streets to schoolchildren: An image mapping study of the effects of traffic on children's cognitive development of spatial knowledge. *Journal of Transport & Health, 5*, 27–41.

Appleyard, D., Gerson, M. S., & Lintell, M. (1981). *Living streets*. Berkeley: University of California Press.

Bandar Abad, A., & Ahmadinejad, F. (2014). Assessment of quality of life with emphasis of habitable cities in region 22 of Tehran. *Research and Urban Planning, 5*(16), 55–74. (in Persian).

Calthorpe, P., & Fulton, W. (2001). *The regional city*. Washington, DC: Island Press.

Couclelis, H. (1990). Urban liveability: A commentary. *Urban Geography, 11*(1), 42–47.

Eisinger, P. (2004). Global competitiveness and livability: Why some cities succeed in the international marketplace. (A review of) H.V. Savitch, P. Kantor; cities in the international marketplace: The political economy of urban development in North America and Western Europe, Princeton University Press, Princeton, NJ, 2002. *Cities, 21*(6), 552–555.

Faryadi, Sh., & Taheri, Sh. (2009). Interconnections of urban green spaces and environmental quality of Tehran. *International Journal of Environmental Research, 3*(2), 199–208.

Gehrke, S. R., & Clifton, K. J. (2017). A pathway linking smart growth neighborhoods to home-based pedestrian travel. *Travel Behaviour and Society, 7*, 52–62.

Golkar, K. (2007). The livability concept in urban planning. *Sofeh, 16*(44), 66–75 (in Persian).

Gough, M. Z. (2015). Reconciling livability and sustainability: Conceptual and practical implications for planning. *Journal of Planning Education and Research, 35*(2), 145–160.

Heatwole Shank, K. S., & Cutchin, M. P. (2016). Processes of developing 'community livability' in older age. *Journal of Aging Studies*, 39, 66–72.

Jokar, A. J., Helbich, M., Kainz, W., & Darvish, B. A. (2013a). Integration of logistic regression, Markov chain and cellular automata models to simulate urban expansion. *International Journal of Applied Earth Observation and Geoinformation*, 21, 265–275.

Jokar, A. J., Helbich, M., & Vaz, E. N. (2013b). Spatiotemporal simulation of urban growth patterns using agent-based modeling: The case of Tehran. *Cities*, 32, 33–42.

Jokar, A. J., Kainz, W., & Mousivand, A. J. (2011). Tracking dynamic land use change using spatially explicit Markov chain based on cellular automata: The case of Tehran. *International Journal of Image and Data Fusion*, 2(4), 329–345.

Kashef, M. (2016). Urban livability across disciplinary and professional boundaries. *Frontiers of Architectural Research*, 5(2), 239–253.

Khorasani, M. A., Rezvani, M. R., Motiei Langroudi, S. H., & Rafieian, M. (2013). Surveying and assessment of livability in peri urban villages (case study: Varamin Township). *Journal of Rural Research*, 3(4), 23–27 (in Persian).

Khorasani, M. A., & Zarghamfard, M. (2017). Analyzing the impacts of spatial factors on livability of peri-urban villages. *Social Indicators Research*, 1–25. doi: 10.1007/s11205-016-1546-4.

Kotus, J., & Rzeszewski, M. (2013). Between disorder and livability: Case of one street in post-socialist city. *Cities*, 32, 123–134.

Leach, J. M., Lee, S. E., Hunt, D. V. L., & Rogers, C. D. F. (2017). Improving city-scale measures of livable sustainability: A study of urban measurement and assessment through application to the city of Birmingham, U.K. *Cities*, 71, 80–87.

Ley, D. (1990). Urban liveability in context. *Urban Geography*, 11(1), 31–35.

Madanipour, A. (2006). Urban planning and development in Tehran. *Cities*, 23(6), 433–438.

Majedi, H., & Bandarbad, A. (2014). The study of the global and local principles of the livable city. *Hoviateshahr*, 8(17), 65–76.

Major Cities Unit. (2010). *State of Australian cities, 2010*. Major Cities Unit, Infrastructure Australia, Commonwealth of Australia.

Marshall, W. E. (2013). An evaluation of livability in creating transit-enriched communities for improved regional benefits. *Research in Transportation Business & Management*, 7, 54–68.

Mesimäki, M., Hauru, K., Kotze, D. J., & Lehvävirta, S. (2017). Neo-spaces for urban livability? Urbanites' versatile mental images of green roofs in the Helsinki metropolitan area, Finland. *Land Use Policy*, 61, 587–600.

Miller, H. J., Witlox, F., & Tribby, C. P. (2013). Developing context-sensitive livability indicators for transportation planning: A measurement framework. *Journal of Transport Geography*, 26, 51–64.

Mofidi, S. M., & Kashani Jou, K. (2010). Emergence of pedestrianisation in Tehran: Obstacles and opportunities. *International Journal of Sustainable Urban Development*, 2(1–2), 121–134.

Monajem, S., & Nosratian, F. E. (2015). The evaluation of the spatial integration of station areas via the node place model; an application to subway station areas in Tehran. *Transportation Research Part D*, 40, 14–27.

Pacione, M. (1990). Urban liveability: A review. *Urban Geography*, 11(1), 1–30.

Pacione, M. (2003). Urban environmental quality and human wellbeing: A social geographical perspective. *Landscape and Urban Planning*, 65, 19–30.

Rafiee, R., Mahiny, A. S., Khorasani, N., Darvisgsefat, A. A., & Danekar, A. (2009). Simulating urban growth in Mashad city, Iran through the SLEUTH model (UGM). *Cities*, 26(1), 19–26.

Rasoolimanesh, S. M., Jaafar, M., & Badarulzaman, N. (2014). Examining the contributing factors for the successful implementation of city development strategy in Qazvin city, Iran. *Cities*, 41, 10–19.

Riahifard, A. (2013). Survey on the appropriate distribution of open space in order to upgrade quality of modern urban residential areas in Tehran. *Hoviateshahr*, 7(15), 71–82.

Robert, M. (2013). *The impact of gender planning in Europe*. I. Sánchez de Madariaga (Ed.). Abingdon, UK: Routledge.

Ruth, M., & Franklin, R. S. (2014). Livability for all? Conceptual limits and practical implications. *Applied Geography*, 49, 18–23.

Sabet Sarvestani, M., Ibrahim, A. L., & Kanaroglou, P. (2011). Three decades of urban growth in the city of Shiraz, Iran: A remote sensing and geographic information systems application. *Cities*, *28*(4), 320–329.

Safavi Sohi, M., Razavian, M. T., & Kohestani Faruj, G. (2014). What kind of cities are "livable"? (Case Study: Tehran, Neighborhood Darake). *Advances in Environmental Biology*, *8*(11), 572–588.

Sasanpour, F., Tavalaie, S., & Jafari Asasabadi, H. (2014). Livability of cities in sustainable urban development, case study of Tehran metropolis. *Geography*, *12*(42), 129–157. (in Persian).

Sasanpour, F., Tavalaie, S., & Jafari Asasabadi, H. (2015). Study of urban livability in twenty-two districts of Tehran metropolis. *Journal of Regional Planning*, *5*(18), 27–42. (in Persian).

Sintusingha, S., & Mirgholami, M. (2013). Parallel modernization and self-colonization: Urban evolution and practices in Bangkok and Tehran. *Cities*, *30*(1), 122–132.

Sintusingha, S., & Mirgholami, M. (2015). An 'applicable framework' to compare 'indigenous modernity'? *Cities*, *45*, 150–151.

Sufian, A. J. M. (1993). A multivariate analysis of the determinants of urban quality of life in the world's largest metropolitan areas. *Urban Studies*, *30*(8), 1319–1329.

Tayyebi, A., Pijanowski, B. C., & Pekin, B. (2011). Two rule-based urban growth boundary models applied to the Tehran metropolitan area, Iran. *Applied Geography*, *31*(3), 908–918.

Tehran Urban Planning Research Center. (2016). *Tehran's commitment toward new urban agenda*.

Zamani, B., & Arefi, M. (2013). Iranian new towns and their urban management issues: A critical review of influential actors and factors. *Cities*, *30*, 105–112.

Zebardast, E. (2006). Marginalization of the urban poor and the expansion of the spontaneous settlements on the Tehran metropolitan fringe. *Cities*, *23*(6), 439–454.

Final Remarks

Each of the 15 chapters that have been written for this book has focused on a particular city for examining livable cities from a global perspective. Dr. Hilda Blanco provided a well-developed and comprehensive introduction that set the stage for this book laying out its parameters.

The book is organized into the five sections: livability in capital city regions, livability and growth and development, livability and equity concerns, livability and metrics, and creating livability. Used as case studies, these chapters, focusing on 15 cities, encompassing 12 countries, have provided insight into what livability encompasses. Each case study presents a unique perspective on how that particular city is grappling with what is a livable city. Virtually all of the cities are wrestling with the meaning and definition of livability within their culture and how to use it in the context of community development. The following seven cities depict these concerns and are representative of the group of cities described in the book.

Austin is an example of a rapidly growing US city where population growth has been occurring since the early 1970s. Residents are trying to come to grips with the meaning of livability and which definition should be emphasized. The effort has polarized the city when it comes to the things that resident's value. The vision of how the city should develop with more residents and improved transit is being reconsidered.

Cape Town, even though it is seeing a continuous massive in flow of people, seeks to try and address the livability of the city. The author sees the term livable cities as "directional rather than finite condition: it describes the direction cities should be advancing to make them more livable". Four performance measures are described in general and are applied to the city of Cape Town. As a result, "it shows that South African Cities are very far from being livable". The reasons for this situation are described in the chapter. As a result, the author describes a different model for addressing this situation.

Helsinki is seen as a livable city by many observers. It has high ratings "in The Economist and Monocle's livability and quality of life indices". Large new urban areas are being built, and critics believe such developments do not meet the needs of a diverse population. This concern of not meeting the needs of citizens is a recurring issue in many of the chapters.

London notes that livable city is often used as a synonym for terms such as sustainable, green, smart, intelligent, resilient, and eco-city. Although using such terms interchangeably, London sees itself differently from other UK cities, as it aims to satisfy global criteria. The London Plan livability is confounded with sustainability and quality of life and encompasses equity and inclusion.

In Melbourne, while taking into account levels of social equity, the city has often ignored "the distribution of the urban goods that underpin the concept of livability—public safety, health and education services, housing access, traffic congestion, environmental quality and cultural life".

In Ottawa, in the National Capital Region, the authors argue "that the concept of livability and place-making, along with the cooperation between municipal governments, community groups, and private developers, can play a large role in ensuring equity and accessibility".

Pune is the second largest city in the Indian state of Maharashtra. The city has a document titled, "Pune Metropolis: A Livable City". The author believes the document misleads the reader into believing the city is truly livable when the reality is that 70% of its population lives in the informal sector. In this situation, it appears that the city report is using the term livable and its livability index to promote the city in a questionable way.

Singapore is a very dense city and rates high among various global surveys. This juxtaposition is unique. Although being dense and rated high as a livable city, it has developed broad principles to guide the city-state. Such principles perhaps could be used by other cities in the world.

Finally, although these cities have been highlighted, they present only a broad overview of the challenges of depicting, describing and implementing livable communities. They are somewhat representative of the others.

Additional Information on Livability for Cities Covered in the Book

Helsinki, Finland

www.hel.fi/hel2/ksv/julkaisut/yos_2013-23_en.pdf

London, United Kingdom

www.ucl.ac.uk/steapp/research/projects/liveable-cities
www.lse.ac.uk/researchAndExpertise/researchImpact/PDFs/liveable-cities.pdf
www.ukgbc.org/news/building-liveable-cities/

Ottawa, Canada

http://greenspace-alliance.ca/wp-content/uploads/2017/02/OP-2014-preliminary_proposals.pdf

Austin, Texas

www.liveablecity.org/about-liveable-city

Warsaw, Poland

http://sarp.warszawa.pl/warsztaty-stare/warszawskie-centra-lokalne/
www.jakosczycia.um.warszawa.pl/
www.um.warszawa.pl/en
http://irm.krakow.pl/en/
www.urbandivercities.eu/warsaw/

Pune, India

www.punesmartcity.in/
http://smartcities.gov.in/upload/uploadfiles/files/LiveabilityStandards.pdf
www.punesmartcity.in/?wicket:bookmarkablePage=:Com.SmartCity.Page.frmsmartcityproject
http://smartcities.gov.in/content/
https://qcmweb.org/

Sydney, Australia

https://theconversation.com/au/topics/liveability-1375
http://urbanlivingindex.com/
www.greater.sydney/
www.domain.com.au/news/domain-liveable-sydney-citys-555-suburbs-ranked/
https://infrastructure.gov.au/infrastructure/pab/soac/files/2012_08_INFRA1360_MCU_SOAC_CHAPTER_5_WEB_FA.pdf.

Tokyo, Japan

www.toshiseibi.metro.tokyo.jp/eng/
https://en.wikipedia.org/wiki/Greater_Tokyo_Area
https://en.wikipedia.org/wiki/Aging_of_Japan

Vancouver, Canada

http://vancouver.ca/home-property-development/urban-planning.aspx
https://unhabitat.org/wp-content/uploads/2010/07/GRHS2009CaseStudyChapter09Vancouver.pdf
www.policyschool.ca/wp-content/uploads/2016/03/livability-conger.pdf
www.eiu.com/Handlers/WhitepaperHandler.ashx?fi=Liveability+Ranking+Summary+Report+-+August+2016.pdf&mode=wp&campaignid=Liveability2016

Singapore

www.clc.gov.sg
www.ura.gov.sg/uol/master-plan/view-master-plan/master-plan-2014/master-plan/Regional-highlights/central-area/central-area/Towards-a-sustainable-and-liveable-city
www.mewr.gov.sg/ssb/

Salt Lake City, Utah

www.slcgreen.com/
www.visitsaltlake.com/about-salt-lake/sustainability/
http://dotnet0.slcgov.com/PublicServices/Sustainability/

Melbourne, Australia

www.communityindicators.net.au/
https://aurin.org.au/projects/lens-sub-projects/nw-melbourne-project/
www.mtf.org.au/MTF-Reports/Most-Liveable-and-Best-Connected-The-Economic-Benefits-of-In.aspx
https://research-repository.griffith.edu.au/bitstream/handle/10072/29808/61038_1.pdf?sequence=2

Rio de Janeiro, Brazil

https://pt-br.facebook.com/BemEstar/ or g1.globo.com/bemestar/ (same source)
https://estilo.uol.com.br
www.ekosbrasil.org

Cape Town, South Africa

http://sasdialliance.org.za
www.dag.org.za/
www.capetown.gov.za/work%20and%20business/invest-in-cape-townm/why-invest-in-capetown/the-liveability-of-cape-town

Tehran, Iran

www.theguardian.com/cities/gallery/2016/aug/18/tehran-economist-intelligence-unit-global-liveability-ranking
http://thisbigcity.net/four-changes-that-made-tehran-a-more-liveable-city/
www.theguardian.com/world/iran-blog/2013/oct/08/tehran-reacts-mayor-ghalibaf-third-term
www.isna.ir/news/96022718052/

Index

Note: Page numbers in italic indicate a figure and page numbers in bold indicate a table.

Active, Beautiful and Clean Waters (ABC Waters) Programme 154, 155
Act on Special Measures Concerning Urban Reconstruction 130
Adelaide, Australia 139; top ten livable cities 6; top ten ranking cities from selected livability indices and surveys **114**
Adler, S. 61
Agenda 21 7
Ahwanee Principles 3
Amsterdam, The Netherlands: economic opportunity 6; housing 6; top ten livable cities 6; top ten ranking cities from selected livability indices and surveys **114**
Appleyard, D.: *Livable Streets* 2, 230
Article 7 9
Article 25 9
Auckland, New Zealand: top ten livable cities 6; top ten ranking cities from selected livability indices and surveys **114**
Augé, M. 197
Austin, TX 59, 61–75, 237; "Austin is Livable" 68, 70; Austinites for Geographic Representation 69; *Austin Tomorrow* 67; Blueprint 73; challenging local regime 69–70; Code Next 70–72; conflicting visions of livability 62–63; context for livability 63–67; defining livable city 67–69; "desired development zone" 64–65; development change 62–63; environmental footprint 64; geographic representation 69–70; HOLC map 65; housing plan 72–74; *Imagine Austin* 67–69, 70, 71, 72, 73; Long-Term Planning 67; Mexican American Cultural Center 66; Neighborhoods Council 68, 71; "residential security" map 64, 65; right to the city 63; Smart Growth 64–65; Watershed Regulation Areas 68
"Austin is Livable" 68, 70
Austinites for Geographic Representation 69
Austin Neighborhoods Council 68, 71
Austin Tomorrow 67
Australia 2, 5, 119, 121, 138; corruption 181; Federal Government 121; public healthcare 181; *State of Australian Cities Report 2010* 226; *see also* Adelaide, Australia; Canberra, Australia; Committee for Economic Development of Australia; Melbourne, Australia; Perth, Australia; Property Council Australia; Sydney, Australia; Urban Taskforce Australia; Victoria, Australia
Australian Bureau of Statistics, Census of Population and Housing 115, 178, 185
Australian Department of Infrastructure and Regional Development 120
Australian Housing Urban Research Institute 119
Australian Urban Research Infrastructure Network 184

Basic Services to Urban Poor 102
Becker, R. 166, 167, 168, 169, 170, 172, 173, 174
Belfast, Ireland 33, 34, 42n8
Berkshire, UK 33
Berlin, Germany, 6, **6**, *114*
Bharatiya Janata Party 102
Bill, A. 111
Birmingham, UK 33, 34, 35, 42n8, 226
Biskupski, J. 166, 169, 173, 174
Blanco, H. 193, *194*, 237
Blasio, B. de 163
Blueprint 73
Bognar, G. 192
Bournemouth, UK 34
Bradford, UK 33, 34, 42n8
Brazil 2, 81; African influence 195, 201; culture 197; favelas 195, 199, 203; housing 199; land use plan 198; urban inequalities 189, 195; *see also* Rio de Janeiro, Brazil
Brexit 38, 42n17
Bright, E. 193
Brighton, UK 33–35
Bristol, UK 33, 34, 42n8
British Columbia 140–141
Brundtland Commission 7
"Building a Liveable Ottawa 2031" 50
BuzzData 120

CACs *see* Community Amenity Contributions
Calgary, Canada 139; top ten livable cities **6**; top ten ranking cities from selected livability indices and surveys **114**
Calthorpe, P. 3
Cambridge, UK 32, 34, **35**
Camp Fortune Ski Centre 55
Canada 2, 138, 139, 145; complex streets 52; housing 140; migration 15; poverty 140; public healthcare 181; renting 139; *see also* Calgary, Canada; Gatineau, Canada; Ottawa, Canada; Toronto, Canada; Vancouver, Canada
Canberra, Australia **114**
Cape Town, South Africa 189, 210, 216–218, 237
capital cities 5, 15, 167, 237; *see also* Helsinki, Finland; London, England; Ottawa, Canada
Cardiff, UK 33, **34**, 35, 42n8
Cardinal, D. 45
Cardoso, A. L. 197
Catholic Social Services 123n6
Caves, R.: *Community Livability*, 192, 193
CAWI 52–53
Centre for Cities 32, 42n7
Centre for Liveable Cities (CLC) 153, 154, 155, 159, 164; *Liveable & Sustainable Cities* 152
Chelsea, Québec 47, 53, 54, 55
"Choosing Our Future" 50
Church of Jesus Christ of Latter-Day Saints (LDS) 167, 172
Cidade de Deus slum 200, 202
Cities PLUS 230
City Creek Canyon 170
City Creek Center 167
City for All Women Initiative (CAWI) 52–53
CLC *see* Centre for Liveable Cities
Code Next 70–72
Commitment Toward a New Urban Agenda 229, 231, 232
Committee for Economic Development of Australia 123n6
Community Amenity Contributions (CACs) 142
Community Development Framework 52
Community Indicators Victoria (CIV) 149, 176–177, 182, 183, 184, 186
community livability, 79, 176
Complementary Law 101 197
Complete Streets 49, 50, 51–52
concept 1–4; biophilic cities 4, 7, **7**; healthy cities movement 3–4, 7; Lynch's *A Theory of Good City Form* 2; new urbanism 3, 8, 47, 227, 230; resilient cities 4, 7, 8, 9, 144, 183, 218; smart growth movement 3, 8, 64, *194*, 227, 230
Conger, B. 7
Congress for the New Urbanism 192, *194*

Copenhagen, Denmark: Climate Plan 163; housing 6; systemic innovation 162; top ten livable cities **6**; top ten ranking cities from selected livability indices and surveys **114**; urbanism 163
Copestake, J.: *Liveability & Cost of Living* 113
Council on Aging Ottawa 52
creating livability 30, 189, 237; *see also* Cape Town, South Africa; Rio de Janeiro, Brazil; Tehran, Iran
Creative Boom **34**
Crossroads Plaza 167
Cumbernauld, Scotland 31
Cycling Plan 49, 50–51

Darlington, UK 33
Davies, A. 113
Deccan College 99
Deloitte 30, 33
Deloitte Access Economics 114
Del Rio, V. 192, 199, 204
Dhanabalan, S. 157–158, 160, 161
Domain Liveable Sydney 2016 114
DPZ (Duany Plater-Zyberk) 53, *54*
Dropping off the Edge report 123n6, 180
Duany Plater-Zyberk (DPZ) 53, *54*
Dundee **34**
Dunham-Jones, E. 48
Dusseldorf, Germany **6**, **114**

Earth Summit 7
East India Company 99
Eccles Theater 168, 173
Economist Intelligence Unit Global Liveability Index, The (EIU) 4, 5, **6**, 7, 37, **114**, 120–121, 138, 227; Melbourne 180, **180**, 181, 186; "most livable city" 176; Sydney 113, 114, 181
Edinburgh, Scotland 33, **34**, 35, 42n8, **114**
Eisinger, P. 227
EIU *see* The Economist Intelligence Unit Global Liveability Index
equity concerns 109; *see also* Sydney, Australia; Tokyo, Japan; Vancouver, Canada
Europe/European Union 2; capitals 21; economy 38; government involvement 145; heritage 195; housing 31; Leipzig Charter 81, 82, 90n3; migration 145; neighborhood diversity 21; polycentric development 83–84; population 37, 38, 99, 145; PwC's Quality of Living rating 6; quality of life surveys 5, 9, 111; renaissance 62; Single European Market 38; UK's decision to leave European Union 38, 42n17, 42n19; World Health Organization 3; *see also specific name of city or country*
European Commission 5, 10n3
Evening Standard 38, 39, 40, 42n18
Expo '86

Faehnle, M. 22
Federation of Citizens' Associations of Ottawa 52
FIFA World Cup 2014 196
Finland 17, 19, 21; *see also* Helsinki
Finnemore, M. 81
First World War 31
Fish Harbour, Kalasatama 18, 23
5000 Doors Initiative 169
Fligstein, N. 81
Florida, R. 18, 61, 144
Foresight 32
"Framing Our Future" 50
Franklin, R. S. 226
Frankfurt, Germany 6, **114**
Fukouka, Japan 6, **114**

Games Monitor 44n40
Gatineau, Canada 45, 46, 50, 53, 55, 56
Gateau Park 53, *54*, 55
Gateway Mall 167
Gehl, J. 88; "Places for People" 163
Geneva, Switzerland 6, **6**, **114**
Ghalibaf, Dr. 228, 229
GHG *see* greenhouse gas emissions
Glasgow, Scotland 31, **33**, 34, 35, 42n8
Gleeson, B. 111, 115, 122
Gokhale Institute of Politics and Economics 100
Gough, M. Z. 176, 226
Grattan Institute 115; *City Limits* 119
Great East Japan Earthquake 131
greenhouse gas emissions 8, 209, 210, 215, 217, 219
growth and development 59; *see also* Austin, TX; Pune, India; Warsaw, Poland
Guan, L. S. 157

Habitat III Conference 9, 229
Hall, E. T. 88
Hamburg, Germany 6, **6**, **114**
Hamel, P.: *Suburban Governance* 47
Harvey, D. 112, 191
hate crime prevention 172
Healthy Cities movement 3–4, 7
Healthy Transportation Coalition 52
Helsinki, Finland 6, 15, 237; "Development Perspective" 19–20; Fish Harbour, Kalasatama 18, 23; frame for analysis 20; frame for production **20**; housing 6; institutional city 20, **20**; Kalasatama case study 18, 23–25, *25*, 26, 27; *Lisää kaupunkia Helsinkiin* 22; new urban, 17–27; planning and liability 21; planning policies 22; politics 18–20; REDI Centre 23, 24–26; soft city 20, **20**, 23, 26; soft planning 20, **20**, 23, 26; top ten livable cities **6**; top ten ranking cities from selected livability indices and surveys **114**; urbanization 21–26; "Urban plan" 21, 22

Hendrick Farm 45, 53–56, *54*; DPZ (Duany Plater-Zyberk) 53, *54*; *see also* LandLab
Hertfordshire, UK **33**
Hindoo College 99
Holden, M. 178
Home Owners Loan Corporation 64
Hong Kong 139, 164; economic opportunity 6; top ten ranking cities from selected livability indices and surveys **114**
Hopkins, R. 32
human rights 9, 197, 213; UN Human Rights Council Special Rapporteur 197; UN Universal Declaration of Human Rights 9
Human Rights Commission 172

ICLEI-Local Governments for Sustainability 7–8
image of the city 19, 26, 94
Imagine Austin 67–69, 70, 71, 72, 73
Index of Relative Socio-Economic Advantage and Disadvantage (IRSAD) 178, *179*
IRSAD *see* Index of Relative Socio-Economic Advantage and Disadvantage
Irvine, J. 111

Jacobs, J. 88, 144, 230
Javaheri: *Four Changes That Made Tehran a More Liveable City* 228
Jawaharlal Nehru National Urban Renewal Mission 102
Jenkins, S. 38
Jesuit Social Services 123n6
Jordan, K. 111
Just Space 40–41

Kaal, H. 19
Kalasatama case study 18, 23–25, *25*, 26, 27
Kashani Jou, K. 230
Kashef, M. 227
Keil, R.: *Suburban Governance* 47
Khorasani, M. A. 231
Koike, Y. 131
Koizumi, J. 130
Kyoto, Japan **6**, **114**

LandLab 45, 53, 54, 55
Lapintie, K. 26
Lauster, N. 143
LDS *see* Church of Jesus Christ of Latter-Day Saints (LDS)
Leach, J. M. 226
Leeds, **33**, 34, 42n8
Lefebvre, H. 111, 112, 122
Leipzig Charter on Sustainable European Cities 81, 82, 90n3
Lisää kaupunkia Helsinkiin 22
livability, sustainability, resilience 7–10; contrasting spatial and temporal standpoints 8; differences and overlaps 8; expansion

of sustainability 7–8; human rights 9; sustainability and resilience 9
Liverpool, UK 33, 34, 35, 42n8
Living Streets 230
LLDC *see* London Legacy Development Corporation
Local Agenda 21 7
London, England 15, 30, 31, 32, 36–42, 42n6, 43n26, 237; Campaign to Protect Rural England 41; "Community Led London Plan" 41; comparative livability index 37; comparative table of selected city livability indices and rank orders 33–35; CPRE 41; economic opportunity 6; enhancement for all 40–41; Great Fire 30, 38; housing 6; Just Space 40–41; livability deficits 38–40; skyscrapers 43n29; top ten livable cities 6; top ten ranking cities from selected livability indices and surveys 114; *see also* United Kingdom
London Legacy Development Corporation (LLDC) 40
Lovability index 89
Lovato, F. 120
Lowe, M. 18
Lynch, K.: *The Image of the City* 2; *A Theory of Good City Form* 2
Lynch, R. 38

Mäenpää, P. 22
Manchester, UK 33, 34, 35, 42n8
Manguinhos slum 202
Maratha Empire 97–98, 99
Maré slum 200;
Marshall, F. 99
Mason, P. 41
McAdam, D. 81
McAdam, S. 45, 53, 54, 55
McElvoy, A. 38
McCrindle Research: *Urban Living Index* 114
McNally, R.: *Places Rated Almanac* 2
Melbourne, Australia 119, 138, 139, 149, 176–186; Commonwealth Rental Assistance 178; Community Housing Associations 178; Economist Intelligence Unit 180, 180; Economist Intelligence Unit's "most livable city" 176; Future Melbourne 2026 163; history 177–180; housing 177–178; Index of Relative Socio-Economic Advantage and Disadvantage (IRSAD) 178, 179; indicators to improve planning 182–183; international livability rankings 180–182; Local Government Area 183, 184; Mercer Quality of Living 176, 180; Monocle Quality of Life Survey 180; "most livable city" 176; "Places for People" 163; Plan Melbourne 163; public transportation 178; spatially enabled indicators 184–185; top ten livable cities 6; top ten ranking cities from selected livability indices and surveys 114; urban goods 237; urban growth boundary 177; Victorian Public Health Survey (VPHS) 183; walkability 183, 184, 185; *see also* Community Indicators Victoria; Transparency International
Mellander, C. 61
Mercer HR & financial services 37
Mercer Quality of Living Survey 4, 5, 6, 6, 7, 10n3, 30, 37, 113, 114, 138, 145, 151, 164n1, 176, 180, 227
metrics 7, 31, 149, 166, 169, 170, 172, 173, 174, 237; *see also* Melbourne, Australia; Salt Lake City, NV; Singapore
Mexican American Cultural Center 66
Millbank, UK 43n32
Mirgholami, M. 231
MMF Mori Memorial Foundation 37
Mofidi, S. M. 230
MoneySuper Market MSM 33, 33
Monocle Quality of Life Survey 4, 5, 6, 6, 17, 30, 37, 113, 114, 176, 180, 237
Mori Institute for Uban Strategies 37
Mori Memorial Foundation 37
Mountain Accord 170
Mumbai Metropolitan Region 93, 98
Munich, Germany 6; top ten livable cities 6; top ten ranking cities from selected livability indices and surveys 114
Municipal Organic Law (LOM) 196–197
Museum of Civilisation 45
Museum of History 45

Nakasone, Y. 129
National Capital Commission (NCC) 46, 50
National Capital Region (NCR) 45–47, 46
National Gallery 45
National Savings Bank 198
NCC *see* National Capital Commission
Negahdari, B. 232
Newcastle upon Tyne, UK 34, 35, 42n8
New Lanark 32
New Port Public-Private Partnership (PPP-PN) 196, 198, 199
New South Wales 122
new urbanism 3, 8, 47, 227, 230
New York, NY: economic opportunity 6; Meatpacking district 24; Office of Long-Term Planning and Sustainability 163; top ten livable cities 6; top ten ranking cities from selected livability indices and surveys 114
New York Times, The 30
NGOs *see* nongovernmental organizations
nongovernmental organizations (NGOs) 7, 93, 97, 122, 163
Nordik Spa 55
Northern Ireland 31
North Lanarkshire, UK 33
North Temple Street 168
North Temple Viaduct 168
Northumberland, UK 33

Norwich, UK 33, 35
Nottingham, UK 33, 34, 42n8

Office for National Statistics 43n34
Okulicz-Kozaryn, A. 10n3
Old Chelsea, Québec 53
Olympic Games 2016 196
One Hundred New Cities Programme 103
Oslo, Norway 6
Ottawa, Canada 15, 45–56, 238; "Building a Liveable Ottawa 2031" 50; Camp Fortune Ski Centre 55; CAWI 52–53; "Choosing Our Future" 50; City for All Women Initiative (CAWI) 52–53; Complete Streets 49, 50, 51–52; community advocacy 52–53; Community Development Framework 52; Council on Aging Ottawa 52; Cycling Plan 49, 50–51; Federation of Citizens' Associations of Ottawa 52; "Framing Our Future" 50; Greenbelt area 49; Healthy Transportation Coalition 52; Infrastructure Master Plan 49; livability, walkability, and sustainability 49–50; Museum of Civilisation 45; Museum of History 45; National Capital Commission 46, 50; National Capital Region (NCR) 45–47, 46; National Gallery 45; Nordik Spa 55; Official Plan 49, 50; Ottawa Neighbourhood Study 52; Pedestrian Plan 49, 50–51; Place du Portage 45; place-making 47–49, 53–56, 238; Social Planning Council of Ottawa 52; Transportation Master Plan 49, 50; walkability 47, 48, 49, 50, 51, 52, 53, 55; *see also* Hendrick Farm; LandLab
Otterson, M. 172
Outer London, UK 33, 35
Owen, R. 32
Oxford, UK 32, 34, 35

Palermo, P. C. 48
Paris, France 6, **6**, **114**
Partners for Livable Communities 2, 18, 192
The Peabody Trust 31
Pearson, L. "Mike" 45
Pedestrian Plan 49, 50–51
Penalosa brothers 48
Penha slum 202
Perth, Australia 6, **114**
Pew Research Center 96
Pickett, K. 140
Pimpri-Chinchwad Municipal Corporation 93
Place du Portage 45
place-making 192, 213; concept 47–49; Ottawa 47–49, 53–56, 238; possibility in NCR 53–56, 238; Salt Lake City 174; Tehran 229; Warsaw 89
Plymouth, UK 33
Polish National Science Centre 87
Ponzini, D. 48
popular global city rating systems 5–7

PPP-PN *see* New Port Public-Private Partnership
precarious settlements 195, 200
Pressman, N. E. P.: *International Experiences in Creating Livable Cities* 2
PricewaterhouseCoopers (PwC) International accountants 37
PricewaterhouseCoopers (PwC) Quality of Living Indicators in their Cities of Opportunity Ranking 4, 5, 6, **6**, 7, 10n5, 30, 113, **114**
Property Council Australia 121
Pune, India 59, 93–107, 238; Balewadi High Street 95; Basic Services to Urban Poor 102; Best Countries to Do Business In 102; Bharatiya Janata Party 102; Deccan College 99; development 102–104; equated monthly installments (EMIs) 93, 105; first and second societies integration 105–106; first society versus second society 93–97; Governance Index 105, 106, 107; Hindoo College 99; income expended on basic needs **100**; Jawaharlal Nehru National Urban Renewal Mission 102; Livability Institutional Theme 106; Livability Index 104–105; livability through history 97–102; map *94*; Metropolitan Region 93, 94, 98; military nerve center 99; One Hundred New Cities Programme 103; Parvati Hill slum *101*; Pimpri-Chinchwad Municipal Corporation 93; Pune Municipal Corporation 93, 95, 103–104; Quantified Cities Movement (QCM) 103, 104; railway 99; right to the city 93; Shaniwar Wada Citadel *98*; slums 93, 95, 96, 101, *101*, 102, 105; Smart Cities 95, 97, 102, 103, 104, 105; social leaders 99–100; Special Economic Zones 102; Urban Corridors 103
Pune Municipal Corporation 93, 95, 103–104
Punter, J. 142
Purcell, M. 112
Putnam, R. 193

quality of life 3, 5, 6, 7, 18, 41, 48, 192, 193, 199, 213, 226; Austin, TX 61, 63, 71; Bogotá, Colombia 164; Europe 10n3; Helsinki, Finland 17, 237; London, England 15, 36, 37, 39, 237; Melbourne, Australia 176,, 180, 181, 182, 183, 185; New York, NY 163; Ottawa, Canada 49; Pune, India 100, 102; Salt Lake City, UT 169, 173; Singapore 151, 153, 155, 164; Sydney, Australia 112, 113, 121; Tehran, Iran 228, 230, 231; United Kingdom 31, 33; Vancouver, Canada 138; Vienna, Austria 10n4, 145; Warsaw, Poland 79, 80, 81, 82, 83, 84, 88, 89; *see also* Mercer Quality of Living Survey; Monocle Quality of Life Survey
Quantified Cities Movement (QCM) 103, 104

246 Index

Raleigh, NC **114**
Randolph, B. 111, 115, 122
rating systems 4–7; popular global city rating systems 5–7; quality of life surveys 5, 6, 10n4 (*see also* Mercer Quality of Living Survey; Monocle Quality of Life Survey); top ten livable cities by global rating **6**
REDI Centre 23, 24–26
resilient cities 4, 7, 8, 9, 144, 183, 218
Riahifard, A. 229
right to the city 19, 41; Austin, TX 63; Pune, India 93; Sydney, Australia 112, 122; Warsaw, Poland 80, 81
Rio de Janeiro, Brazil 7, 189, 191–204; Alemão slum 202; Center for Studies and Solidarity Actions 202; Cidade de Deus slum 200, 202; City Council Commission of Inquiry 199; City Hall 195, 196–197, 199; concept 192–193; Complementary Law 101 197; culture 201–202; favelas 195, 199, 203–204; FIFA World Cup 2014 196; housing 200; Light Rail Train 198; Manguinhos slum 202; Maré slum 200; Marvelous Port 196–199, 203–204; Municipal Organic Law (LOM) 196–197; National Savings Bank 198; New Port Public-Private Partnership (PPP-PN) 196, 198, 199; Olympic Games 2016 196; Penha slum 202; population 195; popular territories answers to unequal and discretionary urbanization 199–203; port area renovation projects 195–199, *198*, 204–204; precarious settlements 195, 200; Rio favelas *201–202*, 203; Rocinha slum 199–200, 202; slums 195, 196, 199, 200, 201, 202; subnormal agglomeration 195; sustainability dimensions *194*; urban inequalities 195; Urban Redevelopment Plan 197
RIO 92 Eco Summit 193
Rismaharini, T. 164
Rocinha slum 199–200, 202
Rolnik, R. 197
Ruth, M. 226

Salt Lake City, UT 149, 166–74; affordable housing 169–170; air quality 173; arts and cultural activities 173; bike infrastructure 168, 169; Church of Jesus Christ of Latter-Day Saints (LDS) 167, 172; City Creek Canyon 170; City Creek Center 167; civic campus 167–168, 174; community gardens *171*, 171–172; Crossroads Plaza 167; Cultural Core Plan 173; Cultural Facilities Master Plan 173; downtown 167–168; Eccles Theater 168, 173; energy use 173–174; 5000 Doors Initiative 169; Gateway Mall 167; hate crime prevention 172; housing 169–170; landfill 166; LEED certification 174; Local Food Microgrant 172; Mayoral Agenda 166; light rail/TRAX 167, 168; mobility 168–169; Mountain Accord 170; natural areas and recreation opportunities 170–171; North Temple Street 168; North Temple Viaduct 168; performing arts center 168; Public Safety Building 167, 168, 174; social equality 172–173; Square Kitchen 172; streetcars 168, 169; Sugar House Streetcar 168, 169; Sustainable Salt Lake 173; sustainability 173–174; TRAX line 167, 168, 169; 24-hour population 167–168; urban agriculture 171–172; Utah Performing Arts Center 173; walkability 173; Wasatch Community Gardens 171, *172*; waste 174; ZCMI Center 167; *see also* Wasatch Mountains
Salt Lake City International Airport 168
Salt Lake Redevelopment Agency 168, 173
San Diego, CA **114**
San Francisco, CA 6, **6**, **114**
Sasanpour, F. 228, 230
Scerri, A. 178
Scotland 31
Secchi, B. 193
Second World War 17, 30, 31, 127, 128, 167, 177, 216
Shaniwar Wada Citadel 98, *98*
Sheffield, UK 33, 34, 42n8
Sikkink, K. 81
Singapore 6, 149, 151–164, 238; accountable, transparent, and incorruptible public sector 160; Active, Beautiful and Clean Waters (ABC Waters) Programme 154, *155*; achievement by balancing outcomes 154; Centre for Liveable Cities (CLC) 152, 153, 154, 155, 159, 164; Chek Jawa 161, *161*; City in a Garden 158; CLC livability matrix *151*; competitive economy 153; Concept Plan 156–157; cultivating robust institutions and processes 160; economic opportunity 6; future change 157–158; global practice 162; government working with community 160–161; high quality of life 153–154; integrated master planning and development 155–156, *156*; livability framework 151, *152*, 152–153, *162*; long-term planning 156–157, 163; Malayan Nature Society 164n2; Mass Rapid Transit 157; Mercer Quality of Living survey *151*, 164n1; natural resources 153; Park Connector Network 158; plan implementation 158; principles of dynamic urban governance *159*; principles of livability 153–154; private sector 161; productive "fights" 157; slums 151, 153; Sungei Buloh Wetland Reserve 157, 158; sustainable environment 153; systemic innovation 172–173; thinking outside the box 158–159; top ten livable cities **6**; top ten ranking cities from selected livability indices and surveys **114**; urban 114; urban governance 159, 163–164; urban planning and governance 155–156, *159*; urban redevelopment 160; Urban Redevelopment Authority Master Plan 154; vision and pragmatism 159–160

Single European Market 38
Sintusingha, S. 231
slums: Pune, India 93, 95, 96, 101, *101*, 102, 105; Rio de Janeiro, Brazil 195, 196, 199, 200, 201, 202; Singapore 151, 153
smart growth movement 3, 8; Austin, TX 64–65; Tehran, Iran 227, 230
social capital 193, *194*, 200, 202, 203
Social Planning Council of Ottawa 52
soft city 20, **20**, 23, 26
soft planning 20, **20**, 23, 26
Sohi, S. 230
Soja, E. 48, 193
Solihull, UK **33**
Sopranos, The 24
South Africa 2, 189, 208–221, 237; aesthetic appeal 214; avoiding hazards and protecting resources 211; climate change 209–210; context-specific developmental filter 215; designing with nature 212; dignity 213; ecological interdependencies 211; economic globalization and structural unemployment 209; efficiency 211; equity and social justice 212; food security 210; fossil fuel dependence 210; integration 212–213; interdependence of landscapes 212; international tendencies 208–209; law 214–215; performance model 215; performance qualities 208–215; planning theory 210–211; population growth and urbanization 209; safety and security 214; sense of place 213; sociability and privacy 213–214; Spacial Planning and Land Use Management Act 214; sustainability 211–212; urban planning and spatial principles 218–221; water scarcity 210; *see also* Cape Town, South Africa
Southampton, UK **33**
South Lanarkshire, UK **33**
spatial capital 193, *194*, 199, 203
Speck, J. 48
Square Kitchen 172
standpoints 1, 6, 8, 33, 41, 227
Statistics Canada 47
Steiner, R. 193
Stilwell, F. 111
Stockholm, Sweden 6, **6**, 114
subnormal agglomeration 195
Sugar House Streetcar 168, 169
Sumitomo 153
Supreme Court 75n1
Sustainable Salt Lake 173
Swee, G. K. 157
Sydney, Australia 6, 109, 111–123, 177; economic opportunity 6; homeownership 139; housing 178; housing tenure 117, **117**, *118*; income levels *116*; inequality 115–122; livability 112–113; relationship between different forms of spatial disadvantage *120*; right to the city 112, 122; Roadmap for a Liveable City 122; Social Sustainability Policy 121; spatial disadvantage 111, 119, *120*; spatial geography 109, 111, 115, 123n1; terrorism 181; top ten livable cities **6**; top ten ranking cities from selected livability indices and surveys **114**; transport 117; see also *Domain Liveable Sydney 2016*
Sydney Morning Herald, The: "Why The Economist says Sydney is no longer one of the world's 10 most liveable cities" 114

Tan, M. B. 158
Tehran, Iran 189, 224–238; academic research 229–231; background 225–226; Better Life Index, 227; Chitgar Lake park *225*; improvements 227–229; locating 226–227; Mercer Quality of Life Survey 227; moving toward a conclusion 231–232; population 224; smart growth 227, 230; sustainability 226; Tehran Vision Plan 2025 229; transportation 227; walkability 227, 230
Telegraph 35
Telegraph, The 33
Teo, S. 19, 27, 114
terrorism 4, 114, **180**, 181
Thameslink 39
third space 48
third worlds 192; *see also* Rio de Janeiro, Brazil
Tilak Maharashtra University 100
Tokyo, Japan 6, 109, 127–137; activities 130; *Act on Special Measures Concerning Urban Reconstruction* 130; aging and household trends 131–132; attractiveness of suburban residential areas 130–131; bubble economy 129; child-rearing environment 134; co-creative projects between residents and businesses 136; collaborative efforts between private business, government, academia, and citizens 135; community living 134–135; community living as concept for *Next-Generation Suburban Machizukuri* 135; comprehensive community care systems 133–134; expansion and changes in metropolitan area in post-war 127–129; expansion of perimeter and damage to urban communities due to bubble economy 129; formation of dense urban areas 128–129; formation of multi-core urban area 127–128; formation of world's largest metropolitan area 127; Great East Japan Earthquake 131; green zones 127; households *132*; housing 128; left-behind elderly households 131, 132–133; merits and demerits of 2020 Olympics 131; *Next-Generation Suburban Machizukuri* 135–136; Olympics 131; mobility 134; population change in metropolitan area *128*; Special Districts for Urban Regeneration 130; suburban residential areas with predominantly left-behind elderly and renewal efforts 131–135; super-aging society 136–137; sustainable

renewal of suburban residential areas 133–136; top ten livable cities 6; top ten ranking cities from selected livability indices and surveys 114; urban housing and urban renewal policies 129–131; urban living as commodity 129–130; urban renewal 130; vacant houses and vacant lots 132–133, *133*; walk-able living areas 135; Yamanote Line 127, 128

top ten ranking cities from selected livability indices and surveys **114**

Toronto, Canada 52; economic opportunity 6; top ten livable cities 6; top ten ranking cities from selected livability indices and surveys **114**, 139

Tract Consultants 114

Transition Network 32

Transparency International *180*, 181

Transportation Master Plan 49, 50

TRAX line 167, 168, 169

Trudeau, P. E. 45

UK *see* United Kingdom

UK Money 33, **34**

UN *see* United Nations

UNISDR (United Nations International Strategy for Disaster Reduction) Making Cities Resilient Campaign 4

United Kingdom (UK): Brexit 38, 42n17; Business Improvement Districts 39; comparative table of selected city livability indices and rank orders **33–35**; decision to leave European Union 38, 42n17, 42n19; definition of livable city 30; livable cities in 31–32; location of livable cities 36; measuring livability of cities 30–36; 'Transition Towns' 32; *see also* London, England

United Nations (UN) 197; Article 7 9; Article 25 9; Commission on Environment and Development 7; Conference on Environment and Development 7; Human Rights Council Special Rapporteur 197; Human Settlements Programme 145; International Strategy for Disaster Reduction (UNISDR) 4; Review of World Cities 212, 216; sustainability 9; UNICEF 104; Universal Declaration of Human Rights 9; World Health Organization (WHO) 3, 193

United States (US) 1–2, 61, 62, 139, 178; air quality 173; complete streets 52; congested corridors 64; healthcare system 181; Healthy Cities movement 3–4; new urbanism 3; PwC's Quality of Living rating 6; smart growth movement 3; urban design movement 3; *see also* Austin, TX; Salt Lake City, UT

United States Department of Agriculture (USDA) 171

United States Forest Service 170

University of Birmingham 42n13

University of Melbourne 149, 182; Faculty of Architecture, Building and Planning 119; Spatial Data Access project 184, 185

Urban Corridors 103

Urban Living Index 114

Urban Taskforce Australia 114

USDA *see* United States Department of Agriculture

U.S. News and World Report 61

uSwitch 33

Utah Performing Arts Center 173

Utah *see* Salt Lake City, UT

Utah Transit Authority 168

Valdermos, A. 172

Vancouver, Canada 49, 109, 138–145, 146n5, 178, 230; Bartholomew Plans 143; bifurcated city 140–141; CityPlan 143; Community Amenity Contributions (CACs) 142; context 139–149; Economist Intelligence Unit Global Liveability Survey 138; Expo '86; hedge city 139; homelessness 140; housing 139, 140, 141, 146n20; livability and quality of life rankings, 138–139; median household incomes and average home prices **139**; Mercer Quality of Living Survey 138; North and South False Creek development *143*; poverty 140–141; top ten livable cities 6; top ten ranking cities from selected livability indices and surveys **114**; what makes Vancouver livable 141–144; World Exposition on Transportation and Communication 142

vehicle kilometers (VKT) 8, 209

Victoria, New South Wales 122; Community Indicators Victoria (CIV) 149, 176–177, 182, 183, 184, 186; housing 178; spatial analysis 182; top ten ranking cities from selected livability indices and surveys **114**

Victorian Public Health Survey (VPHS) 183

Vienna, Austria: housing 6; Mercer Quality of Life 145; Municipal Department 50 144; population 145; quality of life surveys 10n4; top ten livable cities 6; top ten ranking cities from selected livability indices and surveys **114**, 138

VKT *see* vehicle kilometers

Wagner, F.: *Community Livability*, 192, 193

Wales 31, **34**, 42n7

walkability 18, 214, 219, 227, 229; Melbourne, Australia 183, 184, 185; Ottawa 47, 48, 49, 50, 51, 52, 53, 55; Salt Lake City, UT 173; Tehran, Iran 230

Wall, K. 48

Warsaw, Poland, 59, 79–89; Congress of Urban Movements 81; context, 82–83; Convoy Model of Social Relations 88; Fifteen Urban Theses 90n2; local centers 85–87; National

Urban Policy 81, 82; Nine Urban Theses 81, 90n2; revitalization projects 87–88; right to the city 80, 81; urban context, 80–82; Warsaw Local Centers project, 83–85, 87, 89
Warsaw Charter of Polish Association of Architects, 83
Wasatch Mountains 168, 170
WhatsApp 97
Whelan, R. K. 48, 192
Whyte, W. 88
Wilheim, J. 192
Wilkinson, R. 140
Wong, A. 158
Woolcock, G. W. E. 193
World Bank *180*, 181
World Exposition on Transportation and Communication 142

World Health Organization (WHO) 3, 193
World War I 31
World War II 17, 30, 31, 127, 128, 167, 177, 216

Yamanote Line 127, 128
Yellowstone National Park 170
Yew, L. K. 153, 160
York, UK 33

Zarghamfard, M. 231
ZCMI Center 167
Znaniecki, F. 88
Zukin, S., 20, 24, 27
Zurich, Switzerland: top ten livable cities **6**; top ten ranking cities from selected livability indices and surveys **114**